T0339762

THE AUTHENTIC CONSTITUTION

THE AUTHENTIC CONSTITUTION

AN ORIGINALIST VIEW OF AMERICA'S LEGACY

Arthur E. Palumbo

Algora Publishing
New York

Library of Congress Cataloging-in-Publication Data —

Palumbo, Arthur E.
     The authentic constitution: An Originalist View of America's Legacy / Arthur
Palumbo.
       p. cm.
     Includes bibliographical references and index.
     ISBN 978-0-87586-705-2 (trade paper: alk. paper) — ISBN 978-0-87586-706-9 (hard
cover: alk. paper) — ISBN 978-0-87586-707-6 (e-book) 1. United States—Politics and
government—Philosophy. 2. Constitutional history—United States. I. Title.

     JK275.P36 2009
     342.73—dc22
                                    2009005550

Printed in the United States

To the Founders,
for their gift of liberty;
And to the Patriots throughout our history,
who have been its guardians.

"In questions of power then let no more be heard of confidence in man, but bind him
down from mischief by the chains of the Constitution."
— Thomas Jefferson

TABLE OF CONTENTS

INTRODUCTION

Alan Keyes, the Republican presidential candidate in 1996 and 2000, described the relationship between the Declaration and the Constitution of the United States in the following way:

> The doctrine of unalienable rights is to the Constitution what the laws of phys-
> ics are to architecture or engineering. Those laws are not repeated in every plan
> or architect's drawing, but they are assumed and must be respected or the re-
> sults will be defective and dangerous.[1]

Judge Andrew P. Napolitano, Fox News Senior Judicial Analyst and author, described the relationship in this way:

> The significance of the Declaration for constitutional scholars is that it is be-
> lieved to contain the philosophical underpinnings of the Constitution. In other
> words, an understanding of Natural Law, its conferral of rights upon men and
> women, and the relationship between those rights and the role of government
> is fundamental to understand and interpret the Constitution properly.[2]

Finally, noted constitutional law attorney Dr. Edwin Vieira, Jr. described the relationship in this manner:

> [T]he legitimacy of the Constitution depends upon the Declaration of Indepen-
> dence; and therefore the Constitution's powers cannot contradict the Declara-
> tion's principles. For, were the Declaration not an actual law both prior in time
> and superior in authority to the Constitution, and the source of WE THE PEO-
> PLE'S authority to enact the Constitution, the Constitution itself would not
> be valid. After all, before they could enact their own laws, binding on anyone,
> including themselves, Americans had to win legal independence from Great
> Britain. They secured that independence only under the aegis of the Declara-

---

1 Alan Keyes, *By their Fruits*, WorldNetDaily [Internet]; available from http://www.worldnet-
daily.com/news/article.asp?ARTICLE_ID=46709; accessed 6 July 2008.
2 Judge Andrew P. Napolitano, *The Constitution in Exile* (Nashville: Nelson Current, 2006), xix.

tion. Therefore, they could enact only such subsequent laws as were entirely consistent with the principles the Declaration set forth.[1]

Whatever the precise relationship between the two documents may actually be, what is clear is that the founding principles of the Declaration are intimately connected with the Constitution and it would be unwise to ignore them or the bond that the two documents share. Perhaps the best way to explain the relationship is to say that the Declaration provides the source and purpose of proper government *generally*, whereas Constitution provides the structure and function of a *specific* government most appropriate for implementing the stated purpose. Thus, each document requires the other for a full description of our system of government.

In the following pages, I will treat both the Declaration and the Constitution as one document under the title "the "Authentic Constitution"." However, this designation refers to more than simply the union of two founding documents. The "Authentic Constitution" is also the Constitution *as the Founders originally intended it to be understood*. This view conforms to the theory of judicial interpretation known as "originalism," which is the idea that the Constitution should be understood in accordance with the meaning advanced by those who wrote and ratified it. Originalism applies to the constitutional amendments as well. Each amendment should be understood in accordance with the meaning advanced by those who wrote and ratified it, which, of course, would be different for each amendment.

Almost all our nation's problems today are due precisely to the fact that we have essentially abandoned our adherence to the "Authentic Constitution". The federal government has become far too large, too intrusive, and too wasteful with little to restrain its irresponsible actions. Congress spends money as if it has an unlimited source of funding, while saddling our posterity with enormous debt. All kinds of laws are regularly passed based on whatever outlandish ideas the legislators can imagine rather than any written, authoritative code to hold back their impulses. Most of the time, these laws turn out to be either detrimental to the country or petty nuisances that the American people must tolerate. On the other hand, if sensitive political questions should arise, Congress has no qualms about transferring its responsibilities to other branches or departments and thus freeing itself from having to deal with them at all. The truth is that the nine justices of the Supreme Court have become the real rulers of the nation, because we have allowed their judicial decisions to be legally binding not only on the parties to the particular case, but on the President, Congress, and everyone else as well. Our foreign policy is not much better. We have allowed our government to meddle constantly in the affairs of other countries, which accomplishes nothing worthwhile except that it causes increasing numbers of people to hate us around the world.

In the following pages, I will endeavor to describe some of the ways in which the "Authentic Constitution" has been disregarded or distorted and the problems that have emerged as a result. What will become obvious is that we have wandered far off course. Change is a normal aspect of life; and from the Constitution's inception, it was always acknowledged that alterations might very well be needed in the future. History illustrates all too clearly that the twenty-first century is vastly different from the nineteenth, as doubtless the twenty-third will be from the twenty-first. The

---

1 Dr. Edwin Vieira, Jr., "Will The North American Union Be American Patriots' Last Stand?" NewWithViews.com [Internet]; available from http://newswithviews.com/Vieira/edwin49. htm; accessed 6 July 2008.

Founders were wise and provided a means for making alterations, if necessary, which was through the constitutional amendment process found in Article V of the Constitution. Alexander Hamilton alluded to this process in *The Federalist Papers* (# 78):

> Until the people have, by some solemn and authoritative act, annulled or changed the established form, it is binding upon themselves collectively, as well as individually; and no presumption, or even knowledge, of their sentiments, can warrant their representatives in a departure from it, prior to such an act.

The relevant portion of Article V is quoted below:

> The Congress, whenever two thirds of both Houses shall deem it necessary, shall propose Amendments to this Constitution, or, on the Application of the Legislatures of two thirds of the several States, shall call a Convention for proposing Amendments, which, in either Case, shall be valid to all Intents and Purposes, as Part of this Constitution, when ratified by the Legislatures of three fourths of the several States, or by Conventions in three fourths thereof, as the one or the other Mode of Ratification may be proposed by the Congress.

According to Article V, the constitutional amendment process begins with Step 1, the Proposal, which is completed when either 2/3 of both houses of Congress propose an amendment or 2/3 of the state legislatures request that Congress call a Convention of delegates from all the states to propose an amendment. Step 2 is the Ratification. Congress chooses one of two methods for Ratification: Either 3/4 of the state legislatures must ratify the proposed amendment or 3/4 of the Conventions held in each of the States must ratify the proposed amendment.

However, we should not be concerned with *proper* changes of this type. Our great concern should be with certain *unauthorized* changes that have been made over the years. When we read or hear about the Constitution today, reference is usually being made to a fraudulent substitute constitution skillfully crafted from the "Authentic Constitution" in order to allow the federal government to assume more and more powers that it does not really have. It is generally accepted today that the Constitution is a "living document" and must be reinterpreted with the changing times for it to continue being relevant. Since it is difficult to get a constitutional amendment ratified properly via Article V, other improper means have been used to accomplish the same result in lieu of the constitutional amendment process. Some of these are listed below:

- Words in the text are allowed to take on different, wider, or more modern meanings than those originally intended.
- Words in the text are disregarded altogether.
- Clauses are considered "outdated" and no longer have any efficacy or relevance.
- New powers not actually written in the text are "uncovered" by faulty reasoning.
- The Supreme Court regularly amends the Constitution from the bench in lieu of the legitimate constitutional amendment process.
- Treaties are considered to have higher legal authority than the Constitution.
- In addition, and particularly awkwardly, certain constitutional amendments were not ratified as claimed. Evidence clearly shows that such is the case for the Fourteenth, Fifteenth, Sixteenth, and Seventeenth Amendments. The truth is that, because of their flawed ratification, these amendments did not really change the "Authentic Constitution" in any way.

Unfortunately, in researching the ratification of the Fourteenth Amendment one may discover that the ratification process underlying the Fifteenth Amendment was beset with the same fundamental errors as the former and consequently neither one was properly ratified. The Fifteenth Amendment was supposed to give former slaves the right to vote after the Civil War, but it would have a wider significance now. Section 1 of the Amendment states, "The right of citizens of the United States to vote shall not be denied or abridged by the United States or by any State on account of race, color, or previous condition of servitude." Unlike the Fourteenth, Sixteenth, and Seventeenth Amendments, which have been nothing but detrimental to our nation, the Fifteenth Amendment is a worthy addition that deserves inclusion in the "Authentic Constitution". However, this can only be accomplished by going through the amendment process once again to get it ratified properly, which most likely could be completed rather quickly. I offer a unique way of accomplishing this in a later chapter.

Such practices described above pervert the very idea of having a *written* Constitution, since one of its fundamental purposes is to curb the abuse of government power. In 1803, Chief Justice John Marshall stated this fact clearly in the famous Supreme Court case *Marbury v. Madison*:

> [The] ... original and supreme will [the People] organizes the government, and assigns to different departments their respective powers. It may either stop here; or establish certain limits not to be transcended by those departments.
>
> The government of the United States is of the latter description. The powers of the legislature are defined and limited; and that those limits may not be mistaken or forgotten, the constitution is written. To what purpose are powers limited, and to what purpose is that limitation committed to writing; if these limits may, at any time, be passed by those intended to be restrained? The distinction between a government with limited and unlimited powers is abolished, if those limits do not confine the persons on whom they are imposed, and if acts prohibited and acts allowed are of equal obligation. It is a proposition too plain to be contested....
>
> Between these alternatives there is no middle ground. The constitution is either a superior, paramount law, unchangeable by ordinary means, or it is on a level with ordinary legislative acts, and like other acts, is alterable when the legislature shall please to alter it (italics mine).[1]

It would be incorrect to assert that every clause in the Constitution can be clearly understood and do not allow for different interpretations. No document produced by human beings has ever been so perfect. In cases where disparities may *legitimately* exist, government officials should always keep squarely in mind the essential understanding that the federal government is one of *limited* powers, so that the temptation to expand government power will not be attempted. James Madison explained this fact very clearly in *The Federalist Papers* (# 45):

> The powers delegated by the proposed Constitution to the federal government are few and defined. Those which are to remain in the State governments are numerous and indefinite.

A few examples where problems with interpretations may occur in the Constitution would be the "necessary and proper" clause (Article I, section 8, clause 18),

---

1 *Marbury v. Madison* (1803), FindLaw [Internet]; available from http://supreme.lp.findlaw.com/ supreme_court/landmark/marbury.html; accessed 16 July 2008.

the commerce clause (Article I, section 8, clause 3), and the precise meaning of the statement that "Judges ... shall hold their Offices during good Behavior ..." (Article III, section 1).

It is indeed true, as President Andrew Jackson maintained in his veto message regarding the Second Bank of the United States (July 10, 1832), that "each public officer who takes an oath to support the Constitution swears that he will support it as he understands it, and not as it is understood by others."[1] However, the range of possible interpretations permissible must be strictly limited by the actual words of the text and their original meanings, as well as adherence to the founding principles of the Declaration and an understanding of the reasons and objectives held by the Founders in writing the Constitution in the first place. Unfortunately, this boundary has been crossed today by faulty interpretations and even outright deception.

Most politicians in Washington continually talk about the Constitution, but the truth is they are merely giving it lip service in order to promote their own ends. In actuality, they simply ignore it so that unconstitutional legislation can be passed without difficulty. This situation is a perfect example of "talking the talk, but not walking the walk." However, when they urgently need some kind of pseudo-legal justification to endorse specific legislation, do they go to the "Authentic Constitution" for the legal authority they require? Well, no, for doing so would doubtless have just the opposite effect. Instead, they go to where the validation is readily available — the fraudulent substitute constitution.

How can they claim to honor their oath of office truly under these circumstances? The oath of office for all government officers, elected or appointed, except the President, is "I ... do solemnly swear (or affirm) that I will support and defend the Constitution of the United States against all enemies, foreign and domestic; that I will bear true faith and allegiance to the same; that I take this obligation freely, without any mental reservation or purpose of evasion; and that I will well and faithfully discharge the duties of the office on which I am about to enter. So help me God" (U.S. Code 5, section 3331). The President's oath of office is in Article II, section 1, clause 8 of the Constitution and is as follows: "I do solemnly swear (or affirm) that I will faithfully execute the Office of President of the United States, and will to the best of my Ability, preserve, protect and defend the Constitution of the United States."

Ignoring the "Authentic Constitution" or accepting a fraudulent substitute constitution in its place hardly seems like honoring those oaths. For specific examples of the consequences of this evasion, read on!

---

1 President Jackson's Veto Message Regarding the Bank of the United States; July 10, 1832, The American Presidency Project [Internet]; available from http://www.presidency.ucsb.edu/ws/index.php?pid=67043&st=&st1=; accessed 23 July 2008.

Chapter 1: The "Authentic Constitution"—Its Origin and Purpose

The happy Union of these States is a wonder; their Constitution a miracle; their example the hope of Liberty throughout the world.

— James Madison, "Outline" Notes, September 1829

In the Declaration of Independence, we formally declared our separation from Great Britain and listed our reasons for doing so. At the Pennsylvania State House (now known as Independence Hall) in Philadelphia, the Second Continental Congress formed a five-man committee to draw up a Declaration on June 11, 1776. The committee chose one of its members, Thomas Jefferson, to compose an initial draft of the document. On June 28, this draft with some committee revisions was read before Congress. Although officially declaring independence from Great Britain on July 2, Congress continued to work on the draft until an acceptable version of the Declaration was adopted on July 4 and copies were ordered to be printed. By this time, the war with Great Britain had already been going on for more than a year.

The first document describing our fundamental laws and system of government was the Articles of Confederation and Perpetual Union. It went into effect when Maryland, the last of the thirteen states to do so, ratified it on March 1, 1781, while the Revolutionary War was still raging. The war ended when the British general, Cornwallis, surrendered his army on October 19, 1781 after the Battle of Yorktown. However, the Treaty of Paris, which officially ended the war, was not signed until September 3, 1783.

It took less than five years for many influential persons to realize there were serious problems with the Articles that urgently needed correction, if the new government was to survive and the country not fracture into thirteen independent nations. The government's unicameral Congress lacked many powers that the central government of any sovereign nation should rightfully have. Most significantly, it did not really have the power to tax. Although Congress could determine the "mode" and "time" in which taxes would be assessed based on the total real property value of each state, the tax would actually be "laid and levied by the authority and direction of the legislatures of the several States ... (Article VIII)" *not* by Congress. The result was that the states usually did not meet their financial responsibility and the treasury was critically short of funds most of the time.

Because of this defect in the Articles and others, a Convention was finally called up by the Confederation Congress on February 21, 1787 to be held in Philadelphia in order to correct the deficiencies. The resolution that was approved by Congress is quoted from the Journal below:

> Resolved that in the opinion of Congress it is expedient that on the second Monday in May next a Convention of delegates who shall have been appointed by the several States be held at Philadelphia for the sole and express purpose of revising the Articles of Confederation and reporting to Congress and the several legislatures such alterations and provisions therein as shall when agreed to in Congress and confirmed by the States render the federal Constitution adequate to the exigencies of Government and the preservation of the Union.[1]

However, during the hot, humid summer of 1787, instead of merely "revising" the Articles, which they had been entrusted to do, the delegates at the Convention, which met in Independence Hall, created a whole new form of government. A new Constitution was written, and when the task was completed, it was signed by thirty-nine delegates on September 17. The Constitution and the resolutions of the Convention, along with a cover letter from George Washington, who was the President (i.e., the presiding officer) of the Federal Convention, were forwarded to the Congress, which was then meeting in New York City. The resolutions were as follows:

> Resolved,

> That the preceeding Constitution be laid before the United States in Congress assembled, and that it is the Opinion of this Convention, that it should afterwards be submitted to a Convention of Delegates, chosen in each State by the People thereof, under the Recommendation of its Legislature, for their Assent and Ratification; and that each Convention assenting to, and ratifying the Same, should give Notice thereof to the United States in Congress assembled.

> Resolved,

> That it is the Opinion of this Convention, that as soon as the Conventions of nine States shall have ratified this Constitution [this statement is also found in Article VII of the Constitution], the United States in Congress assembled should fix a Day on which Electors should be appointed by the States which shall have ratified the same, and a Day on which the Electors should assemble to vote for the President, and the Time and Place for commencing Proceedings under the Constitution.

What occurred next is described by Stanley L. Klos, author of *President Who? Forgotten Founders*:

> The "New Plan for the Government" arrived in New York on September 20th and its fate was subject to the vote of the United States in Congress Assembled, the very body that would be disassembled should they vote to send it to the states for ratification. The great debate that must have ensued is forever lost due to the veil of secrecy that surrounded Congress. We do know, however,

---

1 Journals of the Continental Congress 1774–1789, Wednesday, February 21, 1787, Volume 32, Page 74, Library of Congress (Thomas) [Internet]; available from http://memory.loc.gov/ cgi-bin/ampage?collId=lljc&fileName=032/lljc032.db&recNum=83&itemLink=r?ammem/ hlaw:@field(DOCID+@lit(jc03225)):%230320084&linkText=1; accessed 16 July 2008.

that ... Congress ... voted, only eight day later, to send the Constitution to the legislature of each state.[1]

The resolution passed by Congress on September 28, 1787, approved the first resolution of the Philadelphia Convention that was quoted above.

Although the ninth state, New Hampshire, actually ratified the new Constitution on June 21, 1788, Congress did not receive notification until July 2, at which time all the state ratifications were sent to a committee in order to determine the procedure for beginning implementation of the new Constitution. Thus, June 21, 1788, became the official date that the Articles of Confederation went out of use and the Constitution took its place. Nevertheless, a resolution was not passed by Congress for putting the Constitution into operation until September 13, 1788, and after a considerable period of debate. This resolution approved the second resolution of the Philadelphia Convention that was quoted above.

According to Article XIII of the Articles of Confederation, any changes in it must be "confirmed by the legislatures of *every* State." Consequently, they were still operational at least in principle until 1790, when the Constitution was ratified by all thirteen states. Rhode Island was the last state to ratify it, on May 29, 1790.

The new Congress was assembled in New York City on March 4, 1789, George Washington was inaugurated President on April 30,[2] and the first Supreme Court was in operation on February 2, 1790, after a failed try on the previous day.

What are the reasons for having a written Constitution? Well, no doubt one reason is to describe in writing the fundamental principles and laws of a nation and the structure and operation of its government. However, there is another more important reason, which Thomas Jefferson provided in a famous quotation from *The Kentucky Resolutions of 1798*:

> ... it would be a dangerous delusion were a confidence in the men of our choice to silence our fears for the safety of our rights: that confidence is every where the parent of despotism: free government is founded in jealousy and not in confidence; it is jealousy and not confidence which prescribes limited Constitutions to bind down those whom we are obliged to trust with power: that our Constitution has accordingly fixed the limits to which and no further our confidence may go.... In questions of power then let no more be heard of confidence in man, but bind him down from mischief by the chains of the Constitution.[3]

In other words, the Constitution also serves as an impartial barrier against the possible abuse of power by our government leaders, who, being imperfect human beings, can be tempted to pursue evil.

Regardless of what we may wish to believe, the Constitution is not perfect either, as nothing created by human beings can ever be. A number of compromises had to be reached by the delegates in order to bring the Constitution to completion and to

---

1 Stanley L. Klos, *President Who? Forgotten Founders* (Carnegie, PA: Estoric.com, 2004), 196.

2 It will come as a surprise to many to discover that George Washington was not really our first President. Indeed, it is true that he was the first President of the United States *under the Constitution*, but ten other individuals before him served as the President of the United States in Congress Assembled from 1781 to 1789, when the Articles of Confederation was still in operation. George Washington was actually the *eleventh* President of the United States. The first President was Samuel Huntington, who served in the office from March 1, 1781 to July 6, 1781. Klos, 15-41.

3 *The Kentucky Resolutions of 1798*, The Papers of Thomas Jefferson Princeton University [Internet]; available from http://www.princeton.edu/~tjpapers/kyres/kyednote.html; accessed 16 July 2008.

save the country from ultimately breaking apart. Nevertheless, on the last day of the Convention (September 17, 1787), but before the delegates signed the Constitution, Benjamin Franklin was able to state, "when you assemble a number of men to have the advantage of their joint wisdom, you inevitably assemble with those men, all their prejudices, their passions, their errors of opinion, their local interests, and their selfish views. From such an assembly can a perfect production be expected? It therefore astonishes me, Sir, to find this system approaching so near to perfection as it does."[1]

Franklin was not the only delegate to voice such a view. About a month later, James Madison, a delegate to the Federal Convention of 1787 and the fourth President of the United States, was able to state in a letter to Thomas Jefferson, who was in France at the time (October 24, 1787), "[writing the Constitution] formed a task more difficult than can be well conceived by those who were not concerned in the execution of it. Adding to these considerations the natural diversity of human opinions on all new and complicated subjects, it is impossible to consider the degree of concord which ultimately prevailed [at the Convention] as less than a miracle." Then, about a month into the following year, George Washington was able to write much the same thing in a letter to Marquis de Lafayette, one of Washington's generals in the Revolutionary War, on February 7, 1788: "It appears to me ... little short of a miracle, that the Delegates from so many different States ... should unite in forming a system of national Government, so little liable to well founded objections."

Of course, even if America *did* possess a perfect Constitution, flawless in every way, it would have little impact in producing a good and just government for a people who are without integrity or morals. Consider the following quotations from John Adams and Samuel Adams, who were second cousins and signers of the Declaration of Independence (John Adams served as the second President of the United States):

> ... we have no government armed with power capable of contending with human passions unbridled by morality and religion. Avarice, ambition, revenge, or gallantry, would break the strongest cords of our Constitution as a whale goes through a net. Our Constitution was made only for a moral and religious people. It is wholly inadequate to the government of any other. — John Adams, Letter to the Officers of the First Brigade of the Third Division of the Militia of Massachusetts, October 11, 1798).

> [N]either the wisest constitution nor the wisest laws will secure the liberty and happiness of a people whose manners are universally corrupt. — Samuel Adams, Essay in *The Public Advertiser*, 1749).

Legendary as an example of integrity, George Washington voluntarily relinquished his authority as Commander in Chief of the American forces after the war with England had been successfully won and the peace treaty signed. He returned to Mt. Vernon as a private citizen. This solemn act took place on December 23, 1783, before Congress, which had then been assembling at Annapolis, Maryland. A portion of his address before the body was as follows: "Having now finished the work assigned to me, I retire from the great Theatre of Action; & bidding an Affectionate farewell to this August Body under whose orders I have so long acted, I here offer my Commission, & take my leave of all the employments of public life." What makes this act most astonishing is that if he so desired he could have marched on Congress with

---

1 James Madison, *Notes of Debates in the Federal Convention of 1787*, Introduction by Adrienne Koch, Bicentennial Edition (New York: W. W. Norton & Company, 1987), 653-4.

his army and declared himself George I, King of America. Because Washington was so admired by the people, it is very likely such a coup would have been successful. Of course, if this step had been taken, the sacrifices that had been made for approximately eight years would have been in vain. The writer and historian, Paul Johnson, describes the public reaction to this startling act as follows:

> No one who knew Washington well was surprised. Everyone else, in varying degrees, was astonished at this singular failure of the corruption of power to work. And, indeed, it was a rare moment in history. In London, George III questioned the American-born painter Benjamin West what Washington would do now he had won the war. "Oh," said West, "they say he will return to his farm." "If he does that," said the king, "he will be the greatest man in the world."[1]

The Constitution begins with the well-known Preamble, which lists very succinctly the six objectives that the government under the Constitution was expected to achieve. Most importantly, by using the phrase "WE THE PEOPLE" written in unusually large letters, it makes clear to the entire world that the People are the true rulers and the sole source of authority in the United States. Let me quote it below in a somewhat enhanced format in order to bring out its full meaning:

WE, THE PEOPLE of the United States,

In Order to form:

a more perfect Union,

establish Justice,

insure domestic Tranquility,

provide for the common defense,

promote the general Welfare,

and secure the Blessings of Liberty to ourselves and our Posterity,

Do ordain and establish this Constitution for the United States of America.

---

1 Paul Johnson, *George Washington: The Founding Father* (New York: HarperCollins Publishers, 2005), 78.

Chapter 2: The Founding Principles

We have it in our power to begin the world over again. A situation, similar to the present, hath not happened since the days of Noah until now. The birthday of a new world is at hand....
— *Thomas Paine, "Appendix," Common Sense (1776)*

The founding principles of our government can be found in the second paragraph of the Declaration of Independence:

> We hold these truths to be self-evident, that all Men are created equal, that they are endowed by their Creator with certain unalienable Rights, that among these are Life, Liberty and the pursuit of Happiness. That to secure these Rights, Governments are instituted among Men, deriving their just powers from the consent of the governed. That whenever any Form of Government becomes destructive of these ends, it is the Right of the People to altar or to abolish it, and to institute new Government, laying its foundation on such principles and organizing its powers in such form, as to them shall seem most likely to effect their Safety and Happiness. Prudence, indeed, will dictate that Governments long established should not be changed for light and transient causes; and accordingly all experience hath shewn, that mankind are more disposed to suffer, while evils are sufferable, than to right themselves by abolishing the forms to which they are accustomed. But when a long train of abuses and usurpations, pursuing invariably the same object, evidence a design to reduce them under absolute Despotism, it is their Right, it is their duty, to throw off such Government, and to provide new Guards for their future security.

It should first be mentioned that "Men" refers to human beings collectively. The Founders agreed that what distinguishes a human being from all other creatures is that the former has the ability to reason. Since all human beings, regardless of their color or gender, are *thinking* beings, they are "equal" in their "unalienable rights." The evil of slavery was that it existed in spite of this fact. With regard to women, consider this quotation from James Otis, a patriot, speaker, and writer from Massachusetts: "Are not women born as free as men? Would it not be infamous to assert that the ladies are all slaves by nature?" (*The Rights of the British Colonies Asserted and Proved*, 1764). A rejection of any human being's unalienable rights is indefensible.

There are three main principles that are described in this paragraph. The first principle is declared "self-evident," which means that it is so obvious that no special proof is required. All human beings are born equal and as such are endowed with "certain unalienable Rights." What does this equality actually mean? Surely, it does not mean that all human beings have the same abilities, which common sense would quickly refute. The answer is that human beings are "created equal" precisely *because* they have "unalienable Rights." These rights are "unalienable" (or inalienable, which is another way to spell the word), in other words inherent, and thus cannot be surrendered, transferred, or taken away. They are also called natural rights, because they are inherent in human beings irrespective of any government that may or may not exist. They originate from what the Declaration calls the "Laws of Nature and of Nature's God." Three of them are mentioned — "Life, Liberty and the pursuit of Happiness," although "among these" implies that there are others.

Is there a means of identifying an unalienable right, and can others be discovered besides life, liberty and the pursuit of happiness? A careful review of the subject reveals that a right is unalienable only if it meets these two requirements: (1) a person can have the right in the absence of any government, in what is usually termed a state of nature, and (2) the having of the right neither diminishes nor takes away another person's rights.

Based on these two requirements, the following rights can be considered unalienable in addition to life, liberty, and the pursuit of happiness, although there are doubtless still others not listed here: (1) the right to self-defense (self-preservation), which obviously includes the right to own weapons for this purpose (2) the right to think and believe what one wishes, (3) the right to practice a religion of one's choosing, (4) the right to communicate and associate with others, (5) the right to move about freely, (6) the right to a livelihood, (7) the right to privacy, 8) the right to raise and educate your children as you choose, (9) the right to make agreements (contracts) with others, and (10) the right to acquire, have, and use property. This last unalienable right is actually mentioned along with life, liberty, and the pursuit of happiness in Article I of the Virginia Bill of Rights, which was adopted on June 12, 1776:

> That all men are by nature equally free and independent, and have certain inherent rights, of which, when they enter into a state of society, they cannot, by any compact, deprive or divest their posterity; namely, the enjoyment of life and liberty, with the means of acquiring and possessing property, and pursuing and obtaining happiness and safety.

It is important to understand that all of these unalienable rights are self-limited by requirement #2. For example, the right to liberty does not include the right to murder someone, which would take away that person's right to life. The right to a livelihood does not include the right to employment, which would diminish someone else's right to use his property (in this case to operate his business) as he chooses. Neither does the right to move about freely include the right to trespass on someone else's property, which would be an intrusion on somebody else's right to privacy.

Of course, other rights are acquired when human beings leave a state of nature and enter into a government by means of a social contract, which in this case is the Constitution. Citizenship rights fall in this category. Examples of these are the right to vote and the right to a trial by jury. Citizenship rights last only as long as the social contract is in force, so they are *not* unalienable. In addition, it may be possible for them to be regulated, changed or rescinded by passing new legislation within the bounds of the social contract at any time. A right granted by the decision of a court is another type of right that falls in this category. An example would be an easement, which a court grants to someone to use another's property for some specified, but limited, purpose. The function of this type of right is usually to make equitable some injustice that existed or occurred between the two parties in a lawsuit. Court-granted rights are usually only temporary at the outset. By contrast, unalienable rights, which are innate in human beings, exist regardless of whether a social contract, and hence a functioning government, is in operation or not.

The most important feature of unalienable rights is that they are not derived from any human authority — be it Congress, the Supreme Court, the President, the Declaration of Independence, the Constitution, the Bill of Rights or any other human source that may come to mind. They are inherent at birth.

John Adams, the second President of the United States, summarized this view of unalienable rights as follows:

> The poor people, it is true, have been much less successful than the great.... This, however, has been known by the great to be the temper of mankind; and they have accordingly labored, in all ages, to wrest from the populace, as they are contemptuously called, the knowledge of their rights and wrongs, and the power to assert the former or redress the latter. I say *rights*, for such they have, undoubtedly, antecedent to all earthly government, — *Rights*, that cannot be repealed or restrained by human laws — *Rights*, derived from the great Legislator of the universe (*A Dissertation on Canon and Feudal Law*, 1765).

Alexander Hamilton, a delegate to the Federal Convention of 1787 and a contributor to *The Federalist Papers*, explained it in this way:

> The sacred rights of mankind are not to be rummaged for among old parchments or musty records. They are written, as with a sunbeam, in the whole volume of human nature, by the hand of Divinity itself, and can never be erased or obscured by mortal power (*The Farmer Refuted*, 1776).

Examined in a practical manner, what is the benefit of believing that rights are not dependent on the generosity of human rulers? Throughout history, kings and tyrants have claimed they had the prerogative to determine who did and who did not have rights and few individuals were in a position to disagree with them. For example, Hitler declared that the Jews did not have any rights and he could do with them what he wanted. Many could disagree intellectually with the details of his racist argument, but if the generally prevailing view was that human beings were the grantors of rights, there would be little basis on which to refute his basic premise. On the other hand, if the generally prevailing view were that such rights are inherent in all humans, Hitler's basic premise would be refuted immediately. No human being, including a dictator, has any authority in this area.

It should also be mentioned that this principle is at the heart of the abortion debate. This highly emotional issue appears to pit the right of a woman against the right of the unborn. By the standard of unalienable rights, legal abortion would hinge entirely on the definition of when human life begins.

Even though certain unalienable rights, and even other rights for that matter, are not *specifically* mentioned in the Constitution, this does not mean they are not included in the document nonetheless. The Ninth Amendment makes this very clear: "The enumeration in the Constitution of certain rights shall not be construed to deny or disparage others retained by the people."

The second principle is "that to secure these rights, Governments are instituted among Men, deriving their just powers from the consent of the governed." The sole purpose of government, in this view, is to protect the unalienable rights of the governed — a view that may seem quite strange today in contrast to all the things the US government does that have nothing to do with safeguarding rights. Nevertheless, this is supposed to be the only legitimate function of the US government. Furthermore, the people ("the governed") authorize a government to act for this purpose. Although there were brief episodes prior to the Declaration when the people ruled (for example, ancient Athens and republican Rome), most of the time it was the government that ruled through a king, an emperor, or some other absolute head of state and he determined what freedoms the people could and could not have. This tyrannical concept fell with a loud crash in 1776 for it was declared with the stroke of a pen that the people are the legitimate rulers and government only exists for their benefit. Government is the servant of the people; the people are not the servants of the government.

Because the purpose of government is to protect citizens' unalienable rights, it may be necessary through due process of law to disregard a person's unalienable rights in order to protect other's rights in society:

> [C]onstitutions recognize the power to deprive persons of their rights under *due process* of law. Strictly speaking, a person may not be deprived of such rights in the sense of taking them away. Natural rights are never lost. Their exercise can, however, be restricted or, to use the proper legal term, *disabled*. While some might question the practical distinction between losing a right and having it disabled, that distinction is important. A right which is disabled under due process may also be re-enabled by the removal of that disability....[1]

This necessity is based on the law of self-preservation, which is in turn derived from the unalienable right of the same name. Thomas Jefferson, the writer of the Declaration and the third President of the United States, described the law in this fashion:

> A strict observance of the written laws is doubtless *one* of the high duties of a good citizen, but it is not the *highest*. The law of necessity, of self-preservation, of saving our country when in danger, are of higher obligation. To lose our country by a scrupulous adherence to written law, would be to lose the law itself, with life, liberty, property, and all those who are enjoying them with us; thus absurdly sacrificing the end to the means ... (Thomas Jefferson, Letter to J. B. Colvin, Sept. 20, 1810).

Therefore, someone's unalienable rights can only be "disabled" through due process of law in order to safeguard the rights of others. Allowing murderers and robbers to continue murdering and robbing would completely defeat government's ability to perform its purpose. Surely, this would be a nonsensical means of "protecting" our unalienable rights.

The third principle states that if a government does not perform its legitimate duty (that is, to protect our unalienable rights), the people can change or eliminate it and create a new government in its place. The only qualification is "that Governments long established should not be changed for light and transient causes," but only "when a long train of abuses and usurpations, pursuing invariably the same object, evidence a design to reduce them under absolute Despotism." In fact, this critical

---

1Jon Roland, "Social Contract and Constitutional Republics," 1994, Basic Principles, Constitution Society [Internet]; available from http://www.constitution.org/soclcont.htm; accessed 17 July 2008.

point had been reached in 1776. The Declaration announced to the world the intention of the colonies to separate from Great Britain and listed, as evidence to support their case, the many acts of tyranny that had been perpetrated by King George III. For example, "he [the King] has refused his Assent to Laws, the most wholesome and necessary for the public Good" and "he has dissolved Representative Houses repeatedly, for opposing with manly Firmness his Invasions on the rights of the People."

At the end of the Declaration, the following pledge was made: "And for the support of this Declaration, with a firm Reliance on the Protection of divine Providence, we mutually pledge to each other our Lives, our Fortunes, and our sacred Honor." The signatures of fifty-six men followed these bold words, even though the very act of signing made them immediately guilty of high treason. An "engrossed" copy (i.e., a specially prepared, handwritten copy) of the Declaration was signed and this one is now exhibited in the National Archives. Most of the delegates signed it on August 2 (not July 4, as is usually thought), although several did so even later. John Hancock, the President of the Second Continental Congress, cautioned them, "there must be no pulling different ways: we must all hang together." Benjamin Franklin with his usual wit then augmented Hancock's warning with the following words, "we must indeed all hang together, or most assuredly we will all hang separately."

If they were not successful in their noble endeavor, and the likelihood of victory was far from certain, the penalty they would receive was actually more ghastly than just hanging: "To be hanged by the head until unconscious. Then cut down and revived. Then disemboweled and beheaded. Then cut into quarters. Each quarter to be boiled in oil. The remnants were scattered abroad so that the last resting place of the offender would remain forever unnamed, unhonored, and unknown."[1]

Although the success they hoped for finally came in 1783 when the Treaty of Paris was signed, the sacrifices that many of them paid all the same were shocking. An anonymous letter that I discovered in Ann Landers' column several years ago described the many hardships that the signers of the Declaration encountered for their heroic act. The accuracy of the information in the letter was later confirmed with other sources:

> Five signers were captured by the British as traitors and tortured before they died. Twelve had their homes ransacked and burned. Two lost their sons who served in the revolutionary Army. Another had two sons captured. Nine of the 56 fought and died from wounds or hardships of the Revolutionary War....
>
> Carter Braxton of Virginia, a wealthy planter and trader, saw his ships swept from the seas by the British Navy. He sold his home and properties to pay the debts, and died in rags.
>
> Thomas McKean was so hounded by the British that he was forced to move his family constantly. He served in Congress without pay, and his family was kept in hiding. His possessions were taken, and poverty was his reward.
>
> Vandals or soldiers looted the properties of Ellery, Hall, Clymer, Walton, Gwinnet, Heyward, Rutledge, and Middleton.
>
> At the Battle of Yorktown, Thomas Nelson, Jr., noted that the British general Cornwallis had taken over the Nelson home for his headquarters. He quietly urged General George Washington to open fire. The home was destroyed, and Nelson died bankrupt.

---

1 W. Cleon Skousen, *The Making of America*, 2nd rev. ed. (Washington, D.C.: The National Center for Constitutional Studies, 1986), 31.

The home of Francis Lewis was destroyed. The enemy jailed his wife, and she died within a few months.

John Hart was driven from the bedside of his dying wife. Their 13 children fled for their lives. His fields and gristmill were laid waste. For more than a year, he lived in forests and caves, returning home to find his wife dead, his children gone. He died shortly thereafter, heartbroken. Morris and Livingston suffered similar fates....[1]

The principles propounded by the Founders were indeed revolutionary. It is true that many of the ideas originated in France and had been expressed at various times before the Declaration was drafted, but they were never before put together in one document and in such a clear and succinct manner. Those holding political power understood that such views meant overturning the world order; and they were not enthusiastic about giving their subjects (or slaves) the liberty that was called for. In the United States, slavery was not abolished until the ratification of the 13th Amendment, in 1865, decades after Great Britain, Spain, France and Latin America had abolished slavery.

With regard the slavery issue, many Americans today accuse Thomas Jefferson and the other Founders of hypocrisy for talking about unalienable rights and yet owning human beings as property. However, even as early as 1776 Jefferson took an initial step in the other direction. He wrote a passage in his first draft of the Declaration that condemned the slave trade and blamed its continued proliferation on the British king. Unfortunately, it was deleted because of a protest made by representatives of the southern states at the Second Continental Congress.

Although Jefferson believed that slavery should be ended as soon as it was possible, he was also convinced that both races — the black and the white — would find it difficult to live together peacefully. Therefore, his solution in the short term was to expatriate and re-colonize the blacks back to Africa. The government would protect them and supply them with everything they needed to make their resettlement successful. In his *Autobiography* in 1821, Jefferson summarized these ideas in this way: "Nothing is more certainly written in the book of fate, than that these people are to be free; nor is it less certain that the two races, equally free, cannot live in the same government. Nature, habit, opinion, have drawn indelible lines of distinction between them."

How can Jefferson's view of human rights be properly reconciled with the fact that he was a slave owner? A letter in a local newspaper offers a useful viewpoint:

A historical approach reverses the question: How could a man raised in a society and world in which slavery was the norm repudiate his own self-interest by proclaiming the inevitability of freedom and democracy?

It is so easy to forget that in Jefferson's world the idea that government existed to protect God-given rights and derived its powers from the consent of the governed was both radical and at odds with common sense and the lessons of history.

In helping to transform these ideas from theoretical abstractions into practical reality, Jefferson helped to set in motion the destruction of an institution he despised but could never give up. He is not unique for owning slaves; he is unique for helping to make a nation in which slavery could not permanently endure.[2]

---

1 *The Boston Globe*, July 4, 2000, E8 (Ann Landers' column).
2 The Boston Globe, July 7, 2000, A22 (Letters to the Editor).

To conclude this chapter, I will quote a portion of Thomas Jefferson's letter to Roger Weightman, which is dated June 24, 1826. It was Jefferson's last letter, prior to his death on July 4. Weightman invited Jefferson to attend the fiftieth anniversary of America's Independence to be celebrated in Washington D.C. Regrettably, Jefferson was unable to accept the invitation because of poor health. In the portion of the letter quoted below, Jefferson expressed his belief that the words of the Declaration would stir the inhabitants of other nations in their turn to break the chains of despotism that they had been suffering under and that ultimately all people would come to share in the blessings of liberty:

> [M]ay ... [the Declaration] be to the world, what I believe it will be, (to some parts sooner, to others later, but finally to all,) the Signal of arousing men to burst the chains, under which monkish ignorance and superstition had persuaded them to bind themselves, and to assume the blessings & security of self-government. [T]hat form which we have substituted, restores the free right to the unbounded exercise of reason and freedom of opinion. [A]ll eyes are opened, or opening, to the rights of man. [T]he general spread of the light of science has already laid open to every view [...] the palpable truth, that the mass of mankind has not been born with saddles on their backs, nor a favored few booted and spurred, ready to ride them legitimately, by the grace of god. [T]hese are grounds of hope for others. [F]or ourselves, let the annual return of this day forever refresh our recollections of these rights, and an undiminished devotion to them (Thomas Jefferson, Letter to Roger Weightman, 1826).

CHAPTER 3: THE AMERICAN REPUBLIC

I pledge allegiance to the Flag of the United States of America, and to the Republic for which it stands, one Nation under God, indivisible, with liberty and justice for all.
— *The Pledge of Allegiance (US Code 4, section 4).*

The media is constantly talking about "our democracy," apparently referring to the form of government operating in the United States. However, anyone who endeavors to study the Founding documents will quickly realize that this is not the case. The term "democracy" is not even found in the Declaration or the Constitution. In fact, in the latter document, article IV, section 4 stipulates, "The United States shall guarantee to every State in this Union a *Republican* Form of Government ... (italics mine)." The United States is *not* a democracy in the sense of a pure or complete democracy, but is actually a Constitutional Republic with some *indirect or representative* democracy. Let me explain.

A pure or complete democracy, which is only possible in states or nations with a small territory and population, is the absolute rule by the majority. Whatever at least 50% plus 1 of the citizens vote for is the law. Unfortunately, this form of government poses serious defects and they usually stem from the chaotic and undisciplined nature of large masses of people and the unchecked power of the majority. It is often forgotten or not realized that an unrestrained majority can be just as dangerous to liberty as a king or a dictator.

A pure or complete democracy has several shortcomings. One major defect of this form of government is that, as one writer puts it, "if the majority wins, then the minority loses."[1] He continues his argument as follows:

> So although everyone has an equal vote, society is still divided into competing factions of majority and minority — or to be more blatant winners and losers.

---

1 Michael Badnarik, *Good to be King: The Foundation of Our Constitutional Freedom* (Cranston, RI: The Writers' Collective, 2004), 34.

If we apply the "majority wins" argument to every situation, the result is that rights do not exist in a democracy. That is because your "rights" can be voted away by the majority of the voters. If your "rights" can be voted away, then you only have privileges granted to you by the will of the majority.[1]

Private property rights, for instance, are always at risk. In a pure or complete democracy, the attitude to private property tends to be communistic. When those without property are the majority, they can pass laws that mandate the redistribution of wealth to all the citizens. Thus, the right to property no longer looks unalienable.

The rights of individuals in specific minorities are also in jeopardy. As often happens, a charismatic leader (a demagogue) will come forward and blame a number of critical problems that the whole society is currently facing on a certain group within it (a minority) by exciting the people's passions and prejudices. Laws can be hastily passed that limit or completely take away that group's rights. The excesses of the majority, persuaded by a leader or group of leaders, sacrifice the rights of the minority (and in recent years, Americans have even been persuaded to give up a wide range of liberties and rights across the board). James Madison explained the situation as follows:

> In all cases where a majority are united by common interest or passion, the rights of the minority are in danger. What motives are to restrain them? A prudent regard to the maxim that honesty is the best policy is found by experience to be as little regarded by bodies of men as by individuals. Respect for character is always diminished in proportion to the number among whom the blame or praise is to be divided. Conscience, the only remaining tie, is known to be inadequate in individuals: In large numbers, little is to be expected from it. Besides, Religion itself may become a motive to persecution & oppression. — These observations are verified by the Histories of every Country antient [sic] & modern.[2]

Assembling all or most citizens to decide every issue is impractical, if not impossible, and this is another significant defect of this form of government. Some important issues need to be decided quickly, for example, the authorization to mobilize the armed forces to stop an anticipated enemy attack. The contentious and long-winded deliberations that this issue would most likely generate would surely not expedite the situation. In addition, sometimes expert knowledge in a certain area is required to make a proper decision and most of the people simply do not have it or cannot learn it quickly enough. An example of this kind would be in the area of monetary policy, which to the average person is as comprehensible as nuclear physics. How can an informed decision by amateurs (most of the citizenry in this case) be expected in this area? Besides, most people need to earn a living and provide for their families. The endless involvement in government business that a pure or complete democracy would necessitate would be overly time consuming and tedious for most people to manage.

Lack of stability is yet another defect of a pure or complete democracy. Since there is no one to direct the actions of the citizens other than themselves, the deliberations often become rash and shortsighted. One day they will vote to increase taxes, but on the next day decrease them; or they will make something illegal on one day, but on the next day make it legal. Demagogues will often move the people back and forth in the highly charged spectacles that usually take place. A confusing, unreliable,

---

1 Ibid.

2 James Madison, *Notes of Debates in the Federal Convention of 1787*, Introduction by Adrienne Koch, Bicentennial Edition (New York: W. W. Norton & Company, 1987), 76.

and arbitrary legal system can be the only result of such an operation. Dissatisfaction, protest, and lawlessness become the characteristics of the day.

Ancient Athens, which in the fifth century BC was a nearly perfect model of a pure or complete democracy, provides us with actual examples of this last defect. The most important part of Athenian government was the Assembly, which usually met more than one time per month and consisted of a quorum of the first 6,000 male citizens who arrived for each meeting. The population of Athens was approximately 400,000, although only about ten percent of the population actually had the right to vote in the Assembly. Those excluded from voting were women, under-age males, slaves, and free foreigners.

In 406 BC, the Assembly voted to execute six Athenian generals for allowing a large number of their men to drown needlessly in sinking ships, because of a naval battle. These generals (actually eight, two did not return to the Athens) had been the commanders in the battle and had actually won a victory for the Athenians, but casualties were high. Because of certain demagogues who came forward to excite the emotions of the Athenian citizens, the Assembly voted for execution without a proper trial or even any kind of defense for the generals. Nevertheless, the prescribed sentence was indeed carried out. Sometime afterwards, regretting what they had done, the Athenians filed actions against the demagogues who had misled them.

As another example, in 428 BC Mitylene, a city on the island of Lesbos, left the Athenian alliance and went over to Sparta. When the Athenians were finally able to drive the Spartans off Lesbos and thus out of Mitylene, the Assembly voted to execute all the Mitylenian males for their disloyalty and to sell their women and children into slavery. A ship was sent to Mitylene to carry out the sentence. Fortunately for them, the next day the Assembly took up the case again and decided to reverse its decision to put the Mitylenians to death.

James Madison provides a summary of the defects of a pure or complete democracy in *The Federalist Papers* (#10):

> [A] pure democracy ... can admit of no cure for the mischiefs of faction. A common passion or interest will, in almost every case, be felt by a majority of the whole; a communication and concert results from the form of Government itself; and there is nothing to check the inducements to sacrifice the weaker party, or an obnoxious individual. Hence it is, that such Democracies have ever been spectacles of turbulence and contention; have ever been found incompatible with personal security, or the rights of property; and have in general been as short in their lives, as they have been violent in their deaths. Theoretic politicians, who have patronized this species of Government, have erroneously supposed, that by reducing mankind to a perfect equality in their political rights, they would at the same time, be perfectly equalized and assimilated in their possessions, their opinions, and their passions.

What is the remedy for all these defects in this form of government? The answer is a Constitutional Republic, which has one prime objective in creating an effective and enduring government:

> Its purpose is to control The Majority strictly, as well as all others among the people, primarily to protect The Individual's God-given, unalienable rights and therefore for the protection of the rights of The Minority, of all minorities, and the liberties of people in general.[1]

---

1 *An Important Distinction: Democracy versus Republic*, The American Ideal of 1776: The Twelve Basic American Principles [Internet]; available from http://www.lexrex.com/enlightened/AmericanIdeal/aspects/demrep.html; accessed 19 July 2008.

A Constitutional Republic has two main characteristics. First, it is an indirect or representative democracy. In *The Federalist Papers* (# 10), Madison describes this characteristic as follows:

> The two great points of difference between a Democracy and a Republic are, first, the delegation of the Government, in the latter, to a small number of citizens elected by the rest: secondly, the greater number of citizens, and greater sphere of country, over which the latter may be extended.

> The effect of the first difference is, on the one hand to refine and enlarge the public views, by passing them through the medium of a chosen body of citizens, whose wisdom may best discern the true interest of their country, and whose patriotism and love of justice, will be least likely to sacrifice it to temporary or partial considerations. Under such a regulation, it may well happen that the public voice pronounced by the representatives of the people, will be more consonant to the public good, than if pronounced by the people themselves convened for the purpose. On the other hand, the effect may be inverted. Men of factious tempers, of local prejudices, or of sinister designs, may by intrigue, by corruption or by other means, first obtain the suffrages, and then betray the interests of the people. ...

> The other point of difference is, the greater number of citizens and extent of territory which may be brought within the compass of Republican, than Democratic Government; and it is this circumstance principally which renders factious combinations less to be dreaded in the former, than in the latter. The smaller the society, the fewer probably will be the distinct parties and interests composing it; the fewer the distinct parties and interests, the more frequently will a majority be found of the same party; and the smaller the number of individuals composing a majority, and the smaller the compass within which they are placed, the more easily will they concert and execute their plans of oppression. Extend the sphere, and you take in greater variety of parties and interests; you make it less probable that a majority of the whole will have a common motive to invade the rights of other citizens; or if such a common motive exists, it will be more difficult for all who feel it to discover their own strength, and to act in unison with each other.

According to Madison, in a Republic the whole people elect representatives from among themselves to run the government for them. With this arrangement, the representatives, who will be better able see the whole picture rather than just bits and pieces, can filter out the more appropriate views from the large number of disparate, prejudiced, hasty, and shortsighted ones that will most likely be expressed by the whole body of the people. Representation will further allow the country to have a larger population and a geographical area than would be possible in a pure or complete democracy. As a result, it will also be more difficult for various groups with similar evil motives to unit and carry out their designs.

However, Madison is surely not referring to representatives who control all aspects of government and have no restraints placed on their power. If he were doing so, the form of government he would be describing would actually be an oligarchy. Just as there is an unrestrained majority in a pure or complete democracy, so there would be unrestrained representatives in this form of government. If the representatives were corrupt, the rights of the people would certainly be at risk. Madison was well aware of the possibility of corruption by the representatives, when he states "men of factious tempers, of local prejudices, or of sinister designs, may by intrigue, by corruption or by other means, first obtain the suffrages, and then betray the interests of the people." There would be little real difference between pure or complete democracy and an indirect or representative democracy of this type.

In 1781–2, Thomas Jefferson, in his *Notes on the State of Virginia*, described Virginia's government an "elective despotism," because, although its members were indeed elected into office by the people, they nevertheless had nearly absolute power. In actuality, the legislature was an oligarchy. The only check that the people really had over it was the election of its members. Prior to the ratification of the Constitution of the Commonwealth of Massachusetts in 1780, "there were no effective State Constitutions to limit the legislatures because most State governments were operating under mere Acts of their respective legislatures which were mislabelled [*sic*] 'Constitutions.'"[1] I quote the relevant section of the *Notes on the State of Virginia* below:

> All the powers of government, legislative, executive, and judiciary, result to the legislative body. The concentrating these in the same hands is precisely the definition of despotic government. It will be no alleviation that these powers will be exercised by a plurality of hands, and not by a single one. 173 despots would surely be as oppressive as one. Let those who doubt it turn their eyes on the republic of Venice. As little will it avail us that they are chosen by ourselves. An *elective despotism* was not the government we fought for; but one which should not only be founded on free principles, but in which the powers of government should be so divided and balanced among several bodies of magistracy, as that no one could transcend their legal limits, without being effectually checked and restrained by the others.[2]

Obviously, a Constitutional Republic, besides having the characteristic of an indirect or representative democracy, must also have some means of restraining government power. This is provided for in its Constitution, which is the second characteristic of this form of government. A Constitutional Republic can therefore be described as follows:

> ... a constitutionally limited government of the representative type, created by a written Constitution—adopted by the people and changeable (from its original meaning) by them only by its amendment—with its powers divided between three separate Branches: Executive, Legislative and Judicial. Here the term "the people" means, of course, the electorate.[3]

Another source describes it as follows:

> A Constitutional Republic is similar to democracy in that it uses democratic processes to elect representatives and pass new laws, etc. The critical difference lies in the fact that a Constitutional Republic has a Constitution that limits the powers of the government. It also spells out how the government is structured, creating checks on its power and balancing power between different branches. The idea was to hold the entire government in check by utilizing the jealousies of the people in each branch over their own areas.[4]

1 Ibid.

2 Thomas Jefferson, *Notes on the State of Virginia*, Query 13, "Constitution" The constitution of the state, and its several charters? Constitution, #4, Electronic Text Center, University of Virginia Library [Internet]; available from http://etext.virginia.edu/toc/modeng/public/JefVirg.html; accessed 19 July 2008.

3 *An Important Distinction: Democracy versus Republic*, The American Ideal of 1776: The Twelve Basic American Principles [Internet]; available from http://www.lexrex.com/enlightened/AmericanIdeal/aspects/demrep.html; accessed 19 July 2008.

4 Pat Baska, *On Republic vs. Democracy*, Liberty and Democracy, Serendipity [Internet]; available from http://www.serendipity.li/jsmill/baska01.htm; accessed 19 July 2008.

The following story will illustrate the difference between unbridled democracy (the unchecked majority or mob) and a republic (represented by the sheriff and his adherence to the law), and the role of the demagogue in influencing the mob:

> In this plot, one that the moviegoer has probably seen a hundred times, the brutal villain rides into town and guns down the unobtrusive town merchant by provoking him into a gunfight. The sheriff hears the gunshot and enters the scene. He asks the assembled crowd what had happened, and they relate the story. The sheriff then takes the villain into custody and removes him to the city jail.
>
> Back at the scene of the shooting, usually in a tavern, an individual stands up on a table (this individual by definition is a Demagogue) and exhorts the crowd to take the law into its own hands and lynch the villain. The group decides that this is the course of action that they should take (notice that the group now becomes a democracy where the majority rules) and down the street they (now called a mob) go. They reach the jail and demand that the villain be released to their custody. The mob has spoken by majority vote: the villain must hang.
>
> The sheriff appears before the democracy and explains that the villain has the right to a trial by jury. The demagogue counters by explaining that the majority has spoken: the villain must hang. The sheriff explains that his function is to protect the rights of the individual, be he innocent or guilty, until that individual has the opportunity to defend himself in a court of law. The sheriff continues by explaining that the will of the majority cannot deny this individual that right. The demagogue continues to exhort the democracy to lynch the villain, but if the sheriff is persuasive and convinces the democracy that he exists to protect their rights as well, the scene should end as the people leave, convinced of the merits of the arguments of the sheriff.[1]

An excellent depiction of this very subject can be found in the 1943 movie titled "The Ox-Bow Incident." In this movie, an illegally deputized posse is sent out to find some alleged cattle rustlers who supposedly also murdered the cattle owner. The posse soon comes upon three men who are sleeping in a forest. Because of certain circumstantial evidence, the posse takes a vote and decides to hang them. On the way back to town, feeling that justice had been done, the men of the posse meet up with the sheriff and his men who inform them that the alleged crimes were actually bogus — no one had been killed and no cattle had been stolen. Those who had voted to hang the three innocent men now had to face not only possible criminal charges but also an immense burden of guilt.

Whether one chooses a pure or complete democracy that has no restraints placed on the majority or an indirect or representative democracy that has no restraints placed on the representatives (an "elective despotism," as Jefferson called it), history illustrates that both types of government will eventually destroy themselves from within. In a letter to John Taylor dated April 15, 1814, John Adams offered this assessment of unbridled democracy:

> Remember, democracy never lasts long. It soon wastes, exhausts, and murders itself. There never was a democracy yet that did not commit suicide. It is in vain to say that democracy is less vain, less proud, less selfish, less ambitious, or less avaricious than aristocracy or monarchy.[2]

Alexander Fraser Tytler (1747–1813), a Scottish jurist, historian, and professor at Edinburgh University, expressed the same reservations:

---

1 A. Ralph Epperson, *The Unseen Hand* (Tucson, AZ: Publius Press, 1985), 34-5.
2 Patrick Diggins, ed., *The Portable John Adams* (New York: Penguin Books, 2004), 429-30.

A democracy cannot exist as a permanent form of government. It can only exist until the voters discover that they can vote themselves largesse from the public treasury. From that moment on, the majority always votes for the candidates promising the most benefits from the public treasury with the result that a democracy always collapses over loose fiscal policy, always followed by a dictatorship.[1]

Eventually a pure or complete democracy will self-destruct, because of the defects described above and others. One possible scenario is that the majority of the people could get into the habit of voting themselves benefits from the treasury followed by the necessity of raising taxes repeatedly to pay for them. There is little doubt that the upper classes would be assessed most of these taxes, since they would be the ones most able to pay them. In due course, poor financial management and class conflict would probably lead to the collapse of the government and the descent into anarchy. In the futile attempt of the people to restore government and order to the society, some form of tyranny would most likely emerge — be it a dictatorship or a monarchy.

The same outcome would also be the fate of an "elective despotism," whose members are actually oligarchs. To continue being elected, they could promise more and more benefits to the people from the state coffers, which would eventually result in the collapse of the government due to lax financial management. Alternatively, they could alter the law, so that their terms of office would be for life. Worse yet, they could end elections by the people altogether and make inheritance the determinant for holding office, which would turn the government into an aristocracy. Of course, the desire for power would not end there. Now the rulers could fight amongst themselves to determine who would have the supreme authority. When all the other leaders were killed off under so-called mysterious circumstances and only one of them remained, a dictatorship or a monarchy would be the result.

The only democratic feature of the Constitutional Republic that is the United States is that the people of the states elect the Representatives in the House of Representatives every two years. Supposedly, in 1913 the ratification of the Seventeenth Amendment provided for the election of the Senators by the people instead of by the state legislatures, as had been the case previously. However, as will be discovered in a later chapter, the Seventeenth Amendment was not really ratified. From the date when the first Senators elected by the people entered into their office up to the present time, the United States has not had a constitutional Senate in Congress. According to the "Authentic Constitution", Senators were and still are to be chosen by the state legislatures. This is not a democratic feature.

As will be learned in a later chapter, although the Electoral College system for electing the President of the United States every four years no longer works as it was originally intended, it still cannot be considered a democratic system. The people do not actually elect the President; they elect a slate of Electors, who then elect the President. In the 2000 Presidential Election, although Al Gore (the Democrat) won

---

1 Two quotations are usually attributed to Alexander Fraser Tytler, but only one has been quoted here. The second one is quoted in Chapter 17. Although both quotations have been cited numerous times as coming from Tytler, the truth is that this attribution cannot be verified. In fact, their true source is currently unknown. For an examination of this question, see Loren Collins, "The Truth About Tytler," Loren Collins [Internet]; available from http://lorencollins.net/sundries.html; accessed 5 July 2008. Regardless of the source, the quotation above still reveals an acknowledged, though often overlooked, truth about unbridled democracy.

the popular vote by 543,816 votes, he still lost the election because President George Bush (the Republican) won the electoral vote by five votes. The total electoral vote count was President George Bush 271 and Al Gore 266.

The judicial branch of government is clearly not democratic either, since the President with the advice and consent of the Senate appoints all Supreme Court justices, court of appeals judges, and district court judges.

Since Article I, section 5, clause 1 of the Constitution states, "a Majority of each [House] shall constitute a Quorum to do Business," only *a majority of a Quorum*, which at a bare minimum is only a majority of members, can pass a bill in each House: *a majority of members* is not required. However, two facts mitigate the likelihood that only a Quorum in each House would vote on an important bill. First, it would not be politically advantageous for members to miss voting on an important piece of legislation, and second, Article I, section 5, clause 1 also states, "a smaller Number [than a Quorum in each House] ... may be authorized to compel the Attendance of absent Members, in such Manner, and under such Penalties as each House may provide." Although a bill can be passed in each House by at least a majority of a Quorum, which can be considered a democratic rule, in order to overcome a President's veto two-thirds of each house must vote on a bill before it can become law. A two-thirds vote is not a democratic rule.

The amendment process, which is found in Article V of the Constitution, should be mentioned as well. For proposing an amendment, either two thirds of each house must vote to do so or else two thirds of the state legislatures must request a special Convention to do so. If this step turns out to be successful, the proposed amendment will become part of the Constitution when ratified by either three fourths of the state legislatures or else by three fourths of the Conventions held in all the states. It is the prerogative of Congress to determine the ratification method.

The percentage required for proposing and ratifying an amendment (two thirds and three fourths respectively) is admittedly rather difficult to achieve. This is certainly an important reason why unconstitutional means have replaced, in many instances, the proper method for amending the Constitution. Nevertheless, a majority vote is not even enough to propose an amendment, let alone to ratify one.

When the new Constitution was presented to the states for ratification, Conventions of delegates chosen by the people of each state decided whether to accept or reject the Constitution. Thus, true to its *republican* form, the people's wishes were expressed through representatives they selected for this purpose.

To conclude this chapter, I would like to recount a well-known story about Benjamin Franklin. In 1787, when the Federal Convention in Philadelphia had ended, a woman approached Franklin, who had been one of the delegates. "Well, Doctor," she asked, "What have we got, a republic or a monarchy?" He replied, "A republic, if you can keep it." Are we keeping a Constitutional Republic? The following chapters will reveal not only that we are *not* keeping it, but like mindless robots we continue via the voting booth to move toward its complete eradication.

CHAPTER 4: THE POWERS OF CONGRESS

If we can prevent the government from wasting the labors of the people, under the pretense of taking care of them, they must become happy.
— *Thomas Jefferson, Letter to Thomas Cooper, January 29, 1802*

The Constitution created a federal government of limited, delegated, and enumerated powers. At the Federal Convention of 1787, the delegates from the states transferred certain powers to the federal government that they believed would be most appropriate for the federal government to have control over, but retained all other powers with the states. Thus, the states created the federal government; it was not the other way around. Those powers that were delegated were specifically enumerated in the Constitution. James Madison explained this very clearly in *The Federalist Papers* (# 45) as follows:

> The powers delegated by the proposed Constitution to the federal government are few and defined. Those which are to remain in the State governments are numerous and indefinite. The former will be exercised principally on external objects, as war, peace, negotiation, and foreign commerce; with which last the power of taxation will, for the most part, be connected. The powers reserved to the several States will extend to all the objects which, in the ordinary course of affairs, concern the lives, liberties, and properties of the people, and the internal order, improvement, and prosperity of the State.

The 10th Amendment to the Constitution states the same idea:

> The powers not delegated to the United States by the Constitution, nor prohibited by it to the States, are reserved to the States respectively, or to the people.

Most of the powers of Congress are listed in Article I, section 8 of the Constitution as follows:

> *Section. 8.* [Clause 1] The Congress shall have Power To lay and collect Taxes, Duties, Imposts and Excises, to pay the Debts and provide for the common Defense and general Welfare of the United States; but all Duties, Imposts and Excises shall be uniform throughout the United States;

[Clause 2] To borrow Money on the credit of the United States;

[Clause 3] To regulate Commerce with foreign Nations, and among the several States, and with the Indian Tribes;

[Clause 4] To establish a uniform Rule of Naturalization, and uniform Laws on the subject of Bankruptcies throughout the United States;

[Clause 5] To coin Money, regulate the Value thereof, and of foreign Coin, and fix the Standard of Weights and Measures;

[Clause 6] To provide for the Punishment of counterfeiting the Securities and current Coin of the United States;

[Clause 7] To establish Post Offices and post Roads;

[Clause 8] To Promote the Progress of Science and useful Arts, by securing for limited Times to Authors and Inventors the exclusive Right to their respective Writings and Discoveries;

[Clause 9] To constitute Tribunals inferior to the supreme [*sic*] Court;

[Clause 10] To define and punish Piracies and Felonies committed on the high Seas, and Offenses against the Law of Nations;[1]

[Clause 11] To declare War, grant Letters of Marque and Reprisal, and make Rules concerning Captures on Land and Water;

[Clause 12] To raise and support Armies, but no Appropriation of Money to that Use shall be for a longer Term than two Years;

[Clause 13] To provide and maintain a Navy;

[Clause 14] To make rules for the Government and Regulation of the land and naval Forces;

[Clause 15] To provide for calling forth the Militia to execute the Laws of the Union, suppress Insurrections and repel Invasions;

[Clause 16] To provide for organizing, arming, and disciplining, the Militia, and for governing such Part of them as may be employed in the Service of the United States, reserving to the States respectively, the Appointment of the Officers, and the Authority of training the Militia according to the discipline prescribed by Congress;

[Clause 17] To exercise exclusive Legislation in all Cases whatsoever, over such District (not exceeding ten Miles square) as may, by Cession of particular States, and the Acceptance of Congress, become the seat of the Government of the United States, and to exercise like Authority over all Places purchased by the consent of the Legislature of the State in which the Same shall be, for the Erection of Forts, Magazines, Arsenals, dockyards, and other needful Buildings; — And

[Clause 18] To make all Laws which shall be necessary and proper for carrying into Execution the foregoing Powers, and all other Powers vested by this Constitution in the Government of the United States, or in any Department or Officer thereof.

---

1 Congress is empowered to first "define" precisely what these "Offenses against the Law of Nations" are and then to "punish" those who violate them. The word "punish" in this context actually means to *prescribe the penalties*, since the executive branch enforces the laws not Congress. You will also note that *Congress* is given the power here, not some international body separate from our government like the United Nations!

Some additional powers of Congress are recorded in other Articles of the Constitution and are quoted below:

Article I, section 2, clause 3. Representatives and direct Taxes shall be apportioned among the several States which may be included within this Union, according to their respective numbers.... The actual Enumeration shall be made within three Years after the first Meeting of the Congress of the United States, and within every subsequent Term of ten Years, in such Manner as they [Congress] shall by Law direct.

Article I, section 2, clause 5 (House Power Only). The House of Representatives ... shall have the sole Power of Impeachment.

Article I, section 3, clause 6 (Senate Power Only). The Senate shall have the sole Power to try all Impeachments. When sitting for that purpose, they shall be on oath or affirmation. When the President of the United States is tried, the Chief Justice shall preside: And no Person shall be convicted without the Concurrence of two thirds of the Members present.

Article II, section. 1, clause 4. The Congress may determine the Time of chusing [sic] the Electors,[1] and the Day on which they shall give their Votes; which day shall be the same throughout the United States.

Article II, section 2, clause 2 (Senate Power Only). [The President] ... shall have Power, by and with the Advice and Consent of the Senate, to make Treaties, provided two thirds of the Senators present concur.

Article II, section 2, clause 2 (Senate Power Only). [The President] ... shall nominate, and by and with the Advice and Consent of the Senate, shall appoint Ambassadors, other public Ministers and Consuls, Judges of the supreme Court, and all other Officers of the United States, whose Appointments are not herein otherwise provided for, and which shall be established by law.

Article II, section 2, clause 2. ... the Congress may by Law vest the Appointment of such inferior Officers, as they think proper, in the President alone, in the Courts of Law, or in the Heads of Departments.

Article III, section. 3, clause 2. The Congress shall have Power to declare the Punishment of Treason, but no Attainder of Treason shall work Corruption of Blood, or Forfeiture except during the Life of the Person attainted.[2]

Article IV, section. 1. Full Faith and Credit shall be given in each State to the public Acts, Records, and judicial Proceedings of every other State. And the Congress may by general Laws prescribe the Manner in which such Acts, Records, and Proceedings shall be proved, and the Effect thereof.

Article IV, section 3, clause 1. New States may be admitted by the Congress into this Union; but no new State shall be formed or erected within the Jurisdiction of any other State; nor any State be formed by the Junction of two or more States, or Parts of States, without the Consent of the Legislatures of the States concerned as well as of the Congress.

Article IV, section 3, clause 2. The Congress shall have Power to dispose of and make all needful Rules and Regulations respecting the Territory or other Property belonging to the United States; and nothing in this Constitution shall be so

---

1 These Electors mentioned in Article II, section. 1, clause 4 are the members of the Electoral College who elect the President and Vice-President of the United States.

2 Although the Congress can determine the penalty for treason, this penalty can never extend to the family of the accused person. In addition, if any property were confiscated as part of the penalty, it had to be returned to the family after the accused person's death.

construed as to Prejudice any Claims of the United States, or of any particular State.

Article V (Proposing Amendments). The Congress, whenever two thirds of both Houses shall deem it necessary, shall propose Amendments to this Constitution, or, on the Application of the Legislatures of two thirds of the several States, shall call a Convention for proposing Amendments,

Article V (Ratifying Amendments). [Proposed amendments] ... shall be valid to all Intents and Purposes, as Part of this Constitution, when ratified by the Legislatures of three fourths of the several States, or by Conventions in three fourths thereof, as the one or the other Mode of Ratification may be proposed by the Congress.

These are all the powers that have been granted in the Constitution to the Congress of the United States. After reading the above list carefully, you may naturally ask the question, "How is it that Congress has passed laws in so many areas that have not been granted to it in the Constitution?" These expansions of power are indeed numerous, but some noteworthy examples are health care (Medicare/Medicaid), retirement security (Social Security), housing subsidies (Housing Choice Vouchers, formerly Section 8), aid to education, farm subsidies, and foreign aid. The answer has primarily to do with the disputed meaning of seventeen words found within clause 1 of Article I, section 8. I quote the portion of clause 1 below with the applicable words in italics:

The Congress shall have Power To [sic] lay and collect Taxes, Duties, Imposts and Excises, *to pay the Debts and provide for the common Defense and general Welfare of the United States*; but all Duties, Imposts and Excises shall be uniform throughout the United States....

What do the italicized words actually mean? James Madison, who was given the name father of the Constitution for is noteworthy work in creating the document, explained their correct meaning in *The Federalist Papers* (# 41) as follows:

Some, who have not denied the necessity of the power of taxation, have grounded a very fierce attack against the Constitution, on the language in which it is defined. It has been urged and echoed, that the power "to lay and collect taxes, duties, imposts, and excises, to pay the debts, and provide for the common defense and general welfare of the United States," amounts to an unlimited commission to exercise every power which may be alleged to be necessary for the common defense or general welfare. No stronger proof could be given of the distress under which these writers labor for objections, than their stooping to such a misconstruction.

Had no other enumeration or definition of the powers of the Congress been found in the Constitution, than the general expressions just cited, the authors of the objection might have had some color for it; though it would have been difficult to find a reason for so awkward a form of describing an authority to legislate in all possible cases....

But what color can the objection have, when a specification of the objects alluded to by these general terms immediately follows, and is not even separated by a longer pause than a semicolon? If the different parts of the same instrument ought to be so expounded, as to give meaning to every part which will bear it, shall one part of the same sentence be excluded altogether from a share in the meaning; and shall the more doubtful and indefinite terms be retained in their full extent, and the clear and precise expressions be denied any signification whatsoever? For what purpose could the enumeration of particular powers be inserted, if these and all others were meant to be included in the preceding general power? Nothing is more natural nor common than first to use a general phrase, and then to explain and qualify it by a recital of particulars. But the idea of an enumeration of particulars which neither explain nor qualify the general meaning, and can have no other effect than to confound and mislead, is an absurdity, which, as we are reduced to the dilemma of charging either on the authors of the objection or on the authors of the Constitution, we must take the liberty of supposing, had not its origin with the latter.

In the supplement to his letter to Andrew Stevenson (November 27, 1830), which was his final discussion of this subject, Madison provided the same view as he did in 1788:

> The result of this investigation is, that the terms "common defence [sic] and general welfare" ... are used ... as general terms, limited and explained by the particular clauses subjoined to the clause containing them; that in this light they were viewed throughout the recorded proceedings of the Convention which framed the Constitution; that the same was the light in which they were viewed by the State Conventions which ratified the Constitution, as is shown by the records of their proceedings; and that such was the case also in the first Congress under the Constitution, according to the evidence of their journals, when digesting the amendments afterward made to the Constitution. It equally appears that the alleged power to appropriate money to the "common defence [sic] and general welfare" is either a dead letter, or swells into an unlimited power to provide for unlimited purposes, by all the means necessary and proper for those purposes. And it results finally, that if the Constitution does not give to Congress the unqualified power to provide for the common defence [sic] and general welfare, the defect cannot be supplied by the consent of the States, unless given in the form prescribed by the Constitution itself for its own amendment.[1]

From the above quoted paragraphs, it can be seen that Madison described the italicized words as being *general spending categories* in which the specified powers should be placed. They do *not* grant other powers to Congress in addition to those specifically listed in Article I, section 8. Madison asked the question, "If these words in the first clause of section 8 give Congress an unlimited scope of powers, what would be the point of enumerating certain powers in the lines below it? Wouldn't they already be included by inference in the first clause?" Obviously, there would be no point in providing such a list, because everything that Congress could possibly do would be included in clause 1: "the Congress shall have Power [t]o lay and collect Taxes, Duties, Imposts and Excises, to pay the Debts and provide for the common Defense and general Welfare of the United States." However, it is clear that the disputed words do not grant additional powers to Congress and that those powers granted are indeed limited:

> The powers of the federal government are enumerated; it can only operate in certain cases; it has legislative powers on defined and limited objects, beyond which it cannot extend its jurisdiction (James Madison, Speech at the Virginia Ratifying Convention, June 6, 1788).

> If Congress can do whatever in their discretion can be done by money, and will promote the general welfare, the government is no longer a limited one possessing enumerated powers, but an indefinite one subject to particular exceptions (James Madison, Letter to Edmund Pendleton, January 21, 1792).

---

1 James Madison to Andrew Stevenson, 27 Nov. 1830, Document 27, The Founders' Constitution [Internet]; available from http://press-pubs.uchicago.edu/founders/documents/a1_8_1s27. html; accessed 11 August 2008.

> With respect to the words, "general welfare," I have always regarded them as qualified by the details of power connected with them. To take them in a literal and unlimited sense would be a metamorphosis of the Constitution ... [that] was not contemplated by the creators. (James Madison, Letter to James Robertson, April 20, 1831).

> Congress has not unlimited powers to provide for the general welfare, but only those specifically enumerated (Thomas Jefferson, Letter to Albert Gallatin, 1817).

> The plan of the convention declares that the power of Congress, or, in other words, of the *national legislature*, shall extend to certain enumerated cases. This specification of particulars evidently excludes all pretension to a general legislative authority, because an affirmative grant of special powers would be absurd, as well as useless, if a general authority was intended. (Alexander Hamilton, *The Federalist Papers*, # 83).

Alexander Hamilton wrote the last quotation above shortly after the Federal Convention of 1787. At that time, he was clearly in agreement with Madison and Jefferson that Congress was given only specific and limited powers, but no more. Unfortunately, when he became Secretary of the Treasury under President Washington, he began arguing for a broader interpretation of the powers of Congress in order to get the bill passed that authorized the creation of the First Bank of the United States. Hamilton's new view was that the phrase "to pay the Debts and provide for the common Defense and general Welfare of the United States" conferred an *additional* power completely independent of the enumerated powers listed after it. The only limitation on this power was that it had to be for a national purpose; it could not be for only a specific section or group within the country. Of course, this view conveniently leaves unanswered the reason for the enumeration of powers in Article I, section 8 in the first place.

However, Hamilton was indeed correct in one sense. Although the phrase "to pay the Debts and provide for the common Defense and general Welfare of the United States" clearly does not give *additional* powers to Congress, the words "common" and "general" do indicate that all the specified powers must be used to benefit the *entire* nation, *not* a specific individual, group, city, state or region only.

Today, following Hamilton's lead, many people accept the view that the Constitution is a "living document" that must be reinterpreted with the changing times for it to continue being relevant. However, the method of change they support is usually not the admittedly difficult amendment process found in the Constitution, but the Supreme Court improperly amending the Constitution from the bench. Walter E. Williams refutes this "living document" hypothesis as follows:

> Many law professors, and others who hold contempt for our Constitution, preach that the Constitution is a living document. Saying that the Constitution is a living document is the same as saying we don't have a Constitution. For rules to mean anything, they must be fixed. How many people would like to play me poker and have the rules be "living"? Depending on "evolving standards," maybe my two pair could beat your flush.

> The framers recognized there might come a time to amend the Constitution, and they gave us Article V as a means for doing so. Early in the last century, some Americans thought it was a good idea to ban the manufacture and sale of alcohol. They didn't go to court asking the justices to twist the Constitution to

accomplish their goal. They respected the Constitution and sought passage of the 18th Amendment.[1]

The last clause (18) of Article I, section 8, which is often called the "necessary and proper" clause or the elastic clause, has been an ongoing object of controversy. However, there is no valid reason for the debate. The purpose of the clause is clear, but those who have been unhappy with limited government and have had a desire to expand its power in lieu of the onerous amendment process have always exaggerated the complexity of the issue. Congress is given the power to pass any law that is "necessary and proper" to put into operation any of the specified powers. How is a law deemed" necessary and proper"? Now here there may indeed be some divergence in opinion.

Thomas Jefferson, as Secretary of State, explained the correct meaning of the "necessary" portion of this clause in a report to President Washington, in which he gave his opinion as to why the bill authorizing the First Bank of the United States was unconstitutional:

> If has been urged that a bank will give great facility or convenience in the collection of taxes. Suppose this were true: yet the Constitution allows only the names which are "*necessary*," not those which are merely "convenient" for effecting the enumerated powers. If such a latitude of construction be allowed to this phrase as to give any non-enumerated power, it will go to everyone, for there is not one which ingenuity may not torture into a *convenience* in some instance *or other*, to *some one* of so long a list of enumerated powers. It would swallow up all the delegated powers and reduce the whole to one power, as before observed. Therefore it was that the Constitution restrained them to the *necessary* means, that is to say, to those means without which the grant of power would be nugatory.... [2]

A law is "necessary" if the specified power would be inoperative without it. It cannot be passed merely because it is "convenient," but only because without its passage the "grant of [the enumerated] power would be nugatory." To do otherwise, "would swallow up all the delegated powers and reduce the whole to one power."[3]

The correct meaning of the "proper" portion of this clause is that "the end or purpose of a law must be within the jurisdiction of Congress to enact [it]...."[4] The law can only be passed to put into force a power specified in the Constitution. Thus, a law is "necessary and proper," if the end (the specified power) actually exists and the means (the law in question) is indispensable to its operation. Nevertheless, some

---

1 Walter E. Williams, *The law or good ideas?* WorldNetDaily [Internet]; available from http://www.worldnetdaily.com/news/article.asp?ARTICLE_ID=43540; accessed 19 July 2008.

2 Jefferson's Opinion on the Constitutionality of a National Bank, 1791, The Avalon Project at Yale Law School [Internet]; available from http://www.yale.edu/lawweb/avalon/amerdoc/bank-tj.htm#bl; accessed 19 July 2008.

3 "It would reduce the whole instrument to a single phrase, that of instituting a Congress with power to do whatever would be for the good of the United States; and, as they would be the sole judges of the good or evil, it would be also a power to do whatever evil they please." Ibid.

4 Randy E. Barnett, "The Original Meaning of the Commerce Clause," Randy E. Barnett [Internet]; available from http://randybarnett.com/pdf/originalmeaning.pdf; accessed 19 July 2008. See also Randy E. Barnett, "The Original Meaning of the Necessary and Proper Clause," Randy E. Barnett [Internet] http://randybarnett.com/pdf/originalNecessary.pdf; accessed 19 July 2008: "A law actually enacted for a purpose or end that was not among those enumerated would exceed its jurisdiction under the Constitution and be improper regardless of the means employed."

disagreement over exactly what falls under the phrase "necessary and proper" is to be expected. In order to reduce it to a minimum, it is important to keep in mind the original purpose of the clause and to remember that the federal government is one of *limited* powers.

What specific sections of the Constitution give Congress the authority to approve budgets (i.e., appropriations bills) for the day-to-day operations of the legislative, executive, and judicial branches of the government? This power is derived from Article I section 8, clause 1, which gives Congress the power "To [*sic*] lay and collect Taxes, Duties, Imposts, and Excises..." and from Article I, section 9, clause 7, which states, "No Money shall be drawn from the Treasury, but in Consequence of Appropriations made by Law; and a regular Statement and Account of the Receipts and Expenditures of all public Money shall be published from time to time." Also applicable would be Article I, section 8, clause 18, which states, "[Congress shall have power] to make all Laws which shall be necessary and proper for carrying into Execution ... all ... Powers vested by this Constitution in the Government of the United States, or in any Department or Officer thereof."

The taxing power, being the primary power that makes possible all the others, begins the enumeration, since all the other powers must be paid for in some fashion. Even the second listed power, "to borrow money on the credit of the United States," must eventually be paid for through taxes. With this obvious fact in mind, I have created Illustration 1, which shows how Article I, section 8 should properly be understood. I have also included the other powers of Congress not found in Article I, section 8, since they are dependent on the taxing power as well.

Article I, section 9 listed some things that Congress is prohibited from doing. Of course, this section does not attempt to list *all* the things that are forbidden, for such a list would be very long indeed, if one could even be written, but only those things that deserved special consideration in the opinion of the Convention delegates. Even so, the view that seems to be accepted today is that as long as something is *not* listed in Article I, section 9, Congress has the power to do it. However, from all that has been explained above, this view is clearly incorrect. I quote this section below:

> *Section. 9.* [Clause 1] The Migration or Importation of such Persons[1] as any of the States now existing shall think proper to admit, shall not be prohibited by the Congress prior to the Year one thousand eight hundred and eight, but a Tax or duty may be imposed on such Importation, not exceeding ten dollars for each Person.
>
> [Clause 2] The Privilege of the Writ of Habeas Corpus shall not be suspended, unless when in Cases of Rebellion or Invasion the public Safety may require it.
>
> [Clause 3] No Bill of Attainder or ex post facto Law shall be passed.
>
> [Clause 4] No Capitation, or other direct, Tax shall be laid, unless in Proportion to the Census or Enumeration herein before directed to be taken.[2]

---

1 The phrase the "Importation of such Persons" actually referred to slaves who were brought into the United States for sale. In order to keep the southern states (Georgia, South Carolina, and North Carolina) in the union, the delegates at the Federal Convention of 1787 reached a compromise, stipulating that the slave trade could not be outlawed for twenty years (i.e., 1787 to 1808). Note that Congress was still given the authority within that twenty-year period to assess a tax of not more than ten dollars on the owners of "such Importation." We will discuss this clause in much more detail in a later chapter.

2 This census or enumeration is also mentioned in Article I, section 2, clause 3. The purpose of the Sixteenth Amendment was to permit an income tax (classified as a direct tax) that

[Clause 5] No Tax or Duty shall be laid on Articles exported from any State.

[Clause 6] No Preference shall be given by any Regulation of Commerce or Revenue to the Ports of one State over those of another: nor shall Vessels bound to, or from, one State, be obliged to enter, clear or pay Duties in another.

[Clause 7] No Money shall be drawn from the Treasury, but in Consequence of Appropriations made by Law; and a regular Statement and Account of the Receipts and Expenditures of all public Money shall be published from time to time.

[Clause 8] No Title of Nobility shall be granted by the United States: and no Person holding any Office of Profit or Trust under them, shall, without the Consent of the Congress, accept of any present, Emolument, Office, or Title, of any kind whatever, from any King, Prince, or foreign State.

So what have been the consequences of the Congress abandoning all constitutional bounds and spending money for any program it wants to without restriction? Well, to begin with, federal spending has increased by 134 percent since 1990, from $1.25 trillion to $2.93 trillion in 2008[1] and much of it is clearly not within constitutional limits. I mentioned some important examples of unconstitutional spending above, such as Medicare, Medicaid, Social Security, aid to education, housing subsidies like Housing Choice Vouchers (formerly Section 8), farm subsidies, and foreign aid, but these are only the largest and most obvious examples. One writer has stated "no matter how long one searches through the Constitution, it is impossible to find any language that authorizes at least 90 percent of the civilian programs that Congress crams into the federal budget today."[2]

A most egregious form of unconstitutional spending is known as "pork-barrel projects." The number of these projects has increased by a whopping 2,026 percent since 1991, from 546 to 11,610 in 2008.[3] In addition, spending for these projects has increased by 455 percent since 1991, from $3.1 billion to $17.2 billion in 2008.[4] According to Citizens Against Government Waste (CAGW), "a pork-barrel project is a line-item in an appropriations or authorization bill that designates funds for a specific purpose in circumvention of the normal procedures for budget review. To qualify as pork, a project must meet one of seven criteria that were developed in 1991 by Citizens Against Government Waste (CAGW) and the Congressional Porkbusters Coalition:

- Requested by only one chamber of Congress;
- Not specifically authorized;
- Not competitively awarded;
- Not requested by the President;
- Greatly exceeds the President's budget request or the previous year's funding;

---

did not need to be apportioned according to this census or enumeration, as direct taxes are required to be according to clause 4. However, we will learn in a later chapter that the Sixteenth Amendment was not constitutionally ratified.

1 Brian M. Riedl, "Federal Spending by the Numbers 2008," Nominal Budget Data and the Budget Baseline, pg. 12, The Heritage Foundation [Internet]; available from http://www.heritage.org/Research/Taxes/wm1829.cfm; accessed 27 June 2008.

2 Stephen Moore, *The Unconstitutional Congress*, Hoover Foundation [Internet]; available from http://www.hoover.org/publications/policyreview/3566517.html; accessed 27 June 2008.

3 Historical Trends, Citizens Against Government Waste (CAGW) [Internet]; available from http://www.cagw.org/site/PageServer?pagename=reports_porkbarrelreport#trends; accessed 27 June 2008.

4 Ibid.

- Not the subject of congressional hearings; or
- Serves only a local or special interest."[1]

CAGW further informs us that "the terms 'pork' and 'earmarks' are often used interchangeably, but they are different. The term 'earmark' generally means any expenditure for a specific purpose that is tucked into a larger bill. Only when the earmark is inappropriately added to the bill is it considered pork."[2]

Unfortunately, it is doubtful that any pork meets constitutional requirements for two reasons: 1) it is probably not authorized by Article I, section 8 and/or 2) since a pork project usually goes to a particular recipient that is located in a certain state or region, it does not "provide for the *common* Defense and *general* Welfare of the United States (italics mine)." Some noteworthy examples of pork-barrel projects from the CAGW are listed for years 2005 and 2006 below:

2005
- In Alaska, $1,790,000 for berry research.
- In West Virginia, $3,638,000 for the Appalachian Fruit Laboratory in Kearneysville.
- In Washington, $250,000 for asparagus technology and production.
- In South Carolina, $469,000 for the National Wild Turkey Federation (NWTF) in Edgefield.
- In New Jersey, $335,000 for cranberry/blueberry disease and breeding (since 1985, $4.3 million has been spent on this research).
- In Montana, Texas, and Wyoming, $300,000 for wool research (since 1984, $4.6 million has been spent for this research).
- In California, $1,250,000 for the American Film Institute's Screen Education Program.
- In California, $150,000 for the Lady B. Ranch in Apple Valley for a Therapeutic Horseback Riding Program.
- In Ohio, $350,000 for the Rock n' Roll Hall of Fame in Cleveland (since 2002, they have received $750,000),
- In Iowa, $231,000 for dairy education.[3]

2006
- In South Carolina, $234,000 more for the National Wild Turkey Federation (NWTF).
- In Michigan, $1,000,000 for the Waterfree Urinal Conservation Initiative.
- In Nevada, $250,000 for the Mojave Bird Study.
- In Alaska, Idaho, Maine, Michigan, Minnesota, Mississippi, North Carolina, Oregon, Tennessee, Washington, and West Virginia, $6,435,000 for wood utilization research (since 1985, $86 million has been spent on this research).
- In New York, $250,000 for the Stanley Theater in Utica.
- In Washington, $550,000 for the Museum of Glass in Tacoma.
- In Alaska, $500,000 for the Arctic Winter Games.
- In Nevada, $100,000 for the Richard Steele Boxing Club in Henderson.
- In Iowa, $250,000 for the National Cattle Congress (NCC) in Waterloo.
- $13,500,000 for the International Fund for Ireland (IFI) — some portion of

1 Tom Finnigan, "All About Pork: The Abuse of Earmarks and the Needed Reforms," Citizens Against Government Waste (CAGW) [Internet]; available from http://www.cagw.org/site/PageServer?pagename=reports_earmarks; accessed 27 June 2008.
2 Ibid.
3 2005 Pig Book Summary, Citizens Against Government Waste (CAGW) [Internet]; available from http://www.cagw.org/site/PageServer?pagename=reports_pigbook2005; accessed on 19 July 2008.

which will be spent for the World Toilet Summit.[1]

According to CAGW, 2007 "breaks a run of seven consecutive years of record dollar amounts of pork, culminating in $29 billion in the 2006 Congressional Pig Book. This lesser barrel of pork can be attributed to the efforts of ... [a few Senators], who prevented the enactment of nine appropriations bills in December, 2006, and the subsequent moratorium on earmarks announced and enforced by the House and Senate Appropriations Committee Chairmen ... in H. J. Res. 20, the bill that funds the government for the remainder of fiscal 2007."[2] Nevertheless, according to CAGW, "there is still enough pork to cause concern for taxpayers, as 2,658 projects were stuffed into the Defense and Homeland Security Appropriations Acts, at a cost of $13.2 billion."[3] Below are a few of the pork-barrel projects found in the Defense Appropriations Act. Let me first stress that this bill is supposedly for *Defense* spending:

- $5,000,000 for Impact Aid for children with disabilities.
- $5,300,000 for the study of marine mammals, which would, of course, include whales.
- $5,000,000 for alcohol breath testers.
- $1,000,000 for the Allen Telescope Array in Mountain View, California, which is part of SETI (Search for Extraterrestrial Intelligence).
- $1,650,000 for improving the shelf life of vegetables.[4]

Finally, some noteworthy examples of pork-barrel projects for 2008 are listed below:

- In South Carolina, $172,782 more for the National Wild Turkey Federation (NWTF).
- $7,556,660 for grape and wine research.
- $460,752 for hops research, the main ingredient of beer.
- In New York, $98,000 for renovations to the Wakely Lodge Resort in Indian Lake, the location of a public nine-hole golf course.
- In Washington, $245,000 for the construction of the Walter Clore Wine and Culinary Center in Prosser.
- In Wisconsin, $178,740 for the Dairy Business Association (DBA).
- In Alaska, $818,232 for alternative salmon products.
- In New York, $1,950,000 to add a library and archives at the Charles B. Rangel Center for Public Service at The City College of New York. The Center, which is sponsored by Rep. Charles Rangel, has been colloquially called the "Monument to Me."
- In Mississippi, $147,660 for the Immanuel Church in Winona.
- In Iowa, $393,760 for the City National Bank Building, a privately owned structure that is being converted into a 26-room hotel.[5]

As a bill moves through the legislative process, additional provisions like pork-barrel projects and other items are inserted into it that often have little or nothing to do with the original title or purpose of the legislation. These provisions are fre-

1 2006 Pig Book Summary, Citizens Against Government Waste (CAGW) [Internet]; available from http://www.cagw.org/site/PageServer?pagename=reports_pigbook2006; accessed on 19 July 2008.

2 2007 Pig Book Summary, Citizens Against Government Waste (CAGW) [Internet]; available form http://www.cagw.org/site/PageServer?pagename=reports_pigbook2007; accessed 27 June 2008.

3 Ibid.

4 Ibid.

5 2008 Pig Book Summary, Citizens Against Government Waste (CAGW) [Internet]; available form http://www.cagw.org/site/PageServer?pagename=reports_pigbook2008; accessed 27 June 2008.

quently "hidden" deep within the bill and can be easily overlooked by legislators. Sometimes, a bill becomes so huge that, prior to its scheduled vote, it is not read in its entirety, so these additions go unnoticed. Furthermore, many of them would never be passed into law in the first place, if they had been on *specific* legislation for that purpose. However, because they are inserted into large bills, they escape detection and become law anyway. This type of legislation can only be called deceptive and should not be allowed.

Article I, section 7, clause 2 of the Constitution describes the process by which a bill becomes law, but does not describe in any detail what comprises a bill. Consequently, a constitutional amendment would probably have to be proposed and ratified in order to prohibit legislation that is a jumble of unrelated laws or spending. The ideal wording for this proposed amendment is already available and it comes from the defunct Constitution of the Confederate States of America. This Constitution officially went into effect for the Confederacy on March 11, 1861. In Article I, Section 9, clause 20 of the document, the following passage is found: "*Every law, or resolution having the force of law [a joint resolution],*[1] *shall relate to but one subject, and that shall be expressed in the title* (italics mine)."[2] This wording, or words very much like it, if properly proposed and ratified as an amendment to the Constitution, would only allow a bill to be enacted that contained legislation pertaining to one topic only. In addition, the topic would be clearly identified by the title of the bill.

Another needed improvement should be made in the legislative process. Some means should be adopted to make it mandatory that each bill is actually read by all the members of Congress who plan to vote for it. Since according to Article I, section 5, clause 2 of the Constitution, "each House may determine the Rules of its Proceedings...," only a bill, as opposed to a constitutional amendment, would be required to make this change. The Downsize DC organization has actually written such a bill, which is titled the "Read the Bills Act of 2006." Among the provisions in this proposed legislation, one requires that all members of both houses who will vote for a bill must sign an affidavit attesting to the fact that they have either carefully listened to a complete reading of the bill or have thoroughly read the entire bill themselves. A copy of the proposed bill can be found on the Downsize DC web site.[3]

When the difference between revenues and expenditures is a deficit in any given year, the federal government must borrow money to pay for the lack of funds.[4] Article I, section 8, clause 2 of the Constitution gives Congress the power to "borrow Money

---

1 According to a document on the US Government Printing Office (GPO Access) web site, "there is no real difference between a bill and a joint resolution." On the other hand, "a concurrent resolution ... does not have the force of law." Congressional Bills: Glossary, Congressional Bills, GPO Access [Internet]; available from http://www.gpoaccess.gov/bills/glossary.html; accessed 25 August 2008.

2 The Constitution of the Confederate States of America, Articles, Filibuster Cartoons [Internet]; available from http://www.filibustercartoons.com/CSA.htm; accessed 18 August 2008.

3 "Read the Bills Act of 2006," Downsize DC [Internet]; available from http://www.downsizedc.org/page/rtba_legislation; accessed August 25 2008.

4 In actuality, "the Government's debt (debt held by the public) is [only] *approximately* the cumulative amount of borrowing to finance deficits.... *Borrowing is not exactly equal to the deficit...*, because of the other means of financing ... [,which] ... can either increase or decrease the Government's borrowing needs... (italics mine)." The Budget System and Concepts, FY 2009 Budget, Budget Management, The White House [Internet]; available from http://www.whitehouse.gov/omb/budget/fy2009/pdf/concepts.pdf; accessed 18 August 2008. However, so as not to make the above explanation overly convoluted, I will not get into any detail about the "other means of financing."

on the credit of the United States." The Bureau of the Public Debt, which is a division of the US Treasury, is given the authority to sell Treasury securities (i.e., bills, notes, bonds, and savings bonds) to the public via the primary and secondary securities markets. At one time, Congress passed legislation to authorize every new issuance of debt that was sold to the public, but this is not the case anymore. Today, Congress only authorizes a debt limit known as the debt ceiling. Under this system, the Bureau of the Public Debt is allowed to sell Treasury securities on its own up to the debt ceiling, but no further. If Congress decides to pass legislation to increase the ceiling, as it has done repeatedly,[1] the Bureau would then be able to sell additional Treasury securities up to the new limit.

When money is borrowed, a national debt is the result. If the yearly deficits accumulate, the national debt grows. Without any restraints on the type or amount of spending, Congress has created over time a national debt that is currently more than $9.5 trillion and growing![2] That is right, not $9.5 million or even $9.5 billion, but $9.5 *trillion (of course, that is separate from and in addition to the states' debts, corporate debt, family debt, etc.).* Of course, the interest payment on this debt cannot be forgotten either, which in 2007 was $430 billion.[3]

This is a staggering amount indeed, but it is only the "tip of the iceberg." When the baby boomer generation (those born in the period from 1946 to 1963) begins to collect Medicare and Social Security (programs that are unconstitutional, by the way), words cannot adequately portray what the financial impact will be. According to Carolyn Lochhead of the *San Francisco Chronicle* (Washington Bureau), "an array of government and private analysts put the actual US 'fiscal gap,' which means all future receipts minus all future obligations, at $40 trillion (Government Accountability Office) to $72 trillion (Social Security Board of Trustees)."[4] She continues, "these are not sums, but present-value figures, heavily discounted to show in today's dollars what it would cost to pay off the debt immediately. The International Monetary Fund estimates the gap at $47 trillion, the Brookings Institution at $60 trillion."[5]

Laurence J. Kotlikoff, a professor of economics at Boston University and a research associate at the National Bureau of Economic Research, states that the "Gokhale and

---

1 For example, in the "Housing and Economic Recovery Act of 2008" that was passed on July 30, 2008 (Public Law 110-289), Section 3083 increased the Debt Ceiling from $9.815 to $10.615 trillion, which is an increase of $800 billion. See H. R. 3221, A bill to provide needed housing reform and for other purposes, Library of Congress (Thomas) [Internet]; available from http://thomas.loc.gov/cgi-bin/bdquery/z?d110:HR03221:|TOM:/bss/d110query.html|; accessed 20 August 2008. Prior to this increase, a bill titled "Increasing the statutory limit on the public debt" that was passed on September 29, 2007 (Public Law 110-91), increased the Debt Ceiling from $8.965 to $9.815 trillion, which is an increase of $850 billion. See H. J. Res. 43, Increasing the statutory limit on the public debt, Library of Congress (Thomas) [Internet]; available from http://thomas.loc.gov/cgi-bin/bdquery/z?d110:HJ00043:|TOM:/bss/d110query.html|; accessed 20 August 2008.

2 The Debt to the Penny and Who Holds It, Treasury Direct [Internet]; available from http://www.treasurydirect.gov/NP/BPDLogin?application=np; accessed 19 July 2008.

3 Internet Expense on the Debt Outstanding, Treasury Direct [Internet]; available from http://www.treasurydirect.gov/govt/reports/ir/ir_expense.htm; accessed 19 July 2008.

4 Carolyn Lochhead, "Speeches ignore impending U. S. debt disaster," Restoring America to Constitutional Principles [Internet]; available from http://eldoradogold.net/pdf/September2004/debt_lochead.pdf; accessed 19 July 2008.

5 Ibid.

Smetters measure of the fiscal gap is a stunning $65.9 trillion!"[1] He then provides his assessment of the seriousness of this approaching financial fiasco:

> This figure is more than five times US GDP and almost twice the size of national wealth. One way to wrap one's head around $65.9 trillion is to ask what fiscal adjustments are needed to eliminate this red hole. The answers are terrifying. One solution is an immediate and permanent doubling of personal and corporate income taxes. Another is an immediate and permanent two-thirds cut in Social Security and Medicare benefits. A third alternative, were it feasible, would be to immediately and permanently cut all federal discretionary spending by 143 percent.[2]

As if this assessment is not serious enough, he further informs us "the $65.9 trillion gap is all the more alarming because its calculation omits the value of contingent government liabilities and relies on quite optimistic assumptions about increases over time in longevity and federal healthcare expenditures."[3]

Whatever the precise size of this fiscal gap may be, it is surely a very grave financial problem for the nation. The truth is that the US federal government's finances are a mess. In fact, in the Government Accountability Office (GAO) Statement attached to the 2007 Financial Report of the United States Government, David M. Walker, the Comptroller General of the United States, stated that "certain material weaknesses[4] in financial reporting and other limitations on the scope of our work[5] resulted in conditions that, for the 11th consecutive year, prevented us from expressing an opinion on the financial statements...." In addition, "the federal government did not maintain effective internal control over financial reporting (including safeguarding assets) and compliance with significant laws and regulations as of September 30, 2007."[6] According to *Government Auditing Standards*, which is usually known as the Yellow Book by auditors, one of the "four AICPA [American Institute of Certified Public Accountants] generally accepted standards of reporting" is that the "auditor must either express an opinion regarding the financial statements, taken as a whole, or state that an opinion cannot be expressed, in the auditor's report. When the auditor cannot express an

1 Laurence J. Kotlikoff, "Is the United States Bankrupt?" The Federal Reserve Bank of St. Louis *Review* (July/August 2006 Vol.88, No.4), The Federal Reserve Bank of St. Louis [Internet]; available from http://www.research.stlouisfed.org/publications/review/06/07/Kotlikoff.pdf; accessed 19 July 2008.

2 Ibid.

3 Ibid.

4 According to the Government Accountability Office (GAO) Auditor's Report, a "material weakness" is "a significant deficiency, or a combination of significant deficiencies, that results in more than a remote likelihood that a material misstatement of the financial statements will not be prevented or detected." Government Accountability Office (GAO) Auditor's Report, 2007 Financial Report of the United States Government, Financial Management Service [Internet]; available from http://fms.treas.gov/fr/07frusg/07gao2.pdf; accessed 27 June 2008.

5 According to the Government Accountability Office (GAO) Auditor's Report, the "other limitations on the scope" were "1) serious financial management problems at the Department of Defense, 2) the federal government's inability to adequately account for and reconcile intragovernmental activity and balances between federal agencies, and 3) the federal government's ineffective process for preparing the consolidated financial statements." Ibid.

6 Government Accountability Office (GAO) Statement, 2007 Financial Report of the United States Government, Financial Management Service [Internet]; available from http://fms.treas.gov/fr/07frusg/07gao1.pdf; accessed 27 June 2008.

overall opinion, the auditor should state the reasons therefore in the auditor's report."[1] Please note that this is not the first year, but the "*11th consecutive year*" that an opinion could not be expressed on the federal government's financial statements.

Unfortunately, while Congress has run amok spending on all kinds of unconstitutional programs that the collective minds of most of the members can dream up, it has not hesitated to transfer many of its legitimate powers over to other bodies. The reason is no doubt to avoid having to make any important, yet politically sensitive, decisions in these areas. Let me provide some examples below:

Although the Constitution states that "all legislative powers ... shall be vested in a Congress of the United States" (Article I, section 1), in many instances it has given this power over to either the President, who often makes law by signing Executive Orders or to the Supreme Court that is allowed to legislate from the bench. Please note that Congress is granted "*all* legislative powers," not just some of them.

Article II of the Constitution states that the "executive Power shall be vested in a President of the United States of America" (Section 1, clause 1) and the President "shall take Care that the Laws be faithfully executed ...." (Section 3). He is clearly not given the power to make law, but only to carry out the laws passed by Congress.

Executive Orders are usually legitimate if they are issued by the President to give guidance to the departments of the executive branch in implementing laws passed by Congress. However, according to ThisNation.com, "Executive Orders are controversial because they allow the President to make major decisions, even law, without the consent of Congress. This, of course, runs against the general logic of the Constitution — that no one should have power to act unilaterally."[2] Paul Begala, former President Clinton advisor, once made the following startling remark about the use of these presidential directives: "Stroke of the pen. Law of the Land. Kinda cool," (*The New York Times*, July 5, 1998).[3]

Article III of the Constitution states that the "judicial Power of the United States, shall be vested in one supreme Court, and in such inferior Courts as the Congress may from time to time ordain and establish" (Section 1). It is as clear as anything can be that the Constitution grants no power to the Supreme Court to make law, but only to interpret, *in the context of a particular case brought before it*, a law passed by Congress or enforced by the President. More will be said about the judicial power of the Supreme Court in a later chapter.

Congress is supposed to "regulate commerce with foreign nations" (Article I, section 8, clause 3), but it has bypassed this power in two important ways. First, it has transferred it over to international organizations that administer so-called free trade agreements, such as NAFTA (North American Free Trade Agreement), CAFTA-DR (Dominican Republic–Central America–United States Free Trade Agreement), and about sixty other agreements handled by the WTO (World Trade Organization). Second, Congress has given the President extraordinary power to negotiate trade agreements with very little participation of its own. This arrangement is called Trade Promotion (TPA) or "Fast Track" Authority. More will be said about the power of Congress to regulate foreign trade in a later chapter.

---

1 *Government Auditing Standards* (The Yellow Book), GAO (US Government Accountability Office) [Internet]; available from http://www.gao.gov/govaud/d07162g.pdf; accessed 19 July 2008.

2 "What is an Executive Order?" ThisNation.com [Internet]; available from http://www.thisnation.com/question/040.html; accessed 19 July 2008.

3 Ibid.

Congress is supposed to "coin money" and "regulate the value thereof" (Article I, section 8, clause 5), but it has given this power over to the Federal Reserve System since 1913 without any constitutional authority. Actually, the "Fed," as it is nicknamed, does not "coin" money, but it prints unconstitutional Federal Reserve notes instead. All the same, it can still be said that the money making power of Congress was transferred over to the Fed. More will be said about the monetary system in the next chapter.

Finally, Congress is supposed to "declare war" (Article I, section 8, clause 11), but it has given this power over to the President. The latter is empowered to administer the conduct of the war as the "Commander in Chief" (Article II, section 2) only after war has been declared, unless on the rare occasions a *national emergency* requiring *immediate action* exists. This subject will be discussed in more detail in a later chapter.

Prior to the 20th century, numerous cases can be pointed out when a Congressman or a President refused to vote for or to sign a piece of legislation that was considered unconstitutional. Let me briefly mention some of them:

In 1794, James Madison, then a member of the House of Representatives, refused to approve $15,000 for French refugees. He stated, "I cannot undertake to lay my finger on that article of the Constitution which granted a right to Congress of expending, on objects of benevolence, the money of their constituents."

In 1796, the Virginian, William Giles, a member of the House of Representatives, sternly disapproved of an aid bill for the victims of a fire. He stated that Congress had not the power to "attend to what generosity and humanity require, but to what the Constitution and their duty require."

In 1817, President Madison vetoed the "Bonus Bill" establishing an internal improvement program, which was to be financed through surplus revenues provided to the federal government by the Second Bank of the United States. His reason for vetoing the bill was that he could find no authorization in the Constitution giving Congress the power to spend funds for such a purpose. The bill failed, because Congress could not prevail over the president's veto.

In 1827, the legendary Colonel Davy Crockett, then a member of the House of Representatives, refused to approve $10,000 for a dead navy officer's widow. He made this noteworthy utterance to the body: "We must not permit our respect for the dead or our sympathy for the living to lead us into an act of injustice to the balance of the living. I will not attempt to prove that Congress has no power to appropriate this money as an act of charity. Every member upon this floor knows it. We have the right as individuals, to give away as much of our own money as we please in charity; but as members of Congress we have no right to appropriate a dollar of the public money." Interestingly enough, apparently because of his statement, the pension bill was defeated.

In 1830, President Andrew Jackson vetoed an internal improvement bill regarding the building of a 60-mile road linking the towns of Maysville and Lexington in Kentucky. The federal government was to purchase $150,000 of stock in a privately owned company in order to finance the building of the road. The objection President Jackson offered was that, since Congress was not given the power to provide funding for internal improvements, especially for such purposes within a single state only, the bill was unconstitutional. It failed to pass, because Congress could not override the president's veto. A few days later, two additional bills of similar type came to President Jackson's desk. He dealt with them by using the technique called the pocket veto.

In 1832, President Andrew Jackson vetoed a bill to renew the Second Bank of the United States. His reason for doing so was that he believed it was unconstitutional. In his veto message, he stated, "each public officer, who takes an oath to support the constitution, swears that he will support it as he understands it, and not as it is understood by others." With our unquestioning acceptance of judicial supremacy today, it is surely surprising that President Jackson took this course of action even though the Supreme Court had already declared the Bank constitutional in *McCulloch v. Maryland* back in 1819.

In 1854, President Franklin Pierce vetoed a bill designed to help the mentally ill. To his critics, he stated, "I cannot find any authority in the Constitution for public charity." He further contended that such spending "would be contrary to the letter and spirit of the Constitution and subversive to the whole theory upon which the Union of these States is founded."

In 1887, President Grover Cleveland vetoed a bill to aid counties in Texas that had been severely affected by a drought. He stated, "I feel obliged to withhold my approval of the plan to indulge in benevolent and charitable sentiment through the appropriation of public funds ... I find no warrant for such an appropriation in the Constitution."

Surely, none of these men were unsympathetic to people in dire need or unaware of the many benefits that could accrue from internal improvements. What was their underlying motivation then in making their decisions? Since the US Constitution created a federal government of limited, delegated, and enumerated powers, they were concerned that if they took a single step away from its dictates the "cat would be let out of the bag." The first transgression would create a precedent for taking another one, then another, and then another, etc., until any restraints once placed on government become ineffective. History has proved them right. Look how enormous the federal government octopus is today with its tentacles in every area of life. Can anyone deny that government has grown far beyond anything that was intended by the Constitution?

When examining the deeds of these great statesmen of the eighteenth and nineteenth centuries, it is very refreshing to see how deeply concerned they were with trying to adhere to the tenets of the Constitution. Their oaths of office seem to have actually meant something to them. Today, there are politicians in Washington, most of whom may utter the words of the oath, but clearly do not take them seriously. How can they, when they give the Constitution little more than lip service? I wonder how many of them have actually ever read the Constitution or the Declaration of Independence? How the times have changed.

Some may ask, "If it is unconstitutional for the federal government to provide, let us say, health care, how can people who need it still get it?" There are only four possible ways:

1. They can find a means of paying for health care themselves. I know that in these days the idea of taking responsibility for your own life is something many of us may not like to hear. All the same, if we truly want to live in liberty and self-government, self-reliance must remain the primary means of obtaining our needs. Nevertheless, a self-reliant lifestyle would not sound like such an impossible feat, if the federal government stayed within constitutional bounds. The favorable result of such restraint would be a government that could operate with significantly less revenue, which means we would be able to keep more of our own money.

2. Charitable organizations can provide it to people who need it. Americans are the most charitable people on earth. Consider this quote from an article in *Philanthropy* magazine:

Is it a coincidence one of the world's freest, most entrepreneurial, and most religious nations is also the world's most philanthropic nation? Americans donate like no other people, whether you look at total donations, per capita giving, size of gifts, or types of giving. And as our wealth increases, so does our generosity.

Two writers for England's *Economist* magazine just wrote a book about America's differences from the rest of the world, and one important difference they note is the way Americans give. After noting that we give far larger proportions of our income to charity, they write, "Crucially, Americans much prefer to give away their money themselves, rather than let their government do it.... This tradition of philanthropy encouraged America to tackle its social problems without building a European-style welfare state, and to embrace modernity without abandoning its traditions of voluntarism, decentralization and experiment."

Similarly, American philanthropist Daniel Rose observed last year that the French "are bemused to learn that American private charitable contributions this year will exceed $200 billion, equal to about 10 percent of the total federal budget; that some 70 percent of US households make charitable cash contributions; and that over half of all US adults will volunteer an estimated 20 billion hours in charitable activities." Nor, Rose adds, are the French alone in their astonishment: "A recent German study reports that on a per capita basis, American citizens contribute to charity nearly seven times as much as their German counterparts and that about six times as many Americans as Germans do volunteer work."[1]

Surely, it would be reasonable to suppose that if Americans were paying far less taxes because of congressional spending remaining within constitutional limits, the donations that would ensue would be even greater than they are now. Numerous charitable organizations would doubtless come into existence to provide all kinds of services for those truly in need.

This charity would not be limited to domestic assistance only, but would doubtless include foreign aid as well. Even with a high tax load, it was concluded in a study by the United States Agency for International Development (USAID), which is an independent federal government agency, that "the United States is the clear leader in all measures of private assistance to the developing world."[2] For 2010, it was estimated that total US international assistance to developing countries would be $84.9 billion. Of this total, government assistance is estimated at $29.9 billion, whereas private assistance is estimated at $55 billion — 65% of the total (low estimate).[3]

The transfer payments of government can never be true charity, because people are forced to give it through taxes.

3. The states can provide health care to their citizens who need it, as long

1 Alexander C. Karp, Gary A. Tobin, Aryeh K. Weinberg, "An Exceptional Nation," *Philanthropy* (Nov./Dec. 2004).

2 *Foreign Aid in the National Interest:Promoting Freedom, Security, and Opportunity*, Released 7 January 2003, Chapter 6, The Full Measure of Foreign Aid, Sources and amounts of private investment lending [html], pg. 134, USAID [Internet]; available from http://www.usaid.gov/fani/Full_Report—Foreign_Aid_in_the_National_Interest.pdf; accessed 19 July 2008.

3 *Foreign Aid in the National Interest: Promoting Freedom, Security, and Opportunity*, Released 7 January 2003, Table 6.4, The full measure of international assistance, pg. 146, USAID [Internet]; available from http://www.usaid.gov/fani/Full_Report—Foreign_Aid_in_the_National_Interest.pdf; accessed 19 July 2008.

as it is not prohibited by the federal Constitution or by each state's own Constitution. The federal Constitution prohibits the states from doing certain things and these are listed in Article I, section 10. I quote this section below:

Section. 10. [Clause 1] No State shall enter into any Treaty, Alliance, or Confederation; grant Letters of Marque and Reprisal; coin Money; emit Bills of Credit; make any Thing but gold and silver Coin a Tender in Payment of Debts; pass any Bill of Attainder, ex post facto Law, or Law impairing the Obligation of Contracts, or grant any Title of Nobility.

[Clause 2] No State shall, without the Consent of the Congress, lay any Imposts or Duties on Imports or Exports, except what may be absolutely necessary for executing it's inspection Laws: and the net Produce of all Duties and Imposts, laid by any State on Imports or Exports, shall be for the Use of the Treasury of the United States; and all such Laws shall be subject to the Revision and Controul [*sic*] of the Congress.

[Clause 3] No State shall, without the Consent of Congress, lay any Duty of Tonnage, keep Troops, or Ships of War in time of Peace, enter into any Agreement or Compact with another State, or with a foreign Power, or engage in War, unless actually invaded, or in such imminent Danger as will not admit of delay.

As you can see, the federal Constitution does not prohibit the states from providing health care, or any other type of social service for that matter, to its citizens. Therefore, as long as a state's own Constitution does not prohibit it, the state can pass a law to provide it. Of course, if health care were prohibited in some way by the state Constitution, it would first have to be amended in the proper manner so that a law could be passed to provide it to its citizens.

If the states retained all the powers that were not specifically delegated to the federal government, a healthy competition would naturally result between the states. Some states would be more liberal and experiment with all types of social service programs, whereas others would be more conservative, and prefer not to get involved in these areas. As a result, the inferior programs would be criticized and discarded and the superior ones would be praised and copied by other states.

Of course, taxes in the more liberal states would tend to be higher than in the more conservative ones. Consequently, those citizens residing in a liberal state who were unhappy with their taxes could either attempt to change the state of affairs through the political process or, if all else failed, move to a more conservative state. On the other hand, those citizens in a conservative state who were dissatisfied with the lack of social services would have the same options — either alter the situation within or relocate. Today's political agenda of instilling social conformity throughout the nation was clearly *not* the idea the Founders had in mind.

> 4. Finally, they can try to get a constitutional amendment proposed and then ratified according to Article V of the Constitution, which would give the federal government the power to provide health care.

An ingenious solution was offered a few years back by Harry Browne, the noted investment advisor, author, and two-time Presidential candidate for the Libertarian party, as a means of solving the social security and national debt problems. The plan would end the former and slash the latter, hopefully to zero. Unfortunately, there would only be one try at it, so before attempting the plan we must be sure that the federal government can never again get involved with funding retirement plans or other unconstitutional programs.

If, in order to guard against possible federal government excesses in the future, a new constitutional amendment needs to be proposed and ratified like the Liberty Amendment for example, so be it. The text of this proposed Amendment to the Constitution reads as follows:

> *Section 1.* The Government of the United States shall not engage in any business, professional, commercial, financial or industrial enterprise except as specified in the Constitution.
>
> *Section 2.* The constitution or laws of any State, or the laws of the United States shall not be subject to the terms of any foreign or domestic agreement which would abrogate this amendment.
>
> *Section 3.* The activities of the United States Government which violate the intent and purpose of this amendment shall, within a period of three years from the date of the ratification of this amendment, be liquidated and the properties and facilities affected shall be sold.
>
> *Section 4.* Three years after the ratification of this amendment the sixteenth article of amendments to the Constitution of the United States shall stand repealed and thereafter Congress shall not levy taxes on personal incomes, estates, and/ or gifts.[1]

Nine states (Wyoming, Texas, Nevada, Louisiana, Georgia, South Carolina, Mississippi, Arizona, and Indiana) have endorsed the Amendment and Congressman Ron Paul of Texas introduced it into the House of Representatives as a joint resolution on January 28, 2003. Since then, it appears that no further action has been taken on it.

Many people may be surprised to learn that the federal government owns almost 29% of all the land in the United States. Most of it is located in the western states, but in Alaska as well. For example, the federal government owns 84.5% of the land in Nevada, 57.5% in Utah, 53.1% in Oregon, and 69.1% in Alaska.[2]

The ownership of this land by the federal government is clearly in violation of the Constitution. The federal government is only authorized to own Washington D.C., ("seat of the Government of the United States") and "Forts, Magazines, Arsenals, dockyards, and other needful Buildings." Article I, section 8, clause 17 reads as follows:

> (Congress shall have power) To exercise exclusive Legislation in all Cases whatsoever, over such District (not exceeding ten Miles square) as may, by Cession of particular States, and the Acceptance of Congress, become the seat of the Government of the United States, and to exercise like Authority over all Places purchased by the consent of the Legislature of the State in which the Same shall be, for the Erection of Forts, Magazines, Arsenals, dockyards, and other needful Buildings.

---

1 The Liberty Amendment [Internet]; available from http://libertyamendment.org/; accessed 19 July 2008.

2 Annual Report 2004 Final, Federal Real Property Profile (FRPP) as of September 30, 2004, GSA [Internet]; available from https://www.realpropertyprofile.gov/Default. aspx?module=Login; accessed 6 July 2006. Unfortunately, on trying to gain access to the web site on July 19, 2008, I found the statement, "you must be a Federal Government employee to access this website." However, a table from the "Countries of the World" web site gives the federally owned land figures for 1998. 381. Total and Federally Owned Land, and by State: 1998, Geography, United States, 2008, Countries of the World [Internet]; available from http://www.allcountries.org/uscensus/381_total_and_federally_owned_land_and. html; accessed 17 August 2008.

Furthermore, the federal government can own, administer, dispose of new territories that have been acquired by the United States through purchase, bequest or other means. The relevant portion of Article IV, section 3, clause 2 reads as follows:

> The Congress shall have Power to dispose of and make all needful Rules and Regulations respecting the Territory or other Property belonging to the United States.

However, it was expected that in due course these territories would be formed into new states, although it was certainly possible that some territories might be administered indefinitely. In any case, the federal government has no authority to own land *within a state* except for the construction of those buildings and structures listed in Article I, section 8, clause 17 (quoted above) and these were to be "purchased by the consent of the Legislature of the State."

Article IV, section 3, clause 1 gives the following rules regarding the formation of new states:

> New states may be admitted by the Congress into this union; but no new states shall be formed or erected within the jurisdiction of any other state; nor any state be formed by the junction of two or more states, or parts of states, without the consent of the legislatures of the states concerned as well as of the Congress.

Almost as soon as the new Constitution went into operation, Congress endorsed the Northwest Ordinance with minor changes, which was originally passed during the Articles of Confederation period. It describes specifically how federal territories would be governed and eventually organized into new states. New states that were formed according to its provisions would enter the Union on an "equal footing" with the other states.[1]

The federal government also owns more than 411,000 buildings and various other structures like pavements, bridges, dams, and railroad, utility, and communication systems. The total acquisition cost for all these assets is approximately $305 billion and in many cases, their "use classifications" are more than questionable from a constitutional point of view. For example, almost 18% of the owned and leased buildings are used for housing, but by comparison, little more than 25 % are used as offices.[2]

Harry Browne describes his plan in the following manner:

> [The Assets] can be sold to the public, putting them in the hands of people who will use them more responsibly and more productively. And the sales will generate the money to clean up the financial mess the politicians have made....
>
> So that the market for these assets won't be depressed, I believe the sales should take place over a six-year period. I'd prefer that it be six days, but that would reduce the proceeds.

---

1 Northwest Ordinance: July 13, 1787, The Avalon Project at Yale Law School [Internet]; available from http://www.yale.edu/lawweb/avalon/nworder.htm; accessed 19 July 2008.

2 Annual Report 2004 Final, Federal Real Property Profile (FRPP) as of September 30, 2004, GSA [Internet]; available from https://www.realpropertyprofile.gov/Default.aspx?module=Login; accessed 6 July 2006. Unfortunately, on trying to gain access to the web site on July 19, 2008, I found the statement, "you must be a Federal Government employee to access this website." However, a table from the "Countries of the World" web site gives the figures for federally owned buildings for 1998. 564. Federal Land and Buildings Owned and Leased, and Predominant Land Usage (1998), Government, United States, 2008, Countries of the World [Internet]; available from http://www.allcountries.org/uscensus/564_federal_land_and_buildings_owned_and.html; accessed 17 August 2008.

It is impossible to know in advance how much money the assets will bring because nothing like this has ever been done before. Estimates of the assets' market value have ranged from $5 trillion to $50 trillion. But if selling the assets brings even $12 trillion, it would solve two thorny problems.

First, the initial proceeds should be used to buy private retirement accounts for everyone now on Social Security — lifetime annuities from stable insurance companies that have never broken their promises.

The government will have no further Social Security liabilities to anyone....

Anyone between age 50 and retirement can receive an annuity that will begin paying out at age 65.

Anyone under 50 will save more from the elimination of the Social Security tax than he gives up in future Social Security benefits.

Second, the remaining proceeds from the asset sales will pay off the entire accumulated federal debt.... The government's yearly interest costs will be reduced to zero.[1]

This is indeed a reform plan of a caliber far beyond the gibberish we constantly hear from most Democrats and Republicans in Congress. It is also precisely the reason why it will never be discussed or even debated in Congress or in the media.

Every thinking person must realize that a very serious financial crisis exists and will not wait too long for a remedy. Some have suggested that a balanced budget amendment would solve the excessive spending problem. This is an unlikely solution, because America is addicted to spending. Soon, like any addict in need of a fix, Congress would devise some means to spend outside the constraints of the balanced budget amendment. Even today, Congress sidetracks the budgetary process with supplemental spending bills. Congressman Ron Paul explains the process in the following manner:

Supplemental spending bills are particularly galling because "emergency" funds are not subject to the same congressional budget rules. This allows Congress to spend billions of dollars completely outside the stated budget, with little or no public attention. It also underscores how meaningless government budgets really are — unlike families and businesses, the political class never has to worry about busting the budget. [2]

In addition, a proposed budget could contain some of the most ludicrous programs that can be imagined, but still be within the spending threshold. *What* is spent is just as important, and perhaps more so, as *how much* is spent. How would a balanced budget amendment control the types of spending?

In order to acquire funds, the first means Congress has available to it is to tax the people (Article I, section 8, clause 1). However, this method has a limit, because if taxes become too high the people will protest and this unwelcome reaction will not be politically beneficial. Unfortunately, Congress has another means of acquiring funds besides taxing the people. As mentioned earlier in this chapter, Congress was given the power "to borrow Money on the credit of the United States" (Article I, section, 8, clause 2). Using this power, Congress has had a nearly unlimited source of funding available to it. A more than $9.5 trillion national debt should be more than

1 Harry Browne, *The Great Libertarian Offer* (Great Falls, Montana: LiamWorks, 2000), 86.
2 "Where is Your Money Going? March 21, 2005, Texas Straight Talk, Representative Ron Paul [Internet]; available from http://www.house.gov/paul/tst/tst2005/tst032105.htm; accessed 12 August 2008.

enough substantiation to prove the truth of this statement. Thomas Jefferson had a novel answer for solving this penchant of Congress to borrow money:

> I wish it were possible to obtain a single amendment to our Constitution. I would be willing to depend on that alone for the reduction of the administration of our government to the genuine principles of the Constitution: I mean an additional article taking from the federal government the power of borrowing. (Thomas Jefferson, Letter to John Taylor, November 26, 1798).[1]

The only reason the borrowing power has been abused is that Congress no longer obeys the constraints placed on it by Constitution. Why have the "chains of the Constitution" been ignored? The answer is obvious. A world empire and a welfare-warfare state could not possibly exist under a government devoted to the "Authentic Constitution". For that reason, the constitutional restraints had to be disregarded or explained away. In addition, such a colossal government undertaking could not possibly be financed through taxation alone, because the people would simply not be able to pay the huge bill. Consequently, a national debt had to be created to support the entire structure. Furthermore, since the people only have to pay the costs gradually under this system, they lose sight of the *total* outlay involved and become complacent with their state of affairs, not realizing the true situation.

Since the Constitution takes the first position as the "supreme Law of the Land," which is stipulated in Article VI, clause 2, Congress is obligated to spend money for only those things specifically authorized by it and nothing more. By so doing, taxation would always be low and borrowing would probably be relegated to use in emergencies only, like financing a war, for example.

ILLUSTRATION 1. THE PROPER UNDERSTANDING OF ARTICLE I, SECTION 8 AND THE OTHER POWERS OF CONGRESS

Congress has power to tax (clause 1):

TO PAY THE DEBTS	TO PROVIDE FOR THE COMMON DEFENSE	TO PROVIDE FOR THE GENERAL WELFARE

However, each general spending category above is limited in scope by the following specified powers:

To borrow money (Clause 2)	To declare war (Clause 11)	To regulate commerce with the foreign nations, among the several states, and with the Indian tribes (Clause 3)
	To grant letters of marque and reprisal (Clause 11)	To establish a uniform rule of naturalization (Clause 4)
	To make rules concerning captures on land and water (Clause 11)	To establish uniform laws on the subject of bankruptcies (Clause 4)

---

1 Martin A. Larson, *Jefferson Magnificent Populist* (Devin-Adair, Publishers: Greenwich, CT, 1984), 207.

	To raise and support armies (Clause 12)	To coin money and regulate the value thereof (Clause 5)
	To provide and maintain a navy (Clause 13)	To fix the standard of weights and measures (Clause 5)
	To make rules for governing and regulating the land and naval forces (Clause 14)	To provide for the punishment of counterfeiting (Clause 6)
	To provide for calling forth the militia (Clause 15)	To establish post offices and post roads (Clause 7)
	To provide for organizing, arming, and disciplining the militia, and governing such part of them as may be employed in the service of the United States (Clause 16)	To establish copyright and patent laws (Clause 8)
	To declare the punishment for treason (Art. III, sec. 3, clause 2)	To constitute tribunals inferior to the supreme court (Clause 9)
		To define and punish piracies and felonies on the high seas (Clause 10)
		To define and punish offenses against the law of nations (Clause 10)
		To oversee the seat of government (Clause 17)
		To oversee federal buildings and other structures (Clause 17)
		To determine the manner in which representatives and direct taxes shall be apportioned among the several states (Art. I, sec. 2, clause 3).
		To impeach officers, including the President (House Power Only, Art. I, sec. 2, clause 5), and to try all impeachments (Senate Power Only, Art. I, sec. 3, clauses 6)

		To determine when the Electors are chosen and when they elect the President (Art. II, sec. 1, clause 4)
		To give advice and consent on treaties negotiated by the President (Senate Power Only, Art. II, sec. 2, clause 2)
		To give advice and consent on ambassadors, Supreme Court judges, and other officers appointed by the President (Senate Power Only, Art. II, sec. 2, clause 2)
		To vest the appointment of such inferior officers, as they think proper, in the President alone, in the courts of law, or in the heads of departments (Article II, sec. 2, clause 2)
		To prescribe the manner in which the acts, records, judicial proceedings of each state shall be given full faith and credit in every other state (Art. IV, sec. 1)
		To admit new states into the union (Art. IV, sec. 3, clause 1)
		To dispose of and make needful rules and regulations respecting the territory and other property of the United States (Art. IV, sec. 3, clause 2)
		To propose amendments to the Constitution whenever two thirds of both houses deem it necessary (Art. V)
		To determine the mode of ratification of a proposed amendment to the Constitution (Art. V)

In addition, all the specified powers must be used to benefit the entire nation, not a specific individual, group, city, state or region only;

Congress can make all laws that are "necessary and proper" for implementing the specified powers (clause 18);

No money can be withdrawn from the treasury unless the law authorizes it (article i, section 9, clause 7a) and;

A statement of receipts and expenditures must be published periodically (article i, section 9, clause 7b).

Chapter 5: Money and Banking

Before money existed, the only means available other than war to obtain commodities that could not be acquired through one's own honest efforts was through the practice known as barter. For example, if a hunter had killed an extra deer and needed a bushel of corn for his family and a farmer had an extra bushel of corn and needed meat, they could both agree to swap the deer and the bushel of corn in an even trade. Of course, the major problem with this method of trade was that it was not always easy to find someone who had something you needed and was willing to swap it for your goods.

The invention of a medium of exchange known as money solved this problem. When everyone accepted some commodity as money, it became much easier to trade goods. The reason for this was that now only one participant in a transaction had to locate a trader in the particular good that he needed, since nearly everyone would naturally store a quantity of the accepted medium of exchange. Let us say, for example, that someone needed a bushel of apples and the accepted medium of exchange was salt. In this case, only a trader of apples would have to be located, since it was expected as a matter of course that the buyer in the transaction would have salt and the seller would accept it.

At some point in the history of humankind the precious metal, gold, with silver taking an important second place, became the accepted medium of exchange. Gold had all the qualities required to fulfill this function admirably. It had a high intrinsic value and was attractive, pure, scarce, and durable. In addition, since it was malleable, homogeneous, divisible, and precisely measurable, gold coins were relatively easy to make.

However, gold was not free of shortcomings. It was heavy and thus cumbersome to carry around, and because it was valuable, theft was a definite possibility if it was not hidden or was left unguarded. For these reasons, a place of safekeeping for a person's gold became something that was needed by most people. When goldsmiths (i.e., artisans and traders in gold) had extra space available for storing gold and offered it to customers for a small fee, banking, through still in its early, undeveloped stage, had begun. When someone stored gold with the goldsmith, he gave the depositor a receipt for the gold, stating that it could be reclaimed when the receipt was returned.

As time went by, the goldsmith's business became more sophisticated. The receipts issued by the goldsmith started being used to pay for purchases instead of the gold itself. The form of the receipt evolved into a promise to pay gold on demand to the holder of the receipt instead of to a specific person. The receipts circulated as money and anytime a holder wanted to get his gold, he simply went to the goldsmith, surrendered the receipt, and received the precise quantity of gold. For the most part, the gold remained in the safekeeping of the goldsmith and the receipts circulated as money.

The goldsmith was not really the owner of his depositors' gold however, but only a custodian for it. This type of arrangement is known in the legal profession as a bailment. In a bailment, the *possession* of property is transferred to someone else (the bailee) for some stated purpose, but the person who transfers the property (the bailor) retains ownership and can take legal action against the former, if the property in his care is broken or destroyed. The late economist, Murray N. Rothbard, stated, "it should be clear that, if the deposit banker, or money-warehouseman, is treated as a regular warehouseman, or bailee, the money deposited for his safe-keeping can never constitute part of the 'asset' column on his balance sheet. In no sense can the money form part of his assets, and therefore in no sense are they a 'debt' owed to the depositor to comprise part of a banker's liability column; as something stored for safekeeping, they are not loans or debts and therefore do not properly form part of his balance sheet at all."[1] Although Rothbard's line of reasoning makes perfect sense, the courts have decided nevertheless to treat money deposited in a bank as the *property* of the bank and not as a bailment. Thus, in the examples below I have treated the storage of gold as a *debt* to the goldsmith or the modern day banker, as the case may be.

Let us say that our goldsmith stores 500 pounds of gold for others. Let us also say that one receipt is issued for each pound of gold stored. Keeping in mind that assets must equal liabilities plus net worth and disregarding for purposes of this example all the other assets, liabilities, and net worth that would normally be recorded, the goldsmith's balance sheet would look like this:

GOLDSMITH'S BALANCE SHEET (SIMPLIFIED)

Assets	Liabilities
500 lbs. of gold	500 receipts to gold
	Net Worth
TOTAL: 500	TOTAL: 500

---

1 Murray N. Rothbard, *The Case Against the Fed* (Auburn, Alabama: Ludwig von Mises Institute, 1994), 41-2.

However, the goldsmith, being a businessman, was always looking for innovative ways to make money. He noticed that only a small percentage of his customers (never more than 10%) surrendered their receipts for the gold. What if he loaned out a portion of the gold stock to those needing money and charged a fee for it? After all, the gold was just sitting in storage, so why not put it to work earning money? Of course, as a precaution, he would always have to make sure at least 10% of the gold remained in reserve in order to accommodate those depositors who (based on his experience) would return to reclaim their gold.

As part of our example, let us say that the goldsmith, who I will now call a banker, loans out 450 pounds of his depositors' gold and that each loan equals one pound. Since he will always maintain at least 10% of the gold in reserve and assuming in our example that no new gold deposits are received, then 50 pounds would be 10% of the stored gold (500 lbs. X 10% = 50 lbs.). In addition, for simplicity's sake I will not show the fees (interest) earned in the examples below. The banker's balance sheet would now look like this:

Banker's Balance Sheet (Simplified)

Assets	Liabilities
50 lbs. of gold	500 receipts to gold
450 loans of gold	Net Worth
TOTAL: 500	TOTAL: 500

As long as no more than the expected 10% of the depositors come to reclaim their gold, the banker would not have any problems. However, if more depositors than anticipated come for their gold and word gets around that the banker cannot supply it, then most likely a "bank run" by the other depositors demanding their gold would occur. Unless he could call in all the loans in order to repossess the gold, the banker would have to declare bankruptcy. It is also important to note that although the total quantity of money *in existence* has not increased, the total quantity of money *in circulation* has increased by 450 hundred pounds of gold.

At this point, the banker gets another brilliant idea. Rather than loan the actual gold out, why not print additional receipts to the gold and loan these out instead of the gold? Let us say that all of the first 450 loans have been paid off. The banker now decides to print and loan out 500 receipts *in addition to* the original 500 receipts. These additional receipts will be issued to the borrowers in place of the gold. He again kept in mind that he would not get into trouble, as long as he had at least 10% gold in reserve (100 lbs.) for the total amount of receipts issued. In this case, he had 500 lbs., which was more than enough. The banker's balance sheet would now look like this:

Banker's Balance Sheet (Simplified)

Assets	Liabilities
500 lbs. of gold	1,000 receipts to gold
500 Loans	Net Worth
TOTAL: 1,000	TOTAL: 1,000

A very interesting thing has occurred. Not only has the money *in circulation* increased by 500 receipts, but now the money *in existence* has increased by 500 receipts (from 500 to 1,000) as well. The dire consequences of this practice, which is known as fractional reserve banking, is that each receipt now represents less than 100% or only a "fraction" of the gold reserve, which in this example is 500 lbs., and the value of each receipt, and thus its purchasing power, is reduced by one half, because the total supply of receipts (i.e., money) has increased by 100%. It should not be difficult to see how the hidden tax known as inflation has negative financial consequences for those holding the receipts. Neither is it difficult to see how profitable it is for the banker to be able to earn interest on loans made possible by the creation of additional receipts.

However, the evolution of the monetary system does not end here. The ability to print receipts (paper money) as needed to pay the bills is surely a godsend for the champions of big government. Raising taxes or borrowing money — the only other viable alternatives — are usually already excessive or not favorable politically. Consequently, the politicians, working in partnership with the bankers, find it advantageous to establish a central bank for creating money as needed to finance their social engineering schemes. Of course, because the temptation is irresistible, it will not take very long before the connection with gold (i.e., the real money backing the paper) is severed completely. Because of this move, the printing presses can proceed without hindrance. Since the paper money in circulation is now completely devoid of any intrinsic value, the government will have little choice but to declare it legal tender in order to prohibit anyone from refusing to use it. A completely fiat monetary system is the result of this whole process and it perfectly represents the present Federal Reserve System.

The Federal Reserve System (nicknamed the Fed) is the central banking system of the United States that was created by the Federal Reserve Act passed on December 23, 1913. It was signed into law by President Woodrow Wilson. The Act created a network of twelve regional Federal Reserve Banks that are each located in a major city of the country. All the member banks throughout the nation are the actual owners of the Fed. The seven-member Board of Governors (also known as the Federal Reserve Board), which is located in Washington D.C., manages the system. Its members (except the Chairman and Vice-Chairman) are appointed by the President and confirmed by the Senate for terms of fourteen years that cannot be repeated. The Chairman and Vice-Chairman, however, are appointed for terms of four years that can be repeated. Ben Bernanke recently replaced Alan Greenspan as the Chairman, who had originally been appointed by President Ronald Reagan on August 11, 1987, but who retired on January 31, 2006.

The primary functions of the Fed are to regulate the operations of the member banks, to undertake check-clearing functions, to lend money to member banks when necessary, and most importantly, to administer the nation's overall monetary policy through the Federal Open Market Committee (FOMC). The last function mainly concerns changing the amount of money by means of three basic tools: undertaking open market operations, adjusting the discount rate, and changing the reserve ratio.

Before going into more detail as to how the Fed manages monetary policy, a preliminary question needs to be answered: "What does our money currently consist of?" The Federal Reserve Bank of Chicago provides the following reply to the question:

> Today, in the United States, money used in transactions is mainly of three kinds — currency (paper money [i.e., Federal Reserve notes] and coins in the pockets and purses of the public); demand deposits (non-interest-bearing checking

accounts in banks); and other checkable deposits, such as negotiable order of withdrawal (NOW) accounts, at all depository institutions, including commercial and savings banks, savings and loan associations, and credit unions. Travelers checks also are included in the definition of transactions money. Since $1 in currency and $1 in checkable deposits are freely convertible into each other and both can be used directly for expenditures, they are money in equal degree. However, only the cash and balances held by the nonbank public are counted in the money supply. Deposits of the US Treasury, depository institutions, foreign banks and official institutions, as well as vault cash in depository institutions are excluded.[1]

According to the above passage, the money supply is made up mainly of currency in the form of Federal Reserve notes and coins, and checking accounts in the form of demand deposits and other check writing deposits. "Well all that seems okay," you may reply, "but surely a commodity like gold or silver must back our money." The surprising answer is that we no longer have commodity money. Today, not one iota of gold or silver represents the true value behind our so-called money. As proof of this statement, let me quote again from the Federal Reserve Bank of Chicago:

> In the United States neither paper currency nor deposits have value as commodities [i.e., gold or silver.]. Intrinsically, a dollar bill is just a piece of paper, deposits merely book entries. Coins do have some intrinsic value as metal, but generally far less than their face value.

> What, then, makes these instruments — checks, paper money, and coins — acceptable at face value in payment of all debts and for other monetary uses? Mainly, it is the confidence people have that they will be able to exchange such money for other financial assets and for real goods and services whenever they choose to do so. [2]

According to the Board of Governors web site, the Fed obtains its currency and coin in the following manner:

Currency

> Federal Reserve notes make up more than 99 percent of all US currency in circulation.... Each year, the Federal Reserve Board determines new currency demand and submits a print order to the Treasury's Bureau of Engraving and Printing (BEP).... The Federal Reserve pays the BEP the cost of printing new currency and arranges and pays the cost of transporting the currency from the BEP facilities in Washington, D.C., and Fort Worth, Texas, to all Reserve Bank cash offices....

Coin

> The Federal Reserve's role in coin operations is more limited than its role in currency.... The US Mint ... determines the annual coin production and monitors the Reserve Banks' coin inventories weekly to identify trends in coin demand.... The Mint transports the coin from its production facilities for circulating coin in Philadelphia and Denver to all of the Reserve Banks.... [3]

On the same web site, a startling fact is revealed about how currency and coin are handled on the Fed's balance sheet:

---

1 *Modern Money Mechanics* (Chicago: Federal Reserve Bank of Chicago, February, 1994), Debt Money, ancient meme [Internet]; available from http://landru.i-link-2.net/monques/mmm2.html#MODERN; accessed 19 July 2008.

2 Ibid.

3 Currency and Coin Services, Board of Governors of the Federal Reserve System [Internet]; available from http://www.federalreserve.gov/paymentsystems/coin/default.htm; accessed 19 July 2008.

Federal Reserve Accounting for Currency and Coin

Federal Reserve notes are liabilities on the Federal Reserve's balance sheet. The asset counterpart to the Federal Reserve liability takes the form of securities of the US Treasury and government-approved enterprises (Treasury and federal agency securities represent the majority of the total collateral for currency in circulation).... When a Reserve Bank makes a currency payment to a depository institution, the Reserve Bank charges the depository institution's [reserve] account ... for the amount of the order [and increases its corresponding liability account "Federal Reserve notes"]. Similarly, when a depository institution returns excess currency to a Reserve Bank, it receives a corresponding credit to its [reserve] account [and the Reserve Bank a decrease to its corresponding liability account "Federal Reserve notes"].

Coin, however, is an asset on the Federal Reserve's balance sheet, and is a direct obligation of the US Treasury. As an asset, the Federal Reserve buys coin from the Mint at face value. When a depository institution orders and deposits coin, its Reserve Bank adjusts the institution's account accordingly.[1]

There you have it. All Federal Reserve notes paid out to member banks are evidence of debt, since the "asset counterpart" of the Fed's liability is "securities of the US Treasury and government-approved enterprises." A booklet published by the Board of governors makes this fact even clearer: "Before being issued to the public, [Federal Reserve] notes must be secured by legally authorized collateral, most of which is in the form of US government and federal agency securities held by the Federal Reserve Banks."[2] On the other hand, coin is "a direct obligation of the US Treasury." This explains why the process of creating money is actually called monetizing debt.

The primary means that the Fed uses to increase or decrease the money supply is through a practice known as open market operations, which consists of the purchase or sale of US government securities. Purchases increase the money supply, whereas sales have the opposite effect. The example given below, which has been simplified considerably, illustrates how the Fed through the purchase of US government securities increases the money supply:

Step 1: The Fed purchases US government securities for $1,000,000 from a reputable securities dealer. Through an electronic transfer of funds, the dealer is notified that $1,000,000 has been credited to his bank account (let us say the dealer's bank is Bank A). Simultaneously, Bank A's reserve account is credited for $1,000,000 at the Fed. Once again, keeping in mind that assets must equal liabilities plus net worth and disregarding for purposes of this example all the other assets, liabilities, and net worth that would normally be recorded, the balance sheets of the Fed and Bank A would look like this:

FED'S BALANCE SHEET (SIMPLIFIED)

Assets	Liabilities
$1,000,000 in US Government Securities	$1,000,000 Reserve Account: Bank A
	Net Worth
TOTAL: $1,000,000	TOTAL: $1,000,000

---

1 Ibid.

2 *The Federal Reserve System: Purpose & Functions*, Second Printing (Washington, D. C.: Board of Governors of the Federal Reserve System, 1985), 105.

BANK A'S BALANCE SHEET (SIMPLIFIED)

Assets	Liabilities
$1,000,000 Reserves at Fed	$1,000,000 Demand Deposit: Securities Dealer
	Net Worth
TOTAL: $1,000,000	TOTAL: $1,000,000

Of course, there is really no money to back up the Fed's electronic "check" — it simply presses a computer key and presto, there is the money. With the wave of its magic wand, the Fed has created $1,000,000 in additional money in the form of a demand deposit to the securities dealer at Bank A.

Step 2: Since the reserve requirement is (let us say) 10%, Bank A is required to keep $100,000 (10% of the $1,000,000 deposit) as reserves. This means that it has excess reserves of $900,000 ($1,000,000–$100,000). In order to keep this example from being overly convoluted, let us say that Bank A uses all its excess reserves to create loans.[1] Bank A's balance sheet would look like this:

BANK A'S BALANCE SHEET (SIMPLIFIED)

Assets	Liabilities
$100,000 Reserves at Fed	$1,000,000 Demand Deposits
$900,000 Loans	Net Worth
TOTAL: $1,000,000	TOTAL: $1,000,000

Step 3: Now let us say, again for the sake of simplicity, that all $900,000 in loans created by Bank A end up as deposits in Bank B. This happens because loans are used to pay bills by writings checks and those who receive the checks deposit them in bank accounts. Although Bank B must hold reserves of $90,000 (10% of $900,000 in deposits), it has $810,000 in excess reserves, which it uses to create loans. Bank B's balance sheet would look like this:

BANK B'S BALANCE SHEET (SIMPLIFIED)

Assets	Liabilities
$90,000 Reserves at Fed	$900,000 Demand Deposits
$810,000 Loans	Net Worth
TOTAL: $900,000	TOTAL: $900,000

Step 4: All $810,000 in loans created by Bank B end up as deposits in Bank C. Bank C retains $81,000 (10% of $810,000 in deposits) as reserves and creates loans totaling $729,000, which is the amount of its excess reserves. Bank C's balance sheet would look like this:

1Actually, investments can be increased as well as loans. According to the Federal Reserve Bank of Chicago, "reserves in excess of … [required reserves] may be used to increase earning assets — loans and investments." *Modern Money Mechanics* (Chicago: Federal Reserve Bank of Chicago, February, 1994), Debt Money, ancient meme [Internet]; available from http://landru.i-link-2.net/monques/mmm2.html#MODERN; accessed 19 July 2008.

BANK C'S BALANCE SHEET (SIMPLIFIED)

Assets	Liabilities
$81,000 Reserves at Fed	$810,000 Demand Deposits
$729,000 Loans	Net Worth
TOTAL: $810,000	TOTAL: $810,000

Step 5: For several weeks, this process continues throughout the banking system. The result is that the initial reserves of $1,000,000 that were created when the Fed purchased $1,000,000 in US securities will give rise within the entire banking system to $9,000,000 in loans and $10,000,000 in deposits. The Federal Reserve Bank of Chicago gives the formula for this calculation very succinctly: "The deposit expansion factor for a given amount of new reserves is ... the reciprocal of the required reserve percentage[, which in this example is] (1/.10 = 10)."[1] Thus, $10,000,000 (10 X $1,000,000) of debt (!) will be created because of the Fed's initial purchase of securities. What is even more amazing, almost all of it will be electronic bookkeeping entries and nothing more. The table below provides a summarization of the process that was describe above:

	Assets			Liabilities
	New Required Reserves	(Excess Reserves)	New Loans	New Demand Deposits
Step 1 — Fed supplies Reserves	$1,000,000	-	-	$1,000,000
Money expansion begins:				
Step 2 — Bank A	$100,000	$900,000	$900,000	$1,000,000
Step 3 — Bank B	$90,000	$810,000	$810,000	$900,000
Step 4 — Bank C	$81,000	$729,000	$729,000	$810,000
Step 5 — Process continues to completion:				
All other Banks	$729,000		$6,561,000	$7,290,000
Process completed	$1,000,000		$9,000,000	$10,000,000

If the entire process is reversed and the Fed *sells* $1,000,000 in US securities on the open market rather than purchase them, the money supply will not be increased but *reduced* by $10,000,000.

A bank's reserves are the total of its vault cash (Federal Reserve notes and coin) and its reserve account at the Fed. If a depositor should cash a check in order to obtain cash to pay a bill instead of paying it directly by check or a borrower should request cash instead of checkbook money, the bank will honor these requests, but paying cash to its customers is not its preferred choice. The reason for this preference is clear:

---

1 Ibid.

When deposits, which are fractional reserve money, are exchanged for currency, which is 100 percent reserve money, the banking system experiences a net reserve drain. Under the assumed 10 percent reserve requirement, a given amount of bank reserves can support deposits ten times as great, but when drawn upon to meet currency demand, the exchange is one to one. A $1 increase in currency uses up $1 of reserves.

Suppose a bank customer cashed a $100 check to obtain currency needed for a weekend holiday. Bank deposits decline $100 because the customer pays for the currency with a check on his or her transaction deposit; and the bank's currency (vault cash reserves) is also reduced $100....

. . .

... Under a 10 percent reserve requirement, the amount of reserves required against the $100 of deposits was only $10, while a full $100 of reserves have been drained away by the disbursement of $100 in currency. Thus, if the bank had no excess reserves, the $100 withdrawal in currency causes a reserve deficiency of $90. Unless new reserves are provided from some other source, bank assets and deposits will have to be reduced ... by an additional $900. At that point, the reserve deficiency caused by the cash withdrawal would be eliminated.[1]

If a member bank needs additional vault cash, it can order it from the Fed by authorizing payment from its reserve account. For example, let us say that a bank needs $10,000 in Federal Reserve notes. The balance sheet entries for the Fed and the bank (let us say Bank A again) would look like this:

FED'S BALANCE SHEET (SIMPLIFIED)

Assets	Liabilities
	($10,000) Reserve Account: Bank A
	$10,000 Federal Reserve Notes
	Net Worth

BANK A'S BALANCE SHEET (SIMPLIFIED)

Assets	Liabilities
$10,000 Vault Cash	
($10,000) Reserves at Fed	Net Worth

Bank A's reserve account at the Fed is reduced by $10,000, but its vault cash is increased by that amount. On the other hand, the Fed's liabilities are increased by $10,000 as "Federal Reserve notes." If a member bank should return Federal Reserve notes to the Fed, the exact opposite accounting entries would be made.

In addition to open market operations, the Fed can take two other actions to change the amount of money in circulation. One of these is adjusting the discount rate. The Fed is known as a bank's bank, because not only do member banks in the

---

1 Ibid.

System have reserve accounts at the Fed, but if necessary, they can borrow money from it as well. The discount rate is the interest that is charged to member banks for borrowing this money. Raising the rate will tend to discourage loans and thus reduce the money supply, while lowering the rate will tend to do just the opposite.

The other action the Fed can take is changing the reserve requirement for member banks. The reserve requirement is the percentage of a bank's reserves that cannot be loaned out, thus limiting the bank's ability to extend credit and expand the money supply. In the example above, 10% was used as the reserve requirement. Raising the reserve requirement will reduce the money supply and lowering it will have the opposite effect.

How these instruments of monetary policy are to be used is determined each month by the Federal Open Market Committee (FOMC). It would not be an exaggeration to assert that the twelve individuals who make up this Committee are probably the most powerful people in the country, for they alone determine the nation's overall monetary policy. Seven of the twelve members are the seven Governors of the Federal Reserve Board and the other five are Presidents of the twelve Federal Reserve Banks. Although the President of the Federal Reserve Bank of New York is always a member, the other eleven Presidents who take turns being members for one-year periods of time fill the remaining four positions.

During the 1980's, the Fed's approach to monetary policy began to change from affecting the *quantity* of reserves to affecting their *price*. The latter is known as the federal funds rate, which is the interest rate banks charge other banks to borrow money overnight from excess reserves they have at the Fed. The FOMC sets the *target* federal funds rate and then, using the monetary tools described above, endeavors to attain its projected goal. The actual federal funds rate that results its efforts is usually close to the projection. A "tight" monetary policy will tend to increase this rate and a "loose" one will tend to accomplish just the opposite. Because of a federal funds rate change, the prime rate will usually move in the same direction, which will influence other interest rates in a like manner as well. Since 1995, the FOMC has publicized the level that is aimed at for federal funds rate. When you hear in the news something like "the Fed raised interest rates for the third time this year," they are talking about the target federal funds rate and its derivative effect on the other interest rates.

So what have been the consequences of having a fiat, debt-based, fractional reserve monetary system? Well, there are several,[1] but for our purposes, only one will be discussed and it can be described in two words: chronic inflation. Inflation can be defined as a rise in consumer prices, and thus a decrease in the purchasing power of money, due to an increase in the supply of currency and credit that is greater than the current value of goods and services.

The Consumer Price Index (CPI) is the main measurement of inflation used by the government. According to the Bureau of Labor Statistics (BLS) website, the CPI "is a measure of the average change over time in the prices paid by urban consumers for a market basket of consumer goods and services."[2] There are actually three indexes. They are the "traditional Consumer Price Index for All Urban Consumers (CPI-U),"

---

1 The "FAME Fact Sheet" lists fifteen defects that have resulted from the Federal Reserve System, FAME (Foundation for the Advancement of Money Education) [Internet]; available from http://www.fame.org/HTM/FAME Fact Sheet 4-6-05.htm; accessed 19 July 2008.

2 What is the CPI? Question #1, Frequently Asked Questions, Consumer Price Index, Bureau of Labor Statistics, The US Department of Labor [Internet]; available from http://www.bls.gov/cpi/cpifaq.htm#Question_1; accessed 29 June 2008.

the "newer Chained Consumer Price Index for All Urban Consumers (C-CPI-U)," and the CPI-W, which "represents about 32 percent of the total US population and is a subset, or part, of the CPI-U's population."[1] The website further reveals, "Each month, BLS releases thousands of detailed CPI numbers to the media," but the media usually concentrates on only the CPI-U, which is "reported on either a seasonally adjusted or an unadjusted basis."[2] In 2007, annual CPI-U (Not Seasonally Adjusted) was 2.8%.[3]

Something does not seem right here. My own experience reveals that prices have risen much higher than this percent indicates. Apparently, I am not the only one who feels this way, since at the beginning of the Shadow Government Statistics website, noted economist John Williams asks the rhetorical question, "Have you ever wondered why the CPI ... run[s] counter to your personal and business experiences?"[4] When I examined the website further, trying to find some explanation for my skepticism, I located an interesting report stating, "Inflation, as reported by the Consumer Price Index (CPI) is understated by roughly 7% per year. This is due to recent redefinitions of the series as well as to flawed methodologies, particularly adjustments to price measures for quality changes."[5] Furthermore, "traditional inflation rates can be estimated by adding 7.0% to the CPI-U annual growth rate...."[6] An annual inflation rate of 9.8% (2.8% + 7%) is definitely more realistic than a rate of 2.8%. Not surprisingly, the May 2008 CPI-U (Not Seasonally Adjusted), which was 4.2%,[7] if corrected in this manner, would be 11.2% (4.2% + 7%). John Williams has a graph on his web site that shows the corrected CPI-U from 1980-2008.[8]

With the help of The Inflation Calculator,[9] let us try to discover how much inflation there has been since the Federal Reserve System began operations on November 16, 1914.[10] For this test, I used $100 for the amount. The Calculator compares the dollar

1 Whose buying habits does the CPI reflect? Question #3, Frequently Asked Questions, Consumer Price Index, Bureau of Labor Statistics, The US Department of Labor [Internet]; available from http://www.bls.gov/cpi/cpifaq.htm#Question_3; accessed 29 June 2008.

2 Which is the "Official CPI" reported in the media? Question #13, Frequently Asked Questions, Consumer Price Index, Bureau of Labor Statistics, The US Department of Labor [Internet]; available from http://www.bls.gov/cpi/cpifaq.htm#Question_13; accessed 29 June 2008.

3 Consumer Price Index — All Urban Consumers, 12 Months Percent Change (Not Seasonally Adjusted), Bureau of Labor Statistics, The US Department of Labor [Internet]; available from http://data.bls.gov/PDQ/servlet/SurveyOutputServlet?data_tool=latest_numbers&series_id=CUUR0000SA0&output_view=pct_12mths; accessed 29 June 2008.

4 John Williams' Shadow Government Statistics [Internet]; available from http://www.shadowstats.com/; accessed 29 June 2008.

5 "Government Economic Reports: Things You've Suspected but Were Afraid to Ask!" John Williams' Shadow Government Statistics [Internet]; available from http://www.shadowstats.com/cgi-bin/sgs/article/id=343; accessed 29 June 2008.

6 Ibid.

7 Consumer Price Index — All Urban Consumers, 12 Months Percent Change (Not Seasonally Adjusted), Bureau of Labor Statistics, The US Department of Labor [Internet]; available from http://data.bls.gov/PDQ/servlet/SurveyOutputServlet?data_tool=latest_numbers&series_id=CUUR0000SA0&output_view=pct_12mths; accessed 29 June 2008.

8 Annual Consumer Inflation — CPI vs. SGS Alternate, John Williams Shadow Government Statistics [Internet]; available from http://www.shadowstats.com/alternate_data; accessed 28 July 2008.

9 The Inflation Calculator [Internet]; available from http://www.westegg.com/inflation/; accessed 7 March 2006.

10 Although the Federal Reserve Act was passed by Congress on December 23, 1913, the Fed did not actually begin its operations until November 16, 1914.

value of one year with another for any two years within the period from 1800 to 2006 and then gives the relative cost of the same merchandise purchased in each year. First, I compared 1800 (the earliest year the Calculator works with) with 1913 (the year before the Fed began operations). The results were as follows:

What cost $100 in 1800 would cost **$56.74** in 1913.

Also, if you were to buy exactly the same products in 1913 and 1800, they would cost you **$100** and **$176.24** respectively.

Then, I compared 1914 (the year the Fed began operations) with 2006 (the latest year the Calculator works with). The results were as follows:

What cost $100 in 1914 would cost **$1967.59** in 2006.

Also, if you were to buy exactly the same products in 2006 and 1914, they would cost you **$100** and **$5.08** respectively.

When 1800 was compared to 1913, purchasing power actually *increased* by 57%; but when 1914 was compared to 2006, purchasing power *decreased* by an astounding 1968%. According to the test, severe inflation shows up only in the period when the Fed has been in operation.

Alan Greenspan actually admitted this fact in a talk that he gave to the Economic Club of New York in New York City on December 19, 2002, titled "Issues for Monetary Policy":

Although the gold standard could hardly be portrayed as having produced a period of price tranquility, *it was the case that the price level in 1929 was not much different, on net, from what it had been in 1800. But, in the two decades following the abandonment of the gold standard in 1933, the consumer price index in the United States nearly doubled. And, in the four decades after that, prices quintupled. Monetary policy, unleashed from the constraint of domestic gold convertibility, has allowed a persistent over issuance of money. As recently as a decade ago, central bankers, having witnessed more than a half-century of chronic inflation, appeared to confirm that a fiat currency was inherently subject to excess.*[1]

In order to make certain that the results from The Inflation Calculator were accurate; I used two other calculators for verification — one from the US Dept. of Labor, Bureau of Labor Statistics,[2] and the other from the Minneapolis Fed.[3] Unfortunately, they both work only for the years from 1913 to 2007. When I compared 1914 to 2006 using these other calculators, I obtained approximately the same results as I did with The Inflation Calculator.

I decided to try another test. I wanted to find out how much inflation has occurred during my own lifetime. The Inflation Calculator was used again and so was the amount of $100. Since I was born in 1950, I used that number and 2006, as the other year. The results were as follows:

What cost $100 in 1950 would cost **$817.30** in 2006.

Also, if you were to buy exactly the same products in 2006 and 1950, they would cost you **$100** and **$12.24** respectively.

1 Remarks by Chairman Alan Greenspan Before the Economic Club of New York, New York City, December 19, 2002, "Issues for Monetary Policy," Board of Governors of the Federal Reserve System [Internet]; available from http://www.federalreserve.gov/boarddocs/speeches/2002/20021219/; accessed 19 July 2008.

2 CPI Inflation Calculator, US Dept. of Labor, Bureau of Labor Statistics [Internet]; available from http://data.bls.gov/cgi-bin/cpicalc.pl; accessed 19 July 2008.

3 "What is a dollar worth?" (Inflation Calculator), Federal Reserve Bank of Minneapolis [Internet]; available from http://www.minneapolisfed.org/Research/data/us/calc/index.cfm; accessed 19 July 2008.

As you can see, when 1950 was compared to 2006, the purchasing power *decreased* by 817%. Everyone must admit that this is indeed serious inflation, especially in only fifty-six years.

Therefore, if you have ever wondered why the same model car purchased new in 1978 and costing $5,000 now costs $25,000 or why a comparable type home purchased in 1968 and costing $25,000 now costs $400,000, you now have the answer. What's more, you now know why in 1955 a postage stamp costing as little as 3 cents today costs 39 cents, and why in that same year an ice cream cone costing around 5 cents today costs at least $2.50. In addition, you now know why there was actually a time when a person could pay his taxes by working less than one and a half months per year, but today needs to work more than five months, and why not too long ago *one* working parent could provide for all the family's needs while holding negligible debt and maintaining an active savings account. Today, sorry to say, the economic realities of the family are quite different, because both parents must work, they are mired in debt and can save nothing at all. All these cases in point are due chiefly to the chronic inflation caused by the fiat, debt-based, fractional reserve monetary system of the US central bank.

In actuality, inflation is probably even worse than the price increases reveal. In order not to increase the prices of consumer products too far beyond the ability of the average customer to pay for them, manufacturers have to resort to using less expensive and less efficient raw materials in the manufacturing process. These materials may keep the prices from going up too high, but they significantly cheapen the quality of the products as well. An excellent example is the use of chrome bumpers and metal bodies on cars built in the 1950s. Today, plastic is the only raw material car exteriors seem to be made of. Anyone who has gotten into a "fender bender" with his car is usually amazed to discover how much auto bodywork is required to repair the damage caused by such a minor collision.

Another method of accomplishing the same end is by giving you less for your money. This method works most effectively for packaged food items. I used to enjoy a particular brand of pre-popped popcorn, which sold for let us say $2.89. Although the price did not seem to go up very much, each time I purchased a bag at the grocery store I noticed it contained a little more air, but a little less popcorn. In this case, the full extent of inflation was being hidden from consumers by reducing how much of the product you actually got, instead of, as was previously noted, by using less expensive raw materials in the manufacture of the product.

The late economist, Murray N. Rothbard, explains the true situation regarding the Fed very eloquently:

> In short: ... we should already get a glimmer of the truth: that the drumfire of propaganda that the Fed in manning the ramparts against the menace of inflation brought about by others is nothing less than a deceptive shell game. The culprit solely responsible for inflation, the Federal Reserve, is continually engaged in raising a hue-and-cry about "inflation," for which virtually *everyone else* in society seems to be responsible. What we are seeing is the old ploy by the robber who starts shouting "Stop, thief!" and runs down the street pointing ahead at others. We begin to see why it has always been important for the Fed, and other Central Banks, to invest themselves with an aura of solemnity and mystery. For ... if the public knew what was going on, if it was able to rip open the curtain covering the inscrutable Wizard of Oz, it would soon discover that

the Fed, far from being the indispensable solution to the problem of inflation, is itself the heart and cause of the problem.[1]

So what is the remedy for this deplorable situation? The answer is to return to a commodity-based (i.e., gold and silver), non-debt bearing, 100% reserve currency and, in fact, this is precisely what the Constitution requires us to have.

Below are the relevant sections of the Constitution that apply to the monetary issue:

Article I, section 8, which lists the powers given to Congress, contain the following clauses:

> [Clause 5] [Congress shall have power] To coin Money, regulate the Value thereof, and of foreign Coin ....

> [Clause 6] [Congress shall have power] To provide for the Punishment of counterfeiting the Securities and current Coin of the United States.

Also, Article I, section 10, which lists the prohibitions of the states, contains the following clause:

> [Clause 1] No State shall ... coin Money; emit Bills of Credit; make any Thing but gold and silver Coin a Tender in Payment of Debts.

The term "dollar" is actually mentioned twice in the Constitution — in Article I, section 9, clause 1, which allowed a tax of not more than "ten dollars" on imported slaves,[2] and in the Seventh Amendment, which guarantees trial by jury "in Suits of common law, where the value in controversy shall exceed twenty dollars ...."

Finally, with regard to the power given Congress "to borrow Money on the credit of the United States" in Article I, section 8, clause 1, the additional power to emit bills of credit (i.e., paper money) was not included with this power as it had been under the Articles of Confederation in Article IX. Thus, under the Constitution, the power to print paper money was taken away from Congress and the states were explicitly prohibited from issuing it in Article I, section 10, clause 1 (quoted above).

As anyone can clearly see, only *Congress* has been given the power "to coin money" and to "regulate the Value thereof," not a quasi-government agency like the Federal Reserve System.[3] In addition, "to *coin* money" can in no way mean to *print* it and in the counterfeiting clause (quoted above) only the "current *coin* of the United States" is referred to *not* bills of credit (i.e., paper money).

As mentioned above, the power to emit bills of credit (i.e., paper money) was deliberately taken away from Congress under the Constitution. This fact can easily be verified by examining James Madison's notes on the Federal Convention of 1787. On Thursday, August 16, 1787, the delegates were discussing whether the phrase "emit bills on the credit of the United States" should be left in or taken out of the first draft of the Constitution. Most of the delegates were clearly opposed to paper money, because etched in their minds were the memories of severe inflation caused by it during the Revolutionary War. The well-known phrase "not worth a Continental" actually originated from this experience.

---

1 Rothbard, 11.

2 Because of a northern and southern state compromise at the Federal Convention in 1787, Congress could not outlaw the importation of slaves until 1808. A law was eventually passed that did make it illegal. It went into effect on January 1, 1808.

3 According to Murray N. Rothbard, "in form as well as in content, the Federal Reserve System is precisely the cozy government-big bank partnership, the government-enforced banking cartel, that big bankers had long envisioned" (Rothbard, 121).

It will suffice to give only a few examples of their views on this subject. Oliver Ellsworth of Connecticut "thought this a favorable moment to shut and bar the door against paper money."[1] James Wilson of Pennsylvania stated, "It will have a most salutary influence on the credit of the U. States to remove the possibility of paper money."[2] Finally, John Langdon of New Hampshire was willing to "reject the whole plan than retain the three words "(and emit bills")."[3] The result was that the removal of the phrase was approved by nine states to two.

Now it is clear that something called a "dollar" must have existed before the Constitution was written, because the term is mentioned twice without defining it. In fact, that "something" was the Spanish milled silver dollar (the peso), which circulated throughout much of the world during the eighteenth century, including the thirteen colonies.[4] One valuable source describes the situation very clearly:

> Thus, prior to the Convention of 1787, Congress had made a factual determination that the common money or currency in use by the people of our country was the Spanish Milled Silver Dollar, and further that experiments, tests and analyses of these coins revealed that they contained 375.64 grains of pure silver. Many members of Congress [under the Articles of Confederation] were also delegates to the Philadelphia Constitutional Convention of 1787 and it was based upon the factual findings made by Congress previously that the word "dollar" as mentioned in the Constitution had meaning.[5]

After the Constitution and the Bill of Rights were both ratified, Congress passed *An Act establishing a Mint, and regulating the Coins of the United States*, which is commonly called the Coinage Act of 1792.[6] Among other things, it confirmed statutorily "that the money of account of the United States shall be expressed in dollars or units (Section 20)" and that "Dollars or Units— [are] each to be of the value of a Spanish milled dollar as the same is now current, and to contain three hundred and seventy-one grains and four sixteenths parts of a grain of pure, or four hundred and sixteen grains of standard silver (Section 9)."[7] Furthermore, the Act authorized the issuance of new gold coins called Eagles. They were "each to be of the value of ten dollars or units, and to contain two hundred and forty-seven grains and four eighths of a grain of pure, or two hundred and seventy grains of standard gold (Section 9)." Half Eagles nd Quar-

---

1 James Madison, *Notes of Debates in the Federal Convention of 1787*, Introduction by Adrienne Koch, Bicentennial Edition (New York: W. W. Norton & Company, 1987), 471.

2 Ibid.

3 Ibid.

4 It is interesting to note that the phrase "piece of eight" actually derived from the practice of physically cutting up the Spanish milled silver dollar into eight pieces or bits to make change. It could also be cut up into fours pieces or quarters and thus a "quarter" became known as "two bits."

5 Larry Becraft, "Memorandum of Law: The Money Issue" (Last updated: September 15, 2002), The Dixieland Law Journal [Internet]; available from http://home.hiwaay.net/~becraft/MONEYbrief.html; accessed 19 July 2008.

6 The Coinage Act of 1792, Debt Money, ancient meme [Internet]; available from http://landru.i-link-2.net/monques/coinageact.html - Chap; accessed 19 July 2008.

7 The reason for the difference in the Spanish milled dollar's weight of 375.64 grains of pure silver before the Constitution was ratified and 371.25 grains afterwards was that Congress accepted the updated findings in Alexander Hamilton's "Report of the Secretary of the Treasury on the Subject of a Mint," which was published in 1791. See page 10 of the entire Report at CoinFacts.com [Internet]; available form http://www.coinfacts.com/mint_history/mint_history_1781_1791/alexander_hamilton_report_1791_page1.htm; accessed 19 July 2008.

ter Eagles were authorized as well.[1] The weights of these new gold coins conformed precisely to Section 11 of the Act, which stated that fifteen parts by weight of pure silver were to be equal in value to one part by weight of pure gold. For example, an Eagle is 247.5 grains of pure gold and equals 10 dollars. Thus, 1 dollar would weigh 24.75 grains. 24.75 grains X 15 = 371.25 grains, which is precisely the weight of 1 dollar of pure silver. Unfortunately, when the government sets a fixed ratio like 15:1 between silver and gold, eventually one of the metals usually disappears from circulation. However, if a fixed ratio were not set, this problem could be avoided.[2]

According to US Code 31, section 5101, "United States money is expressed in dollars ..." and US Code 31, section 5103, "United States coins and currency (including Federal Reserve notes and circulating notes of Federal Reserve banks and national banks) are legal tender for all debts, public charges, taxes, and dues." Furthermore, US Code 12, section 411 states the following:

> Federal Reserve notes ... shall be obligations of the United States and shall be receivable by all national and member banks and Federal reserve banks and for all taxes, customs, and other public dues. They shall be redeemed in **lawful money** on demand at the Treasury Department of the United States, in the city of Washington, District of Columbia, or at any Federal Reserve bank.

If, as we are falsely led to believe, Federal Reserve notes are actually lawful money, then why can they supposedly be "redeemed in lawful money," according to US Code 12, section 411? Obviously, this statement can only mean that Federal Reserve notes are not themselves lawful money. The truth will quickly be revealed when you try to exchange Federal Reserve notes for the real thing at the U. S. Treasury or your local Federal Reserve Bank. You will only receive more of the same, although you can at least request different denominations, token coins[3] instead, or a combination of notes and token coins. You will not receive lawful money (i.e., gold and silver), because no such thing really exists anymore. Therefore, to give Federal Reserve notes the *appearance* of being lawful money; they are declared legal tender by statute. U. S. Code 31, section 5103, which is quoted above, accomplishes this legal deception. As stated earlier in this chapter, fiat money is paper money that is declared legal tender by government decree.

> In actuality, when the Fed first began its operation in 1914, the first series of Federal Reserve notes could be redeemed for gold and silver. Although it had always been a fractional reserve system, the Fed's metamorphosis to a completely fiat system only came gradually. It is very interesting to examine how the Federal Reserve note has evolved over the years to match the transformation. Below is a photograph of a $10 Federal Reserve note from 1914 (front only), which was the first series to be issued.[4]

---

1 In addition, silver coins called Dismes and Half Dismes, and copper coins called Cents and Half Cents were authorized as well. A Disme (now spelt "dime") was one tenth of a dollar and a Cent was one hundredth of a dollar (Section 9 of The Coinage Act of 1792).

2 See Appendix 1. The Bimetallism Problem and Its Solution.

3 According to the Federal Reserve Bank of Chicago, "coins do have some intrinsic value as metal, but generally far less than their face value." *Modern Money Mechanics* (Chicago: Federal Reserve Bank of Chicago, February, 1994), Debt Money, ancient meme [Internet]; available from http://landru.i-link-2.net/monques/mmm2.html#MODERN; accessed 19 July 2008.

4 $10 Federal Reserve note from 1914 (front), Six Kinds of United States Paper Currency [Internet]; available from http://www.friesian.com/images/notes/10-14-ro.gif; accessed 28 July 2008.

The following words can be found on its face:

AUTHORIZED BY FEDERAL RESERVE ACT OF DECEMBER 23, 1913.

In addition, the following paragraph can be found on its back (not shown):

THIS NOTE IS RECEIVABLE BY ALL NATIONAL AND MEMBER BANKS AND FEDERAL RESERVE BANKS AND FOR ALL TAXES, CUSTOMS AND OTHER PUBLIC DUES. IT IS REDEEMABLE IN GOLD ON DEMAND AT THE TREASURY DEPARTMENT OF THE UNITED STATES IN THE CITY OF WASHINGTON, DISTRICT OF COLUMBIA OR IN GOLD OR LAWFUL MONEY AT ANY FEDERAL RESERVE BANK.[1]

This Federal Reserve note was a true note. It "will pay to the bearer on demand ten dollars," which means that it was not in itself the ten dollars. The real ten dollars was the "gold or lawful money" that it represented. It also clearly states, "it is redeemable in gold on demand at the Treasury Department ... or in gold or lawful money at any Federal Reserve Bank."

Below is a photograph of a $10 Federal Reserve note from the 1928 series (front only):[2]

---

1 $10 Federal Reserve note from 1914 (back), Six Kinds of United States Paper Currency [Internet]; available from http://www.friesian.com/images/notes/10-14-rr.gif; accessed 28 July 2008.

2 $10 Federal Reserve note from the 1928 series (front), Six Kinds of United States Paper Currency [Internet]; available from http://www.friesian.com/images/notes/10-28-ro.gif; accessed 28 July 2008.

It was different in some ways from the 1914 series, but was still a valid note (it "will pay to the bearer on demand ten dollars") and could be redeemed in gold. The following words can be found on its face:

REDEEMABLE IN GOLD ON DEMAND AT THE UNITED STATES TREA-
SURY, OR IN GOLD OR LAWFUL MONEY AT ANY FEDERAL RESERVE
BANK.

Federal Reserve notes beginning with the 1934 series were different in significant ways from the 1928 series. Below is a photograph of a $10 Federal Reserve from the 1934 series (front only):[1]

The following words can be found on its face:

THIS NOTE IS LEGAL TENDER FOR ALL DEBTS, PUBLIC AND PRIVATE,
AND IS REDEEMABLE IN LAWFUL MONEY AT THE UNITED STATES
TREASURY, OR AT ANY FEDERAL RESERVE BANK.

As you can see, this Federal Reserve note was no longer redeemable in gold. The obvious reason for this change was that in 1933 it became illegal for Americans to own gold, as a consequence of Executive Order 6102 issued by President Franklin D. Roosevelt on April 5.[2] Yes, you did indeed read the sentence correctly. Except for some items that were exempted, all Americans were ordered to surrender their gold coin and bullion[3] to neighborhood banks in exchange for "an equivalent amount of any other form of coin or currency coined or issued under the laws of the United States" according to Section 4 of the Executive Order. The Federal Reserve note beginning with the 1934 series was also declared legal tender by the passage of the Agricultural Adjustment Act on May 12, 1933.[4] Even so, the note still states that it is "redeemable in lawful money" and it "will pay to the bearer on demand ten dollars."

---

1 $10 Federal Reserve note from the 1934 series (front), Six Kinds of United States Paper Currency [Internet]; available from http://www.friesian.com/images/notes/10-34-ro.gif; accessed 28 July 2008.

2 Franklin D. Roosevelt — Executive Order 6102 — Requiring Gold Coin, Gold Bullion and Gold Certificates to Be Delivered to the Government, April 5, 1933, The American Presidency Project [Internet]; available from http://www.presidency.ucsb.edu/ws/index. php?pid=14611&st=gold+coin&st1; accessed 19 July 2008.

3 The exemptions included gold coins not exceeding $100 per person, gold jewelry, gold used industrially, and gold collector's coins.

4 According to Part 8, Title III, sec. 43 (1) of the Act, "... all ... coins and currencies heretofore or hereafter coined or issued by or under the authority of the United States shall be legal tender for all debts public and private." The Agricultural Adjustment Act, May 12, 1933, Pepperdine University School of Public Policy, The New Deal, New Deal Legislation

At the time, "lawful money" could only have been either more of the same — Federal Reserve notes (including token coins as well) — or silver coin and bullion.[1]

With the printing of the 1963 series, the evolution of the Federal Reserve note was complete and the same phraseology remains on all denominations today. Below is a photograph of a $1 Federal Reserve note from the 1963 series (front only):[2]

The following words can be found on its face:

THIS NOTE IS LEGAL TENDER FOR ALL DEBTS, PUBLIC AND PRIVATE.

This Federal Reserve note is not really a note at all. How can it be, when the statement that it "will pay to the bearer on demand one dollar" is missing? A note can be defined in the following manner:

> A note is the written evidence of a promise to pay with something of value. A bona fide note will specify the item to be paid. Honesty requires that we state the item to be paid and the intention to keep that promise. If the government issues a note without a promise to pay or with a promise to pay without stating the item to be paid, such a promise is meaningless and should not be issued by government officials.[3]

All connection to "lawful money" (i.e., gold and silver) has been completely severed. It is now asserted that the "note" itself is the "legal tender." With the arrival of this Federal Reserve note, the United States was only one small step away from entering the world of one hundred percent fiat currency, but one last link still held the dollar to gold. Foreign governments and their central banks could redeem dollars for gold at the price of thirty-five dollars per ounce. This policy remained in force until the "gold window" was closed on August 15, 1971, as a consequence of Execu-

---

[Internet]; available from http://publicpolicy.pepperdine.edu/faculty-research/new-deal/legislation/aaa051233.htm; accessed 19 July 2008.

1 On August 14, 1974, Public Law 93-373 was passed, which finally allowed Americans to own gold again, effective December 31, 1974.

2 $1 Federal Reserve note from the 1963 series (front), Six Kinds of United States Paper Currency [Internet]; available from http://www.friesian.com/images/notes/1-63-ro.gif; accessed 28 July 2008.

3 Dr. Edward E. Popp, *The Great Cookie Jar Taking the Mysteries Out of the Money System* (Port Washington, Wisconsin: Wisconsin Education Fund, 1978), 172.

---

tive Order 11615 issued by President Richard Nixon.[1] With this last link removed, the United States had indeed taken the disastrous course to complete fiat currency.[2]

Before the Constitution was ratified, the states, not Congress, had the sole power to declare something legal tender. According to Article I, section 10, clause 1, this power was explicitly retained by the states under the Constitution, except that it was restricted to gold and silver only: "No State shall ... make any Thing but gold and silver Coin a Tender in Payment of Debts." One valuable source describes the situation prior to the Constitution's ratification as follows:

> During the War, all of the colonies emitted bills of credit, and most declared the same to be a legal tender, the States claiming unto themselves the right to declare any thing, especially paper, a legal tender. As the Continental Congress did not possess the power to declare a legal tender, it was compelled to enlist the aid of the sovereign States, which thereafter declared the Continental Notes, along with their own notes, a legal tender for debts.[3]

The Constitution changed the situation somewhat as follows:

> In reference to the much-needed revision of the monetary system, Congress had been granted the power to "coin money and regulate the value thereof," virtually the identical powers in reference to the currency which it possessed under the Articles, which did not include the power to declare a legal tender. Further, certain binding, absolute and uncircumventable prohibitions had been placed upon the States in Article 1, § 10, cl. 1, one of which limited the legal tender power of the States to gold and silver coin.[4]

Why were the states allowed to retain this power to declare something legal tender with the only restriction being that it must be gold and silver? Apparently, there were two reasons why this was the case.

The first reason was to manage, concurrently with Congress, the foreign coins that were circulating throughout the nation at the time. According to one source, "foreign coins have been estimated to form 80 percent of American domestic specie circulation in 1800."[5] Since Congress was given the power "to ... regulate the Value ... of foreign Coin ..." in Article I, section 8, clause 5, the original idea seems to have been that Congress would first create a pool of *regulated* foreign gold and silver coins. Each state legislature would then be free to declare which coins within this pool would be legal tender for its own state. Congress did have an *implied* legal tender power simply by not including specific foreign coins within the pool of regulated coins. This would bar the states from making these unregulated coins legal tender, because Congress had chosen not to regulate them and the states were not given this power under the Constitution. Unfortunately, Congress seems to have gone beyond its bounds rather

---

1 Richard Nixon — Executive Order 11615 — Providing for Stabilization of Prices, Rents, Wages, and Salaries, August 15, 1971, The American Presidency Project [Internet]; available from http://www.presidency.ucsb.edu/ws/index.php?pid=60492&st=&st1; accessed 19 July 2008.

2 According to Murray N. Rothbard, "while Fed liabilities are no longer redeemable in gold, the Fed safeguards its gold by depositing it in the Treasury, which issues 'gold certificates' guaranteed to be backed by no less than 100 percent in gold bullion buried in Fort Knox and other Treasury depositories" (Rothbard, 138).

3 Larry Becraft, "Memorandum of Law: The Money Issue" (Last updated: September 15, 2002), The Dixieland Law Journal [Internet]; available from http://home.hiwaay.net/-becraft/MONEYbrief.html; accessed 19 July 2008.

4 Ibid.

5 Rep. Ron Paul and Lewis Lehrman, *The Case for Gold* (Washington, D.C.: Cato Institute, 1982), 32.

---

soon and either *explicitly* granted or denied legal tender status to certain foreign coins at various times from 1791 to 1873.[1]

Secondly, by allowing only gold and silver coin as legal tender, it would prohibit the states from allowing private banks to issue their own fractional reserve notes. By definition, fractional reserve banking entails government paper money or even private bank notes circulating as money that are not fully backed by gold or silver. The states were strictly prohibited from issuing bills of credit (i.e., paper money) on their own authority, according to Article I, section 10, clause 1. However, this did not restrict private banks from issuing their own notes that could be used as money substitutes. Such notes, if based on a one hundred percent reserve requirement, were acceptable, because they represented precisely the gold or silver coin that was in the bank's vaults. However, this was *not* the case for private bank notes based on less than a one hundred percent reserve requirement, since some fraction of these notes would *not* represent the gold or silver coin in the bank's vaults. Unfortunately, because history informs us repeatedly that there is always a temptation to abuse paper money, it is doubtful that any bank would retain a one hundred percent reserve requirement behind its notes for very long. Since the states were only allowed to make "gold and silver Coin a Tender in Payment of Debts," they would have no choice but to prohibit any form of fractional reserve banking.

I would like to conclude this chapter by discussing a paper written by Alan Greenspan back in 1966. The paper appeared in *The Objectivist* titled "Gold and Economic Freedom." It was later reprinted in the paperback book titled *Capitalism: The Unknown Ideal.*[2] In this relatively short essay, Mr. Greenspan made the case that a gold standard is an absolute requirement for a free society. Every American should read it in its entirety. It can be found in the following footnoted website[3] and probably others as well. I will quote only a portion of it below:

> Under a gold standard, the amount of credit that an economy can support is determined by the economy's tangible assets, since every credit instrument is ultimately a claim on some tangible asset. But government bonds are not backed by tangible wealth, only by the government's promise to pay out of future tax revenues, and cannot easily be absorbed by the financial markets. A large volume of new government bonds can be sold to the public only at progressively higher interest rates. Thus, government deficit spending under a gold standard is severely limited.
>
> The abandonment of the gold standard made it possible for the welfare statists to use the banking system as a means to an unlimited expansion of credit. They have created paper reserves in the form of government bonds which — through a complex series of steps — the banks accept in place of tangible assets and treat as if they were an actual deposit, i.e., as the equivalent of what was formerly a deposit of gold. The holder of a government bond or of a bank deposit created by paper reserves believes that he has a valid claim on a real asset. But the fact is that there are now more claims outstanding than real assets.

---

1 The US Monetary Acts from 1791 to 1873, Debt Money, ancient meme [Internet]; available from http://landru.i-link-2.net/monques/monetaryacts.html - U; accessed 19 July 2008. Especially take note of those Acts that refer to regulating foreign coin.

2 Alan Greenspan, "Gold and Economic Freedom" in Ayn Rand, *Capitalism: The Unknown Ideal* (New York City: Signet, 1967), 96–101.

3 Alan Greenspan, "Gold and Economic Freedom," LewRockwell.com [Internet]; available from http://www.lewrockwell.com/north/north204.html; accessed 19 July 2008.

The law of supply and demand is not to be conned. As the supply of money (of claims) increases relative to the supply of tangible assets in the economy, prices must eventually rise. Thus the earnings saved by the productive members of the society lose value in terms of goods. When the economy's books are finally balanced, one finds that this loss in value represents the goods purchased by the government for welfare or other purposes with the money proceeds of the government bonds financed by bank credit expansion.

In the absence of the gold standard, there is no way to protect savings from confiscation through inflation. There is no safe store of value. If there were, the government would have to make its holding illegal, as was done in the case of gold. If everyone decided, for example, to convert all his bank deposits to silver or copper or any other good, and thereafter declined to accept checks as payment for goods, bank deposits would lose their purchasing power and government-created bank credit would be worthless as a claim on goods. The financial policy of the welfare state requires that there be no way for the owners of wealth to protect themselves.

This is the shabby secret of the welfare statists' tirades against gold. Deficit spending is simply a scheme for the confiscation of wealth. Gold stands in the way of this insidious process. It stands as a protector of property rights. If one grasps this, one has no difficulty in understanding the statists' antagonism toward the gold standard.[1]

According to Lawrence Parks of the Foundation for the Advancement of Monetary Education (FAME), he met Alan Greenspan on two separate occasions after the latter had given an address to the Economic Club of New York. The first time was on April 19, 1993. At this meeting, Mr. Parks asked Chairman Greenspan, "Do you still agree with the reasoning and the conclusions in this article ["Gold and Economic Freedom"]? His response was an emphatic 'Absolutely!'" Mr. Parks then described the rest of the meeting as follows:

> Then, I asked, "So why don't you speak out?" Mr. Greenspan said: "Because my colleagues at the institution I represent disagree with me." [Note the absence of proper nouns.] And I responded, "But you know where all of this is leading to [a complete collapse]." He then gave me a very pained look, like I had punched him in the stomach, and walked on.[2]

The second meeting occurred on January 13, 2000. Mr. Parks' description was this:

> We spoke briefly about the merits of gold-as-money, with which he concurred, and then I asked him why, if he understands what is happening and what the implications are, he doesn't speak out more. His answer had a ring of truth and, also, a tinge of desperation. He said: "Nobody wants to hear it." By then, we had reached the elevators on the floor above the main ballroom, and he got in with his wife, Andrea Mitchell, who was most charming.[3]

It is very difficult, if not impossible, to reconcile Alan Greenspan's positive view of "gold-as-money" with the incongruous fact that he was the Chairman of the Board of the Fed, which is a fiat, debt-based monetary system, for nearly twenty years. How can this inconsistency be explained? Could it be that although he was opposed to the system in theory, he was also convinced that any significant change in it was unlikely

---

1 Greenspan in Ayn Rand, *Capitalism: The Unknown Ideal*, 96–101.

2 Lawrence Parks, *What does Mr. Greenspan Really Think?* (New York City The Foundation for the Advancement of Monetary Education, 2001), 83-4.

3 Ibid., 84.

to happen any time soon? On this basis, could it be that he chose to accept the reality of the situation and to work within the system as effectively as he could?

It is worthwhile to read the dialogue between Alan Greenspan and the Texas Congressman, Ron Paul, at the hearings before the US House of Representatives' Committee on Financial Services. Ron Paul is a strong supporter of the gold standard. From these interactions, one can at least catch a glimpse of Alan Greenspan's views on monetary policy from 1997 through 2005.[1]

APPENDIX: THE BIMETALLISM PROBLEM AND ITS SOLUTION

Bimetallism is a monetary system that uses two metals as the standard of value, usually gold and silver, and sets the relative value of the metals by using a fixed mint ratio. During the eighteenth and nineteenth centuries, the United States used a gold and silver bimetallism standard, because the Constitution states, "no state shall ... make anything but gold and silver coin a tender in payment of debts" (Article I, section 10, clause 1). Under the Coinage Act of 1792, the government set the fixed mint ratio between silver and gold at 15:1, i.e., 15 oz. of silver equaled 1 oz. of gold. A silver dollar was 371.25 grains of pure silver, which would equal 24.75 grains of pure gold (371.25/15=24.75).[2] Unfortunately, the two metals are used for various commercial purposes in addition to their use as money, which creates a constantly fluctuating market ratio as well. Because of the two ratios — one artificially fixed and one always changing, Gresham's Law inevitably comes into play. This law states that if a metal has a market value less than its mint value, and is thus overvalued at the mint, it will tend to remain as money in circulation. On the other hand, if a metal that has a market value more than its mint value, and is thus undervalued at the mint, it will tend to be withdrawn from circulation and used for commercial purposes or hoarded.

As an example, let us say that the fixed mint ratio is 15:1, but the current market ratio is 16:1.[3] With a 16:1 market ratio, the 15:1 fixed mint ratio artificially overvalues silver and undervalues gold. As a result of Gresham's Law, gold will eventually disappear as money, since people will realize the economic advantage of using it commercially (making jewelry for example) or storing it in the expectation of future profits, leaving only silver as the medium of exchange. There are two possible solutions to this problem:

- Adopt a gold monometallic standard with the dollar defined as a certain amount of gold by weight, but silver, with no link to the dollar, freely floating in the market, or
- Adopt a silver monometallic standard with the dollar defined as a certain amount of silver by weight, but gold, with no link to the dollar, freely floating in the market.

A gold monometallic standard would perhaps be the more suitable alternative. In either case, both gold and silver would remain mediums of exchange, except that there would be no fixed mint ratio between them.

1 The Greenspan — Paul Congressional Exchanges 1997-2005, Hearings before the US House of Representatives' Committee on Financial Services, USAGOLD [Internet]; available from http://www.usagold.com/gildedopinion/greenspan-gold.html; accessed 29 June 2008.

2 Under the Coinage Act of 1792, there was no actual gold coin worth a dollar and weighing 24.75 grains, but there were Eagles worth ten dollars (247.5 grains of pure gold), Half Eagles worth five dollars (123.75 grains of pure gold), and Quarter Eagles worth two and a half dollars (61.875 grains of pure gold).

3 It is customary to set the *initial* fixed mint ratio the same as the current market ratio in order to counter Gresham's Law, but because of market conditions, the latter inevitably changes.

Chapter 6: Taxation and the Sixteenth Amendment

> *Taxes on consumption [indirect taxes] are always least burdensome, because they are least felt, and*
> *are borne too by those who are both willing and able to pay them; that of all taxes on consumption,*
> *those on foreign commerce are most compatible with the genius and policy of free States.*
> — *James Madison, Address to the States, April 25, 1783.*

The government can assess only two types of taxes on its citizens — direct taxes and indirect taxes. A direct tax is a tax assessed on persons or their property and is paid straight to the government by the individuals that are assessed the tax. Examples of direct taxes would be capitation (head), poll, property, and income taxes. On the other hand, an indirect tax is a tax assessed on commodities. An intermediary (i.e., a tax collector who is a non-government entity) is usually involved in the transfer of the tax from the taxpayer to the government, which makes the process essentially a two-step procedure. First, the taxpayer pays the tax to the tax collector and then the accumulated funds are remitted to the government based on some fixed schedule. However, some indirect taxes are paid directly to government tax collectors as well. Examples of indirect taxes would be customs duties (also called duties, imposts, and tariffs), excises, and sales taxes.

Article I, section 8, clause 1 of the Constitution gives Congress the power to tax:

> The Congress shall have Power To [sic] lay and collect Taxes, Duties, Imposts
> and Excises ... but all Duties, Imposts and Excises shall be uniform throughout
> the United States.

Duties, imposts, and excises are all indirect taxes and, according to the Constitution, the one requirement of this type of tax is that they must be "uniform throughout the United States." This means for example that a tax on cigarettes cannot be assessed only in New England, but must be assessed throughout the entire country. The amount of the tax must be the same as well.

Indirect taxes have two other important characteristics. The first is that they are voluntary. No one is forced to buy a particular good and consequently pay the tax on it. The second characteristic is that there is a built-in limit as to how high the tax can be. If the tax on a commodity should be too excessive, then people will simply stop purchasing it. Of course, these characteristics may not hold for necessities like food, clothing, and shelter, but in any case, exclusions from taxation are often made for these items.

The constitutional requirement for direct taxes is stated in Article I, section 9, clause 4: "No Capitation, or other direct, Tax shall be laid, unless in Proportion to the Census or Enumeration herein before directed to be taken." Article I, section 2, clause 3 further explains the census or enumeration as follows:

> [Representatives and direct Taxes shall be apportioned among the several States which may be included within this Union, according to their respective Numbers, which shall be determined by adding to the whole Number of free Persons, including those bound to Service for a Term of Years, and excluding Indians not taxed, three fifths of all other Persons.] The actual Enumeration shall be made within three Years after the first Meeting of the Congress of the United States, and within every subsequent Term of ten Years, in such Manner as they shall by Law direct. The number of Representatives shall not exceed one for every thirty Thousand, but each State shall have at Least one Representative....

If the Fourteenth Amendment to the Constitution had been truly ratified, then the section placed in brackets above would have been changed by section 2 of the Amendment as follows: "Representatives shall be apportioned among the several States according to their respective numbers, counting the whole number of persons in each State, excluding Indians not taxed." The only significant change from the original clause is that the phrase "three fifths of all other Persons" has been taken out. The reason for this deletion was to repeal the requirement that former slaves were to be counted in the census as three fifths of a person.

This fraction was arrived at through a compromise between the northern and southern states at the Federal Convention of 1787, but it actually had little to do with the racist view that blacks were inferior. The northern states did not want the slaves to be counted at all, but the southern states wanted them to be counted in the normal manner. If the slaves had been counted fully, the southern states would have gained more representatives and thus more political power in the new government. If the slaves were not counted at all, then the northern states would have gotten the upper hand politically. Three-fifths was the compromise between these two views.

Although I am certainly not opposed to abolishing this phrase from the Constitution, the fact remains nonetheless that the Fourteenth Amendment was *not* properly ratified and cannot therefore be a part of the "Authentic Constitution". The phrase would be inoperative anyway, because the Thirteenth Amendment abolished slavery. We will take up this issue in more detail in a later chapter.

The purpose of the census or enumeration is to determine the apportionment population in order to allocate representatives and direct taxes among the states. The first one was performed in 1790 and every ten years thereafter, as is stipulated in the Constitution. Other requirements are that each representative could not have less than thirty thousand constituents and each state had to have at least one representative. Exactly who is included in the apportionment population has changed over the years. The three-fifths requirement was discussed above, and in lieu of the Fourteenth Amendment, it was made inoperative by the Thirteenth Amendment. Furthermore, in 1940 it was determined that there were no longer any Indians that were "not taxed." Currently, according to the US Census Bureau's brochure titled "What You should Know About Apportionment Counts," "the apportionment calculation is based on the total resident population (citizen and noncitizen) of the 50 states. In the Census 2000, the apportionment population also includes US Armed Forces personnel and federal civilian employees stationed outside the United States (and their dependents living with them) that can be allocated, based on administrative records, back to a home state."[1]

Since "the actual Enumeration shall be made ... in such Manner as they [i.e., Congress] shall by Law direct" (Article I, section 2, clause 3), Congress has the authority to determine how the census or enumeration is to be carried out. The first census bill was passed on March 1, 1790 and others followed later. Congress also has the responsibility to determine two other things in order to allocate representatives among the states. First, Congress has to decide the number of representatives that will be apportioned. The number of representatives was fixed at 435 in 1911 and that number has been virtually unchanged since then. Based on the 2000 census, a House member now represents an average population of 646,952 constituents. Second, Congress has to decide how the apportionment calculation will be made. Since the first census in 1790, five different methods for calculating the apportionment of representatives have been used. The current one is called the Method of Equal Proportions, which was first implemented in the 1940 census. According to the US Census Bureau's brochure, under this method of calculation, "first, each state is assigned one seat. Then, the remaining 385 seats are distributed using a formula that computes 'priority values' based on each state's apportionment population."[2]

The apportionment population and number of apportioned representatives by state, based on the 2000 census, are given in Table 1.

Unlike indirect taxes, which are voluntary, direct taxes are unavoidable. In addition, the nature of this type of tax is such that some intrusion on the privacy of individuals is bound to occur. For these reasons, the delegates at the Federal Convention were of the opinion that all the funds needed to pay for the routine operations of the federal government would normally come solely from indirect taxes; direct taxes would be reserved for emergencies only. Of course, if Congress did pass a direct tax bill, there is little chance it would ever be readily accepted by the taxpayers. The latter would probably perceive it as little more than financial mismanagement and their reaction would typically be to vote the culprits out of office in the next election. For this reason, a direct tax bill would usually be proposed only if there were no other choice in the matter.

How would direct taxes be assessed according to the rule of apportionment? Let us try to explain this question by using the following example: The federal government budget for the next fiscal year is $100 billion of which $90 billion will be fully paid for by indirect taxes in the form of excise taxes and tariffs of various types. Unfortunately, this will leave a budget shortfall of $10 billion. In order to obtain the additional $10 billion, Congress decides to enact a direct tax in the form of a property tax, but the legislation leaves the details regarding the manner of assessing and collecting it with the individual states.[3]

---

1 United States Census 2000, Congressional Apportionment, Brochure: "What You Should Know About the Apportionment Counts," U. S. Census Bureau [Internet]; available from http://www.census.gov/dmd/www/pdf/pio00-ac.pdf; accessed 19 July 2008.

2 Ibid.

3 Apparently, Congress has significant flexibility in this area. It could leave the exact manner of assessing and collecting the tax with the individual states, as is being done in the example; or at the other extreme, it could choose to specify every minute detail of the assessment

First, the direct tax ratio for each state would be obtained by dividing the apportionment population of each state by the total apportionment population. If you look at Table 1, you will see that the apportionment population of Alabama is 4,461,130 and the total apportionment population is 281,424,177. Thus, the direct tax ratio for Alabama would be 4,461,130 divided by 281,424,177, which is .01585. The direct tax ratio for each state would be arrived at in the same manner.

Then, based on the above example, each state would be apportioned its share of the $10 billion direct tax, as shown in Table 1. Alabama's share would be $158,500,000 (.01585 direct tax ratio X $10,000,000,000).

Finally, a certified copy of the bill passed by Congress and a statement indicating the amount of the tax it had to collect would be sent to each state. Any other relevant information would be forwarded in the correspondence as well.[1]

In 1894, Congress passed an income tax law titled the Income Tax Act of 1894, which in the following year the Supreme Court declared unconstitutional in *Pollock v. Farmers' Loan & Trust Co.* The reason for the Court's decision was that the income tax was a direct tax that had to be apportioned and the tax bill did not consider this constitutional requirement. In order to remedy the situation, in 1909 Congress proposed the Sixteenth Amendment that would allow an income tax that did not need to be apportioned. This Amendment reads as follows:

> The Congress shall have power to lay and collect taxes on incomes, from whatever source derived, without apportionment among the several States, and without regard to any census or enumeration.

It had been an accepted belief that the Sixteenth Amendment was constitutionally ratified when the Secretary of State, Philander Chase Knox, issued the required Proclamation stating so on February 25, 1913. At the time, there were 48 states in the Union and, since Article V of the Constitution requires approval by three fourths of the states for ratification, 36 states were needed for ratification. In his Proclamation, Knox stated that the Amendment had been ratified by 38 states. Subsequent to the issuance of the Proclamation, four additional states — West Virginia, Vermont, Massachusetts, and New Hampshire — supposedly ratified the Amendment. Of the six remaining states, three had rejected it and three apparently took no action at all on the Amendment. Below is a transcribed copy of this Proclamation (Certificate of Ratification):

Philander C. Knox,
Secretary of State of the United States of America.
To all to Whom these Presents may come, Greeting:
Know Ye that, the Congress of the United States at the first
Session, sixty-first Congress, in the year one thousand nine hundred and
nine, passed a Resolution in the words and figures following: to wit —
"Joint Resolution
Proposing an amendment to the Constitution of
the United States.

---

and collection. Furthermore, Congress could establish more than one type of direct tax in the legislation.

1 For an early example of how direct taxes were assessed based on the apportionment requirement, see Apportionment of Direct Taxes. Communicated to the House of Representatives, May 25, 1798, The Library of Congress [Internet]; available from http://memory.loc.gov/cgi-bin/ampage?collId=llsp&fileName=009/llsp009.db&recNum=592; 19 July 2008.

Resolved, by the Senate and House of Representatives of the United States of America in Congress assembled (two-thirds of each House concurring therein), That the following article is proposed as an amendment to the Constitution of the United States, which, when ratified by the legislatures of three-fourths of the several States, shall be valid to all intents and purposes as a part of the Constitution:

'Article XVI. The Congress shall have power to lay and collect taxes on incomes, from whatever source derived, without apportionment among the several States, and without regard to any census or enumeration.'"

And, further, that it appears from official documents on file in this Department that the Amendment to the Constitution of the United States proposed as aforesaid has been ratified by the Legislatures of the States of Alabama, Kentucky, South Carolina, Illinois, Mississippi, Oklahoma, Maryland, Georgia, Texas, Ohio, Idaho, Oregon, Washington, California, Montana, Indiana, Nevada, North Carolina, Nebraska, Kansas, Colorado, North Dakota, Michigan, Iowa, Missouri, Maine, Tennessee, Arkansas, Wisconsin, New York, South Dakota, Arizona, Minnesota, Louisiana, Delaware, and Wyoming, in all thirty-six.

And, further, that the States whose Legislatures have so ratified the said proposed Amendment, constitute three-fourths of the whole number of States in the United States.

And, further, that it appears from official documents on file in this Department that the Legislatures of New Jersey and New Mexico have passed Resolutions ratifying the said proposed Amendment.

How therefore, be it known that I, Philander C. Knox, Secretary of State of the United States, by virtue and in pursuance of Section 205 of the Revised Statutes of the United States, do hereby certify that the Amendment aforesaid has become valid to all intents and purposes as a part of the Constitution of the United States.

In testimony whereof, I have hereunto set my hand and caused the seal of the Department of State to be affixed.

Done at the city of Washington this twenty-fifth day of February in the year of our Lord one thousand nine hundred and thirteen, and of the Independence of the United States of America the one hundred and thirty-seventh.

[Signed] Philander Case Knox[1]

In 1984, the belief that the Sixteenth Amendment had been constitutionally ratified came crashing down. By the end of that year, Bill Benson of South Holland, Illinois, had visited the capitols of all 48 states, as well as the National Archives in Washington, D.C. in order to review and make certified copies of all the relevant documents regarding the supposed ratification. The results of his investigation were startling to say the least. The required number of states had not really approved the Amendment.

Let us review briefly the amendment process as described in Article V of the Constitution. I quote the relevant portion of the paragraph below:

---

1 Bill Benson & M J. 'Red' Beckman, *The Law That Never Was*, Volume I (South Holland, Illinois: Constitutional Research Associates, 1985), 360-2. The Proclamation (Certificate of Ratification) can also be located on the following web site: Certificate of Ratification 1913 February 25, The Constitution Society [Internet]; available from http://www.constitution.org/tax/us-ic/ratif/cert_16.htm; accessed 19 July 2008.

The Congress, whenever two thirds of both Houses shall deem it necessary, shall propose Amendments to this Constitution, or, on the Application of the Legislatures of two thirds of the several States, shall call a Convention for proposing Amendments, which, in either Case, shall be valid to all Intents and Purposes, as Part of this Constitution, when ratified by the Legislatures of three fourths of the several States, or by Conventions in three fourths thereof, as the one or the other Mode of Ratification may be proposed by the Congress.

In the case of the Sixteenth Amendment, two thirds of each house voted to propose the Amendment and Congress decided that the ratification method to be followed was the one requiring the approval of three fourths of the state legislatures as is stated in the joint resolution passed by the 61st Congress in 1909 and quoted in the above Proclamation.

It is very important to remember that the state legislatures only vote to approve or reject the proposed amendment that is passed by Congress. They are not authorized to change it at all. Therefore, each state legislature must be provided with an exact copy of the amendment as proposed by Congress to vote on one way or the other. With this requirement in mind, on July 26, 1909 the Secretary of State, Philander C. Knox, sent a certified copy of the joint resolution passed by Congress to the Governors of the states. The joint resolution is quoted in the Proclamation (Certificate of Ratification) issued by the Secretary of State on February 25, 1913, which is quoted above.

> Enclosed along with the certified copy of the joint resolution was the following introductory letter:
>
> I have the honor to enclose a certified copy of a Resolution of Congress, entitled 'Joint Resolution Proposing an Amendment to the Constitution of the United States,' with the request that you cause the same to be submitted to the Legislature of your State for such action as may be had, and that a certified copy of such action be communicated to the Secretary of State, as required by Section 205, Revised Statutes of the United States. (See overleaf.) [Note: Reference here is to R. S. Sec. 205 which is quoted infra.]
>
> An acknowledgment of the receipt of this communication is requested.
>
> Section 205 of the Revised Statutes provides:
>
> Whenever *official notice* is received at the Department of State that any amendment proposed to the Constitution of the United States has been adopted, according to the provisions of the Constitution, the Secretary of State shall forthwith cause the amendment to be published in the newspapers authorized to promulgate the laws, with his certificate, specifying the States by which the same may have been adopted, and that the same has become valid, to all intents and purposes, as a part of the Constitution of the United States.[1]

That the states must vote on an *exact* copy of the proposed amendment passed by Congress is essential to the whole process. This is stated very clearly in a memorandum sent by Joshua Reuben Clark, Jr., the Solicitor General, to the Secretary of State on February 15, 1913. I quote the relevant portion below:

---

1 The introductory letter is quoted from a memorandum sent to Secretary of State Knox from the Solicitor General, Joshua Reuben Clark, Jr., on February 15, 1913 (Benson & Beckman, 5-20). The memorandum can also be located on the following web site: State Memorandum 1913 February 15, The Constitution Society [Internet]; available from http://www.constitution.org/tax/us-ic/ratif/memo_130215.htm; accessed 19 July 2008.

Furthermore, under the provisions of the Constitution a legislature is not authorized to alter *in any way* the amendment proposed by Congress, the function of the legislature consisting merely in the right to approve or disapprove the proposed amendment (italics mine).[1]

The revised and updated version of *How Our Laws Are Made* by the Parliamentarian of the U. S. House of Representatives describes the accuracy required in copying a prospective bill that is passed by the House and forwarded to the Senate for its consideration:

> XIII. Engrossment and Massage to Senate
>
> The preparation of a copy of the bill in the form in which it has passed the House can be a detailed and complicated process because of the large number and complexity of amendments to some bills adopted by the House.... Each amendment must be inserted in precisely the proper place in the bill, with the spelling and punctuation exactly as it was adopted by the House. It is extremely important that the Senate receive a copy of the bill in the precise form in which it has passed the House. The preparation of such a copy is the function of the enrolling clerk.[2]

Further on, the document gives the following information:

XV. Final Action on Amended Bill

. . .

> Custody of Papers
>
> A bill cannot become a law of the land until it has been approved in identical form by both Houses of Congress. When the bill has finally been approved by both Houses, all the original papers are transmitted to the enrolling clerk of the body in which the bill originated.[3]

When both houses of Congress have finally agreed to the exact same bill, the meticulous process of "enrollment" is undertaken prior to it being sent to the President for his consideration. This process is described as follows:

> XVII. Enrollment
>
> When the bill has been agreed to in identical form by both bodies-either 1) without amendment by the Senate, 2) by House concurrence in the Senate amendments, 3) by Senate concurrence in House amendments, or 4) by agreement in both bodies to the conference report-a copy of the bill is enrolled for presentation to the President.
>
> The preparation of the enrolled bill is a painstaking and important task because it must reflect precisely the effect of all amendments, either by way of deletion, substitution, or addition, agreed to by both bodies. The enrolling clerk of the House, with respect to bills originating in the House, receives the original engrossed bill, the engrossed Senate amendments, the signed conference report, the several messages from the Senate, and a notation of the final action by the House, for the purpose of preparing the enrolled copy. From these documents the enrolling clerk must meticulously prepare for presentation to the President the final form of the bill as it was agreed to by both Houses. On occasion, as many as 500 amendments have been adopted, each of which must be set out in

---

1 Ibid.

2 "How Our Laws Are Made" (23nd ed.), revised and updated June 30, 2003 by Charles W. Johnson Parliamentarian, U. S. House of Representatives, in consultation with the Office of the Parliamentarian of the US Senate, The Library of Congress, (Thomas) [Internet]; available from http://thomas.loc.gov/home/lawsmade.toc.html; accessed 19 July 2008.

3 Ibid.

the enrollment exactly as agreed to, and all punctuation must be in accord with the action taken.[1]

Clearly, accuracy in the transcription of prospective bills in communications between the two houses of Congress is extremely important in the legislative process. Surely, it is reasonable to expect the same degree of accuracy in the copying of proposed *constitutional* amendments in communications between the Secretary of State's office and the various state governments.

However, the quantity of errors and the downright carelessness discovered by Bill Benson in the supposed ratification of the Sixteenth Amendment is staggering to behold. This assertion holds true at both the state and federal levels of government. Even so, it seems to me that Secretary of State Knox in fairness cannot be faulted for the mistakes and sloppiness that occurred at the state level, regardless of how numerous or serious they may be. His sole responsibility was to obtain a proper certified copy of the decision passed by each state legislature. Indeed, this is what he requested in his introductory letter sent with the certified copy of the joint resolution (quoted above).

What should a state's submittal to the Secretary of State have included at the very minimum? Well, a proper certified copy of the act passed by the state legislature should have had the following items: 1) A statement attesting to the validity and accuracy of the document with the signature of the Secretary of State or even the Governor, 2) the signatures of the presiding officers of the House and the Senate, 3) the vote tallies of the House and the Senate, 4) the copy of the amendment finally agreed to by both the House and the Senate that *exactly agrees* in words, capitalization, and punctuation to the joint resolution passed by Congress, and 5) the Great Seal of the state affixed to the document. If any of these items are missing, unclear, contradictory, or erroneous, the Secretary of State should immediately send a letter to the state's Governor, requesting that he provide him with a proper certified copy of the approved act. Only when it is determined that the submittal is proper can the state then be added to the list of states that ratified the amendment.

There is some question whether the Governor is required to sign a state act that ratifies a constitutional amendment. All Article V of the Constitution states is that an amendment will be "Part of [the] Constitution, when ratified by the Legislatures of three fourths of the several States...." There is no mention here of the state Governors being involved in the state's ratification process. Nevertheless, it is obvious that a Governor *must* sign the act, if his signature is required by his state's own legislative process. However, let me state again that Secretary of State Knox in fairness cannot be faulted for the errors that may have occurred at the state level. If everything else was entirely correct on a state's submittal, but it was missing the Governor's signature, I do not believe he would be committing an indiscretion if he accepted it as a proper certified copy.

As was stated earlier in this chapter, 42 states supposedly ratified the Sixteenth Amendment, three rejected it, and three apparently took no action at all on it. Since there were only 48 states in the Union at the time, 36 states would be required to ratify the Amendment. If it can be shown that at least seven of the states that supposedly ratified it in fact did not, then only 35 states would have approved it and consequently the Sixteenth Amendment would not have been constitutionally ratified. Let us attempt to reduce the number of states that supposedly ratified the Amendment one state at a time by examining some of the evidence discovered by Bill Benson.

---

1 Ibid.

Since, as I maintained above, the sole responsibility of Secretary of State Knox was to obtain a proper certified copy of the act passed by each state legislature, this is what we will focus on.[1]

- *Kentucky.*[2] The submittal received by Secretary of State Knox, although indicating that the Kentucky House voted to approve the Amendment, revealed a discrepancy regarding the Kentucky Senate's vote. One document recorded that the Kentucky Senate approved the Amendment with 27 ayes and 2 nays, but the other, which apparently was the more authoritative one, recorded that the body rejected it with 9 ayes and 22 nays. There is no evidence that Secretary of State Knox made any attempt to investigate further or to obtain a proper certified copy of the state's decision, yet he declared that Kentucky had ratified the Amendment. The tally now is that only 41 states supposedly ratified the Amendment.

- *Minnesota.*[3] In a memorandum sent to Secretary of State Knox on February 15, 1913, Joshua Reuben Clark, Jr., the Solicitor General, related the following information regarding Minnesota's so-called ratification of the Amendment:

  In all cases in which the legislatures appear to have acted favorably upon the proposed amendment, either the Governor or some other state official has transmitted to the Department a certified copy of the resolution passed by the particular legislature, except in the case of Minnesota, in which case the secretary of the Governor merely informed the Department that the state legislature had ratified the proposed amendment and that the Governor had approved the ratification.

Further on, the same memorandum gives the following information:

  The Department has not received a copy of the Resolution passed by the State of Minnesota, but the Secretary of the Governor of that State has officially notified the Department that the Legislature of the State has ratified the proposed 16th amendment. It is believed that this meets fully the requirement with reference to the receipt of "official notice" contained in Section 205 Revised Statutes, and that Minnesota should be numbered with the States ratifying the aforesaid amendment.

It is very curious how in the first paragraph quoted above the statement that the "secretary of the Governor *merely informed* the Department..." metamorphosed into the statement that the "Secretary of the Governor ... has *officially notified* the Department..." in the second paragraph. Actually, it is not known how Secretary of State Knox was "merely informed" by the secretary of the Governor that the state legislature ratified the Amendment and the Governor approved it. In any case, how he could actually have accepted anything else but a proper certified copy of the state legislature's decision on the Amendment is difficult to understand. The issue has not to do with a mere regulation that could change small city government operations, but with a proposed amendment that could change the Constitution. The tally now is that only 40 states supposedly ratified the Amendment.

---

1 Bill Benson's web site is The Law That Never Was [Internet]; available from http://www. thelawthatneverwas.com/new/home.asp; accessed 19 July 2008. Books, CD-Rs, and DVDs on the income tax, the Sixteenth Amendment, and other interesting subjects can be purchased on the site.

2 Bill Benson & M J. 'Red' Beckman, *The Law That Never Was*, Volume I (South Holland, Illinois: Constitutional Research Associates, 1985), 37-44, 343-4.

3 Ibid., 251-6.

- *Illinois.*[1] The submittal attesting to the state's supposed ratification of the Amendment is transcribed in the following manner:

> The Congress shall have power to lay and collect taxes on incomes, from whatever source derived, without apportionment among the several *states*, and without regard to any census or *renumeration*.

The Sixteenth Amendment proposed by Congress reads as follows (note the corresponding italicized words in both versions):

> The Congress shall have power to lay and collect taxes on incomes, from whatever source derived, without apportionment among the several *States*, and without regard to any census or *enumeration*.

Although the submittal did not have the word "States" capitalized, the other error is more serious. Instead of transcribing the correct word "enumeration," which means "the act of counting" according to Dictionary.com, the state officials incorrectly copied "renumeration" — a non-existent word. Check any dictionary if you wish, you will not find it. Dictionary.com will tell you, "No entry found for renumeration." The Sixteenth Amendment is only thirty words in length. One can only wonder why the applicable state officials could not transcribe them correctly, when, as one writer has succinctly put it, "Even a sixth grader can copy, verbatim, 30 words without error."[2] The tally now is that only 39 states supposedly ratified the Amendment.

- *Mississippi.*[3] The submittal attesting to the state's supposed ratification of the Amendment is transcribed in the following manner:

> [ ] Congress shall have power to lay and collect taxes on incomes[ ] from whatever sources derived[ ] without apportionment among the several *states*, and without regard to any census o̲f̲ enumeration[:]

The Sixteenth Amendment proposed by Congress reads as follows (note the corresponding italicized words and punctuation or missing words in brackets in both versions):

> The Congress shall have power to lay and collect taxes on incomes[,] from whatever source derived[,] without apportionment among the several *States*, and without regard to any census o̲r̲ enumeration[.]

The submittal did not have "The" before "Congress" and once again, the word "States" was not capitalized. In addition, commas were missing at the beginning and end of the phrase "from whatever source derived" and there was a colon at the end of the Amendment instead of a period. However, these are not the significant errors. The state officials also copied "of" for "or" between the words "census" and "enumeration." Now, this may seem a minor error until one asks himself the question, "What on earth is a "census *of* enumeration"? The fact of the matter is there is no such thing as this. According to Dictionary.com, a "census" is "an official, usually periodic enumeration of a population, often including the collection of related demographic information" and, as already mentioned above, "enumeration" means "the act of counting." A "census of enumeration" is quite simply nonsense. The tally now is that only 38 states supposedly ratified the Amendment.

- *Idaho.*[4] Curiously, Idaho's submittal to Washington had the same errors as Mississippi ("census *of* enumeration"), except that "The" was copied before

---

1 Ibid., 51-4.

2 Jon Christian Ryter, *Whatever happened to America?* (Tampa, Florida: Hallberg Publishing Corporation, 2000), 162-3.

3 Benson & Beckman, 55-60.

4 Ibid., 101-5.

"Congress" and the punctuation was correct. The tally now is that only 37 states supposedly ratified the Amendment.

- *California.*[1] The submittal to Washington contained the following transcription of the Amendment:

  [ ] Congress shall have power to lay and collect taxes on *income*[ ] from whatever source derived[ ] without apportionment among the several *states*, and without regard to *census enumeration*[;].

The Sixteenth Amendment proposed by Congress reads as follows (note the corresponding italicized words and punctuation or missing words in brackets in both versions):

  The Congress shall have power to lay and collect taxes on *incomes*[,] from whatever source derived[,] without apportionment among the several *States*, and without regard to *any census or enumeration*[.]

The minor errors on the submittal are as follows: "The" is missing before "Congress," the word "incomes" is singular, and the word "States" is not capitalized. Furthermore, commas were missing at the beginning and end of the phrase "from whatever source derived" and there was a semicolon at the end of the Amendment instead of a period. However, of major significance is this error: The word "any" is missing before "census" and "or" is missing before "enumeration." Like the phrase "census of enumeration" used by Mississippi and Idaho, we can only wonder what "census enumeration" is and again we must proclaim it simply nonsense. The tally now is only 36 states, just enough states to ratify the Amendment.

- *Oklahoma.*[2] The submittal attesting to the state's supposed ratification of the Amendment is transcribed in the following manner:

  The Congress shall have power to lay and collect taxes on incomes, from whatever source derived, without apportionment among the several *states*, and *from* any census or enumeration.

The Sixteenth Amendment proposed by Congress reads as follows (note the corresponding italicized words in both versions):

  The Congress shall have power to lay and collect taxes on incomes, from whatever source derived, without apportionment among the several *States*, and *without regard to* any census or enumeration.

The submittal once again has the word "States" spelt without a capital letter. However, the more serious error is that instead of "without regard to" before "any census or enumeration," the word "from" has been copied. The latter clearly has a completely different meaning than the former. The tally now is only 35 states. *It can now be asserted that the Sixteenth Amendment was not constitutionally ratified.* Nevertheless, let us look at three more states with faulty ratifications in order to have ten states that have been reviewed.

- *Georgia.*[3] The submittal attesting to the state's supposed ratification of the Amendment is transcribed in the following manner:

  The Congress shall have power to *levy* and collect taxes on *income*[ ] from whatever *sources* derived[ ] without apportionment among the several States, and without regard to any census or enumeration[,]

---

1 Ibid., 119-23, 364-5.
2 Ibid., 61-7.
3 Ibid., 81-8.

The Sixteenth Amendment proposed by Congress reads as follows (note the corresponding italicized words and punctuation or missing words in brackets in both versions):

> The Congress shall have power to *lay* and collect taxes on *incomes*[,] from whatever *source* derived[,] without apportionment among the several States, and without regard to any census or enumeration[.]

The submittal has "income" instead of "incomes" and "sources" instead of "source." Furthermore, commas were missing at the beginning and end of the phrase "from whatever source derived" and there was a comma at the end of the Amendment instead of a period. However, the major error is that instead of "lay," the word "levy" has been copied. Joseph R. Banister, in his book *Investigating the Federal Income Tax*, provides the best explanation of the dissimilar meanings of the words "lay" and "levy." I quote the passage below:

> Levy refers to taking some kind of action against an object or item to enforce a legal claim or judgment that already exists. Lay refers to the act of administering a demand or requirement upon someone — like paying a tax. For example, the Collection Division of the Internal Revenue Service may levy a bank account to satisfy a tax debt but they do not lay a bank account. Likewise, the US Government may lay a tax on taxpayers but they do not levy a tax on taxpayers. The bottom line is that the words levy and lay are not interchangeable.[1]

- *Missouri*.[2] The state's submittal to Washington had the same error as Georgia in that "levy" was used instead of "lay." However, although both submittals had commas at the end of the Amendment, for Missouri the other minor errors were different in that "Congress" and "States" were not capitalized. The Amendment in the submittal is transcribed as follows:

> The *congress* shall have power to *levy* and collect taxes on incomes, from whatever source derived, without apportionment among the several *states*, and without regard to any census or enumeration[,]

The Sixteenth Amendment proposed by Congress reads as follows (note the corresponding italicized words and punctuation or missing words in brackets in both versions):

> The *Congress* shall have power to *lay* and collect taxes on incomes, from whatever source derived, without apportionment among the several *States*, and without regard to any census or enumeration[.]

- *North Dakota*.[3] The submittal sent to Secretary of State Knox was not a proper certified copy of the state legislature's decision on the Amendment, because it did not have the proper signatures and the Great Seal of North Dakota was not affixed to the document.

Almost as soon as the Sixteenth Amendment was allegedly ratified, controversy surfaced as to what exactly the Amendment actually accomplished. Did it make the income tax a new form of taxation — a direct tax that did not need to be apportioned, or did it take the income tax out of the category of direct taxes all together and make it into an indirect tax? In 1916, *Brushaber v. Union Pacific Railroad Co.* attempted to settle this problem finally, but the unfortunate result was that future court decisions ended

---

1 Joseph R. Banister, *Investigating the Federal Income Tax*, 1st edition, pg. 55. His web site is "Freedom Above Fortune" [Internet]; available from http://www.freedomabovefortune.com/; accessed 19 July 2008. His book can be purchased on this site as well.
2 Benson & Beckman, 191-4.
3 Ibid., 173-8.

up trying to explain the *Brushaber* decision. Although a vast number of federal and state court decisions regarding this issue have been adjudicated since *Brushaber*, the problem has not yet been resolved satisfactorily in the courts.[1]

However, there is no need for this confusion. It is clear that the income tax *is* a direct tax, since it fits the characteristics of such a tax perfectly. Someone's property (in this case someone's income) is being taxed and the taxpayer pays the tax straight to the government. An indirect tax, on the other hand, is a tax on commodities and is usually paid by the taxpayer to a tax collector, who then remits it to the government.

Since the classification of the income tax as a direct tax is clear, the federal government has no constitutional authority to assess and collect this tax on Americans without the proper ratification of the Sixteenth Amendment. Nevertheless, the IRS collected $1,236 billion in personal income taxes in 2006 (the latest year currently available).[2] It is obvious that a government with an appalling 2008 budget of $2.93 trillion[3] and with a relentless proclivity in getting involved in unconstitutional foreign wars in order to make "the world ... safe for democracy"[4] is not going to give up such an indispensable revenue source without a fight. Besides, in a later chapter it will be learned that the federal government actually requires personal income tax revenue to pay the interest on the national debt and a large share of transfer payments to individuals.

Regardless of whether the Sixteenth Amendment was ratified, there are other serious problems with the income tax. It is incredibly difficult to understand much of the law, necessitating that many taxpayers must pay so-called experts to prepare their returns for them. However, stories have been told of these "expects" and even tax preparers trained and employed by the IRS (Internal Revenue Service) being stumped by a particular aspect of the law. For those who *do* make the effort to prepare their own returns, many hours sitting at the kitchen table are often required to accomplish the task.[5] Trying to determine the original "cost basis" of a stock that was purchased twenty or even thirty years ago can be an overwhelming experience to say the least. Surely, a simpler and less time-consuming tax system would not be an unreasonable request.

---

1 "Uncertainty of the Federal Income Tax Laws," The Dixieland Law Journal [Internet]; available from http://fly.hiwaay.net/%7Ebecraft/UNCERTAIN.html; accessed 19 July 2008.

2 Table 466. Internal Revenue Gross Collections by Type of Tax: 2001 to 2006, Federal Government Finances & Employment: Federal Budget — Receipts, Outlays, and Debt, The 2008 Statistical Abstract, US Census Bureau [Internet]; available from http://www.census.gov/compendia/statab/tables/08s0466.pdf; accessed 29 June 2008.

3 Brian M. Riedl, "Federal Spending by the Numbers 2008," Nominal Budget Data and the Budget Baseline, pg. 12, The Heritage Foundation [Internet]; available from http://www.heritage.org/Research/Taxes/wm1829.cfm; accessed 27 June 2008.

4 This well-known quotation is from President Woodrow Wilson's speech before Congress on April 2, 1917, asking for a Declaration of War with Germany prior to the United States' entry into World War I.

5 According to the IRS, the average time needed to completely prepare and file a 1040 form, which would include record keeping, tax planning, and the preparation of applicable schedules and forms, is 14.1 hours for non-business filers and 56.9 hours for business filers. Estimated Average Taxpayer Burden for Individuals by Activity, 2007 Form 1040 Instructions, pg. 84, Internal Revenue Service [Internet]; available from http://www.irs.gov/pub/irs-pdf/i1040gi.pdf; accessed 29 June 2008. What would be the result if Americans were able to use this time for more productive pursuits?

When we file tax returns, which the IRS states is a *mandatory* exercise every year,[1] we provide it with a significant amount of financial and other personal information. By signing the completed 1040 we affirm that we agree with the following declaration:

> Under penalties of perjury, I declare that I have examined this return and accompanying schedules and statements, and to the best of my knowledge and belief, they are true, correct, and complete. Declaration of preparer (other than taxpayer) is based on all information of which preparer has any knowledge.[2]

The IRS also states that it can use this information as evidence against us, if we should be accused of breaking a criminal tax law.[3] However, many individuals have remarked about the serious problem that is presented by this act of filing a tax return. If filing is indeed mandatory, then how can the information we are *forced* to give possibly be used against us in a criminal case? It seems clear that using the information against us in this way violates the Fifth Amendment to the Constitution that states among other things, "No person ... shall be compelled in any criminal case to be a witness against himself...." Only if we *voluntarily* give the information can it be used against us, because only then we are not "compelled" (to use the word of the Fifth Amendment) to give it. Thus, regardless of what the IRS may want us to believe, if the Fifth Amendment has any validity at all and if the information we provide it can in fact be used against us in a criminal case, *then filing a tax return must be voluntary.*

It is interesting in this regard that many IRS documents and manuals actually call the administration of the income tax a *voluntary* compliance system?[4] Yet if we do not volunteer, we all know what will happen. All the same, this alternating use of "mandatory" on one hand and "voluntary" on the other is very peculiar. What is the reason for it? According to Joseph R. Banister, who had been a Special Agent in the IRS Criminal Investigation Division (IRS-CID) before he was forced to resign because of his views on the unconstitutionality of the income tax, provides the following answer:

> During my investigation into why the word voluntary is repeatedly used in conjunction with the federal income tax, I discovered a large volume of constitutional research supporting the conclusion that the creators and curators of the federal income tax system have been *forced* to construct it and administer it as a so-called "voluntary" system, in order to avoid running afoul of the US Constitution. In other words, a way had to be found to pound the "square peg" known as the federal income tax into the "round hole" of the US Constitution. The research shows that this forcing of the "square peg" into the "round hole" has plagued administration and enforcement of the federal income tax since

---

1 "Our legal right to ask for information is Internal Revenue Code sections 6001, 6011, and 6012 (a), and their regulations. They say that you must file a return or statement with us for any tax you are liable for. *Your response is mandatory under these sections* (italics mine)." Disclosure, Privacy Act, and Paperwork Reduction Act Notice, 2007 Form 1040 Instructions, pg. 83, Internal Revenue Service [Internet]; available from http://www.irs.gov/pub/irs-pdf/i1040gi. pdf; accessed 29 June 2008.

2 2007 Form 1040 US Individual Income Tax Return, Internal Revenue Service [Internet]; available from http://www.irs.gov/pub/irs-pdf/f1040.pdf?portlet=3; accessed 29 June 2008.

3 "If you do not file a return, do not provide the information we ask for, or provide fraudulent information, you may be charged penalties *and be subject to criminal prosecution* (italics mine)." Disclosure, Privacy Act, and Paperwork Reduction Act Notice, 2007 Form 1040 Instructions, pg. 83, Internal Revenue Service [Internet]; available from http://www.irs. gov/pub/irs-pdf/i1040gi.pdf; accessed 29 June 2008.

4 Banister, 5–15.

the day it was born. The problem is that the implication of this research is not known or understood by the vast majority of American taxpayers.[1]

Because the Sixteenth Amendment was not constitutionally ratified, does this mean that Americans can stop filing tax returns on April 15 and stop paying income taxes? Those brave, patriotic Americans who have made and are now making the decision to stop filing tax returns must be prepared face the onslaught of the IRS. They need substantial time and money in order to undertake the struggle and they must be prepared to face the possibility of time behind bars. Most Americans, who have families to provide for, simply cannot embark on such a course of action. Nevertheless, one cannot help but remember the sad fate of those noble signers of the Declaration of Independence mentioned in the first chapter.

Perhaps the old maxim that "power is in numbers" may carry some weight here. If *millions* of Americans refused to file or pay income taxes all at once, what could the government possibly do about it? There simply would not be enough prisons and jails available to lock up all the "criminals" and perhaps finally the travesty of the income tax would be ended finally. Unfortunately, because of the rampant indifference infecting the psyche of most Americans today, it is highly unlikely that such a noble endeavor would even get off the ground. On the other hand, if the people would finally use the power of their vote *effectively* and send elected officials to Washington who sincerely follow the Constitution, then perhaps the arduous efforts of such genuine statesmen, as opposed to the sham politicians we mostly elect, could return the tax system to a truly constitutional one. Sad though it is to say, perhaps the title of the old 1937 song, "I Can Dream, Can't I?" fits the reality of the situation far better. In any case, the Sixteenth Amendment was not constitutionally ratified and for that reason, it is not really a part of the "Authentic Constitution".

Population Apportionment, Direct Tax Ratio, and Number of Apportioned Representatives by State, Based on 2000 Census; Example: $10 Billion Direct Tax Apportionment; Number of Senators; Number of Electoral Votes are shown in the next table.

State	Apportionment Population	Direct Tax Ratio	Number of Apportioned Representatives	State Share of $10,000,000,000 Direct Tax Apportionment	Number of Senators	Number of Electoral Votes
Alabama	4,461,130	.01585	7	158,500,000	2	9
Alaska	628,933	.00224	1	22,400,000	2	3
Arizona	5,140,683	.01827	8	182,700,000	2	10
Arkansas	2,679,733	.00952	4	95,200,000	2	6
California	33,930,798	.12057	53	1,205,700,000	2	55

1 Ibid., 15.

State	Apportionment Population	Direct Tax Ratio	Number of Apportioned Representatives	State Share of $10,000,000,000 Direct Tax Apportionment	Number of Senators	Number of Electoral Votes
Colorado	4,311,882	.01532	7	153,200,000	2	9
Connecticut	3,409,535	.01212	5	121,200,000	2	7
Delaware	785,068	.00279	1	27,900,000	2	3
Florida	16,028,890	.05696	25	569,600,000	2	27
Georgia	8,206,975	.02916	13	291,600,000	2	15
Hawaii	1,216,642	.00432	2	43,200,000	2	4
Idaho	1,297,274	.00461	2	46,100,000	2	4
Illinois	12,439,042	.04420	19	442,000,000	2	21
Indiana	6,090,782	.02164	9	216,400,000	2	11
Iowa	2,931,923	.01042	5	104,200,000	2	7
Kansas	2,693,824	.00957	4	95,700,000	2	6
Kentucky	4,049,431	.01439	6	143,900,000	2	8
Louisiana	4,480,271	.01592	7	159,200,000	2	9
Maine	1,277,731	.00454	2	45,400,000	2	4
Maryland	5,307,886	.01886	8	188,600,000	2	10
Massachusetts	6,355,568	.02258	10	225,800,000	2	12
Michigan	9,955,829	.03538	15	353,800,000	2	17
Minnesota	4,925,670	.01750	8	175,000,000	2	10
Mississippi	2,852,927	.01014	4	101,400,000	2	6
Missouri	5,606,260	.01992	9	199,200,000	2	11
Montana	905,316	.00322	1	32,200,000	2	3
Nebraska	1,715,369	.00610	3	61,000,000	2	5
Nevada	2,002,032	.00711	3	71,100,000	2	5
New Hampshire	1,238,415	.00440	2	44,000,000	2	4
New Jersey	8,424,354	.02994	13	299,400,000	2	15
New Mexico	1,823,821	.00648	3	64,800,000	2	5
New York	19,004,973	.06753	29	675,300,000	2	31
North Carolina	8,067,673	.02867	13	286,700,000	2	15

State	Apportionment Population	Direct Tax Ratio	Number of Apportioned Representatives	State Share of $10,000,000,000 Direct Tax Apportionment	Number of Senators	Number of Electoral Votes
North Dakota	643,756	.00229	1	22,900,000	2	3
Ohio	11,374,540	.04042	18	404,200,000	2	20
Oklahoma	3,458,819	.01229	5	122,900,000	2	7
Oregon	3,428,543	.01218	5	121,800,000	2	7
Pennsylvania	12,300,670	.04371	19	437,100,000	2	21
Rhode Island	1,049,662	.00373	2	37,300,000	2	4
South Carolina	4,025,061	.01430	6	143,000,000	2	8
South Dakota	756,874	.00269	1	26,900,000	2	3
Tennessee	5,700,037	.02025	9	202,500,000	2	11
Texas	20,903,994	.07428	32	742,800,000	2	34
Utah	2,236,714	.00795	3	79,500,000	2	5
Vermont	609,890	.00217	1	21,700,000	2	3
Virginia	7,100,702	.02523	11	252,300,000	2	13
Washington	5,908,684	.02100	9	210,000,000	2	11
West Virginia	1,813,077	.00644	3	64,400,000	2	5
Wisconsin	5,371,210	.01909	8	190,900,000	2	10
Wyoming	495,304	.00176	1	17,600,000	2	3
District of Columbia	N/A	N/A	N/A	N/A	N/A	3
TOTALS	281,424,177	1.00002	435	10,000,200,000	100	538

Source: Table 1. Apportionment Population and Number of Representatives, by State: Census 2000, US Census Bureau [Internet]; available from http://www.census.gov/population/cen2000/tab01.pdf; accessed 6 July 2008 and Number of Electoral Votes from "Distribution of 2004 and 2008 Electoral Votes," US Electoral College, Office of the Federal Register, US National Archives and Records Administration (NARA) [Internet]; available from http://www.archives.gov/federal-register/electoral-college/2004/allocation.html; accessed 6 July 2008.

Chapter 7: Regulating Commerce

The power given to Congress by the Constitution does not extend to the internal regulation of the commerce of a State (that is to say, of the commerce between citizen and citizen) which remain exclusively with its own legislature, but to its external commerce only; that is to say, its commerce with another State, or with foreign nations, or with the Indian tribes.
— *Thomas Jefferson: Opinion on Bank, 1791.*

Under the Articles of Confederation, a union was formed in which "each state retains its sovereignty, freedom, and independence, and every power, jurisdiction, and right, which is not by this Confederation expressly delegated to the United States, in Congress assembled" (Article II). This system allowed the states to act almost like independent countries, and since Congress did not have the power to regulate interstate commerce, the states took it upon themselves to do so. Unfortunately, since each state was concerned mainly with its own economic welfare, certain laws regarding trade, including duties on imports from other states, were passed for its own benefit, but to the detriment of the neighboring states. These interstate trade barriers were clearly a hindrance to the new nation's general economic prosperity, but even more serious, they jeopardized the very existence of the union as well.

Congress had some capacity to regulate foreign commerce under the Articles by using its power to negotiate treaties, but since it had no real means of enforcing any of its decrees, the states were able to (and often did) simply ignore the pronouncements of Congress. Even so, although "no State shall lay any imposts or duties, which may interfere with any stipulations in treaties" (Article VI), Congress was still prohibited from negotiating any treaty "whereby the legislative power of the respective States shall be restrained from imposing such imposts and duties on foreigners, as their own people are subjected to, or from prohibiting the exportation or importation of any species of goods or commodities whatsoever ..." (Article IX). Thus, concerned citizens soon realized that the power of Congress to regulate foreign trade under the Articles needed correction.

The inability of Congress to regulate both interstate and foreign trade was one of the main defects in our first form of government that brought the delegates to Philadelphia in 1787. The results of their efforts at the Federal Convention can be found in the following sections of the Constitution:

Article I, section 8, on the powers of Congress:

> [Clause 1] The Congress shall have Power To [*sic*] lay and collect ... Duties, Imposts and Excises ... but all Duties, Imposts and Excises shall be uniform throughout the United States.

> Clause 3: [Congress shall have power] To regulate Commerce with foreign Nations, and among the several States, and with the Indian Tribes.

Article I, section 9, on prohibitions placed on Congress:

> Clause 5: No Tax or Duty shall be laid on Articles exported from any State.

> Clause 6: No Preference shall be given by any Regulation of Commerce or Revenue to the Ports of one State over those of another: nor shall Vessels bound to, or from, one State, be obliged to enter, clear or pay Duties in another.

Article I, section 10, on the prohibitions placed on the states:

> Clause 2: No State shall, without the Consent of the Congress, lay any Imposts or Duties on Imports or Exports, except what may be absolutely necessary for executing it's inspection Laws: and the net Produce of all Duties and Imposts, laid by any State on Imports or Exports, shall be for the Use of the Treasury of the United States; and all such Laws shall be subject to the Revision and Controul [*sic*] of the Congress.

> Clause 3: No State shall, without the Consent of Congress, lay any Duty of Tonnage....

Finally, the means used to regulate commerce with foreign nations and with the Indian tribes is often through the treaty making power of the President with the approval of the Senate. This power is recorded in Article II, section 2, clause 2:

> He [the President] shall have Power, by and with the Advice and Consent of the Senate, to make Treaties, provided two thirds of the Senators present concur.

Since the treaty making power was properly considered a federal one, the states were prohibited from negotiating treaties or forming any kind of pact with other states or with foreign nations:

> Article I, Section. 10. [Clause 1] No State shall enter into any Treaty, Alliance, or Confederation.

> [Clause 3] No State shall, without the Consent of Congress ... enter into any Agreement or Compact with another State, or with a foreign Power....

Let us try to summarize the sections of the Constitution quoted above. Congress is given the power "to regulate Commerce with foreign Nations," "among the several States," and "with the Indian Tribes" (Article I, section 8, clause 3). Although prohibited from taxing exports regardless of their final destination (Article I, section 9, clause 5), Congress can tax imports. Furthermore, it is prohibited from giving the port of one state favored treatment over the port of another state, and from requiring ships coming or going from one state to dock in another state in order to obtain authorization to proceed or to pay a tax (Article I, section 9, clause 6).

The states, on the other hand, are prohibited from taxing imports or exports, as well as the tonnage of merchant ships, without the approval of Congress (Article I, section 10, clauses 2 and 3). However, there is one exception to the approval requirement regarding the taxing of imports and exports. If the revenue is needed solely to carry out their inspection laws, the states are allowed to tax imports and exports without the approval of Congress, but any surplus proceeds have to go into the US Treasury and "all such Laws shall be subject to the Revision and Controul [*sic*] of the Congress" (Article I, section 10, clause 2).

As already stated, the Constitution does not prohibit Congress from taxing imports. Randy E. Barnett, Austin B. Fletcher Professor of Law at the Boston University School of Law, made a detailed study of the Commerce Clause, which Article I, section 8, clause 3 is often called, and reached the following conclusion as to its original meaning:

> "Commerce" means the trade or exchange of goods (including the means of transporting them); "among the several States" means between persons of one state and another; and the term "To regulate" means "to make regular" — that is, to specify how an activity may be transacted — when applied to domestic commerce, but also includes the power to make "prohibitory regulations" when applied to foreign trade. In sum, Congress has power to specify rules to govern the manner by which people may exchange or trade goods from one state to another, to remove obstructions to domestic trade erected by states, and to both regulate and restrict the flow of goods to and from other nations (and the Indian tribes) for the purpose of promoting the domestic economy and foreign trade.[1]

"Prohibitory regulations" includes the use of quotas and tariffs (duties). It is worth noting that before the income tax became our main form of taxation, tariffs, as well as excise taxes, provided the federal government with all the revenue it required. Congress was specifically granted the power to use these types of taxes in Article I, section 8, clause 1, which states, "Congress shall have Power To lay and collect ... Duties, Imposts and Excises ... but all Duties, Imposts and Excises shall be uniform throughout the United States."

A tariff could be a revenue tariff or a protective tariff. The former is used simply to raise revenue and nothing more, whereas the latter has an additional purpose, which is to "protect" the nation's manufacturers from low-priced goods coming in the country from abroad. Protectionism, which is the name given to this type of foreign trade policy, is accomplished by raising the prices of foreign imports by charging tariffs on these goods when they enter the country. The result is that the goods of local manufacturers now have a competitive advantage over the foreign goods.

An example would be helpful here. Let us say a television set manufactured in the United States cost $500, but a similar television set from abroad cost only $300 — the difference in price being due most likely to the lower labor costs in the foreign country. It seems obvious that the US manufacturer is not going to be very successful in reducing his television set inventory when he has to compete with a price so much lower than his own. In order to correct the disparity, a tariff of 40% ($200) or even higher would be placed on the import, which would not only raise revenue for the federal government, but would also give the upper hand to the U. S. manufacturer so he can sell his television sets. The obvious benefit to the nation would be that the U. S. manufacturer would stay in business and, as a result, jobs for Americans would not be lost.

---

1 Randy E. Barnett, "The Original Meaning of the Commerce Clause," Randy E. Barnett [Internet]; available from http://www.bu.edu/rbarnett/Original.htm#F215; accessed 30 June 2008.

One disadvantage for the consumer is that tariffs raise the prices of imported goods. However, what is often overlooked is that *all* taxes increase the prices of goods, not just tariffs. Like all business costs, taxes are transferred to consumers by increasing the prices of the goods sold to them. Thus, regardless of the types of taxes that are placed on goods, the consumer will inevitably pay higher prices for them as a result. Even so, tariffs do provide an important advantage to US industry, which is that the foreign manufacturers end up paying a significant portion, if not all, of the taxes *not* the US companies. By charging tariffs on imported goods, the internal taxes on U. S. businesses like excise, income, and property taxes, can be reduced or even eliminated, because the foreign manufacturers now provide the government with the revenues it needs. In other words, although the consumers will pay the taxes in the end, the initial tax burden is transferred from US businesses to foreign businesses. As a result, U. S. manufacturers are much better able to compete with foreign companies.

History is clear regarding the benefits of a protectionist foreign trade policy, which was the guiding principle of the nation from 1860 to the Great Depression:

> From 1869 to 1900, real wages rose 53 percent, commodity prices fell 58 percent, America's GNP quadrupled, and our national debt fell by two-thirds. Customs duties provided 58 percent of all federal revenues.

> From 1870 to 1913, the US economy grew more than 4 percent a year. Industrial production grew at 5 percent. The Protectionist Era was among the most productive in history. When it began, America was dependent on imports for 8 percent of its GNP. When it ended, America's dependency had fallen to 4 percent. The nation began the era with an economy half the size of Britain's and ended it with an economy more than twice as large as Britain's.[1]

Although tariffs were not the only factor behind the thriving economy of the period, they were certainly a major one. However, the evidence shows that the United States was not the only country to benefit from this type of foreign trade policy:

> ... protectionism has been behind the rise of every great power in modern history: Great Britain under the Acts of Navigation up to 1850, the America of 1860 to 1914, Germany from 1870 to 1914, Japan from 1950 to 1990 and China, which has grown at 9 percent a year for a decade. As China demonstrates, it is a mistake to assume free trade, or even democracy, is indispensable to growth.[2]

Unfortunately, the use of the protective tariff is not the foreign trade policy that is being followed today. Free trade is now in vogue. Anything that restrains trade, especially tariffs, is looked on with disdain. Thus, the goal is to reduce, eventually to zero, all barriers to international trade. The implementation of this policy is currently being accomplished via so-called free trade agreements, such as NAFTA (North American Free Trade Agreement), CAFTA-DR (Dominican Republic — Central America — United States Free Trade Agreement), and about sixty other agreements administered by the WTO (World Trade Organization).

NAFTA is an agreement between the United States, Mexico, and Canada that officially went into effect on January 1, 1994. President Bush signed it into law on December 8, 1993. CAFTA-DR is essentially an expansion of NAFTA to the Central American countries of Guatemala, El Salvador, Honduras, Costa Rica, Nicaragua, and to the Dominican Republic as well. It apparently went into effect when the last

---

1 Patrick J. Buchanan, *Where the Right Went Wrong* (New York: St. Martin's Press, 2005), 155-6.
2 Patrick J. Buchanan, *Riding the Free Trade Raft Over the Falls*, The American Cause [Internet]; available from http://www.theamericancause.org/a-pjb-050418-freetrade.htm; accessed 30 June 2008.

participating nation to approve the agreement — Costa Rica — did so on October 7, 2007. President Bush signed it into law on August 2, 2005. If it is eventually approved, the Free Trade Area of the Americas (FTAA) will be an expansion of the original NAFTA and CAFTA-DR agreements to all of the Western Hemisphere. Although the 34 countries that met at Mar de Plata, Argentina in January 2005 failed to reach an accord, 26 of the countries had made assurances to continue discussions in 2006, but their assurances never came to fruition.

The WTO, which was established on January 1, 1995 and currently has 152 member nations, came into existence because of GATT (General Agreement on Tariffs and Trade) 1994, which was the result of the Uruguay Round of trade negotiations from 1986 through 1994. Its predecessor was the original GATT, which was negotiated shortly after World War II. President Bush signed the updated version into law on December 8, 1994. The WTO web site describes GATT 1994 as follows:

> [It] is now the WTO's principal rule-book for trade in goods. The Uruguay Round also created new rules for dealing with trade in services, relevant aspects of intellectual property, dispute settlement, and trade policy reviews. The complete set runs to some 30,000 pages....[1]

> The table of contents of "The Results of the Uruguay Round of Multilateral Trade Negotiations: The Legal Texts" is a daunting list of about 60 agreements, annexes, decisions and understandings. In fact, the agreements fall into a simple structure with six main parts: an umbrella agreement (the Agreement Establishing the WTO); agreements for each of the three broad areas of trade that the WTO covers (goods, services and intellectual property); dispute settlement; and reviews of governments' trade policies.[2]

Actually, giving the name *free* trade to these agreements is incorrect. Free trade may be the ultimate goal, but the current reality of the situation is quite different. They should more appropriately be called *managed* trade agreements,[3] for the negotiations held between the participating countries created thousands of pages of rules and regulations, including tariff assurances,[4] and authorized the establishment of numerous international bodies, councils, committees, and panels to enforce them. Nevertheless, free trade in the United States seems to be moving steadily forward,

---

1 The WTO in Brief: Part 3, The WTO agreements, World Trade Organization [Internet]; available from http://www.wto.org/english/thewto_e/whatis_e/inbrief_e/inbr03_e.htm; accessed 30 June 2008.

2 Understanding the WTO: The Agreements, Overview: a navigational guide, World Trade Organization [Internet]; available from http://www.wto.org/english/thewto_e/whatis_e/tif_e/agrml_e.htm; accessed 30 June 2008.

3 According to Phyllis Schlafly, "the proper term for NAFTA and GATT is 'Managed Trade,' because it put US trade under the control of new and powerful international bureaucracies." Phyllis Schlafly, "Free Trade, Protectionism, NAFTA, and GATT," The Phyllis Schlafly Report [Internet]; available from http://www.eagleforum.org/psr/1996/mar96/psrmar96.html; accessed 30 June 2008.

4 According to the WTO web site, "the bulkiest results of Uruguay Round are the 22,500 pages listing individual countries' commitments on specific categories of goods and services. These include commitments to cut and "bind" their customs duty rates on imports of goods. In some cases, tariffs are being cut to zero. There is also a significant increase in the number of "bound" tariffs — duty rates that are committed in the WTO and are difficult to raise." Understanding the WTO: The Agreements, Tariffs: more bindings and closer to zero, World Trade Organization [Internet]; available from http://www.wto.int/english/thewto_e/whatis_e/tif_e/agrm2_e.htm; accessed 30 June 2008.

since according to the 2006 U. S. government report for the WTO, "last year nearly 70 percent of all US imports ... entered the United States duty free."[1]

You may be wondering why these trade agreements are not called treaties. The answer, which you will probably be amazed to discover, is not due to simple word preference. By calling them congressional-executive agreements (CEAs) instead of treaties, *which they really are*, they are classified as statutory law only and a majority vote in both houses is all that is required for their passage. Usually only a two-thirds vote in the Senate is necessary for the passage of a treaty (Article II, section 2, clause 2), but if a treaty includes rules for regulating trade between the United States and another country or countries, it would have to be approved by a majority vote in the House of Representatives as well.[2] The reason is that in the Constitution *both* Houses of Congress were given the power to "regulate commerce with foreign nations" (Article I, section 8, clause 3).

Now you may think that a majority vote in both houses is actually more difficult to obtain, but let us look at the facts. For NAFTA, the House vote was 234-200 and the Senate vote was 61-38.[3] Since a two-thirds vote in the Senate would be 67 (the Senate is composed of 100 Senators), NAFTA would not have passed as a treaty. For CAFTA-DR, the House vote was 217-215 and the Senate vote was 55-45.[4] CAFTA-DR would have failed to pass as well. The WTO would have passed, since the House vote was 288-146 and the Senate vote was 76-24.[5] Nevertheless, the fact that two out of three would have failed to pass as treaties shows not only how difficult it is in capturing a two-thirds vote instead of a majority, but also why they were deliberately not classified as treaties in the first place. How convenient it is to call something what it is not, especially in the fantasy world of Washington D.C..

By approving these trade agreements, Congress has clearly transferred its power to "regulate commerce with foreign nations" over to international organizations, and in so doing has completely bypassed the Constitution and its own legislative process. The consequences of this transfer of power to international organizations have been that the sovereignty of the federal and state governments within their proper spheres and the authority of domestic courts to adjudicate disputes have been seriously put in jeopardy.

---

1 Government report (Trade Policy Review Report by the United States, 5 May 2008), Continued openness is key at a time of economic uncertainty, World Trade Organization [Internet]; available from http://www.wto.org/english/tratop_e/tpr_e/tp300_e.htm; accessed 30 June 2008.

2 According to W. Cleon Skousen, "there are some treaties which require the concurrence of the House of Representatives" (W. Cleon Skousen, *The Making of America*, 2nd rev. ed. (Washington, D.C.: The National Center for Constitutional Studies, 1986), 548).

3 H.R. 3450, To implement the North American Free Trade Agreement, Public Law No: 103-182, The Library of Congress THOMAS [Internet]; available from http://thomas.loc.gov/cgi-bin/bdquery/z?d103:HR03450:@@@S; accessed 30 June 2008.

4 H.R. 3045, To implement the Dominican Republic — Central America — United States Free Trade Agreement, Public Law: 109-53, The Library of Congress THOMAS [Internet]; available from http://thomas.loc.gov/cgi-bin/bdquery/z?d109:HR03045:@@@X; accessed 30 June 2008.

5 H.R. 5110, To approve and implement the trade agreements concluded in the Uruguay Round of multilateral trade negotiations, Public Law No: 103-465, Library of Congress, THOMAS [Internet]; available from http://thomas.loc.gov/cgi-bin/bdquery/z?d103:HR05110:@@@R|TOM:/bss/d103query.html; accessed 30 June 2008.

Henry Lamb, the executive vice president of the Environmental Conservation Organization and chairman of Sovereignty International, explains the real situation as follows:

> These trade agreements were sold to Congress, and to the American people, as "Free Trade" agreements. Nothing could be further from the truth. These agreements are actually mountains of regulations, developed and enforced by unelected bureaucrats. They are, in fact, agreements by participating nations, to allow unelected bureaucrats to manage trade among the participants.
>
> These trade agreements have extraordinary legal power. The decisions of an appointed international tribunal have the power to force participating nations to conform their laws to comply with the tribunal's decisions — or face economic penalties.[1]

Dr. Steven Yates, a teacher, writer, and contributing columnist for NewsWith-Views.com, says much the same thing:

> I don't see how one can peruse the official documents of NAFTA and the WTO without realizing that the former was not really a free trade agreement and the latter is not really about free trade. Both are about trade micromanaged and controlled by contingents of bureaucrats, politicians, and politically well-connected corporations and business groups. In other words, what NAFTA created was the *opposite* of free trade.[2]

Further into the article, he notes that the authority of domestic courts and state governments is endangered by these trade agreements as well:

> The reality is that international tribunals created by NAFTA are already arrogating for themselves the authority to overrule US courts in trade spats between American and foreign firms.... [and] The WTO has been considerably more aggressive in handing down judgments against state laws in ways that indicate growing attacks on US sovereignty.[3]

The Public Citizen web site has an article that evaluates NAFTA's performance for the first ten years of its existence. I quote a brief portion of it below:

> Think of NAFTA as a Trojan Horse attack on sovereignty and democracy: hidden beneath the "free trade" cover was an entire ant-democratic governance system under which policies affecting our daily lives in innumerable ways are decided out of our sight or control. When NAFTA was debated in 1993, few realized that this "trade agreement" included hundreds of pages of non-trade policies to which every signatory country was required to conform its domestic laws — even if Congress or state legislatures had opposed the very policies NAFTA's terms required.... Plus, NAFTA established dozens of closed-door committees empowered to set new standards outside the domestic regulatory process — which requires openness and public participation. NAFTA's vast rules are enforced by powerful trade tribunals that lack even the most basic due process guarantees and operate entirely outside the US court system.[4]

---

1 Henry Lamb, "NAFTA, CAFTA and the WTO," WorldNetDaily [Internet]; available from http://www.worldnetdaily.com/news/article.asp?ARTICLE_ID=45521; accessed 30 June 2008.

2 Steven Yates, "Scuttling Bad Trade Agreements," NewsWithViews [Internet]; available from http://newswithviews.com/Yates/steven7.htm; accessed 30 June 2008.

3 Ibid.

4 The Ten Year Track Record of the North American Free Trade Agreement: Undermining Sovereignty and Democracy, Public Citizen [Internet]; available from; http://www.citizen.org/documents/NAFTA_10_democracy.pdf; accessed 30 June 2008.

The article describes further encroachments on our national sovereignty as follows:

> ... state and local policies and governments are bound to NAFTA's dictates but subfederal officials have no right to defend their laws from NAFTA attack and had no role in setting NAFTA's terms or agreeing to their imposition — a remarkable attack against the rights and authority of local or state government.[1]

The Public Citizen web site also describes the WTO's "Dispute Settlement System," which makes it very difficult for a nation charged with an infraction to overcome a ruling:

> One of the most dramatic changes made to the global trade system by the Uruguay Round negotiations of the GATT was the establishment of a new freestanding global commerce agency, the WTO, with a powerful, binding dispute resolution system replete with tribunals whose rulings are automatically binding unless there is unanimous consensus by all WTO Members to *reject* the new interpretation. The new WTO enforcement system replaced the consensus-based GATT contract and its dispute resolution system, which was based on diplomatic negotiation and which required consensus of the GATT countries to adopt a ruling by a GATT dispute resolution.[2]

The same web page then describes how extensive the WTO's powers are:

> The combination of the WTO's powerful new enforcement capacities and the Uruguay Round's expansive new rules encroaching into areas traditionally considered the realm of domestic policy effectively shift many decisions regarding public health and safety and environmental and social concerns from democratically-elected domestic bodies to WTO tribunals.[3]

Ron Paul, a Congressman from Texas and one of the few members of Congress who *does* follow the Constitution, tells the following story in his weekly column about a corporate tax bill that was passed by Congress:

> For years, high-tax Europe has objected to how we tax American companies on their overseas earnings. The EU took its dispute to the WTO grievance board, which voted in favor of the Europeans. The WTO ruling was clear: Congress must change American law to comply with European rules. Make no mistake about it: WTO ministers tell Congress to change American laws, and Congress complies. In fact, congressional leaders obediently scrambled to make sure the corporate tax bill passed before a WTO deadline. Thousands and thousands of bills languish in committees, yet a bill ordered by the WTO was pushed to the front of the line.[4]

In the same weekly column, he mentions "a Congressional Research Service" that reported that "as a member of the WTO, the United States does commit to act in accordance with the rules of the multi-lateral body. It is *legally obligated* to insure that national laws do not conflict with WTO rules."[5]

Of course, we cannot forget the Trade Promotion Authority (TPA) or "Fast Track" Authority given to President Bush in the Trade Act of 2002, which was signed into

---

1 Ibid.

2 The WTO and Democracy: Dispute Settlement System, Public Citizen [Internet]: available from http://www.citizen.org/trade/wto/Dispute/; accessed 30 June 2008.

3 Ibid.

4 Ron Paul, "Bowing and Scraping for the WTO," Texas Straight Talk, Representative Ron Paul [Internet]; available from http://www.house.gov/paul/tst/tst2005/tst022805.htm; accessed 30 June 2008.

5 Ibid.

law on August 6.[1] This "Fast Track" authority transfers extraordinary power to the President to negotiate trade agreements with minimal endorsement from Congress. The President was actually given this authority as far back as 1974, but it had expired by 1994. The Global Exchange web site describes it in the following manner:

> Fast Track is an arrangement by which Congress surrenders its constitutional authority to regulate foreign commerce and gives that power to the executive branch. It sets in advance the conditions for congressional consideration of any trade agreements, thereby limiting public participation in the formation of trade policies. Fast Track would allow the Bush Administration not only to negotiate international trade agreements but also to draft all of the implementing legislation required to bring US law into accordance with these agreements. The resulting agreement and implementing legislation would then be presented to Congress as a package deal for a simple yes-or-no vote with limited debate and no amendments allowed. The time allowed for debate is limited to less than 20 hours. [2]

So what have been the social consequences of Congress surrendering its power to regulate foreign trade, including its use of the protective tariff? According to Thom Hartmann, a bestselling author and a radio talk show host, "the result has been an explosion of cheap goods coming into our nation, and the loss of millions of good manufacturing jobs and thousands of manufacturing companies. Entire industry sectors have been wiped out."[3] However, this is not all. He continues to describe the fallout of this foreign trade policy:

> ... Because our so-called "free trade" policies have left us with an over $700 billion annual trade deficit, other countries are sitting on huge piles of the dollars we gave them to buy their stuff (via Wal-Mart and other "low cost" retailers). But we no longer manufacture anything they want to buy with those dollars.

> So instead of buying our manufactured goods, they are doing what we used to do with Third World nations — they are buying us, the USA, chunk by chunk. In particular, they want to buy things in America that will continue to produce profits, and then to take those profits overseas where they're invested to make other nations strong. The "things" they're buying are, by and large, corporations, utilities, and natural resources.[4]

Patrick J. Buchanan, the well-known syndicated columnist and author, states much the same thing regarding the consequences of this flawed foreign trade policy:

> Since 1971, the trade deficits run by the United States add up to $4 trillion.... These dollars, shipped abroad to buy the products of foreign factories, are now being used by foreigners to buy up our stocks, bonds, companies, and real estate. By 2002, foreigners owned US assets equal to 78 percent of our GDP. They owned 13 percent of our equity market, 22 percent of our corporations, 24 percent of our corporate bonds, [and] 48 percent of the US treasury market. Like

1 To extend the Andean Trade Preference Act, to grant additional trade benefits under the Act, and for other purposes, Public Law #107-210, Library of Congress (THOMAS) [Internet]; available form http://thomas.loc.gov/cgi-bin/bdquery/z?d107:HR03009:@@@L&summ2=m&; accessed 30 June 2008.

2 "What is Fast Track?" Global Exchange [Internet]; available from http://www.globalexchange.org/campaigns/ftaa/fasttrack/faq.html; accessed 30 June 2008.

3 Thom Hartmann, "When Americans No Longer Own America," Common Dreams News Center [Internet]; available from http://www.commondreams.org/views06/0227-20.htm; accessed 30 June 2008.

4 Ibid.

Esau, we are selling our birthright. As Lou Dobbs declaims nightly on CNN, we are "exporting America."[1]

CNN anchor Lou Dobbs states that "between the polar extremes of free trade and isolationism are a wide range of policy choices: In the center of the policy spectrum there is balanced trade."[2] He elaborates:

> Staunch protectionists believe we can turn back the clock and use high tariffs to protect every industry in this country. Their absolutism forces most of us to dismiss their concerns and even their valid points. But the absolutists who demand free trade should be dismissed every bit as quickly. It's time for all of us to realize that a purely ideological commitment to free trade is as foolhardy as absolute protectionism.[3]

In his view, "the real alternative to what we continue to permit Washington and Corporate America to call 'free trade' is balanced trade, in which we negotiate trade agreements that are reciprocal in benefit — unlike the World Trade Organization or trade agreements like NAFTA."[4]

In a short article, balanced trade advocate, Jack Davis, describes this policy as follows:

> Balanced trade described in simple terms is, if a country desires to sell products to the United States, they are required to buy an equal dollar amount of products or services from the United States....
>
> To obtain this balance, the United States will charge a balancing tariff (tax) on imported products. The tariff percentage amounts are variable and will be increased in five-percent increments until the trade balance is obtained.
>
> If the United States exports more dollars in trade than it imports from a specific country, the tariff will be reduced until the trade balance is obtained or the tariff is zero.
>
> The ideal Balanced Trade is equal trade with zero tariffs.[5]

An example of implementing balanced trade would be helpful. In 2007, there was a trade deficit with Taiwan of $11,968 million and total imports from that country totaled $38,278 million.[6] In order to obtain balanced trade with Taiwan in 2008,[7] the trade deficit would first be divided by the total imports, which would give 31% (11,968 divided by 38,278). Then, based on this calculation a tariff of 35% (the next 5% step after 30%) would be placed on all Taiwanese imports. This percentage would provide revenue to the US government of $13,397 million ($38,278 million X 35%), which is somewhat more than the trade imbalance. Although 35% may be considered by some to be a high tariff, if the US trade deficit with Taiwan should improve in the future, the tariff would be reduced likewise with the goal being no tariff at all.

---

1 Patrick J. Buchanan, *Where the Right Went Wrong* (New York: St. Martin's Press, 2005), 162-3.

2 Lou Dobbs, *Exporting America* (New York: Warner Books, 2004), 108.

3 Ibid., 77.

4 Ibid., 108-9.

5 Jack Davis, "Balanced Trade — Not Free Trade." This article was originally on the Save American Jobs web site, as of 17 June 2006, but I can no longer find the web site. However, I still have a copy of the article on file.

6 Exhibit 13. Exports, Imports, and Trade Balance by Country and Area: 2007, US Census Bureau [Internet]; available from; http://www.census.gov/foreign-trade/Press-Release/2007pr/final_revisions/exh13tl.pdf; accessed 30 June 2008.

7 To be even more precise, calculations could be made monthly, which would mean that the numbers would come from the previous month.

The United States must exit the WTO, rescind any unconstitutional trade agreements like NAFTA and CAFTA-DR, and end the President's use of "Fast Track" Authority. In addition, the Constitution must again be followed with regard to our trade dealings with foreign countries. Balanced trade should be our approach, but the goal should always be, as Jack Davis states it, "equal trade with zero tariffs."

As was stated above, the Constitution only grants *Congress* the power to "regulate commerce with foreign nations" (Article I, section 8, clause 3). For trade dealings with some countries, regulating trade would be as simple as Congress passing a tariff bill. Before a ship or plane could enter the United States with goods from that country, the tariff would have to be paid. However, a treaty is often required regarding commercial dealings with a foreign country. In this case, the President would have to negotiate the treaty and then obtain the approval of the Senate (Article II, section 2, clause 2), and in the case of a treaty concerning trade, obtain the approval of the House of Representatives as well, before it can become law (Article VI, clause 2).

Congress is also given the power "to regulate Commerce ... among the several States" (Article I, section 8, clause 3). The operative word is "*among* the several states," which can mean a number of things according to Dictionary.com, but never *within* the states. *Between*[1] could be another word that adequately describes what Congress is allowed to regulate within the area of domestic trade, although it is expressly restricted from taxing the exports of any state (Article I, section 9, clause 5). According to Prof. Randy E. Barnett, "Congress has power to specify rules to govern the manner by which people may exchange or trade goods from one state to another, to remove obstructions to domestic trade erected by states...."[2] The states retain the power to regulate commercial activity within their own borders. Unfortunately, the advocates of big government in Congress, assisted by court decisions, have expanded over the years this limited power far beyond its original intent.

One of the most egregious examples of this expansion of power is the Supreme Court case of *Wickard v. Filburn* (1942),[3] which was decided during the New Deal period of President Franklin Delano Roosevelt. Under the authority granted to it by the Agricultural Adjustment Act (1933),[4] the Department of Agriculture set the amount of wheat that Roscoe Filburn, a small Ohio dairy farmer, could grow on his farm at 11.1 acres. Nevertheless, he ended up growing a total of 23 acres, which was in violation of the allowance set by the Department. Filburn's explanation was that the wheat was solely for his own use — to feed his family and his livestock — and he had no intention of taking the grain off his farm and selling it on the open market. So how could it possibly have any effect on interstate commerce? The government's response was to fine him for producing the excess wheat anyway, so Filburn took the

---

1 "The principal purposes to be answered by Union are these — The common defense of the members — the preservation of the public peace as well against internal convulsions as external attacks — the regulation of commerce with other nations *and between the States* — the superintendence of our intercourse, political and commercial, with foreign countries" (italics mine, Alexander Hamilton, *The Federalist Papers* #23).

2 Randy E. Barnett, "The Original Meaning of the Commerce Clause," Randy E. Barnett [Internet]; available from http://www.bu.edu/rbarnett/Original.htm#F215; accessed 30 June 2008.

3 Wickard v. Filburn, 317 US 111 (1942), FindLaw [Internet]; available from http://caselaw.lp.findlaw.com/scripts/getcase.pl?navby=CASE&court=US&vol=317&page=111; accessed 30 June 2008.

4 The constitutionality of this Act in and of itself is more than questionable, but I will not get into this issue here.

case to court. At the lower court level, Filburn won, but the Secretary of Agriculture, Claude R. Wickard, appealed it to the Supreme Court. The high Court's decision was as follows: Although the Court admitted that Filburn's growing of wheat was solely non-commercial activity within the state, if he had *not* grown the excess grain, he would have had to purchase it on the open market. Although the amount was inconsequential in itself, if viewed collectively (i.e., if other farmers did the same), it would have a significant influence on interstate commerce. Thus, under these circumstances Congress could regulate *intrastate* commerce as well. According to Judge Andrew P. Napolitano, "after *Wickard* it is hard to imagine an activity that Congress could not regulate. The Supreme Court essentially repealed the system of enumerated powers on which the system of checks and balances is based."[1]

Admittedly, there is going to be some disagreement regarding the scope of this power to regulate interstate trade. It is essential that we remember the reason why Congress was given this power in the first place. It was to provide a means of prohibiting the states from setting up trade barriers for their own economic benefit, but to the determent of the neighboring states and the nation as a whole. In other words, the United States was to be a free trade zone, in that its internal commerce was to be completely unhampered by any restraints so that it could grow and prosper. Alexander Hamilton explained this idea in *The Federalist Papers* (# 11), as follows:

> An unrestrained intercourse between the States themselves will advance the trade of each by an interchange of their respective productions, not only for the supply of reciprocal wants at home, but for exportation to foreign markets. The veins of commerce in every part will be replenished, and will acquire additional motion and vigor from a free circulation of the commodities of every part. Commercial enterprise will have much greater scope, from the diversity in the productions of different States. When the staple of one fails, from a bad harvest or unproductive crop, it can call to its aid the staple of another.

In addition, it is important to remember that the federal government is one of *limited* powers.

Congress is also given the power "to regulate Commerce with ... the Indian Tribes" (Article I, section 8, clause 3). Apparently, the original idea was that the Indian tribes, of which there were a significant number at the time of the ratification of the Constitution, were to be treated as sovereign nations. Thus, treaties were to be made with them in the same manner as with foreign countries like France and Germany. For several reasons, which we will not go into here, less than a hundred years later this original policy changed to one of trying to assimilate them into our own nation and culture. This new policy came to the fore most notably with the passage of two pieces of legislation — the Indian Appropriation Act of 1871 and the Indian Citizenship Act of 1924. The former made it a policy of the federal government to no longer recognize Indian tribes as sovereign nations, and thus to no longer negotiate treaties with them. From henceforth, Indian policy would be set by federal statute or executive order. However, treaties passed prior to 1871 were still considered valid. The latter made citizens of all Indians born within the United States and gave them voting rights. Thus, two differing policies that were mutually irreconcilable — segregation and assimilation — began operating concurrently with the emphasis on one or the other being determined by the administration then in power.

Currently, there are more than 550 Indian tribes recognized by the federal government and a number of these tribes have their own federal reservations. There are

---

1 Judge Andrew P. Napolitano, *The Constitution in Exile* (Nashville: Nelson Current, 2006), 164.

approximately 300 of the latter in existence with a land area totaling nearly 56 million acres, and although this land is in reality owned by the federal government, the Bureau of Indian Affairs (BIA) administers it for the benefit of the Indian tribes. It is interesting to note that the largest Indian reservation (the Navajo Nation) comprises a huge land area — approximately 17 million acres. The Indian tribes have their own governments, which are recognized legally as follows:

> [They] are not fully sovereign nations: they are quasi-sovereign rather than sovereign, domestic rather than foreign, and dependent rather than independent nations within our nation. Theirs is a very limited sovereignty that exists solely at the complete discretion and pleasure of the United States Congress. Indian tribes are wards of the federal government since the federal government has taken on the responsibility of "protecting" the tribes from the states. This responsibility is often referred to as the federal government's "fiduciary duty" or "trust responsibility" to the tribes. The tribes are said to have certain inherent governmental powers over their internal affairs free from the state interference, but Congress has plenary or complete power to limit tribal sovereignty. [1]

Apparently, this power "to regulate Commerce with ... the Indian Tribes" has been employed very little by Congress, at least in the sense it was intended to be. According to one source, "about the only area where the commerce clause has been used to control commercial activities among the Indians has been in connection with the sale of alcohol to them."[2]

---

1 "Federal Indian Policy and the Oneida Land Claim," Upstate Citizens for Equality [Internet]; available from http://www.upstate-citizens.org/fip.pdf; accessed 30 June 2008.

2 W. Cleon Skousen, 411.

CHAPTER 8: THE WAR POWER

As war cannot lawfully be commenced on the part of the United States, without an act of Congress, such an act is, of course, a formal official notice to all the world, and equivalent to the most solemn declaration.

— James Kent, Commentaries on American Law (1826), 53-67.

The relevant sections of the Constitution that relate to providing for the nation's defense and carrying out war are as follows:

Article I, section 8, lists the powers of Congress:

[Clause 11] To declare War, grant Letters of Marque and Reprisal, and make Rules concerning Captures on Land and Water;

[Clause 12] To raise and support Armies, but no Appropriation of Money to that Use shall be for a longer Term than two Years;

[Clause 13] To provide and maintain a Navy;

[Clause 14] To make rules for the Government and Regulation of the land and naval Forces;

[Clause 15] To provide for calling forth the Militia to execute the Laws of the Union, suppress Insurrections and repel Invasions.

Article I, section 10, lists the prohibitions placed on the states:

[Clause 1] No State shall ... grant Letters of Marque and Reprisal.

[Clause 3] No State shall, without the Consent of Congress ... keep Troops, or Ships of War in time of Peace ... or engage in War, unless actually invaded, or in such imminent Danger as will not admit of delay.

Article II, section 2, lists the powers of the President:

[Clause 1] The President shall be Commander in Chief of the Army and Navy of the United States, and of the Militia of the several States, when called into the actual Service of the United States.

Let us try to summarize the sections of the Constitution quoted above. First, Congress is empowered to "provide and maintain a Navy" (Article I, section 8, clause 13), but can only "raise and support Armies" through appropriations of money for a period of two years at a time (Article I, section 8, clause 12). Closely connected to clauses 12 and 13 is clause 14, which grants Congress the power to "make rules for the Government and Regulation of the land and naval Forces." The idea seems to be that the navy is to be continually sustained, but armies are to be created only when actually needed. What is the reason for this difference between these two military forces? Well, at the time the Constitution was written a well-equipped navy was certainly necessary to guard the coastlines, but what would have been the point of having armies in peacetime? Besides, the delegates at the Federal Convention of 1787 were not comfortable with the idea of keeping permanent armies. James Madison had this to say about the danger of a standing army:

> A standing military force, with an overgrown Executive will not long be safe companions to liberty. The means of defense against foreign danger have been always the instruments of tyranny at home. Among the Romans it was a standing maxim to excite a war, whenever a revolt was apprehended. Throughout all Europe, the armies kept up under the pretext of defending, have enslaved the people.[1]

Today, we apparently need a permanent army, so Article I, section 8, clause 12 should be amended to the following brief statement: *To provide and maintain an Army.* In any case, if necessary Congress could always federalize the state militias, but for only three reasons: "to execute the Laws of the Union, suppress Insurrections and repel Invasions" (Article I, section 8. clause 15). The state militias will be discussed more fully in a later chapter.

Judge Andrew P. Napolitano asks the following interesting questions: "If the Constitution gives the power to create an army and navy, from whence does Congress have the power to create an air force? Is the air force unconstitutional? How about the coast guard?"[2] I would answer that we should indeed amend the Constitution to include the air force and the coast guard. Almost certainly, such an amendment would be approved with little or no opposition. We should not ever be apprehensive about using the Article V amendment process to bring the Constitution up to date or to change something that has *truly* become out-of-date. It is better than using unconstitutional means to accomplish the change. The words of the Constitution should have *precise* meanings. Ambiguity always allows for the illegitimate expansion of government power.

Establishing and administering the land and naval forces and implementing war were understood by the delegates at the Federal Convention to be federal prerogatives and thus the states were prohibited from conferring Letters of Marque and Reprisal, although this was not the case with regard to Congress (Article I, section 8, clause 11 and section 10, clause 1). The states were also prohibited from maintaining troops[3] without the approval of Congress or war ships during peacetime, and they could not carry out war, "unless actually invaded, or in such imminent Danger as will not admit of delay" (Article I, section 10, clause 3). This federal prerogative for carry-

---

1 James Madison, *Notes of Debates in the Federal Convention of 1787*, Introduction by Adrienne Koch, Bicentennial Edition (New York: W. W. Norton & Company, 1987), 214.

2 Judge Andrew P. Napolitano, *The Constitution in Exile* (Nashville: Nelson Current, 2006), 15.

3 The word "troops" here (Article I, section 10, clause 3) refers to standing armies *not* the states militias.

ing out war also explains why Congress was empowered to "make Rules concerning Captures on Land and Water" (Article I, section 8, clause 11).

Finally, Congress is given the power to "declare war" (Article I, section 8, clause 11) and the President is designated the "Commander in Chief of the Army and Navy of the United States, and the Militia of the several States, when called into the actual Service of the United States." (Article II, section 2). How are these two clauses to be correctly understood?

An interesting discussion is recorded in James Madison's notes on the Federal Convention of 1787. I should note first that the original draft of the Constitution gave Congress the power "to *make* war" instead of "to *declare* War" (Article VII, section 1, draft; Article I, section 8, clause 11 original).[1] Let me quote the discussion below:

> Mr. *Pinkney* opposed the vesting this power in the Legislature. Its Proceedings were too slow. It would meet but once a year. The House of Representatives would be too numerous for such deliberations. The Senate would be the best depositary, being more acquainted with foreign affairs, and most capable of proper resolutions. If the States are equally represented in the Senate, so as to give no advantage to the large States, the power will notwithstanding be safe, as the small have their all at stake in such cases as well as the large States. It would be singular for one authority to make war, and another peace.

> Mr. *Butler*. The objections against the Legislature lie in a great degree against the Senate. He was for vesting the power in the President, who will have all the requisite qualities, and will not make war but when the Nation will support it.

> Mr. *Madison* and Mr. *Gerry* moved to insert "*declare*," striking out "*make*" war; leaving to the Executive the power to repel sudden attacks.

> Mr. *Sherman* thought it stood very well. The Executive should be able to repel and not commence war. "Make" is better than "declare" [,] the latter narrowing the power too much.

> Mr. *Gerry* never expected to hear in a republic a motion to empower the Executive alone to declare war.

> Mr. *Elsworth*. [T]here is a material difference between the cases of making *war* and making *peace*. It should be more easy to get out of war, than into it. War also is a simple and overt declaration [, but] Peace [is] attended with intricate & secret negotiations.

> Mr. *Mason* was against giving the power of war to the Executive, because [he was] not safely to be trusted with it; or to the Senate, because [it was] not so constructed as to be entitled to it. He was for clogging rather than facilitating war; but [was] for facilitating peace. He preferred "*declare*" to "*make*."

> On the motion to insert *declare* — in place of *make*, it was agreed to.[2]

Thus, by the end of the discussion the delegates at the Convention came to the understanding that there were to be only two constitutional means of initiating war: 1) Congress can approve a formal declaration of war and 2) The President can mobilize the military to "repel sudden attacks" without a declaration of war. The main rationale behind the second alternative is that it supports the law of self-preservation

---

1 First Draft of the Constitution (August 6), James Madison, *Notes of Debates in the Federal Convention of 1787*, Introduction by Adrienne Koch, Bicentennial Edition (New York: W. W. Norton & Company, 1987), 385-96.

2 James Madison, 475-6.

that was discussed in the first chapter.[1] Since there would be no time to obtain a declaration of war, the President should be able to mobilize forces in order to protect the country. Saving the nation from an enemy attack must take precedence over the written law, which in this case would be obtaining a declaration of war from Congress. On the rare occasion when the President does act unilaterally however, there is no reason for thinking that Congress is released from formally declaring war as soon as it is able to do so, unless the hostilities subside reasonably quickly and a war declaration is then of no use.

Of course, the brief discussion of the war power at the Convention was not intended to provide all the possible situations in which the President would be allowed to mobilize the military forces without a declaration of war. However, what it does do is give us a clear indication of the President's very limited authority, when acting unilaterally. The word change by the delegates of *"make* war" to *"declare* war" with regard to the congressional power created a narrow window for the President to act on the rare occasions, when a *national emergency* requiring *immediate action* existed. On these occasions, either a declaration of war from Congress would not be considered appropriate based on the nature of the action to be undertaken (a rescue mission, for example) or could not be obtained quickly enough to repel a sudden or anticipated attack. The *defensive* nature of such actions, as opposed to their offensive nature, would always be evident. Some situations that would fall within the President's "narrow window" to act unilaterally (there are doubtless others) would be the following:

- A surprise attack on the nation (already mentioned above).
- Intercepting an enemy attack on the nation or on US embassies abroad, that is actually in progress.
- Pre-empting an anticipated enemy attack on the nation or on US embassies abroad, in which the danger in clear and immediate.
- Rescuing American citizens who are in immediate danger because of political events transpiring in a foreign country.
- Protecting American ships from immediate danger on the high seas.
- Protecting American aircraft from immediate danger in international airspace.[2]
- For most situations however, Congress is the body that decides on war by formally declaring war. James Madison expressed this viewpoint very clearly as follows:

> The power to judge of the causes of war, as involved in the power to declare war, is expressly vested, where all other legislative powers are vested, that is, in the congress of the United States. It is consequently determined by the constitution to be a *legislative power* (James Madison, Letters of Helvidius, #2, August 24 — September 14, 1793).

Then, after Congress has done its duty, the President does his by executing the war as the Commander in Chief.

---

1 "A strict observance of the written laws is doubtless *one* of the high duties of a good citizen, but it is not the *highest*. The law of necessity, of self-preservation, of saving our country when in danger, are of higher obligation. To lose our country by a scrupulous adherence to written law, would be to lose the law itself, with life, liberty, property, and all those who are enjoying them with us; thus absurdly sacrificing the end to the means ..." (Thomas Jefferson, Letter to J. B. Colvin, Sept. 20, 1810).

2 Of course, routine military training exercises with no ulterior motive, such as coercing an enemy nation to attack us in order to initiate a conflict, would also fall within the President's constitutional authority as the Commander in Chief.

In a letter to Thomas Jefferson, Madison explained why Congress instead of the President was given the war power:

> The constitution supposes, what the History of all Gov[ernmen]ts demon-strates, that the Ex[...][ecutive] is the branch of power most interested in war, & most prone to it. It has accordingly with studied care, vested the question of war in the Legisl[ature]. But the Doctrines lately advanced strike at the root of all these provisions, and will deposit the peace of the Country in that De-partment which the Constitution distrusts as most ready without cause to re-nounce it (James Madison, Letter to Thomas Jefferson, April 2, 1798).

Abraham Lincoln also offered an explanation:

> The provision of the Constitution giving the war-making power to Congress, was dictated, as I understand it, by the following reasons. Kings had always been involving and impoverishing their people in wars, pretending generally, if not always, that the good of the people was the object. This our Convention un-derstood to be the most oppressive of all Kingly oppressions; and they resolved to so frame the Constitution that *no one man* should hold the power of bringing this oppression upon us (Abraham Lincoln, Letter to William Herndon, Febru-ary 15, 1848).

In another place, Madison explained why the overall powers for carrying out war were intentionally separated between the legislature and the executive:

> The Constitution expressly and exclusively vests in the legislature the power of declaring a state of war ... [,] raising armies ... [, and] creating offices....

> A delegation of such powers [to the executive] would have struck, not only at the fabric of our Constitution, but at the foundation of all well organized and well checked governments.

> The separation of the power of declaring war from that of conducting it is wise-ly contrived to exclude the danger of its being declared for the sake of its being conducted.

> The separation of the power of raising armies from the power of commanding them is intended to prevent the raising of armies for the sake of commanding them.

> The separation of the power of creating offices from that of filling them is an essential guard against the temptation to create offices for the sake of gratifying favorites or multiplying dependents.

> Where would be the difference between the blending off these incompatible powers, by surrendering the legislative part of them into the hands of the ex-ecutive, and by assuming the executive part of them into the hands of the leg-islature? In either case the principle would be equally destroyed, and the con-sequences equally dangerous (James Madison, "Political Observations," April 20, 1795).

It is also worth mentioning how the delegates at the Convention differentiated between initiating war and peace. They wanted to make it difficult to get into a war, so they reasoned that giving the war power to Congress, which was made up of a large number of persons who would naturally act more deliberately, would tend to guard against the making of a rash decision. On the other hand, they wanted to make it easier to make peace, so they gave this power to the President through his treaty making power, which, after being negotiated with a former enemy, had to be ap-proved by the Senate (Article II, section 2, clause 2).

Can treaties that supposedly obligate the United States to enter a war without a formal declaration by Congress be constitutional? The Korean War (1950-53) is an example of this type of undeclared war. After North Korea's invasion of South Korea on June 25, 1950, the United Nations Security Council passed a resolution condemning the action. As a result, sixteen member nations of the UN, including the United States, joined forces to deal with North Korea's aggressive act. The US Congress never declared war, but President Truman cited the United Nations' resolution as being his authority for entering the war. In a press conference on June 29, 1950, the President replied to some questions regarding North Korea's invasion as follows:

> Q. Mr. President, could you elaborate on this statement that—I believe the direct quote was, "We are not at war." And could we use that quote in quotes?
>
> THE PRESIDENT. Yes, I will allow you to use that. We are not at war.
>
> Q. Could you elaborate sir, a little more on the reason for this move, and the peace angle on it?
>
> THE PRESIDENT. The Republic of Korea was set up with the United Nations help. It is a recognized government by the members of the United Nations. It was unlawfully attacked by a bunch of bandits which are neighbors of North Korea. The United Nations Security Council held a meeting and passed on the situation and asked the members to go to the relief of the Korean Republic.
>
> And the members of the United Nations are going to the relief of the Korean Republic to suppress a bandit raid on the Republic of Korea.
>
> Q. Mr. President, would it be correct, against your explanation, to call this a police action under the United Nations?
>
> THE PRESIDENT. Yes. That is exactly what it amounts to.[1]

Some individuals have argued that treaties do indeed take precedence over the Constitution. In 1952, John Foster Dulles, who was to be the Secretary of State under President Eisenhower, gave a speech before the American Bar Association in Louisville, Kentucky. He argued that, based on the supremacy clause, treaties supersede the Constitution. Below is a portion of John foster Dulles' speech:

> Treaties make international law and they also make domestic law. Under our Constitution, treaties become the Supreme Law of the Land. They are indeed more supreme than ordinary laws, for Congressional laws are invalid if they do not conform to the Constitution, whereas treaty laws can override the Constitution.[2]

Since he based his argument on the supremacy clause of the Constitution (Article VI, clause 2), let me quote it below:

> This Constitution, and the Laws of the United States which shall be made in Pursuance thereof; and all Treaties made, or which shall be made, under the Authority of the United States, shall be the supreme Law of the Land;[3] and the

---

1 Harry S. Truman, The President's News Conference of June 29, 1950, The American Presidency Project, [Internet]; available from http://www.presidency.ucsb.edu/ws/index.php?pid=13544&st=&st1; accessed 30 June 2008. It is worth noting that although a ceasefire was signed between North and South Korea on July 27, 1953, a peace treaty has never been signed.

2 Nathan Tabor, "Bring Back Bricker," The American Conservative Union Foundation [Internet]; available from http://acuf.org/issues/issue37/050601gov.asp; accessed 30 June 2008.

3 The supremacy clause mirrors very closely the passage in the Constitution that defines the scope of judicial authority (Article III, section 2, clause 1): "The judicial Power shall extend to all Cases, in Law and Equity, arising under this Constitution, the Laws of the United States, and Treaties made, or which shall be made, under their [i.e., the United States'] Authority."

Judges in every State shall be bound thereby, any Thing in the Constitution or Laws of any State to the Contrary notwithstanding.

As you can see, the "supreme Law of the Land" consists of the Constitution *first*, then the "Laws of the United States which shall be made in Pursuance thereof," *followed by* "all Treaties made, or which shall be made, under the Authority of the United States." If we go solely by the word order in the clause, laws passed by Congress would actually take precedence over treaties. Nevertheless, the generally accepted understanding is that "treaties are on a par with federal statutes. They supersede prior statutes and may, in turn, be superseded by later ones."[1] This means, "Congress has the power to change or abolish any treaty by enacting legislation superseding it."[2] In any case, what is certain is that *a treaty cannot take precedence over the Constitution.*

Thus, treaties that supposedly obligate the United States to enter a war without a formal declaration by Congress are unconstitutional. If this were not so, the power of the President to make treaties with the approval of the Senate (Article II, section 2, clause 2) would make null and void the power of Congress to declare war (Article I, section 8, clause 11). If such an all-encompassing view of the treaty power were indeed correct, our limited government of checks and balances would most surely be in jeopardy. What constitutional power could not then be made invalid by using the treaty power to supersede it? According to one authority, "... it is the purest absurdity to believe that statesmen who had just wrested our nation's independence from a globe-spanning empire would create a treaty-making provision through which our independence could be signed away."[3]

What is the meaning of the phrase "under the Authority of the United States" that is connected with treaties in the supremacy clause (Article VI, clause 2)? When the Constitution was being ratified, certain treaties were already in existence and still in effect from the period of the Articles of Confederation, most notably the Treaty of Paris in 1783 that ended the Revolutionary War. Some have argued that the phrase "under the Authority of the United States" merely included these treaties within the category of valid treaties that would be enforced under the new government of the Constitution. Unfortunately, I do not believe this argument has much merit. If this had been the true intention, the clause could have been written more to the point as follows (note the changes in italics): "This Constitution, and the Laws of the United States which shall be made in Pursuance thereof; and all Treaties made *under the Articles of Confederation*, or which shall be made *under this Constitution*, shall be the supreme Law of the Land."

I think it more likely that the meaning, as well as the distinct placement of the phrase "under the Authority of the United States,"[4] permitted the President and the Senate to have access to broader powers in negotiating treaties than those specifically enumerated in the Constitution. Flexibility was often required in the negotiations with foreign nations. The phrase "under the Authority of the United States" allowed for this flexibility. However, even if broader powers may be claimed in a particular

---

1 George C. Detweiler, "Treaties and the Constitution," The New American [Internet]; available from http://www.thenewamerican.com/node/1535; accessed 20 July 2008.

2 Ibid.

3 Ibid.

4 The phrase "under the Authority of the United States" in Article VI, clause 2 actually relates to both the verbs "made" *and* "shall be made," not just "made." Note further that the passage in the Constitution that defines the scope of judicial authority (Article III, section 2, clause 1) uses a nearly similar phrase with the same distinct placement: "... and Treaties made, or which shall be made, under their [i.e., the United States'] Authority."

situation, it is certain that a proposed treaty can never be in *conflict* with the Constitution. If this were so, the treaty would then take precedence over the Constitution, which simply does not support the facts.

The "Judges in every State" are subordinated to the "supreme Law of the Land" and the statement "any Thing in the Constitution or Laws of any State to the Contrary notwithstanding" means that the state constitutions and laws cannot override this supreme law. The next clause of Article VI (clause 3) states that all officials of the federal and state governments must swear adherence to the Constitution, but "no religious Test" can be ordered for federal government officials:

> The Senators and Representatives before mentioned, and the Members of the several State Legislatures, and all executive and judicial Officers, both of the United States and of the several States, shall be bound by Oath or Affirmation, to support this Constitution; but no religious Test shall ever be required as a Qualification to any Office or public Trust under the United States.

The War Powers Resolution that was passed by Congress in 1973 is unconstitutional, because it allows the President unilaterally to introduce armed forces into situations where Congress has not yet declared war or even where no *national emergency* requiring *immediate action* exists, which would allow the President to act on his own without a war declaration. Section 4(a) of the Resolution describes the circumstances in which the President can send in military forces "in the absence of a declaration of war." I quote the section below:

> *SEC. 4.* (a) In the absence of a declaration of war, in any case in which United States Armed Forces are introduced—
>
> (1) into hostilities or into situations where imminent involvement in hostilities is clearly indicated by the circumstances;
>
> (2) into the territory, airspace or waters of a foreign nation, while equipped for combat, except for deployments which relate solely to supply, replacement, repair, or training of such forces; or
>
> (3) in numbers which substantially enlarge United States Armed Forces equipped for combat already located in a foreign nation.[1]

The President is required to submit a written report to Congress within forty-eight hours of his sending armed forces into any "hostilities" or "situations" described above [Sec. 4(3)(a)].[2] In this report, he is to give the "circumstances necessitating the introduction of United States Armed Forces," the "constitutional and legislative authority under which such introduction took place," and the "estimated scope and duration of the hostilities or involvement."[3] Furthermore, the President is to "provide such other information as the Congress may request" [Sec. 4(3)(b)][4] and "so long as such armed forces continue to be engaged in such hostilities or situation, report to the Congress periodically on the status of such hostilities or situation as well as on the scope and duration of such hostilities or situation, but in no event shall he report to the Congress less often than once every six months" [Sec. 4(3)(c)].[5]

---

1 War Powers Resolution, Public Law 93–148, 93rd Congress, H.J. Res. 542, November 7, 1973, The Avalon Project at Yale Law School [Internet]; available from http://www.yale.edu/law-web/avalon/warpower.htm; accessed 30 June 2008.

2 Ibid.

3 Ibid.

4 Ibid.

5 Ibid.

Congress is then required to take the following action, as is recorded in Section 5 of the Resolution:

> *SEC. 5.* (b) Within sixty calendar days after a report is submitted or is required to be submitted pursuant to section 4(a)(1), whichever is earlier, the President shall terminate any use of United States Armed Forces with respect to which such report was submitted (or required to be submitted), unless the Congress (1) has declared war or has enacted a specific authorization for such use of United States Armed Forces, (2) has extended by law such sixty-day period, or (3) is physically unable to meet as a result of an armed attack upon the United States. Such sixty-day period shall be extended for not more than an additional thirty days if the President determines and certifies to the Congress in writing that unavoidable military necessity respecting the safety of United States Armed Forces requires the continued use of such armed forces in the course of bringing about a prompt removal of such forces.
>
> (c) Notwithstanding subsection (b), at any time that United States Armed Forces are engaged in hostilities outside the territory of the United States, its possessions and territories without a declaration of war or specific statutory authorization, such forces shall be removed by the President if the Congress so directs by concurrent resolution.[1]

The War Powers Resolution is nothing more than a political tactic of Congress to surrender its legitimate power to the President. As a result, Congress escapes, at least at the beginning of the deployment or hostilities, its own constitutional responsibility and avoids the political consequences that would normally follow from its decisions. If losses turn out to be higher than expected, the blame can always be placed on the President not Congress. The latter can merely say that it adhered to the requirements of the War Powers Resolution by passing the appropriate legislation [i.e., a concurrent resolution per Sec. 5(c)] to take us out of the conflict and save the nation from disaster.

However, why does the President willingly accept this transfer of power with its accompanying responsibilities? The answer is it allows him to use the armed forces without a war declaration from Congress at least at the start of the military actions. In so doing, so-called "police actions" or other undeclared military adventures that have no connection with our own *national* security are no longer difficult for him to undertake. As a result, he has more overall control over his foreign policy initiatives. Having said this, the human desire for power cannot be overlooked either.

A proper declaration of war should at least consist of the following items:

1. The reason(s) for declaring war.
2. A formal declaration of war statement resembling this one: Be it resolved by the Senate and House of Representatives of the United States of America in Congress assembled, that a state of war between the United States and [...] is hereby formally declared.
3. An unambiguous reference to the specific nation(s), organization(s) or even person(s) we are going to war with.
4. A formal authorization giving the President the power to use the military forces and other required resources of the government to conduct the war as the commander-in-chief. This authorization would resemble this one: *The President of the United States is hereby authorized and directed to utilize the military forces of the United States and other resources of the government to conduct*

---

1 Ibid.

war against [...].

5. A clear statement of the commitment of the nation to win the war. This statement would resemble to this one: To attain complete victory in this conflict that has been thrust upon us, all available resources of the country, both tangible and intangible, are hereby pledged by the Congress of the United States.

After the attack on September 11, 2001, Congress passed a joint resolution on September 18, 2001, to "authorize the use of United States Armed Forces against those responsible for the recent attacks launched against the United States." With Osama bin Laden and Al Qaeda alleged to be "those responsible," President Bush authorized the invasion of Afghanistan, which began on October 7, 2001. Catching Osama bin Laden, defeating Al Qaeda, and toppling the Taliban government, since they had given safe haven to bin Laden, were the main reasons asserted for the invasion. The Taliban was essentially ousted by the end of the major military operations, but bin Laden escaped to the mountainous, difficult-to-reach area of northwest Pakistan.

The "authorization of force" resolution passed on September 18, 2001, was not an actual declaration of war but is what the War Powers Resolution terms "specific authorization for such use of United States Armed Forces" [Sec. 5(b)(1)] or "specific statutory authorization" [Sec. 5(c)]. Let us compare an actual declaration of war to this "authorization of force" resolution. First, let me transcribe the declaration of war with Japan, dated December 8, 1941:

> *Joint Resolution* Declaring that a state of war exists between the Imperial Government of Japan and the Government and the people of the United States and making provisions to prosecute the same.
>
> Whereas the Imperial Government of Japan has committed unprovoked acts of war against the Government and the people of the United States of America:
>
> Therefore be it Resolved by the Senate and House of Representatives of the United States of America in Congress assembled,
>
> That the state of war between the United States and the Imperial Government of Japan which has thus been thrust upon the United States is hereby formally declared;
>
> and the President is hereby authorized and directed to employ the entire naval and military forces of the United States and the resources of the Government to carry on war against the Imperial Government of Japan;
>
> and, to bring the conflict to a successful termination, all of the resources of the country are hereby pledged by the Congress of the United States.[1]

Now let me transcribe the joint resolution authorizing the use of military force, dated September 18, 2001:

> Joint Resolution
>
> To authorize the use of United States Armed Forces against those responsible for the recent attacks launched against the United States.
>
> Whereas, on September 11, 2001, acts of treacherous violence were committed against the United States and its citizens; and

---

1 US Historical Documents, Congressional Declaration of War on Japan, December 8, 1941, The University of Oklahoma, College of Law [Internet]; available from http://www.law.ou.edu/ushistory/japwar.shtml; accessed 30 June 2008.

Whereas, such acts render it both necessary and appropriate that the United States exercise its rights to self-defense and to protect United States citizens both at home and abroad; and

Whereas, in light of the threat to the national security and foreign policy of the United States posed by these grave acts of violence; and

Whereas, such acts continue to pose an unusual and extraordinary threat to the national security and foreign policy of the United States; and

Whereas, the President has authority under the Constitution to take action to deter and prevent acts of international terrorism against the United States: Now, therefore, be it

Resolved by the Senate and House of Representatives of the United States of America in Congress assembled,

Section 1. Short Title.

This joint resolution may be cited as the 'Authorization for Use of Military Force'.

Sec. 2. Authorization For Use Of United States Armed Forces.

(a) *In General-* That the President is authorized to use all necessary and appropriate force against those nations, organizations, or persons he determines planned, authorized, committed, or aided the terrorist attacks that occurred on September 11, 2001, or harbored such organizations or persons, in order to prevent any future acts of international terrorism against the United States by such nations, organizations or persons.

(b) War Powers Resolution Requirements-

(1) *Specific Statutory Authorization-* Consistent with section 8(a)(1) of the War Powers Resolution, the Congress declares that this section is intended to constitute specific statutory authorization within the meaning of section 5(b) of the War Powers Resolution.

(2) *Applicability Of Other Requirements-* Nothing in this resolution supercedes any requirement of the War Powers Resolution.[1]

Besides missing a formal declaration of war statement, the next defect that can be noticed in the "authorization of force" resolution is that no specific "nations, organizations or persons" are mentioned as being responsible for the attack on 9/11. The President is just given the blanket authorization "to use all necessary and appropriate force against those" that "he determines planned, authorized, committed, or aided the terrorist attacks ... or harbored such organizations or persons, in order to prevent any future acts of international terrorism against the United States by such nations, organizations or persons" (italics mine). On the other hand, the declaration of war is specific: "The Imperial Government of Japan has committed unprovoked acts of war against the Government and the people of the United States of America."

It is obvious that Congress did not do its homework, but left it to the executive branch to identify the culprits who attacked us on 9/11. When Congress makes the decision to go to war, it must have a clear understanding why we are going, who we are fighting, and what we are trying to achieve, which can be nothing less than com-

---

1 A joint resolution to authorize the use of United States Armed Forces against those responsible for the recent attacks launched against the United States, Public Law # 107-40, Library of Congress (Thomas) [Internet]; available from http://thomas.loc.gov/cgi-bin/bdquery/z?d107:SJ00023:TOM:/d107query.html; accessed 30 June 2008.

plete victory. Precisely how and when the war is to be executed is the responsibility of the President, as the Commander in Chief.

Another serious defect in the "authorization of force" resolution is its sheer lack of any real commitment to defeat the enemy. It only states that the President is "authorized to use all necessary and appropriate force" and to do so "in order to prevent any future acts of international terrorism against the United States." On the hand, the declaration of war states plainly that the "President is hereby authorized and directed to employ the entire naval and military forces of the United States and the resources of the Government to carry on war" and even "all of the resources of the country are hereby pledged by the Congress of the United States." There is no doubt about it. The United States is planning for victory against Japan and defeat is not an option. The declaration even goes further and states that the war is to be brought to a "*successful* termination" (italics mine). Nothing even close to this statement is found in the "authorization of force" resolution.

If Congress had done its constitutional duty, it would have passed a declaration of war with the terrorist organization, Al Qaeda, similar to the declaration of war with Japan quoted above. Simply replacing the name "Imperial Government of Japan" with the "terrorist organization known as Al Qaeda" in the appropriate places of the declaration can provide an excellent example here. The result would look like this (the changes are in italicized letters):

> *Joint Resolution* Declaring that a state of war exists between the *terrorist organization known as Al Qaeda* and the Government and the people of the United States and making provisions to prosecute the same.
>
> Whereas the *terrorist organization known as Al Qaeda* has committed unprovoked acts of war against the Government and the people of the United States of America:
>
> Therefore be it Resolved by the Senate and House of Representatives of the United States of America in Congress assembled,
>
> That the state of war between the United States and the *terrorist organization known as Al Qaeda* which has thus been thrust upon the United States is hereby formally declared;
>
> and the President is hereby authorized and directed to employ the entire naval and military forces of the United States and the resources of the Government to carry on war against the *terrorist organization known as Al Qaeda*;
>
> and, to bring the conflict to a successful termination, all of the resources of the country are hereby pledged by the Congress of the United States.

The resolution to use military force against Iraq, which was passed on October 16, 2002, was *not* a proper declaration of war either. The principal part of the resolution reads:

> Sec. 3. Authorization For Use Of United States Armed Forces.
>
> (a) *Authorization.* The President is authorized to use the Armed Forces of the United States as he determines to be necessary and appropriate in order to
>
> (1) defend the national security of the United States against the continuing threat posed by Iraq; and
>
> (2) enforce all relevant United Nations Security Council Resolutions regarding Iraq.
>
> (b) Presidential Determination.

In connection with the exercise of the authority granted in subsection (a) to use force the President shall, prior to such exercise or as soon there after as may be feasible, but no later than 48 hours after exercising such authority, make available to the Speaker of the House of Representatives and the President pro tempore of the Senate his determination that

(1) reliance by the United States on further diplomatic or other peaceful means alone either (A) will not adequately protect the national security of the United States against the continuing threat posed by Iraq or (B) is not likely to lead to enforcement of all relevant United Nations Security Council resolutions regarding Iraq, and

(2) acting pursuant to this resolution is consistent with the United States and other countries continuing to take the necessary actions against international terrorists and terrorist organizations, including those nations, organizations or persons who planned, authorized, committed or aided the terrorists attacks that occurred on September 11, 2001.[1]

Sec. 3 (a) states, "the President is authorized to use the Armed Forces of the United States *as he determines to be necessary and appropriate...*" (italics mine), which can only mean that the President was given the power to decide whether to attack Iraq or not. This fact is made even more clear by Sec. 3 (b), which states that "in connection with the exercise of the authority granted in subsection (a) to use force the President shall ... make available ... *his determination* that (1) reliance ... on further diplomatic or other peaceful means alone [will not be ineffective] ... and [that] (2) acting pursuant to this resolution is consistent with ... continuing to take the necessary actions against ... terrorists..." (italics mine). Since the President was given authority to determine war or peace at his discretion, it must follow that *the legitimate power of Congress to declare war was unconstitutionally transferred to the President.* Thus, the Iraq War resolution can only be declared unconstitutional.

Furthermore, there is no basis in the argument that the president was empowered to act unilaterally against Iraq, since no *national emergency* requiring *immediate action* existed at the time. The very fact that no military action was undertaken for about six months, from September 12, 2002 when President George Bush gave his speech before the General Assembly of the United Nations until March 20, 2003 when the Iraq War actually began, implies that there was no *immediate* danger, much less any *national* danger, which would have required the President to act without a declaration of war.

No doubt, many members of Congress view a declaration of war as being obsolete or else they would use it. A glaring example of this viewpoint can be seen at the hearings regarding the Authorization to use military force against Iraq (H. J. Resolution 114). On October 3, 2002, Congressman Henry Hyde from Illinois uttered the following shocking statement:

---

1 To authorize the use of United States Armed Forces against Iraq, Public Law # 107-243, Library of Congress (Thomas) [Internet]; available from http://thomas.loc.gov/cgi-bin/bdquery/z?d107:HJ00114:|TOM:/bss/d107query.html|; accessed 30 June 2008. Actually, as far back as October 31, 1998 Congress passed the "Iraq Liberation Act of 1998," which stated among other things "it should be the policy of the United States to seek to remove the regime headed by Saddam Hussein from power in Iraq and to promote the emergence of a democratic government to replace that regime." To establish a program to support a transition to democracy in Iraq, Public Law # 105-338, Library of Congress (Thomas) [Internet]; available from http://thomas.loc.gov/cgi-bin/bdquery/z?d105:HR04655:|TOM:/bss/d105query.html|; accessed 30 June 2008.

There are things in the Constitution that have been overtaken by events, by time. Declaration of war is one of them...There are things no longer relevant to a modern society...Why declare war if you don't have to...We are saying to the President, use your judgment...So, to demand that we declare war is to strengthen something to death. You have got a hammerlock on this situation, and it is not called for. Inappropriate, anachronistic, it isn't done anymore....[1]

The Administration apparently holds to the same viewpoint. In an interview with the press on Air Force Two while headed for Muscat, Oman, Vice President Dick Cheney stated, "yes, I do have the view that over the years there had been an erosion of presidential power and authority, that it's reflected in a number of developments — the War Powers Act, which many people believe is unconstitutional. It's never really been tested.... It will be tested at some point. I am one of those who believe that [it] was an infringement upon the authority of the President."[2] The War Powers Resolution is not unconstitutional because it *takes away* legitimate power from the President, as the Vice-President seems to believe, but, as I have tried to show above, it is unconstitutional because it gives *too much* power to the President in the first place.

---

1 "It Is Now Out In The Open In Congress: Constitution is 'Inappropriate and Anachronistic,'" We The People [Internet]; available from http://www.givemeliberty.org/NoRedress/Update12-31-02.htm; accessed 30 June 2008.
2 Vice President's Remarks to the Traveling Press, December 20, 2005, News & Policies, The White House [Internet]; available from http://www.whitehouse.gov/news/releases/2005/12/20051220-9.html; accessed 30 June 2008.

CHAPTER 9: FOREIGN POLICY

Wherever the standard of freedom and independence has been or shall be unfurled, there will be America's heart, her benedictions and her prayers. But she does not go abroad in search of monsters to destroy. She is the champion and vindicator only of her own.
— *John Quincy Adams, Address, July 4, 1821.*

A noninterventionist foreign policy was advocated by the Founders and it is the one most compatible with the Constitution. Such a foreign policy conforms to the idea that it is in our best interest not to get involved in the affairs of other nations. We should cultivate friendship and trade with all countries that wish to do so, but we should never get involved with them politically. A noninterventionist foreign policy is *not* isolationist, because we would not be cutting ourselves off from the rest of the world. We would just stay clear of negotiating treaties or forming alliances that would obligate us to get involved in the disputes of other nations.

In his Farewell Address (1796), George Washington, the first US President under the Constitution, offered the following guidelines in dealings with foreign nations:

> Observe good faith and justice towards all nations; cultivate peace and harmony with all....

> In the execution of such a plan, nothing is more essential than that permanent, inveterate antipathies against particular nations, and passionate attachments for others, should be excluded; and that, in place of them, just and amicable feelings towards all should be cultivated. The nation which indulges towards another a habitual hatred or a habitual fondness is in some degree a slave. It is a slave to its animosity or to its affection, either of which is sufficient to lead it astray from its duty and its interest. Antipathy in one nation against another disposes each more readily to offer insult and injury, to lay hold of slight causes of umbrage, and to be haughty and intractable, when accidental or trifling occasions of dispute occur.

> Hence, frequent collisions, obstinate, envenomed, and bloody contests. The nation, prompted by ill-will and resentment, sometimes impels to war the govern-

ment, contrary to the best calculations of policy. The government sometimes participates in the national propensity, and adopts through passion what reason would reject; at other times it makes the animosity of the nation subservient to projects of hostility instigated by pride, ambition, and other sinister and pernicious motives. The peace often, sometimes perhaps the liberty, of nations, has been the victim.

So likewise, a passionate attachment of one nation for another produces a variety of evils. Sympathy for the favorite nation, facilitating the illusion of an imaginary common interest in cases where no real common interest exists, and infusing into one the enmities of the other, betrays the former into a participation in the quarrels and wars of the latter without adequate inducement or justification. It leads also to concessions to the favorite nation of privileges denied to others which is apt doubly to injure the nation making the concessions; by unnecessarily parting with what ought to have been retained, and by exciting jealousy, ill-will, and a disposition to retaliate, in the parties from whom equal privileges are withheld. And it gives to ambitious, corrupted, or deluded citizens (who devote themselves to the favorite nation), facility to betray or sacrifice the interests of their own country, without odium, sometimes even with popularity; gilding, with the appearances of a virtuous sense of obligation, a commendable deference for public opinion, or a laudable zeal for public good, the base or foolish compliances of ambition, corruption, or infatuation.

... Against the insidious wiles of foreign influence (I conjure you to believe me, fellow-citizens) the jealousy of a free people ought to be constantly awake, since history and experience prove that foreign influence is one of the most baneful foes of republican government. But that jealousy to be useful must be impartial; else it becomes the instrument of the very influence to be avoided, instead of a defense against it. Excessive partiality for one foreign nation and excessive dislike of another cause those whom they actuate to see danger only on one side, and serve to veil and even second the arts of influence on the other. Real patriots who may resist the intrigues of the favorite are liable to become suspected and odious, while its tools and dupes usurp the applause and confidence of the people, to surrender their interests.

The great rule of conduct for us in regard to foreign nations is in extending our commercial relations, to have with them as little political connection as possible. So far as we have already formed engagements, let them be fulfilled with perfect good faith. Here let us stop.

Europe has a set of primary interests which to us have none; or a very remote relation. Hence she must be engaged in frequent controversies, the causes of which are essentially foreign to our concerns. Hence, therefore, it must be unwise in us to implicate ourselves by artificial ties in the ordinary vicissitudes of her politics, or the ordinary combinations and collisions of her friendships or enmities.

Our detached and distant situation invites and enables us to pursue a different course. If we remain one people under an efficient government, the period is not far off, when we may defy material injury from external annoyance; when we may take such an attitude as will cause the neutrality we may at any time resolve upon to be scrupulously respected; when belligerent nations, under the impossibility of making acquisitions upon us, will not lightly hazard the giving us provocation; when we may choose peace or war, as our interest, guided by justice, shall counsel.

Why forego the advantages of so peculiar a situation? Why quit our own to stand upon foreign ground? Why, by interweaving our destiny with that of any part of Europe, entangle our peace and prosperity in the toils of European ambition, rivalship, interest, humor or caprice?

It is our true policy to steer clear of permanent alliances with any portion of the foreign world....

. . .

Harmony, liberal intercourse with all nations, are recommended by policy, humanity, and interest. But even our commercial policy should hold an equal and impartial hand; neither seeking nor granting exclusive favors or preferences; consulting the natural course of things; diffusing and diversifying by gentle means the streams of commerce, but forcing nothing; establishing (with powers so disposed, in order to give trade a stable course, to define the rights of our merchants, and to enable the government to support them) conventional rules of intercourse, the best that present circumstances and mutual opinion will permit, but temporary, and liable to be from time to time abandoned or varied, as experience and circumstances shall dictate; constantly keeping in view that it is folly in one nation to look for disinterested favors from another; that it must pay with a portion of its independence for whatever it may accept under that character; that, by such acceptance, it may place itself in the condition of having given equivalents for nominal favors, and yet of being reproached with ingratitude for not giving more. There can be no greater error than to expect or calculate upon real favors from nation to nation. It is an illusion, which experience must cure, which a just pride ought to discard.[1]

In his First Inaugural Address on March 1, 1801, President Thomas Jefferson stated the same policy very succinctly in this way: "peace, commerce, and honest friendship with all nations, entangling alliances with none."[2]

President James Monroe advocated the same basic foreign policy, although he did augment it with what became popularly known as the Monroe Doctrine. This new addition to the original policy advised the European powers to desist from subjugating or inhabiting any lands in the Western Hemisphere and to deem any such actions as a threat to the security of the United States. In his seventh Annual Message to Congress on December 2, 1823, President Monroe made the following statement:

> The citizens of the United States cherish sentiments the most friendly in favor of the liberty and happiness of their fellow men on that side of the Atlantic. In the wars of the European powers in matters relating to themselves we have never taken any part, nor does it comport with our policy so to do.
>
> It is only when our rights are invaded or seriously menaced that we resent injuries or make preparation for our defense. With the movements in this hemisphere we are of necessity more immediately connected, and by causes which must be obvious to all enlightened and impartial observers.
>
> . . .
>
> We owe it, therefore, to candor and to the amicable relations existing between the United States and those powers to declare that we should consider any at-

---

1 Washington's Farewell Address, September 19, 1796, The American Presidency Project [Internet]; available from http://www.presidency.ucsb.edu/ws/index.php?pid=65539&st=&st1=; accessed 23 July 2008.

2 Thomas Jefferson First Inaugural Address, March 4, 1801, The American Presidency Project [Internet]; available from http://www.presidency.ucsb.edu/ws/index. php?pid=25803&st=&st1=; accessed 22 July 2008.

tempt on their part to extend their system to any portion of this hemisphere as dangerous to our peace and safety. With the existing colonies or dependencies of any European power we have not interfered and shall not interfere, but with the Governments who have declared their independence and maintained it, and whose independence we have, on great consideration and on just principles, acknowledged, we could not view any interposition for the purpose of oppressing them, or controlling in any other manner their destiny, by any European power in any other light than as the manifestation of an unfriendly disposition toward the United States.

. . .

Our policy in regard to Europe, which was adopted at an early stage of the wars which have so long agitated that quarter of the globe, nevertheless remains the same, which is, not to interfere in the internal concerns of any of its powers; to consider the government de facto as the legitimate government for us; to cultivate friendly relations with it, and to preserve those relations by a frank, firm, and manly policy, meeting in all instances the just claims of every power, submitting to injuries from none.

But in regard to those continents circumstances are eminently and conspicuously different. It is impossible that the allied powers should extend their political system to any portion of either continent without endangering our peace and happiness; nor can anyone believe that our southern brethren, if left to themselves, would adopt it of their own accord. It is equally impossible, therefore, that we should behold such interposition in any form with indifference.[1]

Even by the latter half of the nineteenth century, the government was still advocating a noninterventionist foreign policy. On March 4, 1885, President Grover Cleveland uttered these words in his first inaugural address:

The genius of our institutions, the needs of our people in their home life, and the attention which is demanded for the settlement and development of the resources of our vast territory dictate the scrupulous avoidance of any departure from that foreign policy commended by the history, the traditions, and the prosperity of our Republic. It is the policy of independence, favored by our position and defended by our known love of justice and by our power. It is the policy of peace suitable to our interests. It is the policy of neutrality, rejecting any share in foreign broils and ambitions upon other continents and repelling their intrusion here. It is the policy of Monroe and of Washington and Jefferson — "Peace, commerce, and honest friendship with all nations; entangling alliance with none."[2]

President William McKinley initiated the dangerous drift from a noninterventionist foreign policy to an interventionist one by entering into the Spanish–American War. On February 15, 1898, an explosion in Havana Harbor, Cuba, which killed 266 men, sank the USS Maine. Cuba was then a possession of Spain. The cause of the explosion is still debated; possibilities include an unfortunate accident or a terrorist act that was accomplished by the planting of a mine. Whatever was the cause, the result was that the US Congress declared war on April 25, 1898. When the Treaty of Paris was finally signed on December 10 and approved by the Senate on February 2,

---

1 James Monroe, Seventh Annual Message, December 2, 1823, The American Presidency Project [Internet]; available from http://www.presidency.ucsb.edu/ws/index. php?pid=29465&st=&st1=; accessed 20 July 2008.

2 Grover Cleveland, First Inaugural Address, Wednesday, March 4, 1885, The American Presidency Project [Internet]; available from http://www.presidency.ucsb.edu/ws/index. php?pid=25824&st=&st1=; accessed 22 July 2008.

---

the United States had lost 379 troops in combat and more than 5,000 from disease, but had gained the Spanish possessions of the Philippines, Guam, and Puerto Rico. Cuba was declared independent but with certain restrictions on its status (and a permanent US naval base at Guantanamo).

President McKinley had unlocked the door to interventionism, and President Woodrow Wilson flung the door wide open. In his address before Congress on April 2, 1917, President Wilson advocated the policy that the "world must be made safe for democracy" and asked Congress to declare war on Germany, as a consequence of various provocations. Congress acted quickly on the President's request and declared war on April 6, 1917, officially bringing the United States into World War I.

President Wilson's address before Congress includes an excellent example of an interventionist foreign policy:

> We are accepting this challenge of hostile purpose because we know that in such a Government, following such methods, we can never have a friend; and that in the presence of its organized power, always lying in wait to accomplish we know not what purpose, there can be no assured security for the democratic Governments of the world. We are now about to accept gauge of battle with this natural foe to liberty and shall, if necessary, spend the whole force of the nation to check and nullify its pretensions and its power. We are glad, now that we see the facts with no veil of false pretense about them to fight thus for the ultimate peace of the world and for the liberation of its peoples, the German peoples included: for the rights of nations great and small and the privilege of men everywhere to choose their way of life and of obedience. The world must be made safe for democracy. Its peace must be planted upon the tested founda-tions of political liberty. We have no selfish ends to serve. We desire no con-quest, no dominion. We seek no indemnities for ourselves, no material compen-sation for the sacrifices we shall freely make. We are but one of the champions of the rights of mankind. We shall be satisfied when those rights have been made as secure as the faith and the freedom of nations can make them.

> Just because we fight without rancor and without selfish object, seeking noth-ing for ourselves but what we shall wish to share with all free peoples, we shall, I feel confident, conduct our operations as belligerents without passion and ourselves observe with proud punctilio the principles of right and of fair play we profess to be fighting for.[1]

The cost of World War I in blood and money was staggering. By the war's end, 116,708 Americans had been killed and 204,002 wounded,[2] not to mention the non-civilian casualties of all the other countries that participated in the War. If they are concluded, more than 7 million (lowest calculation) were killed and more than 14 million (lowest calculation) were wounded.[3] In addition, the financial cost to the United States alone was $26 billion in 1918 dollars.[4] Although the task of making the

---

1 President Woodrow Wilson, Address to a Joint Session of Congress Requesting a Declaration of War Against Germany, April 2, 1917, The American Presidency Project [Internet]; avail-able from http://www.presidency.ucsb.edu/ws/index.php?pid=65366&st=&st1; accessed 20 July 2008.

2 Statistical Summary of America's Major Wars [Internet]; available from http://www.civilwar-home.com/warstats.htm; accessed 20 July 2008.

3 World War I Casualties Page [Internet]; available from http://www.nvcc.edu/home/cevans/ Versailles/greatwar/casualties.html; accessed 20 July 2008.

4Statistical Summary of America's Major Wars [Internet]; available from http://www.civilwar-home.com/warstats.htm; accessed 20 July 2008. A cost of $26 billion in 1918 dollars would "world ... safe for democracy" had not been achieved (not surprisingly), alas, the seeds of more sinister actions and untold destruction had been planted in German society:

> The Treaty of Versailles officially ended the war in ... [June] 1919. The crushing effect of this "peace treaty" on an already-reeling Germany is as staggering as it is forgotten. The defeated nation lost nearly one-third of its total land area, along with millions of German citizens. Its foreign colonies were divvied out to the victorious Allies. The brazen and humiliating requirement for the Germans to admit all responsibility for the war — when Serbia, Austria, Russia, and France all held equal or greater roles for its inauguration — set the stage for the half-starved nation to pay financially for the whole war as well, to the tune of $7.5 *trillion* in today's dollars. This, along with later punitive actions taken by France, set the Germans on a course of runaway inflation, Communist uprisings, economic ruin, social chaos, moral breakdown, and Adolf Hitler ... [,] the Nazis [, and World War II].[1]

The enormity of World War II casualties extended well beyond that of World War I. By the end of the conflict, 407,316 Americans had been killed and 670,846 wounded.[2] If the non-civilian casualties of all the other countries are included, it is estimated that more than 17 million were killed and more than 26 million were wounded.[3] Furthermore, the financial burden of the United States alone was $288 billion in 1945 dollars.[4]

According to Texas Congressman, Ron Paul, "a noninterventionist foreign policy is both morally and constitutionally correct. From George Washington to Grover Cleveland, this principle was upheld. The twentieth century has been witness to a complete reversal of this policy and millions have suffered as a consequence. Our foolish foreign policy contributes significantly to our national bankruptcy and presents a threat to our national security."[5] Currently, our total spending for defense and defense-associated items, which would include, among other things, Homeland Security and foreign aid is staggering. Robert Higgs, Editor of *The Independent Review*, has calculated the total outlay as $934.9 billion for 2006.[6]

Especially within the last 30 years, terrorism has become a concern for the United States and other countries around the world. In particular, Muslim men and woman have been blowing themselves up and in the process killing significant numbers of

---

be $417 billion in 2007! This figure was calculated with The Inflation Calculator, available from http://www.westegg.com/inflation/; accessed 20 July 2008.

1 "The United States and World War I," John J. Dwyer, LewRockwell.com [Internet]; available from http://www.lewrockwell.com/orig3/dwyer3.html; accessed 20 July 2008.

2 Statistical Summary of America's Major Wars [Internet]; available from http://www.civilwarhome.com/warstats.htm; accessed 20 July 2008.

3 World War II: Combatants and Causalities (1937-45), Information for Students, Professor Joseph V. O'Brien, Dept. of History, John Jay College of Criminal Justice [Internet]; available from http://web.jjay.cuny.edu/~jobrien/reference/ob62.html; accessed 2 August 2008.

4 Statistical Summary of America's Major Wars [Internet]; available from http://www.civilwarhome.com/warstats.htm; accessed 20 July 2008. A cost of $288 billion in 1945 dollars would be $3,361 billion in 2007! This figure was calculated with The Inflation Calculator, available from http://www.westegg.com/inflation/; accessed 20 July 2008.

5 Ron Paul, *Freedom Under Siege: The US Constitution After 200 Years* Lake Jackson, Texas: Foundation for Rational Economics and Education, Inc., 1987), 55-6.

6 "The Trillion-Dollar Defense Budget Is Already Here," Robert Higgs, March 15, 2007, *The Independent Institute* [Internet]; available from http://www.independent.org/newsroom/article.asp?id=1941; accessed 20 July 2008.

---

other people along with themselves. Why are these terrible acts perpetrated? Do many people in the Muslim world (and elsewhere) hate America, and if so, why?

Jacob Hornberger, the founder and president of The Future of Freedom Foundation, asks a very pertinent "what if" question regarding the cause of terrorism:

> Federal officials argue that terrorism is caused by foreign hatred for America's "freedom and values." So their prescription has been to declare a perpetual war on terrorism, which involves perpetual and ever-increasing infringements on the rights and freedoms of the American people....
>
> But what if the roots of terrorism against Americans instead lie with the US government's interventionist and imperial foreign policy, including its bombs, embargoes, blockades, bribes, torture, assassinations, foreign military occupations, support of brutal democratic and nondemocratic regimes, training of foreign death squads, intimidation of and attacks on weak regimes, sales of weaponry to brutal dictators, arrogance, obnoxiousness, hypocrisy, indefinite incarcerations of foreigners without trial, wars of aggression, invasions, taking sides in longstanding, bitter disputes, and serving as the world's self-appointed international policeman, interloper, and executioner?
>
> What if all that, instead of America's "freedom and values," is why people all over the world now hate America? What if all that is at the root of terrorism against the American people?[1]

This "what if" question is merely rhetorical. There is more than enough evidence to prove that US interventionist foreign policy in the Muslim world is in fact the motivating factor for these terrorist acts. According to Patrick J. Buchanan, the well-known syndicated columnist and author, "we are not hated for who we are. We are hated for what we do. It is not our principles that have spawned hatred of America in the Islamic world. It is our policies."[2] That being said, let me be clear on one point. There is never ever any justification for killing innocent people no matter what the provocation may be perceived to be. Nevertheless, in order to find a solution to the problem, the cause must first be found. There is plenty of evidence.

The "Text of Fatwa Urging Jihad Against Americans," which was published in the London newspaper, *Al-Quds al-'Arabi*, was signed by Osama bin Ladin and others on February 23, 1998. In their own words, these are the reasons given for authorizing attacks on Americans. The essential portion of this fatwa is:

> The Arabian Peninsula has never — since God made it flat, created its desert, and encircled it with seas — been stormed by any forces like the crusader armies spreading in it like locusts, eating its riches and wiping out its plantations. All this is happening at a time in which nations are attacking Muslims like people fighting over a plate of food. In the light of the grave situation and the lack of support, we and you are obliged to discuss current events, and we should all agree on how to settle the matter.
>
> No one argues today about three facts that are known to everyone; we will list them, in order to remind everyone:
>
> First, for over seven years the United States has been occupying the lands of Islam in the holiest of places, the Arabian Peninsula, plundering its riches, dictating to its rulers, humiliating its people, terrorizing its neighbors, and turning

---

1 Jacob G. Hornberger, "A New Year: Time for Hope and Determination," Libertarian International [Internet]; available from http://www.libertarian.to/NewsDta/templates/news1.php?art=art85#top; accessed 20 July 2008.

2 Patrick J. Buchanan, *Where the Right Went Wrong* (New York: St. Martin's Press, 2005), 80.

its bases in the Peninsula into a spearhead through which to fight the neighboring Muslim peoples.

If some people have in the past argued about the fact of the occupation, all the people of the Peninsula have now acknowledged it. The best proof of this is the Americans' continuing aggression against the Iraqi people using the Peninsula as a staging post, even though all its rulers are against their territories being used to that end, but they are helpless.

Second, despite the great devastation inflicted on the Iraqi people by the crusader-Zionist alliance, and despite the huge number of those killed, which has exceeded 1 million… despite all this, the Americans are once against trying to repeat the horrific massacres, as though they are not content with the protracted blockade imposed after the ferocious war or the fragmentation and devastation.

So here they come to annihilate what is left of this people and to humiliate their Muslim neighbors. Third, if the Americans' aims behind these wars are religious and economic, the aim is also to serve the Jews' petty state and divert attention from its occupation of Jerusalem and murder of Muslims there. The best proof of this is their eagerness to destroy Iraq, the strongest neighboring Arab state, and their endeavor to fragment all the states of the region such as Iraq, Saudi Arabia, Egypt, and Sudan into paper statelets and through their disunion and weakness to guarantee Israel's survival and the continuation of the brutal crusade occupation of the Peninsula.

All these crimes and sins committed by the Americans are a clear declaration of war on God, his messenger, and Muslims…. On that basis, and in compliance with God's order, we issue the following fatwa to all Muslims:

The ruling to kill the Americans and their allies — civilians and military — is an individual duty for every Muslim who can do it in any country in which it is possible to do it, in order to liberate the al-Aqsa Mosque [Jerusalem] and the holy mosque [Mecca] … from their grip, and in order for their armies to move out of all the lands of Islam, defeated and unable to threaten any Muslim. This is in accordance with the words of Almighty God, "and fight the pagans all together as they fight you all together," and "fight them until there is no more tumult or oppression, and there prevail justice and faith in God."[1]

As you can see, not a single word is written condemning American freedom, American wealth, or the American manner of living. Their grievances clearly do not stem from a disapproval of our fundamental beliefs and way of life. The three main accusations presented in the fatwa have but one main object in view: *the interventionist policy in the Middle East*, specifically in the Arabian Peninsula, Iraq, and Jerusalem.

In 1998, Ivan Eland, Director of Defense Policy Studies at the Cato Institute, published a study entitled "Does US Intervention Overseas Breed Terrorism?" He listed more than 60 terrorist incidents from 1915 to 1998 that were perpetrated on U. S. interests worldwide and that can be explained as reprisals for US intrusion in foreign affairs. It should be noted that Muslim terrorists did not always commit the instances listed. His conclusion was, "the extensive number of incidents of terrorism linked

---

1 Al Qaeda's Fatwa, Online NewsHour, PBS [Internet]; available from http://www.pbs.org/newshour/terrorism/international/fatwa_1998.html; accessed 20 July 2008. An earlier fatwa by Ossama bin Laden titled "Declaration of War against the Americans Occupying the Land of the Two Holy Places" was published in *Al-Quds al-'Arabi* in August 1996. See Bin Laden's Fatwa, Online NewsHour, PBS [Internet]; available from http://www.pbs.org/newshour/terrorism/international/fatwa_1996.html; accessed 20 July 2008.

to US foreign policy implies that the United States could substantially reduce the chance of catastrophic terrorist attacks if it lowered its military profile overseas."[1]

Scott McConnell of *The American Conservative* interviewed Professor Robert Pape of the University of Chicago, who authored a book titled *Dying to Win*. In the book, he endeavored to explain the true causes of suicide terrorism. According to Professor Pape, "the purpose of a suicide-terrorist attack is not to die. It is the kill, to inflict the maximum number of casualties on the target society in order to compel that target society to put pressure on its government to change policy."[2] What is the policy that the terrorists want changed? Professor Pape describes it as follows:

> The central fact is that overwhelmingly suicide-terrorist attacks are not driven by religion as much as they are by a clear strategic objective: to compel modern democracies to withdraw military forces from the territory that the terrorists view as their homeland. From Lebanon to Sri Lanka to Chechnya to Kashmir to the West Bank, every major suicide-terrorist campaign—over 95 percent of all the incidents—has had as its central objective to compel a democratic state to withdraw.[3]

He then offers a very important line of reasoning, which we should carefully consider when we reflect on a current policy in Iraq:

> Since suicide terrorism is mainly a response to foreign occupation and not Islamic fundamentalism, the use of heavy military force to transform Muslim societies over there, if you would, is only likely to increase the number of suicide terrorists coming at us.[4]

He elaborates on this point further on as follows:

> Another point in this regard is Iraq itself. Before our invasion, Iraq never had a suicide-terrorist attack in its history. Never. Since our invasion, suicide terrorism has been escalating rapidly with 20 attacks in 2003, 48 in 2004, and over 50 in just the first five months of 2005. Every year that the United States has stationed 150,000 combat troops in Iraq, suicide terrorism has doubled.... What is happening is that the suicide terrorists have been produced by the invasion.[5]

In 2004, the US Defense Department issued a Report of the Defense Science Board Task Force on Strategic Communication. Among other things, the report states, "American direct intervention in the Muslim World has paradoxically elevated the stature of and support for radical Islamists, while diminishing support for the United States to single-digits in some Arab societies."[6] The report expands on this point further in the following manner:

> Muslims do not "hate our freedom," but rather, they hate our policies. The overwhelming majority voice their objections to what they see as one-sided support in favor of Israel and against Palestinian rights, and the longstanding, even in-

---

1 Ivan Eland, "Does U. S. Intervention Overseas Breed Terrorism? The Historical Record," Cato Institute [Internet]; available from http://www.cato.org/pub_display.php?pub_id=1574; accessed 20 July 2008.

2 The Logic of Suicide Terrorism, *The American Conservative* [Internet]; available from http://www.amconmag.com/2005a/2005_07_18/article.html; accessed 20 July 2008.

3 Ibid.

4 Ibid.

5 Ibid.

6 Report of the Defense Science Board Task Force on Strategic Communication, Defense Science Board of the Department of Defense [Internet]; available from http://www.acq.osd.mil/dsb/reports/2004-09-Strategic_Communication.pdf; accessed 20 July 2008.

---

creasing support for what Muslims collectively see as tyrannies, most notably Egypt, Saudi Arabia, Jordan, Pakistan, and the Gulf states.

. . .

Furthermore, *in the eyes of Muslims*, American occupation of Afghanistan and Iraq has not led to democracy there, but only more chaos and suffering. US actions appear in contrast to be motivated by ulterior motives, and deliberately controlled in order to best serve American national interests at the expense of truly Muslim self-determination.[1]

A poll conducted in January 2006 by the Program on International Policy Attitudes at the University of Maryland obtained troubling results regarding the views of Iraqis about the US forces stationed in Iraq. According to the poll results, "70% of Iraqis favor setting a timeline for the withdrawal of US forces" [and] "this number divides evenly between 35% who favor a short time frame of 'within six months' and 35% who favor a gradual reduction over two years."[2] In addition, if coalition forces were to leave in six months, "sixty-seven percent say that 'day to day security for ordinary Iraqis' would increase, [which is] a consensus position among all ethnic groups...."[3] However, even more alarming is that "overall, 47% say they approve of 'attacks on US-led forces' (23% strongly)."[4] An earlier poll taken in November 2005 by another organization also revealed that Iraqis were unhappy with the occupation.[5]

A later poll conducted in September 2006 by the Program on International Policy Attitudes at the University of Maryland showed a worsening of the situation. According to the poll results, "a large majority of Iraqis, 71%, say they would like the Iraqi government to ask for US-led forces to be withdrawn from Iraq within a year or less"[6] and "large numbers [78%] say that the United States' military presence is 'provoking more conflict than it is preventing.'"[7] In addition, "support for attacks against US-led forces has increased sharply to 61 percent.... This represents a 14-point increase from January 2006, when only 47 percent of Iraqis supported attacks."[8]

It is as certain as anything can be that the US interventionist foreign policy in the Middle East has been the true cause of the terrorist acts perpetrated against us. Knowing this fact, what should we do in Iraq and Afghanistan and what should be our course of action regarding Al Qaeda?

The Iraqis, as well as the Afghans, are responsible for their own destiny and for the nations that they ultimately bring into existence. We should withdraw our forces from both countries as soon as possible. If a civil war is necessary to determine what group will be in power, then let it be so. Unfortunately, until we finally solve our own energy problems, the United States will continue to need Middle Eastern

---

1 Ibid.
2 "Polls of Iraqis: Public Wants Timetable for US Withdrawal, but Thinks US Plans Permanent Bases in Iraq," World Public Opinion.org [Internet]; available from http://www.worldpublicopinion.org/pipa/articles/brmiddleeastnafricara/165.php?lb=brme&pnt=165&nid=&id=; accessed 21 July 2008.
3 Ibid.
4 Ibid.
5 Ibid.
6 "Most Iraqis Want US Troops Out Within a Year," World Public Opinion.org [Internet]; available from http://www.worldpublicopinion.org/pipa/articles/brmiddleeastnafricara/250.php?lb=brme&pnt=250&nid=&id; accessed 20 July 2008.
7 Ibid.
8 Ibid.

oil. Professor Pape offers what I believe would be an appropriate strategy for dealing with this issue:

> For us, victory means not sacrificing any of our vital interests while also not having Americans vulnerable to suicide-terrorist attacks. In the case of the Persian Gulf, that means we should pursue a strategy that secures our interests in oil but does not encourage the rise of a new generation of suicide terrorists.

> In the 1970s and the 1980s, the United States secured its interest in oil without stationing a single combat soldier on the Arabian Peninsula. Instead, we formed an alliance with Iraq and Saudi Arabia, which we can now do again. We relied on numerous aircraft carriers off the coast of the Arabian Peninsula, and naval air power now is more effective not less. We also built numerous military bases so that we could move large numbers of ground forces to the region quickly if a crisis emerged.

> That strategy, called "offshore balancing," worked splendidly against Saddam Hussein in 1990 and is again our best strategy to secure our interest in oil while preventing the rise of more suicide terrorists.[1]

Based on what is known about Al Qaeda's true motive for perpetrating terrorist acts, it is likely they will cease committing them if the original cause is taken away. This is precisely what "offshore balancing" will accomplish.

This new policy should in no way permit Al Qaeda to get away with its past crimes. Congress should pass a *proper* declaration of war against Al Qaeda in lieu of the flawed joint resolution to "authorize the use of United States Armed Forces against those responsible for the recent attacks launched against the United States" that was discussed in the last chapter. Then, with the authority of this war declaration behind him, the President should use all means at his disposal to find and bring to justice all the leaders of Al Qaeda, including Osama bin Laden, who perpetrated the horrors of 9/11 against us.

What should be our policy with the rest of the world? You may be surprised to discover that the United States has military personnel stationed in 135 nations around the world and this number is a whopping 70 percent of all the countries that exist.[2] Except for a number of important strategic sites that may be required to defend the nation against a possible enemy attack, all of our military forces should be withdrawn from all other areas around the world as soon as possible. Furthermore, Congress should pass legislation to rescind all treaties that have obligated the United States to come to the aide of other nations militarily. This action would include our withdrawal from the United Nations as well. In the Charter of this organization,[3] Chapter VII empowers the Security Council to take military action against a nation that endangers "international peace and security." Military forces and other support that may be required to deal with the threat are to be provided by the member nations. Let me quote a few of the relevant Articles from Chapter VII below:

---

1 The Logic of Suicide Terrorism, *The American Conservative* [Internet]; available from http://www. amconmag.com/2005a/2005_07_18/article.html; accessed 20 July 2008.

2 "The US Global Empire," Laurence M. Vance, March 16, 2004, LewRockwell.com [Internet]; available from http://www.lewrockwell.com/vance/vance8.html; accessed 20 July 2008.

3 Charter of the United Nations, Chapter VII, Acton with Respect to Threats to the Peace, Breaches of the Peace, and Acts of Aggression, Welcome to the United Nations [Internet]; available from http://www.un.org/aboutun/charter/index.html; accessed 20 July 2008.

Article 39

> The Security Council shall determine the existence of any threat to the peace, breach of the peace, or act of aggression and shall make recommendations, or decide what measures shall be taken ... to maintain or restore international peace and security.

Article 42

> ... the Security Council ... may take such action by air, sea, or land forces as may be necessary to maintain or restore international peace and security. Such action may include demonstrations, blockade, and other operations by air, sea, or land forces of Members of the United Nations.

Article 43

> 1. All Members of the United Nations, in order to contribute to the maintenance of international peace and security, undertake to make available to the Security Council, on its call and in accordance with a special agreement or agreements, armed forces, assistance, and facilities, including rites of passage, necessary for the purpose of maintaining international peace and security.

Furthermore, all government foreign aid should be abolished as well, although private aid of this type should be encouraged.

Our intelligence services must have a superior level of competence and sophistication in order to become aware of any potential threats from belligerent groups or nations anywhere in the world. If a credible threat should be discovered, it should be acted on in the appropriate constitutional manner. As was learned from the last chapter, the President has the constitutional authority to pre-empt or intercept an enemy attack on our nation or on our embassies abroad without a declaration of war from Congress, if the danger is a *national emergency* requiring *immediate action*. He should use this power to deal with such threats quickly and effectively. If on the other hand, the threat is not so urgent, but military action is definitely required soon, a declaration of war would have to be obtained from Congress before this could occur.

In order to commence this new foreign policy in a proper manner, the President should inform the nations of the world through a speech given over all the international news services. In the speech, he should tell them that the United States would from now on not involve itself in the political affairs of the world, although it will always strive to be friends with and open channels of trade with all nations that wish to do so. In our trade dealings with other nations, we will no longer join any international trade agreements that manage trade for us and in the process bypass or own constitutional system, but will negotiate and manage our own trade with other nations.

At some point in the speech, the following warning should be stated as unambiguously and as convincingly as possible: If we should henceforward intercept any verifiable intelligence that any nation or group is planning an attack on our shores or on our embassies in other countries, the United States will not hesitate to use all the military might at its disposal to put an end to such aggression immediately and completely.

After the above actions have been taken, we should pledge to follow only a noninterventionist policy from then on. It is vitally important that we never renege on this pledge, since the wellbeing of our nation is at stake if we revert to our old ways.

In a speech before the House of Representatives on April 5, 2006, Congressman Ron Paul described the constitutional, moral, and practical reasons why a noninterventionist foreign policy is in the best interests of the United States:

A strict interpretation of the Constitution mandates it. The moral imperative of not imposing our will on others, no matter how well intentioned, is a powerful argument for minding our own business. The principle of self-determination should be respected. Strict non-intervention removes the incentives for foreign powers and corporate interests to influence our policies overseas. We can't afford the cost that intervention requires, whether through higher taxes or inflation. If the moral arguments against intervention don't suffice for some, the practical arguments should.

Intervention just doesn't work. It backfires and ultimately hurts American citizens both at home and abroad. Spreading ourselves too thin around the world actually diminishes our national security through a weakened military. As the superpower of the world, a constant interventionist policy is perceived as arrogant, and greatly undermines our ability to use diplomacy in a positive manner.

... A policy of trade and peace, and a willingness to use diplomacy, is far superior to the foreign policy that has evolved over the past 60 years.[1]

---

1 "Iran: The Next Neocon Target," April 5, 2006, Speeches and Statements, Representative Ron Paul [Internet]; available from http://www.house.gov/paul/congrec/congrec2006/cr040506.htm; accessed 20 July 2008.

Before a standing army can rule, the people must be disarmed; as they are in almost every kingdom of Europe. The supreme power in America cannot enforce unjust laws by the sword; because the whole body of the people are armed....
— *Noah Webster, An Examination of the Leading Principles of the Federal Constitution, 1787*

The sections of the Constitution that relate to the "Militia of the several States"[1] are as follows:

The Second Amendment confirms the unalienable right to self-defense (self-preservation), which we learned from the second chapter, includes the right to furnish oneself with weapons for this purpose:

A well regulated Militia, being necessary to the security of a free State, the right of the people to keep and bear Arms, shall not be infringed.

- Article I, section 8, lists the powers of Congress:

[Clause 15] To provide for calling forth the Militia to execute the Laws of the Union, suppress Insurrections and repel Invasions;

[Clause 16] To provide for organizing, arming, and disciplining, the Militia, and for governing such Part of them as may be employed in the Service of the United States, reserving to the States respectively, the Appointment of the Officers, and the Authority of training the Militia according to the discipline prescribed by Congress.

- Article II, section 2, lists the powers of the President:

---

1 Each state in principle has its own militia, but Congress has the power to federalize them, or only a portion of them, to "execute the Laws of the Union, suppress Insurrections and repel Invasions" (Article I, section 8, clauses 15 and 16). When the state militias are united as one force for one of the reasons stated above, it is simply called *"the* Militia," or more properly, the "Militia of the several States" (Article II, section 2, clause 1).

[Clause 1] The President shall be Commander in Chief of the Army and Navy of the United States, and of the Militia of the several States, when called into the actual Service of the United States.

The Second Amendment is rarely ever quoted or even understood in its entirety. Those who approve of the right to own guns always tend to quote the second half of the Amendment (i.e., "the right of the people to keep and bear Arms, shall not be infringed"), but avoid quoting the first half (i.e., "a well regulated Militia, being necessary to the security of a free State...."). Although they are quite correct in stressing that this right cannot be "infringed," the first half of the Amendment cannot simply be disregarded, if the right is to be properly understood.

Alternatively, those who are against the right to own guns have little problem in quoting the first half of the Amendment and argue that the right is only applicable to a "well regulated Militia." In this case, the second half of the Amendment is ignored, again making it impossible to obtain a proper understanding of the right. The Amendment can only make proper sense in its entirety.

In order to obtain an accurate comprehension of the Amendment, we first have to determine what the Militia actually is. Constitutional Law Attorney, Dr. Edwin Vieira, Jr., explains it very clearly as follows:

> To be sure, the Constitution does not create any "well regulated Militia". It delegates no power to Congress to "raise and support" (as with an army), to "provide and maintain" (as with a navy), or in any other words to fashion from whole cloth any "well regulated Militia". And it does not even define what constitutes such a Militia. That is because it did not have to: In the late 1700s, every adult American knew that "well regulated Militia" had existed in the Colonies and independent States from the mid-1600s, and were established in every State of the Union even as the Constitution was being drafted and ratified. For that reason, the Constitution simply acknowledged "the Militia of the several States" as already in existence, adopted and incorporated them according to the historical legal principles by which they had long and even then operated, and thereby perpetuated them in that form.[1]

In part two of the same article, he provides us with further information on the Militia:

> In every Colony and independent State from the mid-1600s to the late 1700s immediately prior to ratification of the Constitution, the Militia consisted of every able-bodied male, typically from 16 to 50 or 60 years of age, each of whom was required by law to keep in his personal possession at home a firearm suitable for military use (for most of them a musket or rifle, for some a brace of pistols), together with a supply of ammunition (assembled cartridges, black powder, and lead shot); a bayonet, tomahawk, or sword; and other accoutrements necessary to outfit an infantry soldier or cavalry trooper.
>
> Throughout the original thirteen Colonies and States, the laws required each Militiaman to buy his own arms and ammunition in the free market—thus implicitly guaranteeing the existence and operation of such a market.... And local governments, or very often the Militia, provided publicly owned arms to those individuals too poor to purchase them on their own account. That is, *We the People always required themselves to provide themselves with firearms*, either directly as individuals, or indirectly through the Militia in which they served or the public officials whom they elected.

---

1 Dr. Edwin Vieira, "Are You Doing Your Constitutional Duty For 'Homeland Security'?" Part 1, NewsWithViews.com [Internet]; available from http://newswithviews.com/Vieira/edwin11.htm; accessed 21 July 2008.

. . .

If not explicitly exempted by statute because he held some important public office or practiced some essential profession or trade (such as legislators, physicians, millers, ferrymen, or ministers of religion), every Militiaman was required to bear his firearm and ammunition into the field on a regular basis in order to train in organized formations so as to become proficient with that firearm according to the military tactics of the day.... In addition, many of those technically exempted nevertheless served the Militia, such as public officials (who were often high-ranking Militia officers), physicians (who staffed medical units), and conscientious objectors (who performed not only non-military duties but also the dangerous functions of scouts and spies).

. . .

The Militia were anything but voluntary organizations, their membership anything but limited, the duties they imposed anything but avoidable, and the public services they performed anything but dispensable.[1]

A report of the Senate Subcommittee on the Constitution titled "The Right to Keep and Bear Arms" (1982) stated the same idea regarding the Militia:

> There can be little doubt ... that when the Congress and the people spoke of a "militia", they had reference to the traditional concept of the entire populace capable of bearing arms, and not to any formal group such as what is today called the National Guard. The purpose was to create an armed citizenry, such as the political theorists at the time considered essential to ward off tyranny. From this militia, appropriate measures might create a "well regulated militia" of individuals trained in their duties and responsibilities as citizens and owners of firearms.[2]

On May 8, 1792, Congress passed *An Act more effectually to provide for the National Defense by establishing an Uniform Militia throughout the United States*. Commonly called the Militia Act of 1792, Section 1 describes who is to be enrolled in the Militia and how the enrollment is to be accomplished. It also describes what kind of weapons and accoutrements each Militiaman was to "provide himself with," which in most cases probably meant that the applicable items would be purchased on the open market. He was to acquire them "within six months" after enrollment. Let me quote Section 1 of the Act below:

> *Section 1. Be it enacted by the Senate and House of Representatives of the United States of America*, in Congress assembled, That each and every free able-bodied white male citizen of the respective States, resident therein, who is or shall be of age of eighteen years, and under the age of forty-five years (except as is herein after excepted) shall severally and respectively be enrolled in the militia, by the Captain or Commanding Officer of the company, within whose bounds such citizen shall reside, and that within twelve months after the passing of this Act. And it shall at all time hereafter be the duty of every such Captain or Commanding Officer of a company, to enroll every such citizen as aforesaid, and also those who shall, from time to time, arrive at the age of 18 years, or being at the age of 18 years, and under the age of 45 years (except as before excepted) shall come to

---

1 Dr. Edwin Vieira, Jr., "Are You Doing Your Constitutional Duty For "Homeland Security"? Part 2, NewsWithViews.com [Internet]; available from http://newswithviews.com/Vieira/edwin12.htm; accessed 21 July 2008.

2 Report of the Subcommittee of the Constitution of the Committee on the Judiciary, United States Senate, 97th Congress, Second Session, "The Right to Keep and Bear Arms," Constitution Society [Internet]; available from http://www.constitution.org/mil/rkba1982.txt; accessed 21 July 2008.

reside within his bounds; and shall without delay notify such citizen of the said enrollment, by the proper non-commissioned Officer of the company, by whom such notice may be proved. That every citizen, so enrolled and notified, shall, within six months thereafter, provide himself with a good musket or firelock, a sufficient bayonet and belt, two spare flints, and a knapsack, a pouch with a box therein to contain not less than twenty four cartridges, suited to the bore of his musket or firelock, each cartridge to contain a proper quantity of power and ball; or with a good rifle, knapsack, shot-pouch, and power-horn, twenty balls suited to the bore of his rifle, and a quarter of a pound of power; and shall appear, so armed, accoutred and provided, when called out to exercise, or into service, except, that when called out on company days to exercise only, he may appear without a knapsack. That the commissioned officers shall severally be armed with a sword or hanger, and espontoon, and that from and after five years from the passing of this act, all muskets for arming the militia as herein required, shall be of bores sufficient for balls of the eighteenth part of a pound. And every citizen so enrolled, and providing himself with the arms, ammunition and ac-coutrements, required as aforesaid, shall hold the same exempted from all suits, distresses, executions or sales, for debt or for the payment of taxes.[1]

Thus, the Militia is not some military body separate from the people. Except for women,[2] children, the elderly, mentally and physically handicapped persons, and oth-ers specifically exempted, *it is the people*. Furthermore, this fact is not based on some archaic law, but it is still the law today. The U. S. Code, Title 10, Section 311 describes the "composition and classes" of the Militia as follows:

The militia of the United States consists of all able-bodied males at least 17 years of age and, except as provided in section 313 of title 32,[3] under 45 years of age who are, or who have made a declaration of intention to become, citizens of the United States and female citizens of the United States who are members of the National Guard.

The classes of the militia are —

1. the organized militia, which consists of the National Guard and the Naval Militia; and

2. the unorganized militia, which consists of the members of the militia who are not members of the National Guard or the Naval Militia.[4]

---

1 *An Act more effectually to provide for the National Defense by establishing an Uniform Militia throughout the United States*, Statutes at Large, 2nd Congress, 1st Session, The Library of Congress, (Thomas) [Internet]; available from http://memory.loc.gov/cgi-bin/ampage?collId=llsl&fileName=001/llsl001.db&recNum=394; accessed 21 July 2008.

2 According to Dr. Vieira, "now, with the legal emancipation of women, 'the Militia of the sev-eral States' arguably includes all able-bodied females, who might be called to serve in some capacities in the most critical, last-ditch situations of State and National defense, freeing men for more arduous duties." Dr. Edwin Vieira, Jr., "Are You Doing Your Constitutional Duty For "Homeland Security"? Part 2, NewsWithViews.com [Internet]; available from http://newswithviews.com/Vieira/edwin12.htm; accessed 21 July 2008.

3 Title 32, Section 313 adds that for "original enlistment in the National Guard" or "reenlist-ment" a person has to be "under 64 years of age and a former member of the Regular Army, Regular Navy, Regular Air force, or Regular Marine Corps." In addition, "for appointment as an officer of the National Guard," a person has to be a U. S. citizen and "at least 18 years of age and under 64." U. S. Code, Title 10, Section 311, Cornell Law School U. S. Code Collection [Internet]; available from http://www.law.cornell.edu/uscode/html/uscode32/usc_sec_32_00000313----000-.html; accessed 21 July 2008.

4 U. S. Code, Title 10, Section 311, Cornell Law School U. S. Code Collection [Internet]; available from http://www.law.cornell.edu/uscode/html/uscode10/usc_sec_10_00000311----000-.html; accessed 21 July 2008.

US Code Title 10, Section 312 lists the following persons who are exempt from the Militia:

1. The Vice President.
2. The judicial and executive officers of the United States, and the several States and Territories, and Puerto Rico.
3. Members of the armed forces, except members who are not on active duty.
4. Customhouse clerks.
5. Persons employed by the United States in the transmission of mail.
6. Workmen employed in armories, arsenals, and naval shipyards of the United States.
7. Pilots on navigable waters.
8. Mariners in the sea service of a citizen of, or a merchant in, the United States.

A person who claims exemption because of religious belief is exempt from militia duty in a combatant capacity, if the conscientious holding of that belief is established under such regulations as the President may prescribe. However, such a person is not exempt from militia duty that the President determines to be noncombatant.[1]

Apparently, what these sections of the U. S. Code endeavor to do is to define the National Guard as the *organized* militia and include everyone else that is not exempt from militia duty as being in the *unorganized* militia. However, the latter have been placed most surely in a wretched category. As Dr. Vieira has stated, "If you are lumped into this 'unorganized militia' you are just that: unorganized, unarmed, undisciplined, untrained, unsupplied, undeployed, and unwanted as a matter of statute—thoroughly disregarded by Congress [and the states],[2] wholly disconnected from your necessary constitutional rights and duties, dispensed with, and withal dispersed within an impotent, disoriented rabble."[3]

Indeed, according to Article I, section 8, clause 16 of the Constitution it would seem that Congress has been given the power to classify the Militia into certain groups. Congress is authorized "to provide for organizing, arming, and disciplining, the Militia, and for governing such Part of them as may be employed in the Service of the United States...." The states, in turn, are responsible for "the Appointment of the Officers, and the Authority of training the Militia according to the discipline prescribed by Congress." The main reason for splitting this power between Congress and the states in this way was to make it possible for the separate state militias to function smoothly as one force if they should be federalized. In spite of this authority given to Congress, the National Guard was actually established *as a reserve force for the army* not as a type of militia:

> That the National Guard is not the "Militia" referred to in the second amendment is even clearer today. Congress has organized the National Guard under its

1 U. S. Code, Title 10, Section 312, Cornell Law School U. S. Code Collection [Internet]; available from http://www.law.cornell.edu/uscode/html/uscode10/usc_sec_10_00000312——000-.html; accessed 21 July 2008.

2 "But, other than maintaining their State Guards (which as sub-units of the National Guard are not true State "Militia"), most States have done next to nothing on this score, either." Dr. Edwin Vieira, Jr., "Are You Doing Your Constitutional Duty For "Homeland Security"? Part 2, NewsWithViews.com [Internet]; available from http://newswithviews.com/Vieira/edwin12.htm; accessed 21 July 2008.

3 Ibid.

power to "raise and support armies" [Article I, section 8, clause 12] and not its power to "Provide for organizing, arming and disciplining the Militia" [Article I, section 8, clause 16]. This Congress chose to do in the interests of organizing reserve military units which were not limited in deployment by the strictures of our power over the constitutional militia, which can be called forth only "to execute the laws of the Union, suppress insurrections and repel invasions." The modern National Guard was specifically intended to avoid status as the constitutional militia, a distinction recognized by 10 USC. Sec 311(a).[1]

During the years just prior to the ratification of the Constitution, the idea of a "select militia" was discussed quite often at the state ratification debates. A "select militia" was to be a more thoroughly trained body similar to our National Guard that was to be differentiated from the general Militia.[2] Those who favored a "select militia" argued that it simply would not be practical to train all able-bodied male citizens from 18 to 44 years old to the extent required to create a "well regulated Militia." On the other hand, those that opposed a "select militia" feared that such a body would differ little from a standing army and would thus be a threat to liberty.[3]

Alexander Hamilton was one of those who supported of a "select militia" in *The Federalist Papers* (#29). Let me quote the relevant section of the document below:

> But so far from viewing the matter in the same light with those who object to select corps as dangerous, were the Constitution ratified, and were I to deliver my sentiments to a member of the federal legislature from this State on the subject of a militia establishment, I should hold to him, in substance, the following discourse:
>
> "The project of disciplining all the militia of the United States is as futile as it would be injurious, if it were capable of being carried into execution. A tolerable expertness in military movements is a business that requires time and practice. It is not a day, or even a week, that will suffice for the attainment of it. To oblige the great body of the yeomanry, and of the other classes of the citizens, to be under arms for the purpose of going through military exercises and evolutions, as often as might be necessary to acquire the degree of perfection which would entitle them to the character of a well-regulated militia, would be a real grievance to the people, and a serious public inconvenience and loss. It would form an annual deduction from the productive labor of the country, to an amount which, calculating upon the present numbers of the people, would not fall far short of the whole expense of the civil establishments of all the States.

---

1 Report of the Subcommittee of the Constitution of the Committee on the Judiciary, United States Senate, 97th Congress, Second Session, "The Right to Keep and Bear Arms," Constitution Society [Internet]; available from http://www.constitution.org/mil/rkba1982.txt; accessed 21 July 2008.

2 "When the framers referred to the equivalent of our National Guard, they uniformly used the term 'select militia' and distinguished this from 'militia'." Quoted from the Report of the Subcommittee of the Constitution of the Committee on the Judiciary, United States Senate, 97th Congress, Second Session, "The Right to Keep and Bear Arms," Constitution Society [Internet]; available from http://www.constitution.org/mil/rkba1982.txt; accessed 21 July 2008.

3 "A standing military force, with an overgrown Executive will not long be safe companions to liberty. The means of defense against foreign danger have been always the instruments of tyranny at home. Among the Romans it was a standing maxim to excite a war, whenever a revolt was apprehended. Throughout all Europe, the armies kept up under the pretext of defending, have enslaved the people." Statement by James Madison in James Madison, *Notes of Debates in the Federal Convention of 1787*, Introduction by Adrienne Koch, Bicentennial Edition (New York: W. W. Norton & Company, 1987), 214.

To attempt a thing which would abridge the mass of labor and industry to so considerable an extent, would be unwise: and the experiment, if made, could not succeed, because it would not long be endured. Little more can reasonably be aimed at, with respect to the people at large, than to have them properly armed and equipped; and in order to see that this be not neglected, it will be necessary to assemble them once or twice in the course of a year.

"But though the scheme of disciplining the whole nation must be abandoned as mischievous or impracticable; yet it is a matter of the utmost importance that a well-digested plan should, as soon as possible, be adopted for the proper establishment of the militia. The attention of the government ought particularly to be directed to the formation of a select corps of moderate extent, upon such principles as will really fit them for service in case of need. By thus circumscribing the plan, it will be possible to have an excellent body of well-trained militia, ready to take the field whenever the defense of the State shall require it. This will not only lessen the call for military establishments, but if circumstances should at any time oblige the government to form an army of any magnitude that army can never be formidable to the liberties of the people while there is a large body of citizens, little, if at all, inferior to them in discipline and the use of arms, who stand ready to defend their own rights and those of their fellow-citizens. This appears to me the only substitute that can be devised for a standing army, and the best possible security against it, if it should exist."

On the other hand, Richard Henry Lee, a member of Congress from Virginia, was one of those who opposed a "select militia." Eighteen letters have been accredited to him, although there is apparently some doubt here.[1] His argument can be found in letter #18, which appeared on January 25, 1788. Let me quote the relevant portion of this letter below:

A militia, when properly formed, are in fact the people themselves, and render regular troops in a great measure unnecessary. ... [T]he constitution ought to secure a genuine and guard against a select militia, by providing that the militia shall always be kept well organized, armed, and disciplined, and include, according to the past and general usuage [sic] of the states, all men capable of bearing arms; and that all regulations tending to render this general militia useless and defenceless [sic], by establishing select corps of militia, or distinct bodies of military men, not having permanent interests and attachments in the community to be avoided. I am persuaded, I need not multiply words to convince you of the value and solidity of this principle, as it respects general liberty, and the duration of a free and mild government ... But, say gentlemen, the general militia are for the most part employed at home in their private concerns, cannot well be called out, or be depended upon; that we must have a select militia; that is, as I understand it, particular corps or bodies of young men, and of men who have but little to do at home, particularly armed and disciplined in some measure, at the public expence [sic], and always ready to take the field. These corps, not much unlike regular troops, will ever produce an inattention to the general militia; and the consequence has ever been, and always must be, that the substantial men, having families and property, will generally be without arms, without knowing the use of them, and defenceless [sic]; whereas, to preserve liberty, it is essential that the whole body of the people always possess arms, and be taught alike, especially when young, how to use them; nor does it follow from this, that all promiscuously must go into actual service on every occasion. The mind that aims at a select militia, must be influenced by a truly

---

1 Some scholars believe the letters were actually written by Melancton Smith, a member of Congress from New York, or by both Lee and Smith as collaborators.

anti-republican principle; and when we see many men disposed to practice upon it, whenever they can prevail, no wonder true republicans are for carefully guarding against it.[1]

The fact is that terms like "select militia," "organized militia," "and "unorganized militia" only confuse the issue about what the original definitions of a standing army and a militia are. The National Guard should remain what it was intended to be — a reserve force of the army and *not* the organized Militia. So to, the Militia should remain what it was intended to be — a body of armed citizenry trained thoroughly enough to be called a "well regulated Militia." The millions of citizens throughout the nation who have been relegated to the status of the unorganized Militia should be reinstated to their proper place as the "Militia of the several States".

According to the National Rifle Association (NRA), "there are estimated to be more than 20,000 gun laws in America at the federal state and local levels and laws vary greatly from state to state and, in some states, from locality to locality. Since 1968 virtually every aspect of lawful firearms commerce from manufacture to retail sales has been strictly controlled and regulated by the federal government."[2] All these laws have accomplished little or nothing except to further displace the people from their proper rank as the "Militia of the several States." Although the number of privately owned guns, gun owners, and "right-to-carry" states have increased to unparalleled amounts and although many gun control laws have been either abolished or made less severe, violent crime has nonetheless *decreased* to unprecedented levels.[3] Surely, these statistics do not support the view that more guns and less gun control somehow *increase* violent crime.

In order to ensure that the Militia is "properly armed and equipped" the numerous federal and state laws and restrictions that have been placed on the right of able-bodied citizens to own and use guns should be rescinded. However, no one really has any dispute with the view that certain individuals should most certainly be prohibited from owning and using firearms. The law of self-preservation that was discussed in the first chapter must again come into play.[4] According to federal law, "the following classes of people are ineligible to possess, receive, ship, or transport firearms or ammunition":

- Those convicted of crimes punishable by imprisonment for over one year, except state misdemeanors punishable by two years or less.
- Fugitives from justice.
- Unlawful users of certain depressant, narcotic, or stimulant drugs.
- Those adjudicated as mental defectives or incompetents or those committed

---

1 *Letters from the Federal Farmer*, Letter XVIII, January 25, 1788, The Constitution Society [Internet]; available from http://www.constitution.org/afp/fedfar18.htm; accessed 21 July 2008.

2 FAQ, "What are the laws concerning the purchase, possession, and ownership of firearms for my state or another particular state?" NRA-ILA [Internet]; available from http://www.nraila.org/Issues/FAQ/?s=3; accessed 21 July 2008.

3 Guns, Gun Ownership, & RTC at All-Time Highs, Less 'Gun Control,' and Violent Crime at 30-Year Low, NRA-ILA [Internet]; available from http://www.nraila.org/Issues/FactSheets/Read.aspx?ID=126; accessed 21 July 2008.

4 "A strict observance of the written laws is doubtless *one* of the high duties of a good citizen, but it is not the *highest*. The law of necessity, of self-preservation, of saving our country when in danger, are of higher obligation. To lose our country by a scrupulous adherence to written law, would be to lose the law itself, with life, liberty, property, and all those who are enjoying them with us; thus absurdly sacrificing the end to the means ..." (Thomas Jefferson, Letter to J. B. Colvin, Sept. 20, 1810).

to any mental institution.

* Illegal aliens.
* Citizens who have renounced their citizenship.
* Those persons dishonorably discharged from the Armed Forces.
* Persons less than 18 years of age for the purchase of a shotgun or rifle.[1]
* Persons less than 21 years of age for the purchase of a firearm that is other than a shotgun or rifle.
* Persons subject to a court order that restrains such persons from harassing, stalking, or threatening an intimate partner.
* Persons convicted in any court of a misdemeanor crime of domestic violence.

Persons under indictment for a crime punishable by imprisonment for more than one year are ineligible to receive, transport, or ship any firearm or ammunition. Under limited conditions, relief from disability may be obtained from the US Secretary of the Treasury, or through a pardon, expungement, restoration of rights, or setting aside of a conviction.[2]

There is no reason why enlisting in the Militia could not coincide rather closely to Section 1 of the Militia Act of 1792. When a person reaches seventeen years of age according to US Code, Title 10, Section 311a (quoted above), he presents himself to the Officer commanding the company in his area. The Officer ascertains that he is not included in the "classes of people ... ineligible to possess, receive, ship, or transport firearms or ammunition" (quoted above). If all is well, he is officially enrolled in the Militia; but he only carries out a temporary noncombatant role. Then, on reaching eighteen years old he purchases a rifle and other needed accoutrements, which are required for full Militia duty.

In addition, even Alexander Hamilton, who favored creating a "select militia," did not feel that the rest of the armed citizenry should be completely ignored as they are in the unorganized Militia today. In *The Federalist Papers* (#29), he stated that the "people at large" should at least be "properly armed and equipped; and in order to see that this be not neglected, it will be necessary to assemble them once or twice in the course of a year."

The revitalized Militia would have to undergo appropriate training in order to bring them up to the caliber of a "well regulated Militia." Such instruction would probably include firearm practice and various military drills and exercises, which would first have to be established by Congress (Article I, section 8, clause 16). Although it cannot be expected that the training of the Militia would be anything near the intensity undertaken by the National Guard, those able-bodied citizens not exempted from duty would probably have to undergo training more often than "once or twice in the course of a year," as Alexander Hamilton suggested, or else it is difficult to imagine how they could develop into the "well regulated Militia" of the Second Amendment.

One enormous benefit that would ensue from a restored Militia would be its ability to police itself. Congress, pursuant to its authority under Article I, section 8,

---

1 The only way to make this ineligibility class agree with U. S. Code, Title 10, Section 311 (a), which states that "the militia of the United States consists of all able-bodied males *at least 17 years of age* ... (italics mine)," is to suppose that someone at least seventeen but not yet eighteen years of age would only have a noncombatant role in the militia. How could it be otherwise, since he cannot own a firearm until he reaches eighteen years old?

2 "A Citizen's Guide to Federal Firearms Laws," NRA-ILA [Internet]; available from http://www.nraila.org/GunLaws/Federal/Read.aspx?id=60; accessed 21 July 2008.

clause 16, could pass legislation implementing rules of conduct and proficiency requirements for Militia members. Various disciplinary measures could be prescribed, if the rules of conduct are violated, which could include, for the most serious infringements, dismissal from the Militia. Dismissal would also mean that owning firearms would be prohibited from then on. Proficiency requirements would require members to demonstrate by means of appropriate tests a certain level of skill in the use of firearms, evidence of physical and mental fitness required for Militia duty, proper execution of military drills and other exercises, sufficient leadership ability for officers, and adequate acquisition of knowledge through classroom work, etc. If evidence of competence is below the mark, a number of measures could be implemented. Among them, members could be held back in rank, demoted, or allowed to participate in noncombatant roles only. This self-policing system would be a much more efficient way to regulate firearms than the confusing and unwieldy mass of laws that attempt to do so now.

Dr. Vieira has argued very persuasively that a revived Militia would be the ideal body to handle homeland security:

> Revitalized Militia would mobilize millions upon millions of individuals for hundreds of different programs, and bring with them the innovation and experimentation that emanate from minds not mired in the ruts of rigid bureaucratic centralism, and not incapacitated by some statist ideology from imagining solutions to the conundrums of "homeland security" that are fully compatible with human liberty....
>
> With "homeland security" properly focused in the States and localities, rather than centralized in Washington, D.C., America would return to the Founding Fathers' federalism, rather than continue to expand Franklin Roosevelt's federalization. In the most practical possible way, We the People would finally realize their own personal responsibility to maintain "a Republican Form of Government"—that, in the final analysis, "homeland security" means and demands political control by We the People, which We the People must provide directly.
>
> ...
>
> "homeland security" localized in "the Militia of the several States" is the most effective way to protect Americans against the real threat to their liberties. America will never lose her freedoms because of attacks from some hodge-podge of foreign "terrorists". The actual, acute danger lies in the organized efforts of home-grown subversives, boring from within the political process, the bureaucracies, the courts, the media, academia, the cultural sewers that spew out "entertainment", and all the other critical points of entry into the machinery of mass psychological manipulation, then political power, then usurpation, then tyranny. And which subversives are now using a false concern for "homeland security" as their excuse to amass for themselves ever-increasing, ever-more-abusive powers in its name.[1]

The right of the people to own and use guns cannot be violated, but neither can the corresponding responsibility of Militia duty be merely disregarded, if a proper constitutional understanding of the right to "keep and bear Arms" is to be accepted and practiced.

---

1 Dr. Edwin Vieira, Jr., "Are You Doing Your Constitutional Duty For "Homeland Security"? Part 2, NewsWithViews.com [Internet]; available from http://newswithviews.com/Vieira/edwin12.htm; accessed 21 July 2008.

CHAPTER 11: THE SENATE AND THE SEVENTEENTH AMENDMENT

*The proposed Constitution, so far from implying an abolition of the State Governments, makes them
constituent parts of the national sovereignty by allowing them a direct representation in the Senate,
and leaves in their possession certain exclusive and very important portions of sovereign power.*
— *Alexander Hamilton,* The Federalist Papers (#9).

According to the Constitution, "all legislative Powers herein granted shall be
vested in a Congress of the United States, which shall consist of a Senate and House
of Representatives" (Article I, section 1). The House of Representatives was to represent the People of the nation, whereas the Senate was to represent the States, which
were viewed as sovereign political entities in themselves. Thus, the People chose the
Representatives, but the Senators were chosen by the State legislatures. The Constitution explains it this way:

> The House of Representatives shall be composed of Members chosen every sec-
> ond Year by the People of the several States.... (Article I, section 2, clause 1).

> The Senate of the United States shall be composed of two Senators from each
> State, chosen by the Legislature thereof, for six Years; and each Senator shall
> have one Vote (Article I, section 3, clause 1).

Although there were important differences between the two bodies, the Senate
represents the unicameral Congress under the Articles of Confederation as it has
been preserved under the Constitution. Article V of the Articles describes the requirements of the members (delegates) in Congress as follows:

> For the most convenient management of the general interests of the United
> States, delegates shall be annually appointed in such manner as the legislatures
> of each State shall direct, to meet in Congress on the first Monday in November,
> in every year, with a power reserved to each State to recall its delegates, or any
> of them, at any time within the year, and to send others in their stead for the
> remainder of the year.

> No State shall be represented in Congress by less than two, nor more than seven
> members; and no person shall be capable of being a delegate for more than three

years in any term of six years; nor shall any person, being a delegate, be capable of holding any office under the United States, for which he, or another for his benefit, receives any salary, fees or emolument of any kind.

Each State shall maintain its own delegates in a meeting of the States, and while they act as members of the committee of the States.

In determining questions in the United States in Congress assembled, each State shall have one vote.

The major differences between the Senate and the unicameral Congress of the Articles were that there are only two Senators for each state under the Constitution,[1] whereas there could be as many as seven, but no less than two members in the Congress under the Articles. In addition, under the Constitution each Senator has one vote, whereas under the Articles each state had one vote, regardless of how many members may have attended. Finally, the term of office for a Senator is different from that of the member of Congress under the Articles. Senators are chosen for six years, although because of the initial division of the first Senators into three groups, one-third face possible loss of office every two years.[2] On the other hand, under the Articles "no person shall be capable of being a delegate for more than three years in any term of six years."

The reason why the unicameral Congress under the Articles of Confederation was preserved as the Senate under the Constitution was due to a compromise between the large states and the small states. The small states were concerned that if representation in Congress were based solely on population, the large states, because of their larger populations, would have more representatives and thus more political power in the legislature. Because of this concern, a compromise was reached in which the number of members in the House of Representatives would indeed be based on each state's population, which pleased the large states, but in the Senate, each state would have only two Senators regardless of the number of its inhabitants. Thus, in the Senate, at least there would be equal power politically and this state of affairs satisfied the small states.

It has been an accepted belief that in 1913 the Seventeenth Amendment supposedly gave the people of each state the power to elect their state's Senators and took the power to choose them away from the state legislatures. The Amendment reads as follows:

> The Senate of the United States shall be composed of two Senators from each State, elected by the people thereof, for six years; and each Senator shall have one vote. The electors in each State shall have the qualifications requisite for electors of the most numerous branch of the State legislatures.

---

1 According to W. Cleon Skousen, "there was never an extensive discussion on the number of Senators [at the Federal Convention of 1787]; their only concern was that the number be equal for each state." See W. Cleon Skousen, *The Making of America: The Substance and Meaning of the Constitution* (Washington, D. C.: The National Center for Constitutional Studies, 1985), 290.

2 "Immediately after they [the Senators] shall be assembled in Consequence of the first Election, they shall be divided as equally as may be into three Classes. The Seats of the Senators of the first Class shall be vacated at the Expiration of the second Year, of the second Class at the Expiration of the fourth Year, and the third Class at the Expiration of the sixth Year, so that one third may be chosen every second Year" (Article I, section 3, clause 2 of the Constitution).

When vacancies happen in the representation of any State in the Senate, the executive authority of such State shall issue writs of election to fill such vacancies: Provided, That the legislature of any State may empower the executive thereof to make temporary appointments until the people fill the vacancies by election as the legislature may direct.

This amendment shall not be so construed as to affect the election or term of any Senator chosen before it becomes valid as part of this Constitution.

Three primary reasons have been offered as to why the Seventeenth Amendment was proposed and supposedly ratified. One was the desire for more democracy. Even though the US government was created as a constitutional republic with *some* representative democracy, more of it began to be viewed as an improvement on the old system. This is the main reason why the Electoral College, in which the Electors originally chose the President independently of the people, has evolved into a system in which the people elect a slate of Electors who simply validate the people's choice. Thus, taking the power of electing Senators away from the state legislatures and giving it to the people was viewed as an important reform.

Another reason was that bribery in the state legislatures was often suspected when it came to choosing Senators. Indeed, the Senate had actually investigated several such cases of alleged bribery since its creation.[1] The problem could only be corrected, so it was claimed, by giving the power to elect Senators to the people instead of the state legislatures.

Finally, there were frequent deadlocks in the state legislatures over the choice of Senators, which in some cases, actually caused states to be without Senators for periods of time. In 1866, Congress passed a law in accordance with the power given to it in Article I, section 4, clause 1 of the Constitution,[2] which mandated that a majority in the state legislatures elect Senators instead of a plurality. Apparently, this law made the deadlock problem even worse,[3] so a constitutional amendment was called for to correct the problem once and for all. Todd Zywicki, a law professor at George Mason University, who has done extensive research on the Seventeenth Amendment, believes that the problem of deadlocks could have been corrected in a less complicated manner than by a constitutional amendment. In his view, "amending that [1866] statute to allow for election by a plurality or requiring run-offs would have eliminated the deadlock problem."[4]

Why did the delegates at the Federal Convention of 1787 give the power to elect Senators to the state legislatures anyway? First, it had to do with the idea of a bicam-

---

1 According to Todd Zywicki, law professor at George Mason University, "in the first seventy years that the Constitution was in force, the Senate investigated only one case of election bribery. The next thirty-five years saw nine such cases" (pg. 1022) Todd J. Zywicki, "Senators and Special Interests: A Public Choice Analysis of the Seventeenth Amendment," Professor Todd J. Zywicki's Publications [Internet]; available from http://mason.gmu. edu/~tzywick2/Oregon%20Senators.pdf; accessed 21 July 2008.

2 Article I, section 4, clause 1 of the Constitution provides the following information: "The Times, Places and Manner of holding Elections for Senators and Representatives, shall be prescribed in each State by the Legislature thereof; *but the Congress may at any time by Law make or alter such Regulations, except as to the Places of chusing [sic] Senators*" (italics mine).

3 According to Todd Zywicki, "until about 1860, the system of direct election by state legislatures worked effectively" (pg. 1021) Todd J. Zywicki, "Senators and Special Interests: A Public Choice Analysis of the Seventeenth Amendment," Professor Todd J. Zywicki's Publications [Internet]; available from http://mason.gmu.edu/~tzywick2/Oregon%20 Senators.pdf; accessed 21 July 2008.

4 Ibid (pg. 1025).

eral legislature, which is a legislature consisting of two separate chambers. However, to produce the needed result each chamber had to be different from the other in significant ways. James Madison explains this idea in *The Federalist Papers* (#51) *as* follows:

> In republican government, the legislative authority necessarily predominates. The remedy for this inconveniency is to divide the legislature into *different branches*; and to render them, by *different modes of election* and *different principles of action, as little connected with each other as the nature of their common functions and their common dependence on the society will admit* (italics mine).

He says much the same thing in *The Federalist Papers* (#62):

> It is a misfortune incident to republican government, though in a less degree than to other governments, that those who administer it may forget their obligations to their constituents, and prove unfaithful to their important trust. In this point of view, *a senate, as a second branch of the legislative assembly, distinct from, and dividing the power with, a first*, must be in all cases a salutary check on the government. It doubles the security to the people, by requiring the concurrence of *two distinct bodies* in schemes of usurpation or perfidy, where the ambition or corruption of one would otherwise be sufficient (italics mine).

Second, it had to do with the idea of federalism, which Dictionary.com defines as "a system of government in which power is divided between a central authority and constituent political units." The states, being the "constituent political units," needed to be represented in some manner in the federal government in order to protect their own particular interests. As the people were represented in the Houses of Representatives, so the states were represented in the Senate. At the Massachusetts Convention to ratify the Constitution in 1788, Fisher Ames, the noted federalist and statesman, explained this idea as follows:

> The state governments are essential parts of the system.... The *senators* represent the *sovereignty of the states*; in the other house, individuals are represented. The Senate may not originate bills. It need not be said that they are principally to direct the affairs of wars and treaties. They are in the quality of ambassadors of the states, and it will not be denied that some permanency in their office is necessary to a discharge of their duty. Now, if they were chosen yearly, how could they perform their trust? If they would be brought by that means more immediately under the influence of the people, then they will represent the state legislatures less, and become the representatives of individuals. This belongs to the other house. The absurdity of this, and its repugnancy to the federal principles of the Constitution, will appear more fully, by supposing that they are to be chosen by the people at large.... But whom, in that case, would they represent?—Not the legislatures of the states, but the people. This would totally obliterate the federal features of the Constitution. What would become of the state governments, and on whom would devolve the duty of defending them against the encroachments of the federal government? A consolidation of the states would ensue, which, it is conceded, would subvert the new Constitution.... Too much provision cannot be made against a consolidation. The state governments represent the wishes, and feelings, and local interests, of the people. They are the safeguard and ornament of the Constitution; they will protract the period of our liberties; they will afford a shelter against the abuse of power, and will be the natural avengers of our violated rights.[1]

---

1 Debate in Massachusetts Ratifying Convention, 19 January 1788, The Founders' Constitution [Internet]; available from http://press-pubs.uchicago.edu/founders/documents/a1_3_1-2s10.html; accessed 21 July 2008.

What have been the consequences of giving the power to elect Senators to the people of the states and taking it away from the state legislatures? First, the election of Senators in this fashion distorts the whole idea of a bicameral legislature with two *different* houses by turning the Senate into little more than a second House of Representatives. The members of both Houses are now elected by precisely the same constituents and in precisely the same manner. How can each House be an effective check on the other, when they resemble each other so closely?

Second, no body exists in the federal government any longer that can be a staunch protector of the rights of the states. Author and columnist, Bruce Bartlett, explained it very clearly this way:

> When senators represented states as states, rather than just being super House members as they are now, they zealously protected states' rights. This term became discredited during the civil rights struggle of the 1960s as a code word for racism — allowing Southern states to resist national pressure to integrate. But clearly this is an aberration. States obviously have interests that may conflict with federal priorities on a wide variety of issues that defy easy ideological classification.[1]

Finally, John Dean, FindLaw columnist and former Counsel to the President of the United States, offered the interesting observation that "before the Seventeenth Amendment the federal government remained stable and small. Following the Amendment's adoption it has grown dramatically." He further elaborates on his observation in this way:

> The conventional wisdom is that it was FDR's New Deal that radically increased the size and power of federal government. But scholars make a convincing case that this conventional wisdom is wrong, and that instead, it was the Seventeenth Amendment (along with the Sixteenth Amendment, which created federal income tax and was also adopted in 1913) that was the driving force behind federal expansion.[2]

The Seventeenth Amendment was declared ratified by a Proclamation issued by Secretary of State, William Jennings Bryan, on May 31, 1913. At the time, there were 48 states in the Union and, since Article V of the Constitution requires approval by three-fourths of the states for ratification, it was assumed that 36 states were needed for ratification. In his Proclamation, the Secretary of State declared that the Amendment had been ratified by 36 states. Subsequent to the issuance of the Proclamation, one additional state (Louisiana) ratified the Amendment and another (Utah) rejected it. The ten remaining states took no action at all on the Amendment. Thus, 37 states in all supposedly ratified it. Below is a transcribed copy of this Proclamation (Certificate of Ratification):

William Jennings Bryan,
Secretary Of State Of The United States Of America.

To all to Whom these Presents may come, Greeting:

Know Ye that, the Congress of the United States at the second Session, sixty-second Congress, in the year one thousand nine hundred and twelve, passed a Resolution in the words and figures following: to wit —

---

1 Bruce Bartlett, "The problem with the 17th," Citizen Review Online [Internet]; available from http://www.citizenreviewonline.org/may2004/problem.htm; accessed 21 July 2008.

2 John W. Dean, "The Seventeenth Amendment: Should It Be Repealed?" FindLaw [Internet]; available from http://writ.corporate.findlaw.com/dean/20020913.html; accessed 21 July 2008.

"Joint Resolution

Proposing an amendment to the Constitution providing that Senators shall be elected by the people of the several States of the United States.

Resolved, by the Senate and House of Representatives of the United States of America in Congress assembled (two-thirds of each House concurring therein), That in lieu of the first paragraph of section three of Article I of the Constitution of the United States, and in lieu of so much of paragraph two of the same section as relates to the filling of vacancies, the following article be proposed as an amendment to the Constitution, which shall be valid to all intents and purposes as a part of the Constitution when ratified by the legislatures of three-fourths of the several States:

'The Senate of the United States shall be composed of two Senators from each State, elected by the people thereof, for six years; and each Senator shall have one vote. The electors in each State shall have the qualifications requisite for electors of the most numerous branch of the State legislatures.

When vacancies happen in the representation of any State in the Senate, the executive authority of such State shall issue writs of election to fill such vacancies: Provided, That the legislature of any State may empower the executive thereof to make temporary appointment[s] until the people fill the [v]acancies by election as the legislature may direct.

'This amendment shall not be so construed as to affect the election or term of any Senator chosen before it becomes valid as part of this Constitution.' "

And, further, that it appears from official documents on file in this Department that the Amendment to the Constitution of the United States proposed as aforesaid has been ratified by the Legislatures of the States of Massachusetts, Arizona, Minnesota, New York, Kansas, Oregon, North Carolina, California, Michigan, Idaho, West Virginia, Nebraska, Iowa, Montana, Texas, Washington, Wyoming, Colorado, Illinois, North Dakota, Nevada, Vermont, Maine, New Hampshire, Oklahoma, Ohio, South Dakota, Indiana, Missouri, New Mexico, New Jersey, Tennessee, Arkansas, Connecticut, Pennsylvania, and Wisconsin.

And, further, that the States whose Legislatures have so ratified the said proposed Amendment, constitute three-fourths of the whole number of States in the United States.

Now therefore, be it known that I, William Jennings Bryan, Secretary of State of the United States, by virtue and in pursuance of Section 205 of the Revised Statutes of the United States, do hereby certify that the Amendment aforesaid has become valid to all intents and purposes as a part of the Constitution of the United States.

In Testimony Whereof, I have hereunto set my hand and caused the seal of the Department of State to be affixed.

Done at the city of Washington this thirty first day of May in the year of our Lord one thousand nine hundred and thirteen, and of the Independence of the United States of America the one hundred and thirty-seventh.

[Signed] William Jennings Bryan[1]

---

1 Bill Benson, *Proof the 17th Amendment Was Not Ratified* (Constitutional Research Associates, 1985).

Let us review briefly the amendment process as described in Article V of the Constitution. I quote the relevant portion of the paragraph below:

> The Congress, whenever two thirds of both Houses shall deem it necessary, shall propose Amendments to this Constitution, or, on the Application of the Legislatures of two thirds of the several States, shall call a Convention for proposing Amendments, which, in either Case, shall be valid to all Intents and Purposes, as Part of this Constitution, when ratified by the Legislatures of three fourths of the several States, or by Conventions in three fourths thereof, as the one or the other Mode of Ratification may be proposed by the Congress.

In the case of the Seventeenth Amendment, two thirds of each house voted to propose the Amendment and Congress decided that the ratification method to be followed was the one requiring the approval of three fourths of the state legislatures as is stated in the joint resolution passed by the 62nd Congress in 1912 and quoted in the above Proclamation.

However, Article V, after describing the amendment process, provides a very important restriction on the process: "Provided ... that no State, without its Consent, shall be deprived of its equal Suffrage in the Senate." Now as stated above, one state rejected it and ten states took no action at all on the Seventeenth Amendment. Therefore, these eleven states clearly did not give their "consent ... [to] be deprived of ... [their] equal Suffrage in the Senate." Because of this restriction on the amendment process, the only way the Seventeenth Amendment could have been ratified is *if all forty-eight states approved it and thus consented to lose their vote in the Senate.* The three-fourths requirement cannot hold here, because its means that some states (in this case eleven states) did not give their permission to lose their votes.

Of course, some will say that none of the states really lost their vote in the Senate, because the Seventeenth Amendment just transferred it from the state legislatures to the people of the states. A statement such as this one merely reveals a person's lack of knowledge about the precise meanings of the terms "states" and "people" in the Constitution. Let me try to elucidate these meanings with contractual terms.

Two separate and distinct parties approved the Contract, i.e., the Constitution. *Party A* is "We the People," as is stated in the Preamble:

> We the People of the United States, in Order to form a more perfect Union, establish Justice, insure domestic Tranquility, provide for the common defense, promote the general Welfare, and secure the Blessings of Liberty to ourselves and our Posterity, do ordain and establish this Constitution for the United States of America.

Party B is the "States," as is acknowledged in Article VII, clause 1:

> The Ratification of the Conventions of nine States, shall be sufficient for the Establishment of this Constitution between the States so ratifying the Same.

Party A elects members to the House of Representatives to represent its interests and *Party B* elects members to the Senate via the state legislatures to represent its interests.

In order for any subsidiary contract (i.e., a bill) to have legal force (i.e., become law), two signatures — that of *Party A* and *Party B* — are required on the document. *Party A* supplies its signature through its agent in the House of Representatives, the Speaker of the House, and *Party B* through its agent in the Senate, the President of the Senate. Without these two signatures, the contract (i.e., the bill) is invalid and is unenforceable as a legal document.[1]

Thus, the term "State" found in the sentence "no State, without its Consent, shall be deprived of its equal Suffrage in the Senate" can only refer to states as sovereign political entities and can in no way refer in some nebulous fashion to the *people* of the state.

A very important question now needs to be asked: "If the Seventeenth Amendment were indeed ratified, who would represent *Party B* (i.e., the States) in the Constitution (i.e., the Contract)? The answer is: nobody. *Party B* would be left out of the Contract altogether and the consequences of this state of affairs were noted earlier in this chapter.

Now even *if* we were still to accept the requirement that only three-fourths of the state legislatures needed to approve the Seventeenth Amendment, the necessary number of states would still not have done so. Yes, you read the sentence correctly. When Bill Benson did his research on the Sixteenth Amendment in 1984, he also discovered that the Seventeenth Amendment had the same type of problems regarding its ratification, as did the former. The Sixteenth Amendment and Bill Benson's research on it were already discussed in Chapter 6.

It is very important to remember that the state legislatures only vote to approve or reject the proposed amendment that is passed by Congress. They are not authorized to change it at all. Therefore, each state legislature must be provided with an exact copy of the proposed amendment to vote on one way or the other. With this requirement in mind, on May 15, 1912 the Secretary of State, William Jennings Bryan, sent a certified copy of the joint resolution passed by Congress to the Governors of the states. The joint resolution is quoted in the Proclamation (Certificate of Ratification) issued by the Secretary of State on May 31, 1913, which was quoted above.

Enclosed along with the certified copy of the joint resolution was the following introductory letter:

> I have the honor to enclose a certified copy of a Resolution of Congress, entitled "Joint Resolution Proposing an amendment to the Constitution providing that Senators shall be elected by the people of the several States." with the request that you cause the same to be submitted to the Legislature of your State for such action as may be had, and that a certified copy of such action be communicated to the Secretary of State, as required by Section 205, Revised Statutes of the United States. (See overleaf.) [Note: Reference here is to R. S. Sec. 205 which is quoted infra.]

> An acknowledgment of the receipt of this communication is requested.

Section 205 of the Revised Statutes provides:

> Whenever official notice is received at the Department of State that any amendment proposed to the Constitution of the United States has been adopted, according to the provisions of the Constitution, the Secretary of State shall forthwith cause the amendment to be published in the newspapers authorized to promulgate the laws, with his certificate, specifying the States by which the

---

1 Both houses are required to approve all bills. This fact is clearly acknowledged in Article I, section 7, clause 2: "Every Bill which shall have passed the House of Representatives and the Senate, shall, before it becomes a Law, be presented to the President of the United States." The President's signature is not always required to pass a bill, because a presidential veto can be overcome by a two-thirds vote of both houses.

same may have been adopted, and that the same has become valid, to all intents and purposes, as a part of the Constitution of the United States.[1]

As explained in Chapter 6, it was the responsibility of the Secretary of State to obtain a proper certified copy of the state legislature's decision on the Amendment and this is precisely what he requested from them in his introductory letter sent with the certified copy of the joint resolution (quoted above). If anything in a state's submittal is judged missing, unclear, contradictory, or erroneous, the Secretary of State must immediately inform the Governor, asking him for a proper certified copy of the state's decision. Once the new submittal is deemed a proper certified copy, he will be able to include the state as having ratified the amendment when he finally issues his Proclamation. In addition, it cannot be overly stressed that the amendment approved by the state legislature must be an *exact* copy of the amendment proposed by Congress.

As was stated earlier in this chapter, 37 states supposedly ratified the Seventeenth Amendment, one rejected it, and ten took no action at all on it. Since there were only 48 states in the Union at the time, if we accept the three-fourths requirement, 36 states would be required to ratify the Amendment. Should it be shown that at least two of the states that supposedly ratified it in fact did not, then only 35 states would have approved it and consequently the Seventeenth Amendment would not have been constitutionally ratified. Let us attempt to reduce the number of states that ratified the Amendment one state at a time by examining some of the evidence discovered by Bill Benson.[2]

- *Minnesota.* Secretary of State Bryan did not receive a proper certified copy of the state legislature's decision on the Amendment, as he himself requested in his May 15, 1912 introductory letter sent with the certified copy of the joint resolution passed by Congress (quoted above). In a memorandum sent to the Secretary of State on May 10, 1913 from the Office of the Solicitor, the following notation is made regarding the so-called "official notice" that the Secretary of State received from Minnesota:

  [A] Copy of [the] Resolution [was] not received by the Department. [The] Secretary of State of Minnesota notified [the] Department that [the] legislature had ratified proposed amendment.

Further on, the same memorandum gives the following information:

  The Department has not received a copy of the Resolution passed by the Legislature of the State of Minnesota ratifying the amendment proposed by Congress but the Secretary of the State of Minnesota has officially notified the Department that the Legislature of that State has passed a Resolution ratifying the proposed amendment. It is believed that this meets fully the requirement with reference to receipt of "official notice" contained in Section 205, Revised Statutes o the United States (quoted supra page 20) and that Minnesota should therefore be numbered with the States ratifying the amendment.

How Secretary of State Bryan could actually accept anything else but a proper certified copy of the state legislature's decision on the Amendment is remarkable. Remember, we are discussing no small issue here, but the supposed ratification of a proposed amendment to the Constitution of the United States. The tally now is only 36 states — just enough to ratify the Amendment.

---

1 Bill Benson, *Proof the 17th Amendment Was Not Ratified* (Constitutional Research Associates, 1985).
2 Ibid.

- *Montana.* The proposed Amendment is shown below, the errors italicized, and what was actually transcribed in the state's submittal placed in brackets:

  The Senate of the United States shall be composed of two Senators from each State, elected by the people thereof, for six years; and each Senator shall have one vote. The electors in each State shall have the qualifications requisite for electors of the most numerous branch of the State legislatures.

  When vacancies happen in the representation of any State in the Senate, the executive authority of *such* [each] State shall issue writs of election to fill such vacancies: Provided, That the legislature of any State may empower the executive thereof to make temporary appointments until the people fill the vacancies by election as the legislature may direct.

  This amendment shall not be so construed as to *affect* [effect] the election or term of any Senator chosen before it becomes valid as part of this Constitution.

Although the word "effect" instead of "affect" was transcribed in the last paragraph of the proposed Amendment, the other error is more serious. Instead of transcribing the correct word "such" before the word "State" in the second paragraph, the word "each" was transcribed in its place. As anyone can see, the word "each" completely changes the intended meaning of the paragraph. It is supposed to mean that if vacancies occur in a state's representation in the Senate, *the governor of that state* is required to "issue writs of election to fill such vacancies." However, with the word change it gives the impression that when vacancies occur in a state, *all the state governors* are required to "issue writs of election to fill such vacancies." Secretary of State Bryan should have requested a proper certified copy from the Governor, but he did nothing of the kind. The tally now is only 35 states. *It can now be asserted that the Seventeenth Amendment was not constitutionally ratified.* And there are five more states with faulty ratifications.

- *Tennessee.* Tennessee made the same major error in its submittal as Montana. It transcribed the word "each" instead of "such" before the word "State" in the second paragraph of the proposed Amendment.
- *New Jersey.* The submittal from New Jersey had various minor errors of capitalization and punctuation. However, the major error can be found in the first paragraph of the proposed Amendment. I quote that paragraph below, italicize the location of the error, and place in brackets what was actually transcribed in the submittal:

  The Senate of the United States shall be composed of two Senators from each State, elected by the people thereof, for six years; and each Senator shall have one vote. The *electors* [election] in each State shall have the qualifications requisite for electors of the most numerous branch of the State legislatures.

This change completely distorts the meaning of the last sentence of the paragraph. The actual meaning is that the voters who elect the Senators must have the same "qualifications" (i.e., credentials, like age for example) as the voters who elect members to the largest chamber of the state legislature. This same sentence can be found in Article I, section 2, clause 1 of the Constitution, which is intended to describe the qualifications of the voters who elect members to the House of Representatives.

- *New York.* The submittal from New York had various minor errors of capitalization and punctuation. Also, "whenever" was transcribed for "when" in the second paragraph of the proposed Amendment. However, the major error is the same as that of New Jersey. I quote the applicable paragraphs of the Amendment below and note the locations of the errors and the actual transcriptions in the same manner as above:

The Senate of the United States shall be composed of two Senators from each State, elected by the people thereof, for six years; and each Senator shall have one vote. The *electors* [election] in each State shall have the qualifications requisite for electors of the most numerous branch of the State legislatures.

When [Whenever] vacancies happen in the representation of any State in the Senate, the executive authority of such State shall issue writs of election to fill such vacancies: Provided, That the legislature of any State may empower the executive thereof to make temporary appointments until the people fill the vacancies by election as the legislature may direct.

- *New Mexico.* The submittal from New Mexico had various minor errors of capitalization. Other minor errors are that "the" is transcribed for "such" in the second paragraph of the proposed Amendment and "effect" is transcribed for "affect" in the last paragraph. However, the major error can be found in the last paragraph. I quote the relevant paragraphs of the Amendment below, italicize the locations of the errors, and place in brackets what was actually transcribed in the submittal:

When vacancies happen in the representation of any State in the Senate, the executive authority of *such* [the] State shall issue writs of election to fill such vacancies: Provided, That the legislature of any State may empower the executive thereof to make temporary appointments until the people fill the vacancies by election as the legislature may direct.

This amendment shall not be so construed as to *affect* [effect] the election *or* [of] term of any Senator chosen before it becomes valid as part of this Constitution.

Although at first it may seem like a minor error, what does an "election *of* term" mean? It means nothing, because it is nothing more than gibberish. Surely, the Secretary of State should have requested a proper certified copy from the Governor.

- *Washington.* The submittal from Washington had various minor errors of capitalization and punctuation. However, the major error can be found in the first paragraph of the proposed Amendment. I quote that paragraph, italicize the location of the error, and place in brackets what was actually transcribed in the submittal:

The Senate of the United States shall be composed of two Senators *from* [for] each State, elected by the people thereof, for six years; and each Senator shall have one vote. The electors in each State shall have the qualifications requisite for electors of the most numerous branch of the State legislatures.

This error significantly changes the meaning of the first sentence of the paragraph. The word "from" could be understood to mean that the Senators must be residents of the particular state they are representing. On the other hand, the word "for" could be understood to mean that the Senators do not have to be residents of the state at all. Now even though Article I, section 3, clause 3 of the Constitution states "no Person shall be a Senator ... who shall not, when elected, be an Inhabitant of that State for which he shall be chosen," to have accepted anything other than a proper certified copy can only be considered ineptness of the highest degree.

Based on all that has been discussed above, the bottom line is that the Seventeenth Amendment was not constitutionally ratified and cannot therefore be a part of the "Authentic Constitution". This means that from the time the first Senators elected by the people entered into office until now, there has been no constitutional Senate in operation.

In a strictly legal sense, this fact constitutes an enormous problem, because it also means that any legislation or treaty approved by the Senate is without legal validity. It also means that any ambassadors, Supreme Court judges, and other officials nominated by the President and approved by the Senate have no real authority to be in office in the first place.

If we took action based solely on the legal reality of the situation, the government would be at a standstill for a significant period until a new Senate could be chosen by the state legislatures. Then, new laws and treaties would have to be passed and new appointments to government offices would have to be made. It would be a long and difficult process and potentially dangerous, since we would be vulnerable to attack.

Fortunately, the law of self-preservation, which we discussed in earlier chapters, must come to the rescue here. This law takes precedence over any written law. As Thomas Jefferson said:

> A strict observance of the written laws is doubtless *one* of the high duties of a good citizen, but it is not the *highest*. The law of necessity, of self-preservation, of saving our country when in danger, are of higher obligation. To lose our country by a scrupulous adherence to written law, would be to lose the law itself, with life, liberty, property, and all those who are enjoying them with us; thus absurdly sacrificing the end to the means ... (Thomas Jefferson, Letter to J. B. Colvin, Sept. 20, 1810).

The Senate must be returned to its original constitutional form as soon as possible, which is that Senators must again be chosen by state legislatures. However, based on the law of self-preservation, we need not scrap laws, treaties, and appointments *that are in every other sense proper* simply because an improperly constituted Senate approved them. If we do, we are as Jefferson stated above, "absurdly sacrificing the end to the means...."

CHAPTER 12: THE BILL OF RIGHTS AND THE FOURTEENTH AMENDMENT

Clearly ... the Fourteenth Amendment was never constitutionally ratified, even if it had been constitutionally proposed.
— *Forrest McDonald, Professor of History (1991).*[1]

What we commonly called the Bill of Rights is actually the first ten Amendments to the Constitution that were ratified by the states on December 15, 1791. Actually, twelve amendments were submitted to the states legislatures for their decision, but two of them that had to do with congressional representation and congressional pay were not ratified. However, the Amendment on congressional pay that was rejected as a part of the Bill of Rights was finally ratified when Michigan voted affirmatively on May 7, 1992. It became the Twenty-Seventh Amendment to the Constitution. Let me quote it below:

No law, varying the compensation for the services of the Senators and Representatives, shall take effect, until an election of Representatives shall have intervened.

The ten Amendments that became the Bill of Rights are as follows:

Amendment I

Congress shall make no law respecting an establishment of religion, or prohibiting the free exercise thereof; or abridging the freedom of speech, or of the press; or the right of the people peaceably to assemble, and to petition the Government for a redress of grievances.

Amendment II

A well regulated Militia, being necessary to the security of a free State, the right of the people to keep and bear Arms, shall not be infringed.

Amendment III

---

1 Forrest McDonald, "Was the Fourteenth Amendment Constitutionally Adopted?" *Georgia Journal of Southern Legal History* 1 (Spring/Summer 1991): 18.

No Soldier shall, in time of peace be quartered in any house, without the consent of the Owner, nor in time of war, but in a manner to be prescribed by law.

Amendment IV

The right of the people to be secure in their persons, houses, papers, and effects, against unreasonable searches and seizures, shall not be violated, and no Warrants shall issue, but upon probable cause, supported by Oath or affirmation, and particularly describing the place to be searched, and the persons or things to be seized.

Amendment V

No person shall be held to answer for a capital, or otherwise infamous crime, unless on a presentment or indictment of a Grand Jury, except in cases arising in the land or naval forces, or in the Militia, when in actual service in time of War or public danger; nor shall any person be subject for the same offense to be twice put in jeopardy of life or limb; nor shall be compelled in any criminal case to be a witness against himself, nor be deprived of life, liberty, or property, without due process of law; nor shall private property be taken for public use, without just compensation.

Amendment VI

In all criminal prosecutions, the accused shall enjoy the right to a speedy and public trial, by an impartial jury of the State and district wherein the crime shall have been committed, which district shall have been previously ascertained by law,[1] and to be informed of the nature and cause of the accusation; to be confronted with the witnesses against him; to have compulsory process for obtaining witnesses in his favor, and to have the assistance of counsel for his defense.

Amendment VII

In Suits at common law, where the value in controversy shall exceed twenty dollars, the right of trial by jury shall be preserved, and no fact tried by a jury, shall be otherwise reexamined in any Court of the United States, than according to the rules of the common law.

Amendment VIII

Excessive bail shall not be required, nor excessive fines imposed, nor cruel and unusual punishments inflicted.

Amendment IX

The enumeration in the Constitution, of certain rights, shall not be construed to deny or disparage others retained by the people.

Amendment X

The powers not delegated to the United States by the Constitution, nor prohibited by it to the States, are reserved to the States respectively, or to the people.

The purpose of proposing these Amendments is clearly described in the introductory section preceding their insertion in the Constitution. The applicable portion says:

> The Conventions of a number of the States, having at the time of their adopting the Constitution, expressed a desire, in order to prevent misconstruction or

---

1 See also Article III, section 2, clause 3: "The Trial of all Crimes, except in Cases of Impeachment; shall be by Jury; and such Trial shall be held in the State where the said Crimes shall have been committed; but when not committed within any State, the Trial shall be at such Place or Places as the Congress may by Law have directed."

abuse of its powers, that further declaratory and restrictive clauses should be added: And as extending the ground of public confidence in the Government, will best ensure the beneficent ends of its institution.

Thus, the Bill of Rights was intended to guarantee the people of the United States certain rights *by placing additional restrictions on what the federal government could do.*

Unfortunately, the federal government has been seriously chipping away at the Bill of Rights, especially since 9/11. Entire books have been written on this subject alone, including Judge Andrew P. Napolitano: *Constitutional Chaos: What Happens When the Government Breaks Its Own Laws* (Nashville: Thomas Nelson, 2006), *The Constitution in Exile: How the Federal Government Has Seized Power by Rewriting the Supreme Law of the Land* (Nashville: Nelson Current, 2006), *A Nation of Sheep* (Nashville: Thomas Nelson, 2007), and C. William Michaels: *No Greater Threat–America After September 11 and the Rise of a National Security State* (New York: Algora Publishing 2005).

The Bill of Rights was in no way meant to apply to the states. Besides, each state had its own enumeration of rights included in its Constitution, which had precisely the same purpose at the state level, as the Bill of Rights had at the federal level.[1]

The various state enumerations of rights are not exactly the same, and in some cases have significant differences, but the Founders believed it should be this way. They did not advocate the idea of one Bill of Rights being uniform throughout the nation. This kind of national homogeny is a modern idea. They expected that a state's Constitution and laws would support local viewpoints and lifestyles. If you feel inclined to do so, you can review all the state Constitutions by going to the "Barefoot's World Links" web site.[2]

The principle that the Bill of Rights applied only to the federal government and had no application to the states remained in effect until the supposed ratification of the Fourteenth Amendment on July 9, 1868. A Proclamation issued by the Secretary of State, William H. Seward, on July 28, 1868, declared the ratification to be so.[3] This is the entire Amendment:

> *Section 1.* All persons born or naturalized in the United States, and subject to the jurisdiction thereof, are citizens of the United States and of the State wherein they reside. No State shall make or enforce any law which shall abridge the privileges or immunities of citizens of the United States; nor shall any State deprive any person of life, liberty, or property, without due process of law; nor deny to any person within its jurisdiction the equal protection of the laws.

---

1 The Commonwealth of Massachusetts has the oldest Constitution of any state or even any country. It went into effect in 1780 and was written chiefly by John Adams, the famous patriot, statesman, scholar, and second President of the United States.

2 Barefoot's World Links, [Internet]; available from http://www.barefootsworld.net/bftwl. html; accessed 21 July 2008.

3 No. 13, Certifying that the Fourteenth Amendment of the Constitution has been adopted, July 28, 1868, Library of Congress (Thomas) [Internet]; available from http://memory.loc. gov/cgi-bin/ampage?collId=llsl&fileName=015/llsl015.db&recNum=741; accessed 21 July 2008. Actually, the Secretary of State issued a Proclamation on July 20, 1868 declaring that the Fourteenth Amendment had been ratified. See No. 11 — Certifying that the fourteenth amendment has been adopted, if, &c., July 20, 1868, Library of Congress (Thomas) [Internet]; available from http://memory.loc.gov/cgi-bin/ampage?collId=llsl&fileName=015/ llsl015.db&recNum=739; accessed 21 July 2008. However, Congress, not being satisfied with the ambiguous wording of the Proclamation, passed a concurrent resolution on July 21, 1868 that declared the Fourteenth Amendment to be ratified. This resolution is quoted in the July 28, 1868 Proclamation. Apparently, the Secretary of State issued the revised Proclamation of July 28, 1868 in order to placate Congress.

Section 2. Representatives shall be apportioned among the several States according to their respective numbers, counting the whole number of persons in each State, excluding Indians not taxed. But when the right to vote at any election for the choice of electors for President and Vice President of the United States, Representatives in Congress, the Executive and Judicial officers of a State, or the members of the Legislature thereof, is denied to any of the male inhabitants of such State, being twenty-one years of age, and citizens of the United States, or in any way abridged, except for participation in rebellion, or other crime, the basis of representation therein shall be reduced in the proportion which the number of such male citizens shall bear to the whole number of male citizens twenty-one years of age in such State.

Section 3. No person shall be a Senator or Representative in Congress, or elector of President and Vice President, or hold any office, civil or military, under the United States, or under any State, who, having previously taken an oath, as a member of Congress, or as an officer of the United States, or as a member of any State legislature, or as an executive or judicial officer of any State, to support the Constitution of the United States, shall have engaged in insurrection or rebellion against the same, or given aid or comfort to the enemies thereof. But Congress may by a vote of two-thirds of each House, remove such disability.

Section 4. The validity of the public debt of the United States, authorized by law, including debts incurred for payment of pensions and bounties for services in suppressing insurrection or rebellion, shall not be questioned. But neither the United States nor any State shall assume or pay any debt or obligation incurred in aid of insurrection or rebellion against the United States, or any claim for the loss or emancipation of any slave; but all such debts, obligations and claims shall be held illegal and void.

Section 5. The Congress shall have power to enforce, by appropriate legislation, the provisions of this article.

Section 1 has enormous importance, which we will presently discuss. The most important part of Section 2 annuls the requirement in Article I, section 2, clause 2 of the Constitution that a slave must be counted as three-fifths of a person in the census that is undertaken every ten years. However, it is difficult to understand what relevance the three-fifths requirement can really have anyway, since the Thirteenth Amendment abolished slavery. Sections 3 and 4 have no relevance for us today. The purpose of Section 3 was to deny any future political office to those persons that first took an oath to support the Constitution, but later joined the Confederacy. The purpose of Section 4 was to declare the debt incurred by the United States in the Civil War legally binding, but the debt incurred by the Confederacy null and void. In addition, this same section absolved the United States from being held liable for any losses due to the emancipation of the slaves. Section 5 is important because it allows Congress to pass enabling legislation to enforce the other sections of the Amendment.

Section 1 of the Amendment is the most important section and there are really two main parts to it. The first part reads as follows:

All persons born or naturalized in the United States, and subject to the jurisdiction thereof, are citizens of the United States and of the State wherein they reside.

This part states that any person born on United States land is, with few exceptions, automatically a citizen of the United States and of the particular state he/she resides in. An exception would be a child born to a foreign diplomat, because the latter is not "subject to the jurisdiction ... [of the United States]." Apparently, even a child born in the United States to illegal immigrants is legally a citizen of the United States and the state of residence at the time of birth. However, can illegal immigrants and their offspring be considered "subject to the jurisdiction ... [of the United States]"? Apparently, they can be. For this reason, Congressman Ron Paul has proposed a constitutional amendment[1] that would allow citizenship only to children born in the United States who have at least one parent who is a US citizen or "a person who owes permanent allegiance to the United States."[2] This part of section 1 also mentions, "persons ... naturalized in the United States." Naturalization is the process by which a foreigner becomes a citizen.

The second part of section 1 reads as follows:

> No State shall make or enforce any law which shall abridge the privileges or immunities of citizens of the United States;[3] nor shall any State deprive any person of life, liberty, or property, without due process of law;[4] nor deny to any person within its jurisdiction the equal protection of the laws.

When the Union was formed under the Constitution, the states transferred certain specified powers to the federal government, but those powers not transferred were left to the states. The Tenth Amendment states this fact very clearly: "The powers not delegated to the United States by the Constitution, nor prohibited by it to the States, are reserved to the States respectively, or to the people." In fact, the term "state's rights" refers to the prerogative of each state to put into effect those powers that it retained. This part of section 1 has allowed the federal courts to intrude on these rights. In his excellent book, *The Politically Incorrect Guide™ to American History*, Thomas E. Woods, Jr., states, "an entire book needs to be written about the ways in which the Fourteenth Amendment has encroached upon the self-governing rights of the states."[5] The result of this process has been a gradual loss of state power and a centralization of power in the federal government.

Through a series of court decisions beginning in the 1940s, the US Supreme Court has allowed the Bill of Rights to become more and more applicable to the states. This process has been accomplished by means of the legal doctrine called "selective incorporation," which is that the rights secured by the first eight Amendments in the Bill of Rights are included or "incorporated" in the "due process" and "equal protection"

---

1 H. J. RES. 46, Proposing an amendment to the Constitution of the United States to deny United States citizenship to individuals born in the United States to parents who are neither United States citizens nor persons who owe permanent allegiance to the United States, Library of Congress, (Thomas) [Internet]; available from http://thomas.loc.gov/cgi-bin/bdquery/D?d110:46:./list/bss/d110HJ.lst::|TOM:/bss/110search.html|; accessed 21 July 2008.

2 The latter category ("a person who owes permanent allegiance to the United States") would include Lawful Permanent Residents (LPR's). Such persons, though not entitled to all the rights and privileges of a citizen, can live permanently in the United States, can take employment, and in due course receive an identification card commonly called a "green card" that must be kept in their possession at all times. Also included in this category would be those US Nationals, who are citizens of certain possessions of the United States.

3 This first statement is actually derived from Article IV, section 2, clause 1 of the Constitution: "The Citizens of each State shall be entitled to all Privileges and Immunities of Citizens in the several States."

4 This second statement is actually derived from a portion of the Fifth Amendment to the Constitution: "[No person shall] ... be deprived of life, liberty, or property, without due process of law."

5 Thomas E. Woods, Jr., *The Politically Incorrect Guide™ to American History* (Washington, DC: Regnery Publishing, 2004), 84.

clauses found in Section 1 of the Fourteenth Amendment. By utilizing this doctrine, the Supreme Court has over time been able to "incorporate" the entire First, Fourth, Sixth, Eighth, and portions of the Fifth and Seventh Amendments into the Fourteenth Amendment and use them against the rights retained by the states. However, as we have seen, each state has its own enumeration of rights, so what is the practical need of making the Bill of Rights applicable to the states? There is only one real purpose for selective incorporation: It is to consolidate power in Washington to the detriment of the states.

Indeed, there was a need after the Civil War and the abolishment of slavery to make certain that the emancipated slaves would be accorded the same rights and privileges as the white citizens. This could have been accomplished by assuring through a constitutional amendment that each state's enumeration of rights would be applied equally to all the citizens of that state, regardless of race. There was no need to apply the Bill of Rights to the states and thus begin the process of destroying the rights of the states, as the courts have done with the Fourteenth Amendment.

However, using the Fourteenth Amendment to centralize power in Washington has been in vain, since there is clear and indisputable evidence that the Fourteenth Amendment, like the Sixteenth and Seventeenth Amendments that were discussed in earlier chapters, was not properly ratified either. Let us look at the evidence.

First, it is important to state that after the Civil War the exact manner in which the reconstruction of the South should have proceeded was far from straightforward. The reason for the uncertainty was that the Founders never envisioned anything like a war between the states and consequently never addressed the issue in the Constitution. Two main plans were advanced to solve the problem. Because of the novel situation created by the Civil War, neither plan can be considered the right one.

Presidents Abraham Lincoln and then Andrew Johnson advocated the idea that the Confederate states, although they did rebel and voice their disloyalty for a time, never really left the Union, since the latter was considered indivisible. Under this plan, all that was necessary after the rebellion was put to an end was that the Confederate states should create new state governments composed of citizens loyal to the federal government. When this step was accomplished, they could then enter the Union with the same status they had before.

On the other hand, Congress under the control of the extreme wing of the Republican Party known as the Radical Republicans advocated the idea that the Confederate states did indeed sever their connection with the Union. As a result, they completely lost their previous status as states and were to be treated as mere conquered territories. The legal basis behind this plan was derived from the two clauses in Article IV, section 3 of the Constitution, which describe the authority of Congress to govern territories and to create new states from them. One source describes the congressional plan for reconstruction in the following manner:

> The Constitution gave Congress specific power to govern the territories; hence the South properly should be under direct congressional control. If Congress saw fit to do so, it could presumably govern the South indefinitely as unorganized territory. Moreover, Congress has sole power to create new states and admit them to the Union. Certainly the President could not do so. The presidential program was at best tentative; at worst, it was illegal. Since the congressional power to admit new states was discretionary, Congress could impose conditions precedent upon the new states prior to their admission. Conditions

imposed might well include disfranchisement of Confederate supporters, a guarantee of Negro civil rights, and Negro suffrage.[1]

The presidential plan was put into operation first. By July 1865, provisional governments were set up in all the ex-confederate States. The federal government must have had confidence in the legitimacy of these governments, since they were allowed to decide on whether or not to make the Thirteenth Amendment, which abolished slavery, a part of the Constitution. Let me quote this Amendment below:

> *Section 1.* Neither slavery nor involuntary servitude, except as a punishment for crime whereof the party shall have been duly convicted, shall exist within the United States, or any place subject to their jurisdiction.

> *Section 2.* Congress shall have power to enforce this article by appropriate legislation.

Since there were thirty-six states in the Union at the time, if we include the former Confederate states, twenty-seven states were required to ratify the Amendment.[2] Eight of twenty-seven states that did ratify it were the former Confederate states of Virginia, Louisiana, Tennessee, Arkansas, South Carolina, Alabama, North Carolina, and Georgia. Ratification was completed on December 6, 1865 and the Secretary of State, William H. Seward, issued a Proclamation declaring this to be the case on December 18, 1865.[3]

However, on December 5, 1865 the loyal states of the 39th Congress refused to seat the Senators and Representatives from the ex-Confederate states. The full complement of Senators was seventy-two, but twenty-two from the eleven former Confederate states were denied seats in the Senate. For the House, the full complement of Representatives was two hundred and forty, but fifty-eight from the ex-Confederate states were denied their seats as well. Thus, only the 50 Senators and 182 Representatives from the loyal states were allowed admittance into their respective chambers. By refusing to seat the members from the former Confederate states, the loyal states in Congress were essentially denying the legitimate status of their state governments. By this action, Congress also confirmed that the new governments set up under Presidents Lincoln and Johnson were indeed interim governments only.

If Congress had been consistent in its reasoning from this point on, it could have proceeded along one of two paths in the amendment ratification process. Path 1: Congress could continue to refuse seating the ex-confederate Senators and Representatives and allow only the loyal states to propose a constitutional amendment. Then only those state legislatures could vote to ratify it. Since there were twenty-six such states, including Nebraska, which was admitted into the Union as a new state on March 1, 1867, twenty would be required to ratify an amendment. Congress could then require the ex-Confederate states to accept a ratified amendment, as one of the conditions for attaining statehood once again. Path 2: Congress could have set up a process that would allow the ex-Confederate states to come back into the Union as

---

1 Alfred H. Kelly & Winfred A. Harbison, *The American Constitution: Its Origins and Development* (New York: W.W. Norton & Company, Inc., 1970), 455-6.

2 According to Article V of the Constitution, a proposed amendment must be "ratified by the Legislatures of three fourths of the several States, or by Conventions in three fourths thereof, as the one or the other Mode of Ratification may be proposed by the Congress."

3 No. 52, Certifying that the Thirteenth Amendment of the Constitution has been adopted, December 18, 1865, Liberty of Congress (Thomas) [Internet]; available from http://memory.loc.gov/cgi-bin/ampage?collId=llsl&fileName=013/llsl013.db&recNum=803; accessed 21 July 2008.

legitimate states. Then, when this was accomplished and the ex-confederate Senators and Representatives were properly seated in Congress, *all* the states could propose an amendment and their state legislatures could then vote to ratify it. In this case, since there would have been thirty-seven states, including Nebraska and the eleven former Confederate states, twenty-eight states would be required for ratification. Unfortunately, Congress chose a contradictory, and one must say the unconstitutional, route instead.

Two glaring examples of this inconsistency should be mentioned here. The first one is that Congress never even questioned the legality of the ratification of the Thirteenth Amendment, even though all eleven ex-confederate "states" were involved in the process and eight of them had actually approved it.

Fortunately, today, the Thirteenth Amendment can still be accepted as having been ratified because the inclusion of the ex-Confederate states really did not affect its ratification. There were twenty-five legitimate states in the Union at the time, so nineteen would have been required to ratify it, and this is precisely the number of legitimate states that did approve it.[1] Thus, the Amendment was ratified, regardless of what the ex-Confederate states did. It is then valid to make the extrapolation that the ex-Confederate states, by voluntarily joining the Union once they were allowed to have representation in Congress, had accepted the *amended* Constitution as one of the conditions for re-admittance to it.

The second inconsistency is that when Congress passed a resolution proposing the Fourteenth Amendment on June 13, 1866, a certified copy was sent to *all* thirty-six states — not thirty-seven, because Nebraska would not be a state until March 1, 1867. However, if the ex-confederate "states" did not have legitimate state governments, as Congress apparently had decided by denying seats to their Senators and Representatives, how could they be expected to vote on a constitutional amendment? One source describes this contradictory situation quite clearly as follows:

> In declaring the Southern states to be politically dead and yet at the same time insisting that they ratify a constitutional amendment as a prelude to readmission to Congress, the Radicals had put themselves in a hopelessly inconsistent constitutional position. The seceded states were without rights; yet they could perform the highest sovereign trust reserved to a state — the power to amend the Constitution.[2]

As the 39th Congress was ending on March 4, 1867, it was clear that the Fourteenth Amendment was not going to be ratified based on the thirty-seven state plan of Congress. In fact, all the ex-confederate "states" except Tennessee had rejected it. As a result, Congress decided to take drastic action. A series of Reconstruction Acts were passed from March 2, 1867 through March 11, 1868. All of the ex-Confederate states except Tennessee (most likely because it *did* ratify the Amendment on July 19, 1866) were divided into five districts and placed under martial law. The first Reconstruction Act that was passed on March 2, 1867, is the significant one for our purposes.

The beginning portion of this Act makes the following statement:

---

1 By December 6, 1865, the following nineteen legitimate states ratified the Thirteenth Amendment: Illinois, Rhode Island, Michigan, Maryland, New York, Pennsylvania, West Virginia, Missouri, Maine, Kansas, Massachusetts, Ohio, Indiana, Nevada, Minnesota, Wisconsin, Vermont, Connecticut, and New Hampshire.

2 Kelly & Harbison, 466.

Whereas no legal State governments or adequate protection for life or property now exist in the rebel States of Virginia, North Carolina, South Carolina, Georgia, Mississippi, Alabama, Louisiana, Florida, Texas, and Arkansas; and whereas it is necessary that peace and good order should be enforced in said States until loyal and republican State governments can be legally established: Therefore

Be it enacted by the Senate and House of Representatives ..., That said rebel States shall be divided into military districts and made subject to the military authority of the United States, as hereinafter prescribed, and for that purpose Virginia shall constitute the first district; North Carolina and South Carolina the second district; Georgia, Alabama, and Florida the third district; Mississippi and Arkansas the fourth district; and Louisiana and Texas the fifth district.

In Section 5, the same Act continues as follows:

And be it further enacted, That when the people of any one of said rebel States shall have formed a constitution of government in conformity with the Constitution of the United States in all respects, framed by a convention of delegates elected by the male citizens of said State ... and when such constitution shall be ratified by a majority of the persons voting on the question ... and when such constitution shall have been submitted to Congress for examination and approval, and Congress shall have approved the same, and when said State, by a vote of its legislature elected under said constitution, shall have adopted the amendment to the Constitution of the United States, proposed by the Thirty-Ninth Congress, and known as article fourteen, and when said article shall have become a part of the Constitution of the United States, said State shall be declared entitled to representation in Congress, and Senators and Representatives shall be admitted therefrom on their taking the oaths prescribed by law, and then and thereafter the preceding sections of this act shall be inoperative in said State.[1]

If you examine Section 5 of the Act quoted above, you will see that five conditions must be met by an ex-confederate "state" before it can be "declared entitled to representation in Congress, and Senators and Representatives shall be admitted therefrom on their taking oaths prescribed by law." They are as follows: 1) A constitutional convention must draft a Constitution, 2) the people of the state must approve it, 3) Congress must approve it, 4) the legislature of the state must ratify the fourteenth Amendment, and 5) the Amendment must become part of the Constitution.

The original inconsistency still exists; only now it is in writing. According to Forrest McDonald, Professor of History at the University of Alabama, "it remains a fact that the southern state governments could have a voice in ratifying the amendment only if they were duly recognized as governments *at the time they acted on the amendment.* Congress had taken it upon itself — properly or improperly, it does not matter for present purposes — to be the arbiter of whether the governments were legitimate."[2] Congress decided that the former Confederate states except Tennessee[3] did not have legitimate governments. The very beginning of the Act states that "no legal State governments ... now exist in the rebel States of Virginia, North Carolina, South Carolina, Georgia, Mississippi, Alabama, Louisiana, Florida, Texas, and Arkansas." Even

---

1 Chap. CLIII — *An Act to provide for the more efficient Government of the Rebel States,* Library of Congress (Thomas) [Internet]; available from http://memory.loc.gov/cgi-bin/ampage?collId=llsl&fileName=014/llsl014.db&recNum=459; accessed 21 July 2008.

2 McDonald, 16.

3 Congress passed legislation on July 24, 1866 that allowed Tennessee to have representation in Congress and thus make it a legitimate state, but it was still a non-state when it ratified the Fourteenth Amendment on July 19, 1866 (see Table 2).

if Congress had properly approved a new Constitution for it beforehand, the "state" would still not be legitimate until it was "entitled to representation in Congress." Clearly, only such a state had the authority to vote on a constitutional amendment. Of course, actual admittance to the appropriate chamber would only be allowed after the proper "oaths prescribed by law" had been taken by the Senators and Representatives, but this requirement would only be a mere formality once the state was "entitled to representation in Congress" (i.e., became a state).

On June 25, 1868, Congress passed another Act that changed this process slightly for six of the ex-confederate "states." The relevant portion of this Act makes the following statement:

> Be it enacted by the Senate and House of Representatives ..., That each of the States of North Carolina, South Carolina, Louisiana, Georgia, Alabama, and Florida, shall be entitled and admitted to representation in Congress as a State of the Union when the legislature of such State shall have duly ratified the amendment to the Constitution of the United States proposed by the Thirty-ninth Congress, and known as article fourteen ....[1]

For Georgia, there was the additional proviso that its legislature had to pass legislation declaring a specific section of its Constitution invalid before it would be permitted to have representation in Congress. The President was given the responsibility of issuing a proclamation declaring that each of the six "states" had ratified the Amendment within ten days of receiving official notice from each "state."

The original inconsistency has not been avoided by this Act either. It is still expected that non-states will vote to ratify a constitutional amendment before they can become states.

Let us compare the date when each of the ex-confederate "states" voted to ratify the Fourteenth Amendment with the date that they were "entitled to representation in Congress." This comparison is provided in Table 2.

As can clearly be seen, in all eleven cases a non-state voted to ratify the Fourteenth Amendment prior to its being officially declared a state (i.e., its senators and representatives being allowed in Congress). This means that when the Amendment was supposedly ratified by July 9, 1868, the twenty-eight states that did so included the six non-states of Tennessee, Arkansas, Florida, North Carolina, Louisiana, and South Carolina. Thus, only twenty-two legitimate states actually ratified the Amendment[2] — not enough to declare the Amendment ratified according to the congressional plan, which would require twenty-eight out of thirty-seven "states" to ratify it.

Perhaps we can still conclude that today the Fourteenth Amendment was ratified in spite of the inconsistencies. What if we disregard the vote of the former confederate "states" altogether and only count the twenty-two legitimate states that approved it? As stated earlier in this chapter, twenty of these states would be required

---

1 Chap. LXX — *An Act to admit the States of North Carolina, South Carolina, Louisiana, Georgia, Alabama, and Florida, to representation in Congress*, June 25, 1868, Library of Congress (Thomas) [Internet]; available from http://memory.loc.gov/cgi-bin/ampage?collId=llsl&fileName=015/llsl015.db&recNum=106; accessed 21 July 2008.

2 It should be noted here that two states that ratified the Amendment rescinded their ratifications by July 9, 1868. They were Ohio (ratification rescinded on January 15, 1868) and New Jersey (ratification rescinded on March 24, 1868). Congress — rightly or wrongly — refused to accept them as valid and only recognized their previous ratifications. Oregon also rescinded its ratification on October 15, 1868, but it was after the Amendment had already been officially declared ratified.

to ratify the Amendment, so on this basis the Amendment would have been ratified.[1] We could then make the valid extrapolation that the ex-Confederate states, by voluntarily sending Senators and Representatives to Congress once they were permitted to do so, had merely recognized by their action the validity of the Amendment that had already become a part of the Constitution.

Unfortunately, another problem regarding the ratification of the Fourteenth Amendment needs to be dealt with here. We already encountered it in the supposed ratifications of the Sixteenth and Seventeenth Amendments. It has to do with the fact that the certified copies of the state ratifications that were sent to Washington do not quote the Amendment exactly as proposed by Congress. In a memorandum sent to Secretary of State Knox from the Solicitor General, Joshua Reuben Clark, Jr., on February 15, 1913 regarding the ratification of the Sixteenth Amendment, the following important information is revealed:

> In the resolutions of the state legislatures on file in the Department [of State], ratifying the 14th amendment to the Constitution, there are many errors of punctuation, capitalization, and wording, some of the errors in wording being substantial errors....[2]

That the states must vote on an *exact* copy of the proposed amendment passed by Congress is essential to the whole ratification process, as was learned in the earlier chapters regarding the supposed ratifications Sixteenth and Seventeenth Amendments. This fact is stated very clearly in the same memorandum just quoted above:

> Furthermore, under the provisions of the Constitution a legislature is not authorized to alter *in any way* the amendment proposed by Congress, the function of the legislature consisting merely in the right to approve or disapprove the proposed amendment (italics mine).[3]

Of the twenty-two legitimate states that ratified the Amendment, fifteen had errors in the wording and some were quite substantial.[4] Thus, we have to reduce twenty-two states to seven and this is far below the number required to ratify the Amendment.

Other "states" approved the Fourteenth Amendment after the ratification process was completed by July 9, 1868. They were Alabama (July 13, 1868), Georgia (July 21, 1868), Virginia (October 8, 1869), Mississippi (January 17, 1870), Texas (February 18, 1870), Delaware (February 12, 1901), Maryland (April 4, 1959), California (May 6, 1959), and Kentucky (March 18, 1976). Unfortunately, five of these "states" were actually non-states when they voted on the Amendment (i.e., Alabama, Georgia, Virginia, Mississippi, and Texas, see Table 2), so they cannot be included in the count. By the

---

1 Not including the eleven ex-confederate states, there would be twenty-six legitimate states. Three-fourths of these would be twenty states.

2 Bill Benson & M J. 'Red' Beckman, *The Law That Never Was*, Volume I (South Holland, Illinois: Constitutional Research Associates, 1985), 5-20. The memorandum can also be located on the following web site: State Memorandum 1913 February 15, The Constitution Society [Internet]; available from http://www.constitution.org/tax/us-ic/ratif/memo_130215.htm; accessed 21 July 2008.

3 Ibid.

4 The fifteen states are Connecticut, New Hampshire, Vermont, New York, Ohio, West Virginia, Nevada, Indiana, Rhode Island, Wisconsin, Pennsylvania, Michigan, Massachusetts, Nebraska, and Iowa. If I had included capitalization and punctuation errors as well, then all twenty-two legitimate states would have to be included in the list! It is also worth noting that all eleven former confederate states quoted the Amendment incorrectly and of these, only Tennessee had errors solely of capitalization and punctuation.

time Delaware ratified the Amendment in 1901, eight more states had been added to the Union[1] and would have had to vote on the Amendment as well. For this reason, it is impossible to speculate on whether the Amendment would have been ratified at that time or even later. Thus, we can only conclude that, based on the evidence now available to us, the Fourteenth Amendment was not properly ratified and cannot be a part of the "Authentic Constitution" for this reason.

Was the Fifteenth Amendment properly ratified? Here it is:

> *Section 1.* The right of citizens of the United States to vote shall not be denied or abridged by the United States or by any State on account of race, color, or previous condition of servitude.
>
> *Section 2.* The Congress shall have power to enforce this article by appropriate legislation.

By February 3, 1870, the ratification of the Amendment was completed, since twenty-eight out of the thirty-seven states supposedly approved it. For that reason, the Secretary of State, Hamilton Fish, issued a Proclamation on March 30, 1870 declaring that the Amendment was officially a part of the Constitution.[2] He listed thirty states that supposedly ratified it prior to the issuance of the Proclamation.[3] Unfortunately, since four "states" that did so were still non-states at the time they voted on the Amendment (i.e., Virginia, Mississippi, Georgia, and Texas, see Table 2), the count was actually twenty-six — not enough states to ratify the Amendment.

After the ratification process was supposedly completed by February 3, 1870, the Amendment was subsequently ratified by New Jersey on February 15, 1871, Delaware on February 12, 1901, Oregon on February 24, 1959, California on April 3, 1962, Kentucky on March 18, 1976, and Tennessee on April 8, 1997. New Jersey can be added to the count, because that state approved the Amendment before any new states were added to the Union and they would have had to vote on it as well. With New Jersey added to the tally, only twenty-seven states would have ratified the Amendment — still not enough to make it a part of the Constitution. Sorry to say, we must conclude that the Fifteenth Amendment was not properly ratified either.

Based on all the evidence provided above, it would not be far-fetched to propose a new Fourteenth Amendment and to include Section 1 of the Fifteenth Amendment within it. The new Amendment could be worded in the following manner, but of course, it would have to be proposed and ratified properly to become a part of the Constitution:

> 1. Any person born after the date of the ratification of this article to a mother and father, neither of whom is a citizen of the United States nor a person who owes permanent allegiance to the United States, shall not be a citizen of the United States or of any State solely by reason of birth in the United States.

---

1 The states were Colorado (August 1, 1876), North Dakota (November 2, 1889), South Dakota (November 2, 1889), Montana (November 8, 1889), Washington (November 11, 1889), Idaho (July 3, 1890), Wyoming (July 10, 1890), and Utah (January 1, 1896).

2 No. 10 — Certifying that the fifteenth amendment has become valid, and a part of the Constitution of the United States, March 30, 1870, Library of Congress (Thomas); available from http://memory.loc.gov/cgi-bin/ampage?collId=llsl&fileName=016/llsl016. db&recNum=1166; accessed 21 July 2008.

3 Although New York ratified the Amendment on April 14, 1869, it rescinded it on January 5, 1870. As was the case with the rescissions connected with the ratification of the Fourteenth Amendment, Congress refused to accept it and only accepted the state's earlier ratification. For what its worth, New York did cancel the rescission on March 30, 1970.

2. No person in any State shall ever be counted as less or more than one person in the Census or Enumeration herein before directed to be taken.

3. No state shall make or enforce any law that shall deny or abridge the privileges and immunities of its Constitution or Laws to any of its citizens for any reason whatsoever, except as a punishment for crime.

4. The United States shall not make or enforce any law or treaty that shall deny or abridge the privileges and immunities of the Bill of Rights to any citizen for any reason whatsoever, except as a punishment for crime. Nor shall the United States make or enforce any law or treaty that shall cause the privileges and immunities of the Bill of Rights to infringe on the privileges and immunities of the Constitutions or Laws of the states.

5. The right of citizens of the United States to vote shall not be denied or abridged by the United States or by any State on account of race, color, or previous condition of servitude.

6. The Congress shall have power to enforce these articles by appropriate legislation.

Clause 1 is derived directly from the constitutional amendment proposed by Congressman Ron Paul that was mentioned above. It would allow citizenship only to children born in the United States who have at least one parent who is a US citizen or "a person who owes permanent allegiance to the United States."

Since the Thirteenth Amendment abolished slavery, the phrase "three fifths of all other Persons" in Article I, section 2, clause 2 of the Constitution, which required that slaves be counted as three-fifths of a person in the census, became a useless expression. Nevertheless, clause 2 would formally expunge this phrase from the Constitution anyway.

Clause 3 would prohibit a state from passing any legislation that would take away or limit the protections of its enumeration of rights ("the privileges and immunities of its Constitution or Laws") "to any of its citizens for any reason whatsoever, except as a punishment for crime." Some illegitimate reasons for taking away or abridging these protections would be a person's race, religion, or sex. If a citizen of a state believed that a certain right in that state's enumeration of rights was being denied to him, clause 3 would allow him to take the issue to a federal court for a decision.

Clause 4 would have two purposes at the federal level. First, it would prohibit the federal government from passing any legislation or approving any treaty that would take away or limit the protections of the Bill of Rights "to any citizen for any reason whatsoever, except as a punishment for [federal] crime." If a citizen believed that a certain right enumerated in the Bill of Rights was being denied to him at the federal level, clause 4 would allow him to take the issue to a federal court to obtain a decision. Second, it would disallow the federal government from passing any law or approving any treaty that would make the Bill of Rights applicable in any way to the states. If a citizen of a state believed that a federal law was impinging on that state's enumeration of rights, he could also bring the case before a federal court. Thus, under this new Fourteenth Amendment, the Bill of Rights and state enumerations of rights would never infringe on each other. Of course, this approach would not allow for uniformity throughout the nation, but it does better accord with the original founding idea of federalism.

Clause 5 is actually Section 1 of the original Fifteenth Amendment. It would be very appropriate to make it a part of the new Fourteenth Amendment. Besides, by proposing and ratifying the latter, the former would officially become a part of the Constitution as well.

Finally, Clause 6 would allow Congress to pass legislation as required to make the clauses of the Amendment operational and enforceable.

TABLE 2. DATES OF RATIFICATION COMPARED TO DATES
"ENTITLED TO REPRESENTATION IN CONGRESS"

State	Date 14th Ratified	Date 15th Ratified	Date "Entitled to Representation in Congress"
North Carolina	July 4, 1868[1]	March 5, 1869	July 4, 1868 (per Act of June 25, 1868, automatically "entitled to Representation" after 14th ratification)
South Carolina	July 9, 1868[2]	March 15, 1869	July 9, 1868 (per Act of June 25, 1868, automatically "entitled to Representation" after 14th ratification)
Louisiana	July 9, 1868[3]	March 5, 1869	July 9, 1868 (per Act of June 25, 1868, automatically "entitled to Representation" after 14th ratification)
Alabama	July 13, 1868[4]	November 16, 1869	July 13, 1868 (per Act of June 25, 1868, automatically "entitled to Representation" after 14th ratification)
Florida	June 9, 1868	June 14, 1869	June 25, 1868 (the date the June 25, 1868 Act was passed)[5]
Georgia	July 21, 1868[6]	February 2, 1870	July 15, 1870[7]
Arkansas	April 6, 1868	March 15, 1869	June 22, 1868[8]
Texas	February 18, 1870	February 18, 1870	March 30, 1870[9]
Mississippi	January 17, 1870	January 17, 1870	February 23, 1870[10]
Virginia	October 8, 1869	October 8, 1869	January 26, 1870[11]
Tennessee	July 19, 1866	April 8, 1997 (first rejected November 16, 1869)	July 24, 1866[12]

1 No. 7, *Announcing ratification of the fourteenth amendment of the Constitution by North Carolina, July 11, 1868, Library of Congress (Thomas) [Internet]; available from http://memory.loc.gov/cgi-bin/ampage?collId=llsl&fileName=015/llsl015.db&recNum=736; accessed 21 July 2008.*

2 *No. 8, Announcing ratification of the fourteenth amendment of the Constitution by South Carolina, July 18, 1868, Library of Congress (Thomas) [Internet]; available from http://memory.loc.gov/cgi-bin/ ampage?collId=llsl&fileName=015/llsl015.db&recNum=737; accessed 21 July 2008.*

3 *No. 9, Announcing ratification of the fourteenth amendment of the Constitution by Louisiana, July 18, 1868, Library of Congress (Thomas) [Internet]; available from http://memory.loc.gov/cgi-bin/ ampage?collId=llsl&fileName=015/llsl015.db&recNum=737; accessed 21 July 2008.*

4 *No. 10, Announcing the ratification of the fourteenth amendment of the Constitution by Alabama, July 20, 1868, Library of Congress (Thomas) [Internet]; available from http://memory.loc.gov/cgi-bin/ ampage?collId=llsl&fileName=015/llsl015.db&recNum=738; accessed 21 July 2008.*

5 *Article I, section 9, clause 3 of the Constitution states that "no ... ex post facto Law shall be passed." Florida ratified the Fourteenth Amendment on June 9, 1868 before Congress passed the Act of June 25, 1868, which automatically allowed a state to have representation in Congress when it approved the Amendment. In the case of Florida anyway, the Act of June 25, 1868 is being applied retroactively and is thus operating as an unconstitutional ex post facto law. Congress should have passed a separate resolution allowing Florida's Senators and Representatives in Congress after the state had ratified the Amendment on June 9 in order to avoid this problem.*

6 *No. 12, Announcing the ratification of the fourteenth amendment of the Constitution by Georgia, July 27, 1868, Library of Congress (Thomas) [Internet]; available from http://memory.loc.gov/cgi-bin/ ampage?collId=llsl&fileName=015/llsl015.db&recNum=741; accessed 21 July 2008.*

7 *Chap. CCXCIX — An Act relating to the State of Georgia, July 15, 1870, Library of Congress (Thomas) [Internet]; available from http://memory.loc.gov/cgi-bin/ampage?collId=llsl&fileName=016/llsl016. db&recNum=398; accessed 21 July 2008.*

8 *Chap. LXIX — An Act to admit the State of Arkansas to Representation in Congress, June 22, 1868, Library of Congress (Thomas) [Internet]; available from http://memory.loc.gov/cgi-bin/ ampage?collId=llsl&fileName=015/llsl015.db&recNum=105; accessed 21 July 2008.*

9 *Chap. XXXIX — An Act to admit the State of Texas to Representation in the Congress of the United States, March 30, 1870, Library of Congress (Thomas) [Internet]; available from http://memory.loc.gov/cgi-bin/ ampage?collId=llsl&fileName=016/llsl016.db&recNum=115; accessed 21 July 2008.*

10 *Chap. XIX — An Act to admit the State of Mississippi to Representation in the Congress of the United States, February 23, 1870, Library of Congress (Thomas); available from http://memory.loc.gov/cgi-bin/ ampage?collId=llsl&fileName=016/llsl016.db&recNum=102; accessed 21 July 2008.*

11 *Chap. X — An Act to admit the State of Virginia to Representation in the Congress of the United States, January 26, 1870, Library of Congress (Thomas); available from http://memory.loc.gov/cgi-bin/ ampage?collId=llsl&fileName=016/llsl016.db&recNum=97; accessed 21 July 2008.*

12 *No. 73 — Joint Resolution restoring Tennessee to her Relations to the Union, July 24, 1866, Library of Congress (Thomas) [Internet]; available from http://memory.loc.gov/cgi-bin/ampage?collId=llsl&fileName=014/ llsl014.db&recNum=395; accessed 21 July 2008.*

13 *The Federal Debt amounts are for September 2007 and were taken from Table FD-1. — Summary of Federal Debt, Federal Debt, Table OFS-1. — Distribution of Federal Securities by Class of Investors and Types of Issues, and Table OFS-2. — Estimated Ownership of US Treasury Securities, Ownership of Federal Securities, Treasury Bulletin: Current Issue 2008, Financial Management Service, A Bureau of the US Department of the Treasury [Internet]; available from http://www.fms.treas.gov/bulletin/index.html; accessed 13 July 2008.*

14 *Except for the Fed's earnings on US Treasury securities ($40,298) that came specifically from its 94th Annual Report 2007 that is referenced above, the interest earnings for Federal agencies issuing their own securities, Government account holdings, Foreign and international holdings, and Depository institutions holdings were calculated by first determining the average "End of Month" interest rate for September 2007 from Table MY-1. — Treasury Market Bid Yields at Constant Maturities: Bill, Notes, and Bonds, Market Yields, Treasury Bulletin: Current Issue 2008, Financial Management Service, A Bureau of the US Department of the Treasury [Internet]; available from http://www.fms.treas.gov/bulletin/index.html; accessed 13 July 2008; and then multiplying the applicable figure in the Federal Debt column on the left by the average interest rate thus obtained (4.21%).*

CHAPTER 13: ELECTING THE PRESIDENT

A small number of persons, selected by their fellow citizens from the general mass, will be most likely to possess the information and discernment requisite to so complicated an investigation.
— Alexander Hamilton, *The Federalist Papers (#68).*

One of the questions that the delegates at the Federal Convention of 1787 strove to answer was "Who would select the Chief Executive of the United States in the new government?" Although the delegates put forward several possibilities including Congress, the Senate, the state Governors, the state Legislatures, and the people through a popular vote, they finally settled on the Electoral College system.[1]

Article II, section 1, clauses 2, 3, and 4 of the Constitution provide the original description of this system. Let me quote the relevant clauses of Article II, section 1 below:

> *Section 1.* [Clause 1] The executive Power shall be vested in a President of the United States of America ... and, together with the Vice President, chosen for the same Term, be elected, as follows:

> [Clause 2] Each State shall appoint, in such Manner as the Legislature thereof may direct, a Number of Electors, equal to the whole Number of Senators and Representatives to which the State may be entitled in the Congress: but no Senator or Representative, or Person holding an Office of Trust or Profit under the United States, shall be appointed an Elector.

---

1 "Although the term is not found in the Constitution, the electors have been known collectively as the electoral college since the early days of the republic, an expression that may be misleading, since the college has no continuing existence, never meets in plenary session, and ceases to exist immediately after the electors have performed their function." Quoted from Thomas H. Neale, "The Electoral College: How It Works in Contemporary Presidential Elections," September 28, 2004, US Politics and Government, Congressional Research Service Reports (CRS) and Issue Briefs, Reports, Foreign Press Centers, US Dept. of State [Internet]; available from http://fpc.state.gov/documents/organization/36762.pdf; accessed 21 July 2008.

[Clause 3] The Electors shall meet in their respective States, and vote by Ballot for two Persons, of whom one at least shall not be an Inhabitant of the same State with themselves. And they shall make a list of all the Persons voted for, and of the Number of Votes for each; which List they shall sign and certify, and transmit sealed to the Seat of the Government of the United States, directed to the President of the Senate. The President of the Senate shall, in the Presence of the Senate and House of Representatives, open all the Certificates, and the Votes shall then be counted. The Person having the greatest Number of Votes shall be the President, if such Number be a Majority of the whole Number of Electors appointed; and if there be more than one who have such Majority, and have an equal Number of Votes, then the House of Representatives shall immediately chuse [sic] by Ballot one of them for President; and if no person have a Majority, then from the five highest on the List the said House shall in like Manner chuse the President. But in chusing the President, the Votes shall be taken by States, the Representation from each State having one Vote; A quorum for this purpose shall consist of a Member or Members from two thirds of the States, and a Majority of all the States shall be necessary to a Choice. In every Case, after the Choice of the President, the Person having the greatest Number of Votes of the Electors shall be the Vice President. But if there should remain two or more who have equal Votes, the Senate shall chuse from them by Ballot the Vice President.

[Clause 4] The Congress may determine the Time of choosing the Electors, and the Day on which they shall give their Votes; which Day shall be the same throughout the United States.

The original Electoral College system worked in the following manner: First, each state selected its allotment of Electors "in such Manner as the Legislature thereof may direct" (Article II, section 1, clause 2). Originally, the two main methods for choosing Electors were by the state legislature and less frequently by dividing a state into electoral districts and having the voters of each district choose one of them. The number of Electors that each state was entitled to was equal to the sum of its Senators and Representatives in Congress. Table 1 lists the current number of Representatives, Senators, and Electoral Votes by State. It was the responsibility of Congress to determine when the states would choose their Electors and when the latter would cast their votes, but the second of these two determinations had to be uniform throughout the United States. The only restriction regarding the choice of the Electors was that "no Senator or Representative, or Person holding an Office of Trust or Profit under the United States, shall be appointed an Elector" (Article II, section 1, clause 2).

On a day determined by Congress, the Electors met in their particular state to give their votes. They cast *two* votes for President, but at least one of the candidates voted for could not live in their own state. After voting, the Electors of each state made a list of all the persons who received votes for President, along with the number of votes each person received, and transmitted the list — signed, certified, and sealed — to the President of the Senate (actually the Vice-President currently in office). Then, before a joint session of Congress, the President of the Senate opened the lists and counted the votes. The person having the most votes, as long as it was a majority of the votes cast, became the President and the person having the second largest number of votes became the Vice-President.

However, if more than one person received a majority and there was a tie, then the House of Representatives would have to choose the President from among these individuals. Regardless of how many Representatives a state actually had, each state could only cast one vote and the person finally selected had to receive a majority of the total votes cast. A quorum for the purpose was one or more members from at least two-thirds of the states. If no person received a majority of votes in the first attempt, the House would then have to widen the choice to the top five persons who received electoral votes and try again. After the selection of the President, the office of Vice-President would go to the person remaining who received the highest number of electoral votes. However, if there were still a tie vote among two or more persons, then the Senate would have to choose the Vice-President from among them.

By the 1800 presidential election, political parties became a significant factor in elections. The Electors pledged to the Republican Party sponsored their party's candidates, namely Thomas Jefferson and Aaron Burr. Their expectation was that Jefferson would be President and Burr would be Vice-President, but since Article II, section 1, clause 3 did not allow a separate vote for each office, both candidates received the same number of votes. Because of the tie, the House of Representatives had to decide the election. Jefferson became the President and Burr the Vice-President, but only by the thirty-sixth vote.

On June 15, 1804, the Twelfth Amendment was ratified to correct the problem that surfaced in the 1800 presidential election. Let me quote the Twelfth Amendment below:

> The Electors shall meet in their respective states and vote by ballot for President and Vice-President, one of whom, at least, shall not be an inhabitant of the same state with themselves; they shall name in their ballots the person voted for as President, and in distinct ballots the person voted for as Vice-President, and they shall make distinct lists of all persons voted for as President, and of all persons voted for as Vice-President, and of the number of votes for each, which lists they shall sign and certify, and transmit sealed to the seat of the government of the United States, directed to the President of the Senate; — The President of the Senate shall, in the presence of the Senate and House of Representatives, open all the certificates and the votes shall then be counted;—the person having the greatest number of votes for President, shall be the President, if such number be a majority of the whole number of Electors appointed; and if no person have such majority, then from the persons having the highest numbers not exceeding three on the list of those voted for as President, the House of Representatives shall choose immediately, by ballot, the President. But in choosing the President, the votes shall be taken by states, the representation from each state having one vote; a quorum for this purpose shall consist of a member or members from two-thirds of the states, and a majority of all the states shall be necessary to a choice. [And if the House of Representatives shall not choose a President whenever the right of choice shall devolve upon them, before the fourth day of March next following, then the Vice-President shall act as President, as in the case of the death or other constitutional disability of the President -] The person having the greatest number of votes as Vice-President, shall be the Vice-President, if such number be a majority of the whole number of Electors appointed, and if no person have a majority, then from the two highest numbers on the list, the Senate shall choose the Vice-President; a quorum for the purpose shall consist of two-thirds of the whole number of Senators, and a majority of the whole number shall be necessary to a choice. But no person constitutionally ineligible to the office of President shall be eligible to that of Vice-President of the United States.

The Twelfth Amendment changed Article II, section 1, clause 3 in four significant ways. First, the Electors now voted *separately* for the President and the Vice-President. The Amendment states, "they shall name in their ballots the person voted for as President, and in distinct ballots the person voted for as Vice-President, and they shall make distinct lists of all persons voted for as President, and of all persons voted for as Vice-President...." Second, if no one received a majority of electoral votes for President, the decision went to the House of Representatives and the President was chosen from among the three top persons who received electoral votes. Third, if the decision went to the House of Representatives, but the office of President was still vacant by Inauguration Day on March 4,[1] the Vice-President still in office was to be the acting President until a new President was chosen. Fourth, if no one received a majority of electoral votes for Vice-President, the decision went to the Senate and the Vice-President was chosen from among the two top persons who received electoral votes. A quorum for the purpose was at least two-thirds of all the Senators and the person finally selected had to receive a majority of the total votes cast.

In addition, although it had only been implied in the original Constitution that the Vice-President was to have the same qualifications for office as the President, the Twelfth Amendment now specifically stated so: "no person constitutionally ineligible to the office of President shall be eligible to that of Vice-President of the United States."

On March 29, 1961, another change came to the Electoral College system, when the Twenty-Third Amendment became part of the Constitution. The Amendment gave the District of Columbia three Electoral votes. Before this Amendment, since the District of Columbia was not a state, it could have no Electoral votes and consequently the residents thereof could not vote for President and Vice-President. Let me quote this Amendment below:

> *Section 1.* The District constituting the seat of Government of the United States shall appoint in such manner as the Congress may direct:
>
> A number of electors of President and Vice President equal to the whole number of Senators and Representatives in Congress to which the District would be entitled if it were a State, but in no event more than the least populous State; they shall be in addition to those appointed by the States, but they shall be considered, for the purposes of the election of President and Vice President, to be electors appointed by a State; and they shall meet in the District and perform such duties as provided by the twelfth article of amendment.
>
> *Section 2.* The Congress shall have power to enforce this article by appropriate legislation.

Unfortunately, the Electoral College system never functioned as it was intended almost from its inception. The primary reason was that the delegates at the Federal Convention never considered the formation of political parties. Political parties are inherently inimical to the system's original mode of operation. The reason is that Electors, rather than voting according to their own independent will, are obligated to vote for their party's candidate. According to one source, "by 1800 the principle was fairly well established that electors were mere creatures of party will and could exercise no personal discretion in voting, but instead must vote for the designated

---

[1] The Inauguration Day of the President and the swearing in of the Vice-President were changed to January 20, when the Twentieth Amendment was ratified on January 23, 1933. In addition, the bracketed section of the Twelfth Amendment was replaced by section 3 of the Twentieth Amendment.

party candidates for President and Vice-President."[1] It appears that instead of making an effort to restrain political parties from compelling Electors to vote a certain way, accommodations were actually made for them, which completely distorted rather quickly the original blueprint for the system's operation. Based on the *republican* form of government that the Founders sanctioned, the people's wishes regarding their choice of President were to be expressed through representatives (i.e., Electors in this case) who selected the President for them. The Electoral College system, especially when functioning as originally intended, is merely one more of the nondemocratic features that make up our Constitutional Republic. One source briefly summarizes the system's original modus operandi in the following manner:

> The function of the College of Electors in choosing the president can be likened to that in the Roman Catholic Church of the College of Cardinals selecting the Pope. The original idea was for the most knowledgeable and informed individuals from each State to select the president based solely on merit and without regard to State of origin or political party.[2]

Today, the United States has a strange amalgamation of a direct popular vote combined with the constitutional requirement that Electors choose the President and Vice-President. On Election Day, which takes place on the Tuesday following the first Monday in November in any given presidential election year, the people of each state choose their Electors by popular vote (US Code 3, sec. 1). What actually happens is that during the previous summer each political party of a state chooses its own slate of Electors, which in each case equals the state's prescribed allotment of electoral votes. When the people vote on Election Day, the party's slate of Electors whose candidates for President and Vice-President win the majority of the state's popular vote becomes that state's *official* set of Electors. Since all of these Electors are obviously pledged to the winning candidates, the winning candidates take all that state's electoral votes. This is popularly known as the "winner-take-all" method of choosing Electors. Then, on the first Monday after the second Wednesday in December (US Code 3, sec. 7), all the Electors officially cast their votes in their respective states, but except for the occasional faithless Elector, they vote as expected for their party's candidate.[3] The final step in the election process takes place when Congress counts the electoral votes on January 6 of the following year (US Code 3, sec. 15). Of course, this step is really only ceremonial. At least a majority of electoral votes is required for a presidential — vice-presidential ticket to win the election, which is currently 270 of the 538 electoral votes (50% of 538, which is 269 plus 1 = 270).

1 Alfred H. Kelly & Winfred A. Harbison, *The American Constitution: Its Origins and Development* (New York: W.W. Norton & Company, Inc., 1970), 135, note 5.

2 William C. Kimberling, Deputy Director of FEC Office of Election Administration, "The Electoral College," revised May 1992 [Internet]; available from http://www.fec.gov/pdf/eleccoll.pdf; accessed 6 July 2008.

3 "Although 24 states seek to prohibit faithless electors by a variety of methods, including pledges and the threat of fines or criminal action, most constitutional scholars believe that electors, once chosen, remain constitutionally free agents, able to vote for any candidate who meets the requirements for President and Vice President. Faithless electors have, however, been few in number ... and have never influenced the outcome of a presidential election." Quoted from Thomas H. Neale, "The Electoral College: How It Works in Contemporary Presidential Elections," September 28, 2004, US Politics and Government, Congressional Research Service Reports (CRS) and Issue Briefs, Reports, Foreign Press Centers, US Dept. of State [Internet]; available from http://fpc.state.gov/documents/organization/36762.pdf; accessed 21 July 2008.

Even though the likelihood of returning the Electoral College system to its intended mode of operation is very unlikely, the following modifications would in any
case go a long way towards achieving this result:

1. Political parties should no longer choose Electors. Each state should
   choose one official slate of Electors "in such Manner as the Legislature
   thereof may direct" (Article II, section 1, clause 2), but in a completely
   non-partisan manner.
2. Prior to voting for President and Vice-President, each Elector should sign
   an affidavit stating that the votes he/she is about to cast are completely
   his/her own and are being made without any third party obligation or
   coercion of any kind. It should be illegal for any Elector knowingly to
   break this pledge. In the rare case when an Elector is not able to sign
   the affidavit, a means should be put in place to choose another Elector
   reasonably quickly in order to complete the election process.
3. It should be illegal for anyone to bribe or to any way coerce an Elector to
   vote a certain way.
4. Since Electors are chosen "in such Manner as the Legislature [of each
   State] ... may direct" (Article II, section 1, clause 2), a constitutional
   amendment would need to be proposed and ratified to make the above
   changes uniform throughout the nation.

Most likely, if these modifications were instituted, nearly all the states would opt
for some sort of popular vote to select their Electors, but the voters would be truly
voting for the Electors *not* for presidential and vice-presidential candidates as they do
now. One method of choosing Electors by popular vote is to split the state up into
electoral districts — one for each Elector allotted to the state. At election time, the
voters of each district would then cast their votes for their choice of Elector from a
number of candidates running for the office in that district. Alternatively, the Electors can be split up by congressional district with the two of them that correspond to
the state's senatorial seats being selected by *all* the voters of the state. Either method
would work satisfactorily, but as I have stated above, restoring the Electoral College
system to its proper mode of operation is a highly unlikely undertaking.

Should we abolish the Electoral College system and replace it with a direct popular election of the President and Vice-President? This is an often asked and much
debated question. As was stated earlier in this chapter, the current system is an awkward synthesis of two mutually incompatible ideas: a direct popular vote merged
with the constitutional requirement that Electors choose the President and Vice-
President. It clearly does not operate in the manner it was originally meant to operate.
Under the circumstances, it would make sense to amend the Constitution to abolish
the Electoral College system and institute a direct popular election of the President
and Vice-President. In addition, to make all federal elections (not only the presidential ones) truly accurate and meaningful, we should make the following five changes.[1]

---

1 The states have initial authority through their state legislatures to change the "Times, Places,
  and Manner" for conducting elections for Senators and Representatives, but Congress
  "may at any time ... make or alter such Regulations, except as to the Places of chusing
  [sic] Senators," if it deems it necessary (Article I, section 4, clause 1). However, since the
  Seventeenth Amendment was not constitutionally ratified, as was discovered in Chapter 11,
  the state legislatures still have the power to choose Senators according to Article I, section
  3, clause 1. In addition, the states have sole authority to change how Electors for President
  and Vice-President are chosen, including how direct elections are carried out, if Electors of
  a particular state are chosen in this manner (Article II, section 1, clause 2).

The states should seriously consider instituting these changes in their elections for state offices as well.

The first change is that we need to relax the requirements that allow third party candidates access to the polls. The most important of these requirements is the number of signatures that a third party is required to obtain to get its candidate listed on a state ballot. The specific number varies for each state. In a well-researched article, Richard Winger, the editor of *Ballot Access News*, has calculated that in order to get a presidential candidate on the ballot in all fifty states for the 2004 election year, a new party had to obtain almost 635,000 signatures. The sheer size of this number will become clear when it is realized that a Democratic presidential candidate trying to get on all state primary ballots had to obtain only 27,000 signatures and a Republican presidential candidate only 22,000 signatures.[1]

Certainly, it would be unreasonable to expect every third party that comes along and offers a candidate for a particular office to get on a ballot, because the unfortunate result would almost certainly be confusion for the voter. According to Richard Winger, "if a state requires as few as 5,000 signatures [for a third party to get on the ballot], it is virtually guaranteed to have a statewide ballot that is not crowded."[2]

Furthermore, all third party candidates that do get on the ballot should be allowed to participate in any debates that take place, because the voters have a right to know the views of *all* the candidates that have attained this standing. In a presidential election, how many state ballots a candidate gets on will also have relevance for determining his/her participation in a debate. The Commission on Presidential Debates currently uses three criteria in determining whether a candidate can be in a debate. They are as follows:

1. The candidate must actually be eligible to be President under the Constitution (Article II, section 1, clause 5).
2. The candidate's name must be on a sufficient number of state ballots to make it at least possible to receive enough electoral votes to win the election.
3. The candidate must "have a level of support of at least 15% (fifteen percent) of the national electorate as determined by five selected national public opinion polling organizations, using the average of those organizations' most recent publicly-reported results at the time of the determination."[3]

The second criterion of the Commission that allows only those candidates in the debates that are on enough state ballots to receive conceivably enough Electoral votes to win the election is a sensible criterion. What would be the point of allowing candidates in the debates who could not possibly win the presidential election in the first place? These marginal candidates would only take away time from the other candidates and create needless confusion for the voters.

Even if the Electoral College system were abolished, third party participation in a presidential debate may still have to be restricted somewhat, especially if too many candidates were running for the office. Attempting to conduct an informative debate with an overly large number of participants would end up being disappointing waste

---

1 Richard Winger, "How Many Parties Ought To Be on the Ballet?: An Analysis of *Nader v. Keith*, *Election Law Journal*, Vol. 5, # 2 (2006): 175, 176 (note 40).

2 Ibid, 183.

3 Commission on Presidential Debates' Nonpartisan Candidate Selection Criteria for 2008 General Election Debate Participation, Commission on Presidential Debates [Internet]; available from http://www.debates.org/pages/candsel2008.html; accessed 21 July 2008.

of time. Perhaps the criterion could be that participation in the debates would be limited to those candidates that are on at least three-fourths of the state ballots.

The third criterion is the most difficult one for nearly all third parties to fulfill. In actuality, it puts the proverbial "cart before the horse." A third party desperately needs exposure initially to gain support later. A significant number of voters may have no idea that such a party even exists. The primary means of disseminating its political platform are via paid advertising, free media coverage, and participation in debates. If a third party is denied access to the debates, getting its message out to a wide audience is significantly hampered, especially in the initial stages of its operations, when funds to pay for political advertising are often hard to come by. Free media coverage in the early stages is usually a stroke of luck at best. Furthermore, since a third party would tend to gain acceptance, as a bona fide political party by its participation in the debates, being allowed to take part in them would certainly be advantageous to its image. The beneficial result would almost certainly be more free media coverage and additional financial support to pay for needed political advertising. Thus, criterion 3 assumes that a third party already has significant support initially. In reality, such support only has real substance for the two major parties and rarely ever applies to third parties.

What is the real purpose of the third criterion anyway? As was mentioned earlier in this chapter, in the Electoral College system, the candidate who receives at least 270 *electoral* votes wins the election *not* the one who receives a majority of the popular vote. Thus, there is doubtless an ulterior motive for having the third criterion. Its real purpose is easy to see — it is to curtail third party participation in presidential debates in order to deny them a vehicle to air their views to a larger audience.

The second change needed in the way we carry out federal elections is that voter participation in elections needs to be significantly improved. In the November 2004 presidential election, only 46% of those eligible to vote actually voted.[1] Voter turnout was even worse in the November 2002 congressional election. Only 31% of those eligible to vote actually voted.[2] Clearly, voter participation is not what it should be. In the 19th century, for example, voter turnout was significantly higher. As one writer has stated, "according to Census Bureau figures, almost 80% of the eligible population went to the polls from 1876 to 1892."[3]

Does it even need to be stated that self-government requires citizen participation? One cannot possibly exist without the other. Self-government is essentially hard work. Couch potatoes encourage corruption in government, not to mention the far more grave dangers of incipient dictators or tyrants eventually seizing power. Perhaps when third party participation in elections has improved, voter turnout will increase as well, since the choice of candidates would then be greater, and thus more mentally stimulating, than it is now.

---

1 Voting and Registration in the Election of November 2004 (P20-556), Issued March 2006, US Census Bureau [Internet]; available from http://www.census.gov/prod/2006pubs/p20-556. pdf; accessed 21 July 2008 (only 72% of voting-age citizens were registered to vote, and of these, only 64% actually voted, so 64% of 72% = 46%). ;

2 Voting and Registration in the Election of November 2002 (P20-552), Issued July 2004, US Census Bureau [Internet]; available from http://www.census.gov/prod/2004pubs/p20-552. pdf; accessed 21 July 2008 (only 67% of voting-age citizens were registered, and of these, only 46% voted, so 46% of 67% = 31%).

3 Richard Winger, "The Importance of Ballot Access," Ballot Access News [Internet]; available from http://www.ballot-access.org/winger/iba.html; accessed 21 July 2008.

The third change is that all Direct Record Electronic (DRE) voting machines should be discarded and replaced with the most accurate manual paper trail systems available. Bruce Schneier, the noted security technologist and author, describes DRE voting machines in the following manner:

> In these systems the voter is presented with a list of choices on a screen, perhaps multiple screens if there are multiple elections, and he indicates his choice by touching the screen. These machines are easy to use, produce final tallies immediately after the polls close, and can handle very complicated elections. They also can display instructions in different languages and allow for the blind or otherwise handicapped to vote without assistance.[1]

Unfortunately, the main problems encountered with these machines are twofold — software error and lack of a paper audit trail. Software error could be due to an undetected fault in the original programming or to an intentionally introduced program, which changes the voting results. A paper audit trail is definitely required in order to recount the vote if, for whatever reason, the results of the vote need to be verified. If a software error should be detected, a paper audit trail would be the only means of authenticating the outcome of the election. Bruce Schneier gives the following examples of software errors that actually occurred in voting machines and adds, "there are literally hundreds of similar stories":

> In Fairfax County, VA, in 2003, a programming error in the electronic voting machines caused them to mysteriously subtract 100 votes from one particular candidates' totals.

> In San Bernardino County, CA in 2001, a programming error caused the computer to look for votes in the wrong portion of the ballot in 33 local elections, which meant that no votes registered on those ballots for that election. A recount was done by hand.

> In Volusia County, FL in 2000, an electronic voting machine gave Al Gore a final vote count of negative 16,022 votes.

> The 2003 election in Boone County, IA, had the electronic vote-counting equipment showing that more than 140,000 votes had been cast in the Nov. 4 municipal elections. The county has only 50,000 residents and less than half of them were eligible to vote in this election.[2]

There is little doubt that the old-fashioned paper ballot should be restored as the ballot of choice in elections, even if it does take longer to get the election results. Accuracy must take precedence over speed.

The use of DRE voting machines is only one of the problems that need to be corrected in our voting systems and procedures. Other non-technical problems need to be fixed as well and this is the fourth change that is required in the present manner of conducting elections. According to Bruce Schneier, "in the 2004 US election, problems with voter registration, untrained poll workers, ballot design, and procedures for handling problems resulted in far more votes not being counted than problems with the technology."[3]

The fifth change is that, in order to make the act of voting truly meaningful, we should place certain restrictions on who can vote. Back in Chapter 2, it was learned

1 Bruce Schneier, "The Problem with Electronic Voting Machines," (November 10, 2004), Schneier on Security [Internet]; available from http://www.schneier.com/blog/archives/2004/11/the_problem_wit.html; accessed 21 July 2008.

2 Ibid.

3 Ibid.

that the right to vote is a citizenship right *not* an unalienable right and thus the government could indeed regulate it.

The Constitution allows the states to determine voter qualifications for electing members of the House of Representatives. Article I, section 2 stipulates that the "Electors[1] in each State shall have the Qualifications requisite for Electors of the most numerous Branch of the State Legislature." The Seventeenth Amendment makes precisely the same assertion for electing Senators. However, since this Amendment was not constitutionally ratified, as was discovered in Chapter 11, it is without legal force. For this reason, the state legislatures still have the power to choose Senators according to Article I, section 3, clause 1. This is why Congress was not given authority in the original Constitution to alter the "Places of chusing Senators" in Article I, section 4, clause 1, since the "Place" would naturally be wherever the various state legislatures assembled to conduct their business.

As one can see, the power of the states to determine the qualifications of voters (Electors) who elect members of the House of Representatives is actually set in a roundabout way. The voters (Electors) of House members were to have the same qualifications as the voters (Electors) who elect the members of the largest body of the state legislature. In other words, when the state legislatures determine by law the qualifications for the latter, the former immediately acquire the same qualifications.

In addition, the states determine the voter qualifications for direct popular elections that are undertaken to choose the Electors for President and Vice-President as well. This authority is included in Article II, section 1, clause 2, which stipulates, "each State shall appoint, in such Manner as the Legislature thereof may direct, a Number of Electors...."[2]

Of course, in determining voter qualifications, the states must adhere to the following constitutional amendments:

- The Nineteenth Amendment states that the right to vote "shall not be denied or abridged ... on account of sex."
- The Twenty-fourth Amendment states that the right to vote "shall not be denied or abridged ... by reason of failure to pay any poll tax or other tax."
- The Twenty-sixth Amendment states that the right to vote "shall not be denied or abridged ..." to citizens "who are eighteen years of age or older...."[3]

Besides being a citizen of the United States and of the state where one registers to vote, setting the following five additional restrictions on the franchise should be given serious consideration:

1. A person must not be mentally handicapped, as determined by a court of law. Most states already have such a restriction.
2. A person must not be incarcerated or on parole as a convicted felon. In addition, when the sentence is completed, there should be at least a two-year waiting period before voting is allowed again. Most states already bar a person from voting who is in prison or on parole for a felony conviction.

---

1 The term "Electors" mentioned twice in Article I, section 2 of the Constitution is *not* to be confused with the members of the Electoral College who elect the President and Vice-President.

2 The term "Electors" mentioned in Article II, section 1, clause 2 of the Constitution *does* refer to members of the Electoral College.

3 The Fifteenth Amendment, which states the right to vote "shall not be denied or abridged ... on account of race, color, or previous condition of servitude," would be included in this list as well, but it was not properly ratified. A unique way of solving this problem is provided in Chapter 12.

3. A person must be able to read and write English adequately, and have at least a rudimentary comprehension of mathematics, geography, and history.

4. A person must not be receiving any type of public support and from the time support is terminated, there should be at least a two-year waiting period before voting is again permitted.

5. A person must be an active taxpayer and not owe any unpaid taxes. In addition, the restriction would not apply after someone officially retires, as long as all prior taxes in arrears have been paid.

Since the authority to determine voter qualifications, which would include restrictions, belongs solely to the states, we naturally cannot expect uniformity in this area. Nevertheless, placing the above restrictions on the franchise, as well as making the other changes in federal elections that were suggested above, would go a long way towards producing results that are truly accurate and meaningful instead of being merely tallies of unsubstantiated and valueless votes.

Chapter 14: Immigration

But, why is ... [legal immigration] desirable? Not merely to swell the catalogue of people. No, sir, 'tis to increase the wealth and strength of the community, and those who acquire the rights of citizenship, without adding to the strength or wealth of the community; are not the people we are in want of.

— James Madison, Speech in Congress, February 3, 1790

Even though we have been led to believe that the federal government has the sole responsibility to control immigration into the United States, when we go to the Constitution, we discover a different state of affairs. The true situation is revealed by Article I, section 9, clause 1, which I quote below:

> The Migration or Importation of such Persons as any of the States now existing shall think proper to admit, shall not be prohibited by the Congress prior to the Year one thousand eight hundred and eight, but a Tax or duty may be imposed on such Importation, not exceeding ten dollars for each Person.

James Iredell (1751–1799), who was a member of the North Carolina Supreme Court and a delegate of the state ratifying convention, provides us with the most credible interpretation of this clause:

> Now, sir, observe that the Eastern States, who long ago have abolished slaves, did not approve of the expression *slaves*; they therefore used another, that answered the same purpose. The committee will observe the distinction between the two words *migration* and *importation*. The first part of the clause will extend to persons who come into this country as free people, or are brought as slaves. But the last part extends to slaves only. The word *migration* refers to free persons; but the word *importation* refers to slaves, because free people cannot be said to be imported. The tax, therefore, is only to be laid on slaves who are imported, and not on free persons who migrate.... Is it not the plain meaning of it, that after twenty years they may prevent the future importation of slaves? It does not extend to those now in the country. There is another circumstance to be observed. There is no authority vested in Congress to restrain the states, in

the interval of twenty years, from doing what they please. If they wish to pro-hibit such importation, they may do so.[1]

Thus, the term "Importation" actually referred to slaves who were brought into the United States for resale. Since slaves were considered property, importation would be most appropriate when referring to them. In order to keep the southern states (Georgia, South Carolina, and North Carolina) in the union, the delegates at the Federal Convention of 1787 reached a compromise, stipulating that the slave trade could not be outlawed for twenty years (i.e., 1787 to 1808). However, it should be noted that Congress was still given the authority within that twenty-year pe-riod to assess a tax of not more than ten dollars per slave on the owners of "such Importation."

On December 2, 1806, in his "Sixth Annual Message to Congress," President Thomas Jefferson appealed to Congress to prohibit the importation of slaves into the United States as soon as it was constitutionally able to do so. On March 2, 1807, Congress chose to act in accordance with the President's request by passing a law that made it illegal to import slaves from outside the United States, which went into effect on January 1, 1808.[2]

Although the importation of slaves no longer has any relevance for us today, the term "Migration" found in Article I, section 9, clause 1 most certainly does and it refers to free people or foreigners[3] coming into the United States. Prior to 1808, each state was given complete authority to control the entry of "such Persons" across its own borders, as it chose to allow. However, beginning in 1808, this authority was restricted somewhat. Congress acquired the power to prohibit specific categories of people from entering the United States, but two important points should be kept squarely in mind. First, the power of Congress was *limited* in that it could only pro-hibit or ban the immigration of certain people into the country. Consequently, as long as the states conformed to any bans that Congress might pass, each state was free to control immigration across its borders, as it saw fit. Second, the intent of this clause was definitely not to prohibit the immigration of persons beneficial to the country, but only those detrimental to it. James Madison in a letter to Robert Walsh dated November 27, 1819, stated that "the term migration ... might apply ... to foreign malefactors sent or coming into the country."[4] Furthermore, in the *Federalist Papers* (#42) Madison makes the following statement:

> Attempts have been made to pervert this clause into an objection against the Constitution, by representing it on one side as a criminal toleration of an illicit

1 Debate in North Carolina Ratifying Convention (July 26, 1788), Partial Statement of James Iredell, The Founders' Constitution [Internet]; available from http://press-pubs.uchicago.edu/founders/documents/a1_9_1s15.html; accessed 21 July 2008.

2 Chap. XXII — *An Act to prohibit the importation of Slaves into any port or place within the jurisdiction of the United States, from and after the first day of January, in the year of our Lord one thousand eight hundred and eight*, Library of Congress (Thomas) [Internet]; available from http://memory.loc.gov/cgi-bin/ampage?collId=llsl&fileName=002/llsl002.db&recNum=463; accessed 21 July 2008

3 Of course, before slavery was abolished, the term "Migration" would include slaves owned by foreigners coming into the country that were not intended for resale, i.e., they were a part of the immigrant's household. This explains the phrase used by James Iredell that migra-tion "will extend to persons who come into this country as free people, *or are brought as slaves*" (italics mine).

4 Edited with Introduction and Commentary by Marvin Meyers, *The Mind of the Founder: Sources of the Political Thought of James Madison*, rev. ed. (Hanover and London: Published for Brandeis University Press by University Press of New England, 1981), 321.

practice, and on another as calculated to prevent voluntary and beneficial emigrations from Europe to America. I mention these misconstructions, not with a view to give them an answer, for they deserve none, but as specimens of the manner and spirit in which some have thought fit to conduct their opposition to the proposed government.

However, the situation is entirely different regarding naturalization, which is the process by which a foreigner becomes a citizen. Congress is exclusively granted the power "to establish an uniform Rule of Naturalization ..." in the Constitution (Article I, section 8, clause 4) and "to make all Laws which shall be necessary and proper for carrying into Execution the forgoing Power]...." (Article I, section 8, clause 18).

Not long after the Civil War, the question began to be asked whether it might not be more practical to have a national policy on immigration rather than have different laws in each state. Congress began to assert itself more in this area and the Supreme Court, most notably in *Henderson v. Mayor of the City of New York* (1875),[1] decided that immigration, as well as naturalization, should be the sole responsibility of the federal government. Consequently, by the beginning of the 20th century the federal government assumed full authority over these matters. Unfortunately, although this consolidation of control in the federal government was probably the right course to take at the time, it was accomplished in an entirely unconstitutional manner. Only an amendment to the Constitution in accordance with Article V would have made this alteration truly legitimate.[2] I would suggest that to make it so now a constitutional amendment should be proposed and ratified. It could be written succinctly as follows: *Congress shall have power to establish uniform Rules for Immigration into the United States.*

Since the current reality of the situation is that the federal government is wholly in control of both immigration and naturalization, we will assume for the remainder of this chapter that the required constitutional amendment has in fact been ratified. Furthermore, we will acknowledge that the federal laws and regulations currently existing are valid as well. Nevertheless, in order to put the matter in proper accord with the Constitution a constitutional amendment at least similar to the one suggested above must be ratified. Interestingly enough, the act of approving such an amendment might have an unexpected boon in addition to the fact that it would be an exemplar of constitutional compliance instead of defiance. It may force the federal government at last to do its duty and take serious steps to control illegal immigration across national borders.

---

1 *Henderson v. Mayor of the City of New York*, 92 US 259 (1875), FindLaw [Internet]; available from http://caselaw.lp.findlaw.com/cgi-bin/getcase.pl?court=us&vol=92&invol=259; accessed 21 July 2008. A portion of the decision is as follows: "We are of opinion that this whole subject has been confided to Congress by the Constitution; that Congress can more appropriately and with more acceptance exercise it than any other body known to our law, state or national; that by providing a system of laws in these matters, applicable to all ports and to all vessels, a serious question, which has long been matter of contest and complaint, may be effectually and satisfactorily settled."

2 If Supreme Court cases like *Henderson v. Mayor of the City of New York* really have the legal clout to amend the Constitution, then this proves beyond doubt that we are no longer a Constitutional Republic, but a Krytocracy, i.e., a nation ruled by judges. If Congress had chosen to act *in a constitutional manner* on the Supreme Court's opinion, it should have first proposed a constitutional amendment and sent it to the states for ratification. Once ratified, then and only then, Congress would have been free to pass legislation to implement the federal government's new power.

With the passage of the Immigration Act of 1891, an Office of the Superintendent of Immigration was set up within the Treasury Department. It had extensive authority over all facets of immigration into the United States. This office was to evolve into the United States Immigration and Naturalization Service (INS). In 1940, President Franklin Delano Roosevelt moved the INS from the Department of Labor, where it had been relocated in 1903, to the Department of Justice. Then in 2003, the INS ended, but nearly all its functions were split up among three separate agencies inside the newly formed Department of Homeland Security. These agencies are the US Citizenship and Immigration Services (USCIS), which manages and dispenses all immigration and naturalization services; the US Immigration and Customs Enforcement (ICE), which enforces the immigration and naturalization laws, but has an investigative role as well; and the US Customs and Border Protection (CBP), which conducts customs inspections and guards the borders.

The following definitions are important for a comprehension of the topic:

Alien

An individual who is not a US citizen or US national.

US National

An individual who owes his sole allegiance to the United States, including all US citizens, and including some individuals who are not US citizens. These individuals would include citizens of certain US possessions such as American Samoa and Northern Mariana Islands....

Immigrant

An alien who has been granted the right by the USCIS [United States Citizenship and Immigration Services] to reside permanently in the United States and to work without restrictions in the United States. Also known as a Lawful Permanent Resident (LPR). All immigrants are eventually issued a "green card" (USCIS Form I-551), which is the evidence of the alien's LPR status. LPR's who are awaiting the issuance of their green cards may bear an I-551 stamp in their foreign passports.

Nonimmigrant

An alien who has been granted the right by the USCIS to reside temporarily in the United States. Each nonimmigrant is admitted into the United States in the nonimmigrant status, which corresponds to the class of visa with which, or purpose for which, he entered the United States (e.g., a foreign student may enter the United States on an F-1 visa, which corresponds to the F-1 student status in which he was admitted to the United States)....

Illegal Alien

Also known as an "Undocumented Alien," is an alien who has entered the United States illegally and is deportable if apprehended, or an alien who entered the United States legally but who has fallen "out of status" and is deportable.

Nonimmigrant Visas

A nonimmigrant visa allows a nonimmigrant to enter the United States in one of several different categories, which correspond to the purpose for which the nonimmigrant is being admitted to the United States. For example, a foreign student will usually enter the United States on an F-1 visa, a visitor for business on a B-1 visa, an exchange visitor (including students, teachers, researchers, trainees, alien physicians, au pairs, and others) on a J-1 visa, a diplomat on an A or G visa, etc....[1]

The United States has always accepted and encouraged *legal* immigration. In fact, except for the American Indians, our ancestors were all immigrants to this country at some point in the past. In 2007, 1,052,415 persons became LPRs of the United States[2] and 660,477 persons became naturalized.[3]

The Statue of Liberty, which was a gift given by the people of France to the people of the United States in 1886, has always been a riveting symbol of hope and freedom for immigrants escaping the poverty and oppression of their own country and coming to the United States to build a new life for themselves. In 1903, the famous sonnet titled *The New Colossus* by Emma Lazarus (1849-87) was engraved on a bronze plaque that was fixed to the inner wall of the pedestal on which the Statue of Liberty stands. It reads as follows:

> Not like the brazen giant of Greek fame,
>
> With conquering limbs astride from land to land;
>
> Here at our sea-washed, sunset gates shall stand
>
> A mighty woman with a torch, whose flame
>
> Is the imprisoned lightning, and her name
>
> Mother of Exiles. From her beacon-hand
>
> Glows world-wide welcome; her mild eyes command
>
> The air-bridged harbor that twin cities frame.
>
>
> "Keep, ancient lands, your storied pomp!" cries she
>
> With silent lips. "Give me your tired, your poor,
>
> Your huddled masses yearning to breathe free, The wretched refuse of your teeming shore.
>
> Send these, the homeless, tempest-tost to me,
>
> I lift my lamp beside the golden door!"[4]

In order to become a citizen of the United States, following requirements must be satisfied. In some cases, there are variations or exceptions to these general requirements:

1. The applicant must be at least 18 years old.
2. The applicant must be an LPR.
3. The applicant must, prior to filing the Application for Naturalization

---

1 Immigration Terms and Definitions Involving Aliens, Internal Revenue Service (IRS) [internet]; available from http://www.irs.gov/businesses/small/international/article/0,,id=129236,00. html; accessed 21 July 2008.

2 US Legal Residents: 2007, Immigration Statistics, Homeland Security [Internet]; available from http://www.dhs.gov/xlibrary/assets/statistics/publications/LPR_FR_2007.pdf; accessed 21 July 2008.

3 Naturalizations in the United States: 2007, Immigration Statistics, Homeland Security [Internet]; available from http://www.dhs.gov/xlibrary/assets/statistics/publications/natz_ fr_07.pdf; accessed 21 July 2008.

4 Statue of Liberty National Monument and Ellis Island, The National Park Service [Internet]; available from http://www.nps.gov/archive/stli/prod02.htm; accessed 21 July 2008.

(N-400),[1] have maintained a residence in the US for at least five years, been physically present for at least thirty months of the five-year period, and been a resident of a state or district for at least three months.

4. The applicant must show that he/she is a "person of good moral character."

5. The applicant must show support for the Constitution and have a positive attitude to the United States.

6. The applicant must understand, read, write, and speak commonly used English.

7. The applicant must have knowledge of US history and the form and principles of its government.

8. The applicant must take the Oath of Allegiance,[2] which reads as follows:

I hereby declare, on oath, that I absolutely and entirely renounce and abjure all allegiance and fidelity to any foreign prince, potentate, state, or sovereignty of whom or which I have heretofore been a subject or citizen; that I will support and defend the Constitution and laws of the United States of America against all enemies, foreign and domestic; that I will bear true faith and allegiance to the same; that I will bear arms on behalf of the United States when required by the law; that I will perform noncombatant service in the Armed Forces of the United States when required by the law; that I will perform work of national importance under civilian direction when required by the law; and that I take this obligation freely without any mental reservation or purpose of evasion; so help me God.[3]

The situation regarding illegal aliens is completely different and poses nothing less than a grave threat to the welfare and security of the United States. The number of illegal aliens currently living in the United States is considerable. The *Christian Science Monitor* states, "depending on the source, the numbers range widely — from about 7 million up to 20 million or more."[4] According to a Pew Hispanic Center report, "as of March 2005, the undocumented population has reached nearly 11 million including more than 6 million Mexicans, assuming the same rate of growth as in re-

---

1 Application for Naturalization (N-400), US Citizenship and Immigration Services (USCIS) [Internet]; available from http://www.uscis.gov/portal/site/uscis/menuitem.5af9bb95919f3 5e66f614176543f6d1a/?vgnextoid=480ccac09aa5d010VgnVCM10000048f3d6a1RCRD&vgn extchannel=db029c7755cb9010VgnVCM10000045f3d6a1RCRD; accessed 21 July 2008.

2 The requirements for attaining US citizenship are clearly and succinctly described at the following web address: General Naturalization Requirements, US Citizenship and Immigration Services (USCIS) [Internet]; available from http://www.uscis.gov/portal/ site/uscis/menuitem.5af9bb95919f35e66f614176543f6d1a/?vgnextoid=12e596981298d010Vg nVCM10000048f3d6a1RCRD&vgnextchannel=76719c7755cb9010VgnVCM10000045f3d6 a1___; accessed 21 July 2008.

3 Oath of Allegiance, US Citizenship and Immigration Services (USCIS) [Internet]; available from http://www.uscis.gov/portal/site/uscis/menuitem.5af9bb95919f35e66f614176543f6d1 a/?vgnextoid=931696981298d010VgnVCM10000048f3d6a1RCRD&vgnextchannel=d6f419 4d3e88d010VgnVCM10000048f3d6a1RCRD; accessed 21 July 2008.

4 Brad Knickerbocker, "Illegal immigrants in the US: How many are there?" The Christian Science Monitor [Internet]; available from http://www.csmonitor.com/2006/0516/p01s02-ussc.html; accessed 21 July 2008.

---

cent years."[1] `The same report further states, "About 80 to 85 percent of the migration from Mexico in recent years has been undocumented."[2]

What have been the consequences of allowing the influx of illegal aliens to get so out of hand? Some of the many economic costs and social problems created by this serious situation are listed below:

- According to a study by the Center of Immigration Studies, "illegal alien households are estimated to use $2,700 a year more in services than they pay in taxes, creating a total fiscal burden of nearly $10.4 billion on the federal budget in 2002"[3] and "among the largest federal costs [are] Medicaid ($2.5 billion); treatment for the uninsured ($2.2 billion); food assistance programs ($1.9 billion); the federal prison and court systems ($1.6 billion); and federal aid to schools ($1.4 billion)."[4] Furthermore, "if illegal aliens were legalized and began to pay taxes and use services like legal immigrants with the same education levels, the estimated annual fiscal deficit at the federal level would increase from $2,700 per household to nearly $7,700, for a total federal deficit of $29 billion."[5]

- NewsMax.com reports from *Investors Business Daily* in March 2005 that "the US Justice Department estimated that 270,000 illegal immigrants served jail time nationally in 2003. Of those, 108,000 were in California. Some estimates show illegals now make up half of California's prison population, creating a massive criminal subculture that strains state budgets and creates a nightmare for local police forces."[6]

- According to the City Journal (Winter 2004), "in Los Angeles, 95 percent of all outstanding warrants for homicide (which total 1,200 to 1,500) target illegal aliens. Up to two-thirds of all fugitive felony warrants (17,000) are for illegal aliens."[7]

- According to the source just cited, "a confidential California Department of Justice study reported in 1995 that 60 percent of the 20,000-strong 18th Street Gang in southern California is illegal; police officers say the proportion is actually much greater. The bloody gang collaborates with the Mexican Mafia, the dominant force in California prisons, on complex drug-distribution schemes, extortion, and drive-by assassinations, and commits an assault or robbery every day in L.A. County. The gang has grown dramatically over the last two decades by recruiting recently arrived youngsters, most of them illegal, from Central America and Mexico."[8]

- According to Freedom Alliance, "in all, the US government says it spent $5.8

1 Jeffrey S. Passel, "Estimates of the Size and Characteristics of the Undocumented Population," Pew Hispanic Center [Internet]; available from http://pewhispanic.org/reports/report. php?ReportID=44; accessed 21 July 2008.

2 Ibid.

3 "The Costs of Illegal Immigration," Center for Immigration Studies [Internet]; available from http://www.cis.org/articles/2004/fiscalrelease.html; accessed 21 July 2008.

4 Ibid.

5 Ibid.

6 "Justice Dept. Figures on Incarcerated Illegals," NewsMax.com [Internet]; available from http://www.newsmax.com/archives/ic/2006/3/27/114208.shtml?s=ic; accessed 21 July 2008.

7 Heather Mac Donald, "The Illegal-Alien Crime Wave," City Journal [Internet}; available from http://www.city-journal.org/html/14_1_the_illegal_alien.html; accessed 21 July 2008.

8 Ibid.

billion incarcerating illegal aliens between 2002 and 2005."[1]

- According to USA TODAY, "states where immigrants' share of the labor force jumped the most from 2000 to 2005 have seen some of the sharpest declines in labor force participation by less-educated Americans. In Maryland, the percentage of unskilled Americans working fell from 73.2% to 65.5%, while immigrants as a share of the workforce rose from 12.7% to 22.1%, [Steven] Camarota [of the Center for Immigration Studies] says. Similar sharp increases were noted in North Carolina, Tennessee and Georgia."[2]

- According to Freedom Alliance, "while precise numbers are not possible, based on figures from four areas alone health care-related costs for immigrants easily surpasses $1 billion annually (Texas, $393 million; Florida, $40 million; Los Angeles, $350 million; US–Mexico border counties, $300 million)."[3]

- According to the source just cited, "in some hospitals, almost two-thirds of operating costs are generated by illegal immigrants."[4]

- According to the Washington Times, "Contagious diseases are entering the United States because of immigrants, illegal aliens, refugees and travelers, and World Health Organization officials say the worst could be yet to come."[5] Furthermore, "in a recent statement, Mr. Tancredo [Rep. Tom Tancredo of Colorado], chairmen of the House Immigration Reform Caucus, cited the 'serious consequences' associated with the 'smuggling' of illegals into the United States without proper medical screening" and "among them are the possibilities of the spread of diseases for which we have few, if any, antidotes, he said."[6]

- The United States' blood supply may be in jeopardy. According to the above-cited source, "federal data suggest that as many as 10 percent of the approximately 1,000 Mexicans who emigrate to the United States daily probably are infected with Chagas, said Dr. Louis V. Kirchhoff, a Chagas specialist and a professor at the University of Iowa's medical school."[7] The article adds, "The American Red Cross estimates that nationally, the risk of a blood donor having antibodies to Chagas or being infected with the disease is 1 in 25,000. The risk is 1 in 5,400 in Los Angeles and 1 in 9,000 in Miami. The Red Cross says it will begin screening donors for Chagas, once a suitable test is found."[8]

- According to the Federation for American Immigration Reform (FAIR), "*the total K–12 school expenditure for illegal immigrants costs the states nearly $12 billion*

1 Jon Dougherty, "Illegal Immigration's Financial Impact," Freedom Alliance [Internet]; available from http://www.freedomalliance.org/view_article.php?a_id=642; accessed 21 July 2008.

2 David J. Lynch and Chris Woodyard, "Immigrants claim pivotal role in economy," USA TODAY [Internet]; available from http://www.usatoday.com/money/economy/2006-04-10-immigrants-economic-impact_x.htm; accessed 21 July 2008.

3 Jon Dougherty, "Illegal Immigration's Financial Impact," Freedom Alliance [Internet]; available from http://www.freedomalliance.org/view_article.php?a_id=642; accessed 21 July 2008.

4 Ibid.

5 "Disease, unwanted import," February 13, 2005, The (DC) Washington Times. The article is available from NewsLibrary.com [Internet], the supplier for the Washington Times Archives, but you need to pay a small fee to get the entire article. I paid the fee and have a copy on file.

6 Ibid.

7 Ibid.

8 Ibid.

annually, and when the children born here to illegal aliens are added, the costs more than double to $28.6 billion.[1] The report continues, "This enormous expenditure ... does not ... represent the total costs. Special programs for non-English speakers are an additional fiscal burden as well as a hindrance to the overall learning environment. A recent study found that dual language programs represent an additional expense of $290 to $879 per pupil depending on the size of the class. In addition, because these children of illegal aliens come from families that are most often living in poverty, there is also a major expenditure for them on supplemental feeding programs in the schools."[2]

- According to WorldNetDaily, a Zogby International survey "found that 58 percent of Mexicans agree with the statement, 'The territory of the United States' southwest rightfully belongs to Mexico.' Zogby said 28 percent disagreed, while another 14 percent said they weren't sure."[3] Furthermore, "a similar number — 57 percent — agreed that "Mexicans should have the right to enter the US without US permission," while 35 percent disagreed and 7 percent were unsure." Can we realistically expect persons with views such as these to become loyal citizens of the United States? The answer to this question is obvious.

The solution to the problem is clear and can be accomplished if we sincerely have the desire to do it. First, we must enforce the immigration laws that currently exist, especially those regarding employment. With the passage of the Immigration Reform and Control Act of 1986, all US employers are required to complete an Employment Eligibility Verification form (Form I-9) for each employee hired after November 6, 1986. In the process of completing the Form, each prospective employee must offer documentation from "Lists of Acceptable Documents" in order to corroborate his/her employment eligibility and identity. According to the US Citizenship and Immigration Services (USCIS) web site, the employer must then make a judgment on the authenticity of the documents that were offered to him/her in the following manner:

> The employer must examine the document(s) and accept them if they reasonably appear to be genuine and to relate to the employee who presents them.... If the documentation presented by an employee does not reasonably appear to be genuine or relate to the employee who presents them, employers must refuse acceptance and ask for other documentation from the list of acceptable documents that meets the requirements. An employer should not continue to employ an employee who cannot present documentation that meets the requirements.[4]

According to the M-279, Handbook For Employers on the same web site, employers can face civil penalties for "fail[ing] to properly complete, retain, and/or make

---

1 Jack Martin, "Breaking the Piggy Bank: How Illegal Immigration is Sending Schools Into the Red," Federation for American Immigration Reform (FAIR) [Internet]; available from http://www.fairus.org/site/PageServer?pagename=research_researchf6ad; accessed 21 July 2008.

2 Ibid.

3 Jon Dougherty, "Mexicans: Southwest US is ours," WorldNetDaily [Internet]; available from http://www.worldnetdaily.com/news/article.asp?ARTICLE_ID=27941; accessed 21 July 2008.

4 About Form I-9, Employment Eligibility Verification, US Citizenship and Immigration Services (USCIS) [Internet]; available from http://www.uscis.gov/portal/site/uscis/menuitem.5af9bb95919f35e66f614176543f6d1a/?vgnextoid=0572194d3e88d010VgnVCM10 000048f3d6a1RCRD&vgnextchannel=1847c9ee2f82b010VgnVCM10000045f3d6a1RCRD; accessed 21 July 2008.

available for inspection Forms I-9 as required by law...."[1] In addition, employees can face criminal penalties for "us[ing] fraudulent identification or employment eligibility documents, or documents that were lawfully issued to another person," or for "mak[ing] a false statement or attestation for purposes of satisfying the employment eligibility verification requirements...."[2] Furthermore, there are civil and criminal penalties for "knowingly hiring unauthorized aliens (or continuing to employ aliens knowing that they are or have become unauthorized to work in the United States)...."

Amnesty of any kind should not be an option. Such a capitulation would be nothing more than a "slap in the face" to those immigrants who have made the effort to become US citizens by way of the legal naturalization procedure.

Even though President Bush continually advocates the creation of a "guest worker" program for illegal aliens, the truth of the matter is that visas already exist for this purpose. They are the nonimmigrant visas for temporary or seasonal agricultural workers (classification H-2A) and temporary or seasonal nonagricultural workers (classification H-2B).[3] Temporary workers with these types of visas are allowed an initial stay of up to one year with a three-year extension limit made up of increments of one year each.[4]

Second, we must secure the borders. If this means building a wall, so be it. In fact, a bill has recently been passed that will create a 700 mile fence along the least secured section of US–Mexico border.[5] Unfortunately, the cost of the fence has not been determined and the bill does not appropriate any money for it. However, according to NewsMax.com, "a homeland security spending measure the president signed earlier this month makes a $1.2 billion down payment on the project. The money also can be used for access roads, vehicle barriers, lighting, high-tech equipment and other tools to secure the border."[6]

Third, all benefits that illegal aliens are receiving must be stopped, as these are often inducements for their coming over the border in the first place. As mentioned earlier in this chapter, the federal programs with the highest costs for illegal aliens are Medicaid, treatment for the uninsured, food assistance programs, the federal prison and court systems, and federal aid to schools. Except for continuing to provide medical services for life threatening health conditions only, all other federal pro-

---

1 M-279, Handbook for Employers (instructions for completing Form I-9), US Citizenship and Immigration Services (USCIS) [Internet]; available from http://www.uscis.gov/files/nativedocuments/m-274.pdf; accessed 21 July 2008.

2 Ibid.

3 Temporary Workers, US Department of State [Internet]; available from http://www.travel.state.gov/visa/temp/types/types_1271.html; accessed 21 July 2008.

4 Temporary Workers, US Citizenship and Immigration Services (USCIS) [Internet]; available from http://www.uscis.gov/portal/site/uscis/menuitem.5af9bb95919f35e66f614176543f6d1a/?vgnextoid=a7cc6138f898d010VgnVCM10000048f3d6a1RCRD&vgnextchannel=48819c7755cb9010VgnVCM10000045f3d6a1RCRD; accessed 21 July 2008.

5 To establish operational control over the international land and maritime borders of the United States (Secure Fence Act of 2006), Public Law # 109-367, Library of Congress (Thomas) [Internet]; available from http://thomas.loc.gov/cgi-bin/bdquery/z?d109:HR06061:@@@L&summ2=m&|TOM:/bss/d109query.html|; accessed 21 July 2008.

6 "Bush to Sign Bill for US–Mexico Border Fence," NewsMax.com [Internet]; available from http://www.newsmax.com/archives/articles/2006/10/26/65951.shtml; accessed 21 July 2008.

grams for illegal aliens should be terminated. The states should do the same with their programs as well.

Of course, if the Constitution were actually being followed, there would not be any federal programs of this type in the first place. However, the reality is that such programs *do* currently exist. Therefore, the first step is to end the participation of illegal aliens in them immediately and then they can gradually be discontinued all together by means of a transition period.

> When the President enters office, he takes an oath to "preserve, protect, and defend the Constitution of the United States" (Article II, section 1, clause 8). In addition, Article IV, section 4 of the Constitution states, "the United States shall guarantee to every State in this Union a Republican Form of Government, *and shall protect each of them against invasion*" (italics mine). Pat Buchanan, the noted author and syndicated columnist, has offered a novel way of getting the President to realize his legitimate responsibility under the Constitution:

> [Since] ... we are being invaded, and the president of the United States is not doing his duty to protect the states against that invasion. Some courageous Republican, to get the attention of this White House, should drop into the hopper a bill of impeachment, charging George W. Bush with a conscious refusal to uphold his oath and defend the states of the Union against "invasion."[1]

---

1 Patrick J. Buchanan, "A National Emergency," WorldNetDaily [Internet]; available from http://www.worldnetdaily.com/news/article.asp?ARTICLE_ID=46019; accessed 21 July 2008.

CHAPTER 15: THE JUDICIARY

> *You seem ... to consider the judges the ultimate arbiters of all constitutional questions; a very dangerous doctrine indeed, and one which would place us under the despotism of an oligarchy.*
> — *Thomas Jefferson, Letter to W. C. Jarvis, 1820*

In the Constitution, Article III, sections 1 and 2, describe the composition of the federal judiciary and the scope of its powers. Let me quote the relevant portions of these sections below:

Section 1. The judicial Power of the United States, [sic] shall be vested in one supreme [sic] Court, and in such inferior Courts as the Congress may from time to time ordain and establish. The Judges, both of the supreme [sic] and inferior Courts, shall hold their offices during good Behaviour [sic], and shall, at stated Times, receive for their Services, a Compensation, which shall not be diminished during their Continuance in office.

Section 2. The judicial Power shall extend to all Cases, in Law and Equity, arising under this Constitution, the Laws of the United States, and Treaties made, or which shall be made, under their Authority; — to all Cases affecting Ambassadors, other public Ministers and Consuls; — to all Cases of admiralty and maritime Jurisdiction; — to Controversies to which the United States shall be a Party; — to Controversies between two or more States; — [between a State and Citizens of another State; -] between Citizens of different States; — between citizens of the same State claiming Lands under Grants of different States, [and between a State, or the Citizens thereof, and foreign States, Citizens or Subjects].

In all Cases affecting Ambassadors, other public Ministers and Consuls, and those in which a State shall be Party, the supreme [sic] Court shall have original Jurisdiction. In all the other Cases before mentioned, the supreme [sic] Court shall have appellate Jurisdiction, both as to Law and Fact, with such Exceptions, and under such Regulations as the Congress shall make.

According to Section 1, the federal judiciary is composed of a Supreme Court and a number of lower courts that are created by Congress. Currently, there are twelve regional circuits each with a US Court of Appeals. The regional circuits are subdi-vided into 94 judicial districts each with a US District Court. In addition to these federal courts, others have special functions including Bankruptcy Courts, a Court of International Trade, and a US Court of Federal Claims.[1]

It is usually thought that federal judges serve for life, but this is not true. Accord-ing to Section 1, they "shall hold their offices during good Behaviour." Although it is correct that judges usually *do* hold their offices for life, this does not have to be the case. Unacceptable conduct can be grounds for impeachment and removal from of-fice, although what is considered "unacceptable" is sometimes not clear. Nevertheless, everyone would agree that certain things, like treason or bribery, would certainly lie outside the realm of "good Behaviour."[2] Section 1 also stipulates that judges be paid for their services, but their salary "shall not be diminished during their Continuance in office."

Section 2, clause 1 begins with the statement that "the judicial Power shall ex-tend to all Cases, in Law and Equity, arising under this Constitution, the Laws of the United States, and Treaties made, or which shall be made, under their [i.e., the United States'] Authority." "Law and Equity" are the two components of the judicial power of the United States. "Law" refers to the written law, i.e., the Constitution followed by the statutes and treaties made according to its precepts. The supremacy clause (Article VI, clause 2), which very closely mirrors this portion of Section 2, clause 1, calls these legal sources taken as a whole the "supreme Law of the Land."[3] "Equity," on the other hand, refers to the principle of fair-mindedness rather than the strict, automatic application of the written law. In England, two separate court systems had come into existence by the seventeenth century — courts of law and courts of equity — and they did not finally merge as one until 1873. Early on, the United States followed the two-system approach of England, but began the consolidation of both systems by 1848. Today, the courts employ both components, but generally apply equity when no satisfactory resolution is available in the law.

The rest of Section 2, clause 1 lists the type of "cases" or "controversies" that the federal courts have jurisdiction over. Without getting overly involved in the specific types of actions, it should be mentioned that the Eleventh Amendment, which was ratified February 7, 1795, excluded two types from the list. Let me quote the Eleventh Amendment below:

> The Judicial power of the United States shall not be construed to extend to any suit in law or equity, commenced or prosecuted against one of the United States by Citizens of another State, or by Citizens or Subjects of any Foreign State.

The two exclusions are that citizens of one state cannot sue another state and citizens or subjects of a foreign state cannot sue a US state. The phrases in Section 2, clause 1 that were changed by the Amendment are in brackets in the quotation of Article III, section 2, clause 1 that was quoted at the beginning of this chapter.

---

1 US Courts [Internet]; available from http://www.uscourts.gov/index.html; accessed 10 July 2008.

2 Article II, section 4 states that "the President, Vice President and all civil Officers of the United States, shall be removed from Office on Impeachment for, and Conviction of, Treason, Bribery, or other high Crimes and Misdemeanors."

3 The relevant portion of the supremacy clause (Article VI, clause 2) is as follows: "This Constitution, and the Laws of the United States which shall be made in Pursuance thereof; and all Treaties made, or which shall be made, under the Authority of the United States, shall be the supreme Law of the Land."

Section 2, clause 2 differentiates between those cases or controversies in which the Supreme Court has "original" or "appellate jurisdiction." Original jurisdiction means that the action must be commenced in the Supreme Court and appellate jurisdiction means that it must first be heard in a lower court. The end of Section 2, clause 2 makes the very important statement that "the supreme [*sic*] Court shall have appellate Jurisdiction, both as to Law and Fact, with such Exception and under such Regulations as the Congress shall make." Many people are unaware that Congress has the power to not only control the Supreme Court's appellate jurisdiction, but also to exclude certain actions that can come before its purview in this area.

What appears to be an ironclad opinion today is that the Supreme Court has the final authority as to the meaning of the Constitution. This power typically goes under the name judicial review. As usually understood, it is the principle by which the Supreme Court can declare an act of the executive branch or a law of the legislative branch unconstitutional. Since the power is not found in Article III, sections 1 and 2, a question that naturally comes up is "what is the source of this power?" The answer usually given is that in the case of *Marbury v. Madison*, which was decided during President Thomas Jefferson's first term of office in 1803, the Supreme Court declared that *it* had the final say as to the Constitution's meaning. The Chief Justice, John Marshall, asserted in that case, "it is emphatically the province and duty of the judicial department to say what the law is."[1]

However, this traditional view of *Marbury v. Madison* is not really on the mark. According to Joel B. Grossman, Professor of Political Science at the John Hopkins University, the argument in *Marbury v. Madison* that the judiciary is the final arbiter over the meaning of the Constitution is far from convincing:

> Certainly Marshall made a strong argument for judicial review as a power of the Supreme Court. But his argument for exclusive "monopoly" power is weak at best. He argued that "it is, emphatically, the province and duty of the judicial department, to say what the law is." But while he establishes fidelity to the Constitution as the judiciary's duty, he does not necessarily demonstrate that it is only the judiciary's province — as opposed to the province of all three branches of government. For example, Marshall notes that in a written constitution of enumerated powers, the constitution is superior to ordinary law. But his deductive argument that this implies *exclusive* judicial review is not compelling.
>
> Marshall noted that the judges take an oath to honor the Constitution. But he neglected to say that so do members of the other branches of government, and therefore they are equally bound to act constitutionally. Why is the judgment of constitutionality the Court's job alone?[2]

Robert Lowry Clinton, Associate Professor of Political Science at Southern Illinois University at Carbondale, takes the argument a step further and states categorically, "No exclusive power to interpret the fundamental law is claimed for the Court ... anywhere ... in *Marbury*."[3]

---

1 Marbury v. Madison (1803), FindLaw [Internet]; available from http://supreme.lp.findlaw.com/supreme_court/landmark/marbury.html; accessed 22 July 2008.

2 Joel B. Grossman, "The 200th Anniversary of Marbury v. Madison: The Reasons We Should Still Care About the Decision, and the Lingering Questions It Left Behind," FindLaw [Internet]; available from http://writ.news.findlaw.com/commentary/20030224_grossman.html#bio; accessed 22 July 2008.

3 Robert Lowry Clinton, "How the Court Became Supreme," First Things [Internet]; available from http://www.firstthings.com/article.php3?id_article=3085; accessed 22 July 2008.

In actuality, it was not until 1958 in the case of *Cooper v. Aaron* that the Supreme Court really asserted its exclusive authority to determine the meaning of the Constitution, but remarkably, it used *Marbury v. Madison* to defend this position:

> Article VI of the Constitution makes the Constitution the "supreme Law of the Land." In 1803, Chief Justice Marshall, speaking for a unanimous Court, referring to the Constitution as "the fundamental and paramount law of the nation," declared in the notable case of Marbury v. Madison, 1 Cranch 137, 177, that "It is emphatically the province and duty of the judicial department to say what the law is." *This decision declared the basic principle that the federal judiciary is supreme in the exposition of the law of the Constitution*, and that principle has ever since been respected by this Court and the Country as a permanent and indispensable feature of our constitutional system (italics mine).[1]

The Constitution divides the federal government into three separate and co-equal branches — the judicial, executive, and legislative. Each branch is independent of the others, except in so far as each one is provided with certain constitutionally specified mechanisms (i.e., "checks and balances") to restrain the power of the others. The possible abuse of power and dominance by any one branch are thereby circumscribed. Examples of such "checks and balances" would be the power of the President to veto legislation passed by Congress and the power of the Senate to approve or reject a treaty negotiated by the President with a foreign nation.

If the usual understanding of judicial review were indeed correct, then in actuality it should be called judicial supremacy, because it makes the judicial branch into the most powerful of the three branches. Having the sole power to declare any actions by the other branches unconstitutional and hence invalid, and requiring the entire government and everyone else to be bound by its decisions, can only be called absolute power! The fact is that Congress was provided with means in the Constitution to curb judicial power, but the mechanisms have been used only rarely, if at all. One way is to impeach judges for unacceptable conduct (Article III, section 1; Article I, section 2, clause 5 and section 3, clauses 6 and 7) and the other is to exclude actions from the appellate jurisdiction of the Supreme Court (Article III, section 2, clause 2). As a rule though, the only curb on judicial power has been *the judiciary's own self-restraint*, but history provides scant evidence for its efficacy. This ascendancy of one branch over the government (in this case the judiciary branch) is surely not the purpose of the separation of powers doctrine that is embodied in the Constitution. The absolute rule by the nine judges of the Supreme Court could indeed by called an "oligarchy," which is the rule by a few, but the more accurate term is a "krytocracy," which is the rule by judges.

The truth is there is simply no basis in the Constitution or in statute that gives the judiciary branch the power to determine the constitutionality of laws or acts for the other branches of government. Each branch of the government — the judicial, executive, and legislative — being separate from and co-equal with the others, can determine for itself the constitutionality of some act or law that comes before its own sphere of authority. Thus, in reality there are three types of constitutional review: judicial, executive, and legislative review, but when functioning simultaneously their tripartite operation can most appropriately be called concurrent constitutional review. Dr. Edwin Vieira explains it as follows:

---

1 *Cooper v. Aaron* (1958), FindLaw [Internet]; available from http://caselaw.lp.findlaw.com/scripts/printer_friendly.pl?page=us/358/1.html; accessed 22 July 2008.

... concurrent "constitutional review" by Congress, the Executive, and the Supreme Court, each operating independently within the ambit of its own authority, and none claiming "supremacy" over the others in its power of review, is far more plausible in a representative government, and especially a representative government based upon separation of powers and checks and balances, than is the exclusive "judicial review" that rationalizes the Court's "judicial supremacy."[1]

President Thomas Jefferson explained this form of constitutional review in a passage from his Draft of the First Annual Message to Congress in 1801. Unfortunately, it was deleted from the final version of the message. Let me quote it below:

> Our country has thought proper to distribute the powers of its government among three equal & independent authorities, constituting each a check on one or both of the others, in all attempts to impair its constitution. To make each an effectual check, it must have a right in cases which arise within the line of its proper functions, where, equally with the others, it acts in the last resort & without appeal, to decide on the validity of an act according to its own judgment, & uncontrolled by the opinion of any other department. We have accordingly, in more than one instance, seen the opinions of different departments in opposition to each other, & no ill ensue. The constitution, moreover, as a further security for itself, against violation even by a concurrence of all the departments, has provided for its own reintegration by a change in the persons exercising the functions of those departments (Draft of First Annual Message to Congress, 1801).[2]

He also explained it in several of his letters. Here are the relevant portions of a few of them:

> The judges, believing the law constitutional, had a right to pass a sentence of fine and imprisonment, because that power was placed in their hands by the constitution. But the Executive, believing the law to be unconstitutional, was bound to remit the execution of it; because that power has been confided to him by the constitution. That instrument meant that its co-ordinate branches should be checks on each other. But the opinion which gives to the judges the right to decide what laws are constitutional, and what not, not only for themselves in their own sphere of action, but for the legislature and executive also in their spheres, would make the judiciary a despotic branch (Thomas Jefferson, Letter to Abigail Adams, 1804).[3]

> In denying the right they usurp of exclusively explaining the Constitution, I go further than you do, if I understand rightly your quotation from the *Federalist*, of an opinion that 'the judiciary is the last resort in relation *to the other departments* of the government, but not in relation to the rights of the parties to the compact under which the judiciary is derived.' If this opinion be sound, then indeed is our Constitution a complete *felo de se* [act of suicide]. For intending to establish three departments, coordinate and independent, that they might check and balance one another, it has given, according to this opinion, to one of them alone, the right to prescribe rules for the government of the others, and to that one too, which is unelected by, and independent of the nation. For experience has already shown that the impeachment it has provided is not even a scare-crow.... The Constitution, on this hypothesis, is a mere thing of wax in the hands of the

---

1 Dr. Edwin Vieira, *How To Dethrone the Imperial Judiciary* (San Antonio: Vision forum Ministries, 2004), 228.

2 William J. Quirk, R. Randall Bridwell, *Judicial Dictatorship* (Transaction Publishers: New Brunswick, NJ, 2003), 13.

3 Ibid.

judiciary, which they may twist and shape into any form they please. It should be remembered, as an axiom of eternal truth in politics, that whatever power in any government is independent, is absolute also; in theory only, at first, while the spirit of the people is up, but in practice, as fast as that relaxes. Independence can be trusted nowhere but with the people in mass. They are inherently independent of all but moral law. My construction of the Constitution is very different from that you quote. It is that each department is truly independent of the others, and has an equal right to decide for itself what is the meaning of the Constitution in the cases submitted to its action; and especially, where it is to act ultimately and without appeal (Thomas Jefferson, Letter to Spencer Roane, 1819).

You seem ... to consider the judges the ultimate arbiters of all constitutional questions; a very dangerous doctrine indeed, and one which would place us under the despotism of an oligarchy. Our judges ... and their power [are] the more dangerous as they are in office for life, and are not responsible, as the other functionaries are, to the elective control. The Constitution has erected no such single tribunal, knowing that to whatever hands confided, with the corruptions of time and party, its members would become despots. It has more wisely made all the departments co-equal and co-sovereign within themselves.... When the legislative or executive functionaries act unconstitutionally, they are responsible to the people in their elective capacity. The exemption of the judges from that is quite dangerous enough. I know of no safe depository of the ultimate powers of the society, but the people themselves.... (Thomas Jefferson, Letter to William C. Jarvis, 1820).[1]

President Andrew Jackson stated a similar viewpoint in his Veto Message regarding the Second Bank of the United States in 1832. Let me quote the relevant portion of this document below:

It is maintained by the advocates of the bank that its constitutionality in all its features ought to be considered as settled by precedent and by the decision of the Supreme Court. To this conclusion I can not assent. Mere precedent is a dangerous source of authority, and should not be regarded as deciding questions of constitutional power except where the acquiescence of the people and the States can be considered as well settled....

If the opinion of the Supreme Court covered the whole ground of this act, it ought not to control the coordinate authorities of this Government. The Congress, the Executive, and the Court must each for itself be guided by its own opinion of the Constitution. Each public officer who takes an oath to support the Constitution swears that he will support it as he understands it, and not as it is understood by others. It is as much the duty of the House of Representatives, of the Senate, and of the President to decide upon the constitutionality of any bill or resolution which may be presented to them for passage or approval as it is of the supreme judges when it may be brought before them for judicial decision. The opinion of the judges has no more authority over Congress than the opinion of Congress has over the judges, and on that point the President is independent of both. The authority of the Supreme Court must not, therefore, be permitted to control the Congress or the Executive when acting in their legislative capacities, but to have only such influence as the force of their reasoning may deserve.[2]

---

1 Martin A. Larson, *Jefferson Magnificent Populist* (Devin-Adair, Publishers: Greenwich, CT, 1984), 138.

2 President Jackson's Veto Message Regarding the Bank of the United States; July 10, 1832, The American Presidency Project [Internet]; available from http://www.presidency.ucsb.edu/

Of course, under concurrent constitutional review it is expected that the other branches of the government will evaluate carefully each judicial decision and then act, if appropriate, within their own area of responsibility, but that is the extent of any obligation on their part.

The President's own honest assessment or executive review, as to the constitutionality of the statute purportedly violated, governs whether the executive branch would actually enforce the sentence of a federal court. If he determines it is unconstitutional, whereas the court, through judicial review, has decided just the opposite, he would have two possible remedies. The least contentious one would be his "Power to grant Reprieves and Pardons for Offenses against the United States" (Article II, section 2, clause 1). Using this power, the President could simply pardon the person accused in the specific case and in any similar cases in the future that are adjudicated by a court. The other remedy would be more controversial. He could simply refuse to enforce the court's decision and any future decisions, based on his own determination of the statute's illegality. In addition, Congress would get involved as well. Legislative review could determine that the statute is constitutionally flawed. Under the circumstances, Congress might deem it prudent to rescind the original statute and pass a revised one that would allow the rift to be healed between the judicial and executive branches. On the other hand, Congress, through legislative review, could determine that the statute is constitutionally sound and pass a concurrent resolution stating this fact. If the President remains unyielding in his view of the statute's unconstitutionality, the House could attempt to pass a bill of impeachment against the President (Article I, section 2, clause 5). If successful, the Senate would have to try the impeachment (Article I, section 3, clauses 6 and 7). Whether the President is actually removed from office or not, the next presidential election — either taking place immediately or when the current President's term expires, would hopefully resolve the problem. In any event, the above example shows how all three branches — the judicial, executive, and legislative — could act appropriately within their own areas of responsibility and according to their own separate determinations of the statute's constitutionality.

Of course, under concurrent constitutional review, an impasse may naturally arise between the branches over the constitutionality of a particular action or law and it cannot be resolved through the normal means. How could such a conflict be finally resolved? Dr. Edwin Vieira offers the most appropriate answer to the question as follows:

> ... "judicial supremacy" — the claim that "the federal judiciary is supreme in the exposition of the law of the Constitution" and that "the interpretation of the [Constitution] enunciated by th[e Supreme] Court ... is the supreme law of the land" — affronts both the Constitution's declaration that "WE THE PEOPLE ... do ordain and establish this Constitution and the Constitution's mandate that only WE THE PEOPLE, through their representatives in Congress, State "Legislatures," and the State "Conventions," are authorized to amend it. Moreover, the panegyrists of "judicial supremacy" forget that, because "[t]he power to enact carries with it *final authority to declare the meaning of the legislation*," the "ultimate interpreter of the Constitution" cannot possibly be the Supreme Court, and its "interpretation of the [Constitution]" cannot possibly be "the supreme

law of the land." Rather, the ultimate interpreter, whose decision *ex necessitate* become the supreme law, must always be WE THE PEOPLE.[1]

In other words, the People through the proper channels have the authority to correct a constitutional deadlock via the amendment process found in Article V of the Constitution. Jefferson provides the same remedy in one of his letters. Let me quote the relevant portion of the letter below:

> But the Chief Justice says, 'There must be an ultimate arbiter somewhere.' True, there must; but does that prove it is either party? The ultimate arbiter is the people of the Union, assembled by their deputies in convention, at the call of Congress or of two-thirds of the States. Let them decide to which they mean to give an authority claimed by two of their organs. And it has been the peculiar wisdom and felicity of our Constitution, to have provided this peaceable appeal, where that of other nations is at once to force (Thomas Jefferson, Letter to William Johnson, 1823).

Having shown that each branch of the government has the authority to determine the constitutionality of an act or law within its own sphere of competence via concurrent constitutional review how would genuine *judicial* review operate? In order to look for the answer, here is a more extensive quote from *Marbury v. Madison*:

> It is emphatically the province and duty of the judicial department to say what the law is. Those who apply the rule to *particular cases*, must of necessity expound and interpret that rule. If two laws conflict with each other, the courts must decide on the operation of each. So if a law be in opposition to the constitution: if both the law and the constitution apply to *a particular case*, so that the court must either decide *that case* conformably to the law, disregarding the constitution; or conformably to the constitution, disregarding the law: the court must determine which of these conflicting rules governs *the case. This is of the very essence of judicial duty.*
>
> If then the courts are to regard the constitution; and the constitution is superior to any ordinary act of the legislature; the constitution, and not such ordinary act, must govern *the case* to which they both apply (italics mine).[2]

Chief Justice Marshall used the term "case(s)" five times in the above paragraphs. This is no coincidence, since a case is the most basic component of the judicial process and the focal point of judicial review in its *true* form. Genuine judicial review can be described as the process of deciding a *specific case* that comes before a court. If in this process, a federal court finds that a statute is in conflict with the Constitution, the latter, taking first position as the "supreme Law of the Land,"[3] must take precedence over the former and the statute must be disregarded. However, the important point to keep squarely in mind is this: Except for issues regarding concurrent constitutional review described above, under genuine *judicial* review, *only the parties to the case can be bound by a court's decision.* When we allow federal court decisions, particularly those of the Supreme Court, to have authority that extends outside the judicial do-

---

1 Dr. Edwin Vieira, *How To Dethrone the Imperial Judiciary* (San Antonio: Vision forum Ministries, 2004), 228-9.

2 *Marbury v. Madison* (1803), FindLaw [Internet]; available from http://supreme.lp.findlaw.com/supreme_court/landmark/marbury.html; accessed 22 July 2008.

3 According to Article VI, clause 2 of the Constitution, "*this Constitution*, and the Laws of the United States which shall be made in Pursuance thereof; and all Treaties made, or which shall be made, under the Authority of the United States, *shall be the supreme Law of the Land*; and the Judges in every State shall be bound thereby, any Thing in the Constitution or Laws of any State to the Contrary notwithstanding" (italics mine).

main, courts become ipso facto *legislators*, which is definitely not the business of the judiciary.

Dr. Edwin Vieira explains true judicial review in the following manner:

> ... nowhere does the Constitution delegate to judges any power that amounts to "judicial supremacy." Rather, WE THE PEOPLE delegated merely "[t]he judicial Power," and that only in "Cases" and "Controversies." Nothing in "[t]he judicial Power" so limited leads inexorably (or even at all) to the conclusion that an opinion of the Supreme Court on some constitutional issue necessary to decide a "Case[ ]" or "Controvers[y]," involving particular litigants, under a set of facts peculiar to that litigation, binds *everyone else in the world* on that question, notwithstanding that no one else has had a hearing in that "Case[ ]" or "Controvers[y]." To the contrary, such an universalistic misconstruction of "t]he judicial Power" offends the first principle of due process of law, that "[p]arties whose rights are to be affected are entitled to be heard."[1]

Since applying the law to a specific case is the very foundation of its responsibility, the judicial branch can use "stare decisis" and choose to be obligated by it. The doctrine of "stare decisis" is adhering to the findings of prior court decisions (i.e., precedent) in deciding subsequent cases in which the facts are similar. However, the use of precedent in making its decisions would not impinge on the other branches nor would it create law that others outside the judiciary would be legally bound to follow.

President Abraham Lincoln concurred with this opinion of judicial review, as can be seen in the following passage from his First Inaugural Address on Monday, March 4, 1861:

> I do not forget the position assumed by some that constitutional questions are to be decided by the Supreme Court, nor do I deny that such decisions must be binding in any case upon the parties to a suit as to the object of that suit, while they are also entitled to very high respect and consideration in all parallel cases by all other departments of the Government. And while it is obviously possible that such decision may be erroneous in any given case, still the evil effect following it, being limited to that particular case, with the chance that it may be overruled and never become a precedent for other cases, can better be borne than could the evils of a different practice. At the same time, the candid citizen must confess that if the policy of the Government upon vital questions affecting the whole people is to be irrevocably fixed by decisions of the Supreme Court, the instant they are made in ordinary litigation between parties in personal actions the people will have ceased to be their own rulers, having to that extent practically resigned their Government into the hands of that eminent tribunal. Nor is there in this view any assault upon the court or the judges. It is a duty from which they may not shrink to decide cases properly brought before them, and it is no fault of theirs if others seek to turn their decisions to political purposes.[2]

On the television program *Uncommon Knowledge*, hosted by Peter Robinson and produced by the Hoover Institution, an interesting discussion occurred between Lawrence Alexander, Warren Distinguished Professor of Law at the University of San Diego, and Robert George, McCormick Professor of Jurisprudence and Direc-

---

1 Dr. Edwin Vieira, *How To Dethrone the Imperial Judiciary* (San Antonio: Vision forum Ministries, 2004), 229-30.

2 Abraham Lincoln, First Inaugural Address (Monday, March 4, 1861), The American Presidency Project [Internet]; available from http://www.presidency.ucsb.edu/ws/index.php?pid=25818&st=&st1=; accessed 22 July 2008.

tor of the James Madison Program in American Ideals and Institutions at Princeton University. The title of the program was "The High (And Mighty) Court: Judicial Supremacy" and it was filmed on October 27, 2003. Robert George supported President Lincoln's view that decisions of the Supreme Court are only "binding ...upon the parties to a suit as to the object of that suit," whereas Lawrence Alexander favored judicial review, as it is usually understood.

In one part of the program, the discussion turned to the Supreme Court case of *Bush v. Gore* that settled the 2000 presidential election in favor of George W. Bush.[1] In this case, the US Supreme Court in a 7–2 opinion on December 12, 2000 decided that the varying standards for performing vote recounts in different parts of Florida violated the Fourteenth Amendment's "due process" and "equal protection" clauses. The state would have to create new, uniform standards and implement them, if any vote recount was to be undertaken. Furthermore, an additional 5–4 opinion set down the appropriate remedy that was based on the state's deadline for certifying its Electoral Votes, which was midnight December 12. Since *Bush v. Gore* had been decided only hours before this cut-off date, the Court concluded that a proper recount by the state authorities could not be completed in time, which essentially ended all recounts. Consequently, Secretary of State, Katherine Harris, was able to certify that George W. Bush won Florida's 25 Electoral Votes, which gave him enough Electoral Votes to gain the Presidency.

How would this crisis have turned out, if Lincoln's position had been in effect? Here is the relevant portion of the program:

> *Lawrence Alexander:* Let me just give you one other case ...
>
> *Peter Robinson:* Yeah, sure. Go ahead.
>
> *Lawrence Alexander:* ... where judicial supremacy would have been, you know, where you can see the value of it and that's *Bush v. Gore*.
>
> Peter Robinson: Right.
>
> *Lawrence Alexander:* Assume for a moment that the other political branches did not feel bound by the Supreme Court opinion. You can imagine various scenarios in which politics wouldn't settle the matter because it's the very rules of politics that themselves would be at issue. And there would be disagreements. There could have been disagreements about whether, you know, which delegation from Florida should be recognized, about how the votes could be — there were a number of constitutional questions up in the air. And if you don't assume the power of the Court to arbitrate in that — to come up with a definitive interpretation of the Constitution as it applies ...
>
> *Peter Robinson:* Binding on the state court in Florida, binding on the Florida legislature, binding on ...
>
> *Lawrence Alexander:* Binding on Congress.
>
> *Peter Robinson:* ... binding on Congress, binding on the President, the Vice President. That was important.
>
> *Lawrence Alexander:* I mean, one of the things that *Cooper v. Aaron* does is it prevents — assuming the Court doesn't go completely mad and wild, it prevents major constitutional crises ....

---

1 George W. Bush, et al., Petitioners v. Albert Gore, Jr., et al. (December 12, 2000), FindLaw [Internet]; available from http://caselaw.lp.findlaw.com/scripts/getcase.pl?court=US&vol=000&invol=00-949; accessed 22 July 2008.

Peter Robinson: Absent the assumption of judicial supremacy, absent that, what would *Bush v. Gore* have looked like?

Robert George: Let me make three points about it.

Peter Robinson: Sure.

Robert George: First, according to Lincoln's own standards, *Bush v. Gore* would be settled law because it's binding on the parties to the case. That is Bush and Gore. Secondly ...

Peter Robinson: He's got you there, no?

Lawrence Alexander: Well it's true that in terms of ...

Peter Robinson: We'll get your other two points if we need to but the first one seems decisive, no?

Lawrence Alexander: It's true that in terms of the counting of the ballots in Florida, it was binding on the parties. That did not necessarily conclude anything else.

Peter Robinson: Okay. Other two points. Sorry.

Robert George: Well the second point is that often it will be prudent for statesmen in the executive and legislative branches by Lincoln's own terms here, to comply with Supreme Court rulings, not because they're necessarily the final word but because in the circumstances, the public wheel does require that. So compliance with *Bush v. Gore* would have been probably a prudent thing to do even if a particular person didn't believe he was constitutionally required to ...

Peter Robinson: Are you asserting, Robert, that if your view had prevailed, we just wouldn't have any more constitutional crises than we've had? We would have been ...

Robert George: No, we would have constitutional crises but we would not call them constitutional crises. We would call it constitutional politics, I think.[1]

If Lincoln's viewpoint had been in operation, no significant political crisis would have ensued, since George W. Bush and Al Gore were the litigants to the suit and for that reason, they would have been bound by the Court's decision.

---

1 "The High (And Mighty) Court: Judicial Supremacy," *Uncommon Knowledge*, Hosted by Peter Robinson, Filmed on October 27, 2003, Hoover Institution [Internet]; available from http://www.hoover.org/multimedia/uk/2992941.html; accessed 22 July 2008.

CHAPTER 16: YEAR OF INFAMY

The views of men can only be known, or guessed at, by their words or actions.
— George Washington, Letter to Patrick Henry, January 15, 1799

We can properly call 1913 the Year of Infamy, since it then that the downward spiral away from the government of the "Authentic Constitution" really began in full force. This attack on US liberties and the intended form of government came in three steps:

1. Step one: The American people were falsely led to believe that the ratification of the Sixteenth Amendment was completed on February 3, 1913. As we learned in a previous chapter, the purpose of this Amendment was to make the income tax legal.

2. Step two: The American people were again falsely led to believe that the ratification of the Seventeenth Amendment was completed on April 8, 1913. In a previous chapter, we learned that the purpose of this Amendment was to allow the people of each state to elect Senators instead of the state legislature.

3. Step three: The unconstitutional Federal Reserve Act was passed on December 23, 1913, just before the Christmas recess. As we learned in a previous chapter, the purpose of this Act was to create the Federal Reserve System (the Fed), which took the power to create money away from Congress and gave it to a cabal of private bankers. In actuality, such a radical change in the Constitution could only have been accomplished by a properly ratified constitutional amendment.

Was this threefold attack mere happenstance; or was it actually orchestrated by powerful forces operating behind the scenes? Over the years, various writers have speculated about the existence of a worldwide super-elite made up of exceedingly rich and powerful banking families and other high-ranking people, who have been diligently working for some time to consolidate the nations of the world into a socialistic, totalitarian "new world order" for their own nefarious purposes.

Those who have written on this subject have often been rashly described as para-noid, sensationalistic, conspiracy nuts writing on the fringe of journalism. However, the surprising disclosures made in a book of more than 1,300 pages titled *Tragedy and Hope: A History of the World in Our Time* by Dr. Carroll Quigley should have largely discredited any such characterizations. Dr. Quigley was most definitely *not* a sensa-tionalist, fringe writer, but a distinguished professor of history at the Foreign Service School of Georgetown University until his death in January 1977. Prior to his profes-sorship at Georgetown University, he also taught at Princeton and Harvard. It is also worth mentioning that Dr. Quigley was one of President Bill Clinton's professors during his earlier years at Georgetown University and the latter even mentions him in one of his speeches given at that very school.[1]

According to W. Cleon Skousen in his book titled *The Naked Capitalist*, which is a valuable review and commentary on Dr. Quigley's huge book, "the real value of *Tragedy and Hope* is not so much as a 'history of the world in our time' (as its subtitle suggests), but rather as a bold and boastful admission by Dr. Quigley that there actu-ally exists a relatively small but powerful group which has succeeded in acquiring a choke-hold on the affairs of practically the entire human race."[2]

Just before making this startling disclosure, Dr. Quigley describes what he calls the "radical Right fairy tale":

> This radical Right fairy tale, which is now as accepted folk myth in many groups in America, pictured the recent history of the United States, in regard to domes-tic reform and in foreign affairs, as a well-organized plot by extreme Left-wing elements, operating from the White House itself and controlling all the chief avenues of publicity in the United States, to destroy the American way of life, based on private enterprise, laissez faire, and isolationism, in behalf of alien ideologies of Russian Socialism and British cosmopolitanism (or international-ism). This plot, if we are to believe the myth, worked through such avenues of publicity as *The New York Times* and the *Herald Tribune*, the *Christian Science Monitor* and the *Washington Post*, the *Atlantic Monthly* and *Harper's Magazine* and had at its core the wild-eyed and bushy-haired theoreticians of Socialist Harvard and the London School of Economics. It was determined to bring the United States into World War II on the side of England (Roosevelt's first love) and Soviet Russia (his second love) in order to destroy every finer element of American life and, as part of this consciously planned scheme, invited Japan to attack Pearl Har-bor, and destroyed Chiang Kai-shek, all the while undermining America's real strength by excessive spending and unbalanced budgets.[3]

In the next paragraph, Dr. Quigley makes his statement about the "network," which is the name he gives to the group mentioned by Mr. Skousen above:

> This myth, like all fables, does in fact have a modicum of truth. There does exist, and has existed for a generation, an international Anglophile network which operates, to some extent, in the way the radical Right believes the Communists act. In fact, this network ... has no aversion to cooperating with the Commu-nists, or any other groups, and frequently does so. I know of the operations of this network because I have studied it for twenty years and was permitted for

1 Remarks at the Edmund A. Walsh School of Foreign Service at Georgetown University, November 10, 1994, The American Presidency Project [Internet]; available from http://www.presidency.ucsb.edu/ws/index.php?pid=49469&st=Carroll&st1=Quigley; accessed 26 July 2008.
2 W. Cleon Skousen, *The Naked Capitalist* (Salt Lake City: Private Edition by Reviewer, 1970), 6.
3 Carroll Quigley, *Tragedy and Hope: A History of the World in Our Time* (New York: The Macmillan Company, 1966), 949.

two years, in the early 1960's, to examine its papers and secret records. I have no aversion to it or to most of its aims and have, for much of my life, been close to it and to many of its instruments. I have objected, both in the past and recently, to a few of its policies ... but in general my chief difference of opinion is that it wishes to remain unknown, and I believe its role in history is significant enough to be known.[1]

According to the above paragraph, Dr. Quigley informs us that the "network" wants to stay anonymous, although he was not in agreement with them on this point. He also tells us he was allowed for a time to examine its secret documents. This is truly an amazing admission, but it is only the beginning. Who finances the activities of this "network"? Dr. Quigley answers this question as follows:

Since 1925 there have been substantial contributions from wealthy individuals and from foundations and firms associated with the international banking fraternity, especially the Carnegie United Kingdom Trust, and other organizations associated with J. P. Morgan, the Rockefeller and Whitney families, and the associates of Lazard Brothers and of Morgan, Grenfell, and Company.

The chief backbone of this dynasties copied but rarely excelled organization grew up along the already existing financial cooperation running from the Morgan Bank in New York to a group of international financiers in London led by Lazard Brothers.[2]

However, Dr. Quigley makes clear that the source of its power is not the "network" itself, but actually those who finance its activities from behind the scenes:

It must be recognized that the power that these energetic Left-wingers [the "network"] exercised was never their own power or Communist power but was ultimately the power of the international financial coterie....[3]

This is what Dr. Quigley says about the grand plan of this "international financial coterie":

In addition to ... [certain] pragmatic goals, the powers of financial capitalism ["international financial coterie"] had another far-reaching aim, nothing less than to create a world system of financial control in private hands able to dominate the political system of each country and the economy of the world as a whole. This system was to be controlled in a feudalist fashion by the central banks of the world acting in concert, by secret agreements arrived at in frequent private meetings and conferences. The apex of the system was to be the Bank for International Settlements in Basle, Switzerland, a private bank owned and controlled by the world's central banks which were themselves private corporations. Each central bank, in the hands of men like Montagu Norman of the Bank of England, Benjamin Strong of the New York Federal Reserve Bank, Charles Rist of the Bank of France, and Hjalmar Schacht of the Reichsbank, sought to dominate its government by its ability to control Treasury loans, to manipulate foreign exchanges, to influence the level of economic activity in the country, and to influence cooperative politicians by subsequent economic rewards in the business world.[4]

There you have it. The plan of the 'international financial coterie" or international bankers is to create a financial structure capable of controlling politics and economics on a global scale. You will note that the Fed is one of the central banks mentioned

---

1 Quigley, 950.
2 Ibid., 951.
3 Ibid., 954.
4 Ibid., 324.

in this worldwide system, since all the central banks of the world are linked through the Bank for International Settlements in Basle, Switzerland. By first gaining control of a nation's money supply, the bankers in time could acquire virtually complete power over the nation by creating inflation or recession at will, and by saddling the people, as well as the government, with enormous debt. It is worth mentioning that the eighteenth century European banker, Meyer Amschel Rothschild, is alleged to have said, "Give me control of a nation's money supply and I care not who makes its laws." When all nations were controlled in this fashion, the final step would be to extend their control worldwide.

Dr. Quigley provides us with some very interesting additional information about how the banking families created their huge financial empire and how they established their families into dynasties similar to the European royal families:

> The merchant bankers of London had already at hand in 1810–1850 the Stock Exchange, the Bank of England, and the London money market when the needs of advancing industrialism called all of these into the industrial world which they had hitherto ignored. In time they brought into their financial network the provincial banking centers, organized as commercial banks and savings banks, as well as insurance companies to form all of these into a single financial system on an international scale which manipulated the quantity and flow of money so that they were able to influence, if not control, governments on one side and industries on the other. The men who did this, looking backward toward the period of dynastic monarchy in which they had their own roots, aspired to establish dynasties of international bankers and were at least successful at this as were many of the dynastic political rulers. The Greatest of these dynasties, of course, were the descendants of Meyer Amschel Rothschild (1743–1812) of Frankfort, whose male descendants, for at least two generations, generally married first cousins or even nieces. Rothschild's five sons, established at branches in Vienna, London, Naples, and Paris, as well as Frankfort, cooperated together in ways which other international banking dynasties copied but rarely excelled.
>
> . . .
>
> The names of some of these banking families are familiar to all of us and should be more so. They included Baring, Lazard, Erlanger, Warburg, Schröder, Seligman, the Speyers, Mirabaud, Mallet, Fould, and above all Rothschild and Morgan.... These bankers came to be called "international bankers".... In all countries they carried on various kinds of banking and exchange activities, but everywhere they were sharply distinguishable from other, more obvious, kinds of banks, such as savings banks or commercial banks.
>
> One of their less obvious characteristics was that they remained as private unincorporated firms, usually partnerships, until relatively recently. Offering no shares, no reports, and usually no advertising to the public.... This persistence as private firms continued because it ensured the maximum of anonymity and secrecy to persons of tremendous public power who dreaded public knowledge of their activities as an evil almost as great as inflation. As a consequence, ordinary people had no way of knowing the wealth or areas of operation of such firms, and often were somewhat hazy as to their membership.
>
> . . .
>
> The influence of financial capitalism and the international bankers who created it was exercised both on business and on governments, but could have done neither if it had not been able to persuade both these to accept two "axioms" of its own ideology. Both of these were based on the assumption that politicians were too weak and too subject to temporary popular pressures to be trusted

with control of the money system; accordingly, the sanctity of all values and the soundness of money must be protected in two ways: by basing the value of money on gold and by allowing bankers to control the supply of money.[1] To do this it was necessary to conceal, or even to mislead, both governments and people about the nature of money and its methods of operation.[2]

Near the beginning of his review and commentary, Mr. Skousen offers his explanation why Dr. Quigley wrote his book in the first place:

> When Dr. Quigley decided to write his ... book ... he knew he was deliberately exposing one of the best kept secrets in the world. As one of the elite "insiders," he knew the scope of this power complex and he knew that its leaders hope to eventually attain total global control. Furthermore, Dr. Quigley makes it clear throughout his book that by and large he warmly supports the goals and purposes of the "network." But if that is the case, why would he want to expose this world-wide conspiracy and discloses many of its most secret operations? Obviously, disclosing the existence of a mammoth power network which is trying to take over the world could not help but arouse the vigorous resistance of the millions of people who are its intended victims. So why did Dr. Quigley write this book?
>
> His answer appears in a number of places.... He says, in effect, that it is now too late for the little people to turn back the tide, In the spirit of kindness he is therefore urging them not to fight the noose which is already around their necks. He feels certain that those who do will only choke themselves to death. On the other hand, those who go along with the immense pressure which is beginning to be felt by all humanity will eventually find themselves in a man-made millennium of peace and prosperity. All through his book, Dr. Quigley assures us that we can trust these benevolent, well-meaning men who are secretly operating behind the scenes. THEY are the *hope* of the world. All who resist them represent *tragedy.* Hence, the title for his book.[3]

Then, towards the ending of his work, Mr. Skousen offers his assessment of what is really happening, based on the startling disclosures of Dr. Quigley:

> Actually, what we are witnessing is a very carefully and methodically executed program designed to destroy constitutional government as we have known it and make shambles of the society which has wanted to keep the Constitution alive, Only then can a highly centralized, socialist state be established.
>
> To achieve this, the middle class in America must be ruthlessly squeezed out of existence. That is the message which looms large from many passages in Dr. Quigley's book and which will be found as a favorite theme in the books, magazines and newspapers of the Establishment's liberal press. Just as Marx and Engels waged war against the middle class to set up a socialist state, so does Dr. Quigley and the global network.
>
> The middle class is to be identified as the "petty bourgeoisie," the "neo-isolationists," the broad masses of Americans who are described by Dr. Quigley as "often very insecure, envious, filled with hatreds, and are generally the chief recruits for the Radical Right, fascists, or hate campaigns against any group that

---

1 It should be noted here that Dr. Quigley is describing the period that he calls "Financial Capitalism," which he dates from 1850 to 1931. During this period, there was indeed a gold standard, so the "value of money [was based] on gold," but there was also fractional reserve banking, which means that "bankers [were allowed] to control the supply of money."

2 Quigley, 51-3.

3 Skousen, 4 — 5.

is different or which refuse to conform to middle-class values"(p. 1243). What are Middle-class values?

Middle-class values, of course, are represented by the Constitutional concepts of limited government, states' rights, rights of property, a competitive economy, the solving of problems on a local level if possible and, in any event, with a minimal of government meddling. But all this, Dr. Quigley would seem to suggest, is anathema. It has to go. People who think this way are middle-class mentalities. They are described by Dr. Quigley as the same kind of people as those who supported "the Nazis in Germany thirty years ago" (p.1244). [1]

Although the need for the passage of the Federal Reserve Act is obvious for the operation of the bankers' plan, what was the purpose for the supposed ratifications of the Sixteenth and Seventeenth Amendments?

In 1984, during the presidency of Ronald Reagan, a shocking admission about the income tax was made in the cover letter of the Grace Commission Report, which is also called the President's Private Sector Survey on Cost Control (PPSS). I quote the applicable portion of the letter below:

> Resistance to additional income taxes would be even more widespread if people were aware that:
> * One third of all their taxes is consumed by waste and inefficiency in the Federal Government as we identified in our survey.
> * Another one-third of all their taxes escapes collection from others as the underground economy blossoms in direct proportion to tax increases and places even more pressure on law abiding taxpayers, promoting still more underground economy-a vicious cycle that must be broken.
> * With two-thirds of everyone's personal income taxes wasted or not collected, 100 percent of what is collected is absorbed solely by interest on the Federal debt and by Federal Government contributions to transfer payments. In other words, all individual income tax revenues are gone before one nickel is spent on the services which taxpayers expect from their Government. [2]

The sad truth is that all personal income taxes collected by the federal government actually pay for only two things: the "interest on the Federal debt" and "contributions to transfer payments." This fact is made clear by the statement that "all individual income tax revenues are gone before one nickel is spent on the services which taxpayers expect from their Government."

According to the Grace Commission Report, the first thing personal incomes taxes pay is "interest on the Federal debt." Currently, the Federal (National) debt is more than $9.5 trillion and growing,[3] and in 2007, the interest payment on the debt was $430 billion.[4] In 2006 (the latest year currently available), total personal income tax collections were $1,236 billion.[5] Paying the Federal Debt interest first would leave $806 billion of the collections for "contributions to transfer payments."

---

1 Ibid., 115.

2 The Grace Commission Report (PPSS) Cover Letter from the NTIS (National Technical Information Service), Welcome to uhuh.com [Internet]; available from http://www.uhuh. com/taxstuff/gracecom.htm; accessed 26 July 2008.

3 The Debt to the Penny and Who Holds It, Treasury Direct [Internet]; available from http:// www.treasurydirect.gov/NP/BPDLogin?application=np; accessed 13 July 2008.

4 Internet Expense on the Debt Outstanding, Treasury Direct [Internet]; available from http:// www.treasurydirect.gov/govt/reports/ir/ir_expense.htm; accessed 13 July 2008.

5 Table 466. Internal Revenue Gross Collections by Type of Tax: 2001 to 2006, Federal Government Finances & Employment: Federal Budget — Receipts, Outlays, and Debt, The

---

How much revenue does the US banking system take in from the Federal Debt interest? In a booklet published by the Board of Governors of the Federal Reserve System (the Fed), it states that "the Federal Reserve Banks derive their earnings primarily from interest on their proportionate share of the System's holdings of securities acquired through open market operations...."[1] It further explains that "earnings of Federal Reserve Banks are allocated first to the payment of expenses (including assessments by the Board of Governors to defray its expenses), the statutory 6 percent dividend on Federal Reserve stock that member institutions are legally required to purchase, and additions to surplus necessary to maintain each Reserve Bank's surplus equal to its paid-in capital stock. Remaining earnings are then paid into the US Treasury."[2]

In 2007, the Fed's "Current Income" was $42,576 million, $40,298 million of which came from US Treasury securities. Its net income after expenses, but before payments to the Treasury, was $38,716 million. This amount was then reduced by $992 million, which was the dividends paid to member banks (i.e., the stockholders of the Fed) and $3,126 million, which was the amount transferred to the Fed's surplus account. The remainder, which was $34,598 million, was paid to the US Treasury.[3] As can be seen, the Fed's income is significantly reduced by the Treasury payment, which is actually the amount of interest earned on US Treasury securities held as collateral for Federal Reserve notes. In 2007, the Fed's earnings from US Treasury securities was $5,700 ($40,298 reduced by $34,598).

In addition, all depository institutions in the country (commercial banks, savings institutions, and credit unions) earn interest income on US Treasury securities. This revenue is computed as approximately $4,985 million according to the table below. Thus, in 2007 the total revenue earned by the US banking system on its ownership of US Treasury securities was approximately $10,685 million.

However, the ownership of US Treasury securities is not the only channel used by the US banking system to obtain revenue from Federal Debt interest. Where do all the interest earnings received by individuals, corporations, state and local governments, and others eventually end up? The answer is, of course, in banks. When deposits in banks increase, their reserves increase as well, which allows banks to use any excess reserves they may acquire to create new loans.[4] According to the Federal Reserve Bank of Chicago, "the deposit expansion factor for a given amount of new reserves is ... the reciprocal of the required reserve percentage...."[5] Thus, if the reserve requirement is 10%, loans can be increased to *ten times* the amount of new reserves

2008 Statistical Abstract, US Census Bureau [Internet]; available from http://www.census.gov/compendia/statab/tables/08s0466.pdf; accessed 29 June 2008.

1 *The Federal Reserve System: Purpose & Functions*, Second Printing (Washington, D. C.: Board of Governors of the Federal Reserve System, 1985), 9.

2 Ibid.

3 Reports to Congress, 94th Annual Report 2007, Federal Reserve Operations, Income and Expenses, Board of Governors of the Federal Reserve System [Internet]; available from http://www.federalreserve.gov/boarddocs/rptcongress/; accessed 7 July 2008.

4 According to the Federal Reserve Bank of Chicago, "reserves in excess of ... [required reserves] may be used to increase earning assets — loans and investments." *Modern Money Mechanics* (Chicago: Federal Reserve Bank of Chicago, February, 1994), Debt Money, ancient meme [Internet]; available from http://landru.i-link-2.net/monques/mmm2.html#MODERN; accessed 13 July 2008. However, so as not to make the above explanation overly complicated, I will not consider investments, but only loans.

5 Ibid.

(1/.10 = 10). In addition, it is important to mention, "the most important nonbank depositor [at the Fed] is the US Treasury.... Disbursements by the Treasury ... are made against its balances at the Federal Reserve."[1]

Distribution of 2007 Federal Debt

2007 Federal Debt and Interest, and Revenue Earned by the US Banking System on Federal Debt (US only, Amounts in millions, Approximate only)

Description	Federal Debt[13]	Interest[14]	Revenue Earned by the US Banking System on Federal Debt	
Total Federal Debt	$9,030,612	$430,000		
Less: Securities issued by Federal Agencies other than the US Treasury	($22,959)	($967)		
Total US Treasury (Public Debt) Securities	$9,007,653	$429,033		
Less: Government account holdings	($3,958,411)	($166,649)		
Less: Fed holdings	($774,913)	($40,298)	Interest on US Treasury securities: $40,298 (Less: portion paid to Treasury: $34,598)	$5,700
Total US Treasury (Public Debt) Securities held privately	$4,274,329	$222,086		
Less: Foreign and International holdings	($2,244,100)	($94,477)		
Less: Depository institutions holdings	($118,400)	($4,985)	Interest on US Treasury securities	$4,985
Remaining Federal Debt	$1,911,829	$122,624	Total Revenue Earned	$10,685

All $122,624 million of the remaining interest on the Federal debt shown in the table above is paid from the US Treasury Account at the Fed to the various recipients mentioned above, who in turn deposit the checks received in their respective banks. For purposes of the illustration below, I will designate all banks together, but not including the Fed, the US Banking System. Keeping in mind that assets must equal

---

1 Ibid.

liabilities plus net worth and disregarding for purposes of this example all the other assets, liabilities, and net worth that would normally be recorded, the balance sheets of the Fed and the US Banking System would look like this:

FED'S BALANCE SHEET (SIMPLIFIED)

Assets	Liabilities
	($122,624,000,000) US Treasury Account
	$122,624,000,000 Reserve Account: Banking System
	Net Worth

US BANKING SYSTEM'S BALANCE SHEET (SIMPLIFIED)

Assets	Liabilities
$122,624,000,000 Reserves at Fed	$122,624,000,000 Demand Deposits
	Net Worth
TOTAL: $122,624,000,000	TOTAL: $122,624,000,000

If the reserve requirement is 10%, when the deposit expansion process finally reaches its end, the US Banking System will have increased its deposits by *ten times* the initial reserves of $122,624 million to $1,226,240 million by increasing its loans to $1,103,616 million. The balance sheet of the US Banking System would look like this:

US BANKING SYSTEM'S BALANCE SHEET (SIMPLIFIED)

Assets	Liabilities
$122,624,000,000 Reserves at Fed	$1,226,240,000,000 Demand Deposits
$1,103,616,000,000 Loans	Net Worth
TOTAL: $1,226,240,000,000	TOTAL: $1,226,240,000,000

Loans of $1,103,616 million multiplied by the prime rate (7.96% in 2006, the latest year currently available),[1] means $87,848 million in interest earnings. These are rather substantial earnings. No wonder the bankers wanted to get the Sixteenth Amendment ratified.

According to the Grace Commission Report, the second thing personal incomes taxes pay is "contributions to transfer payments." Transfer payments are money paid to individuals by the government that is not given as compensation for goods or services and that the latter never uses itself, but "transfers" from one group of people to another to provide the latter with certain monetary benefits. In 2005 (the latest year

---

1 Table 1166. Money Market Interest Rates and Mortgage Rates: 1980 to 2006, Banking, Finance, & Insurance: Money Stock, Interest Rates, Bond Yields, The 2008 Statistical Abstract, US Census Bureau [Internet]; http://www.census.gov/compendia/statab/tables/08s1166.pdf; accessed 13 July 2008.

currently available), the total of government transfer payments to individuals was $1,446 billion.[1]

In 2006 (the latest year currently available), total personal income tax collections were $1,236 billion.[2] Paying the Federal Debt interest of $430 billion first would leave $806 billion of the collections for paying "contributions to transfer payments," but the balance would only cover 56% of the latter (1,236 — 430 = 806, 806 / 1,446 = 56%). Can you see what is happening here? Individual income tax collections are being "absorbed" (to use the Grace Commission's word) by interest and transfer payments like a dry sponge soaking up water in a parched and barren desert. Indeed, this proves like nothing else can the truth of the Grace Commission Report statement that "all individual income tax revenues are gone before one nickel is spent on the services which taxpayers expect from their Government."

Another important point must be mentioned. When the individuals who receive these transfer payments get them, where do they deposit them? The answer is again in banks. As a result, based on the deposit expansion factor described above, the banks are able to create more loans and thus earn more profits. I hope you can now understand why, when you see a new bank building just completed, it always seems to look more imposing than the previous one and reaches a little higher into the sky.

Furthermore, it is easy to see that transfer payments, as well as the income tax system itself, are really wealth redistribution systems. Besides the usual kinds of transfer payments like retirement & disability insurance benefit payments, including Social Security; medical payments, including Medicare; income maintenance benefit payments, including Supplemental Security Income (SSI), family assistance, and food stamps; unemployment insurance benefit payments; veterans benefit payments; and federal education & training assistance payments; there is an "Other payments" category, as well. In 2005 (the latest year currently available), the total amount of this category was $4,841 million. It included "Bureau of Indian Affairs payments, education exchange payments, Alaska Permanent Fund dividend payments, compensation of survivors of public safety officers, compensation of victims of crime, disaster relief payments, compensation for Japanese internment, and other special payments to individuals."[3]

With regard to the income tax system, in 1946 Beardsley Ruml, who was the Chairman of the Federal Reserve Bank of New York, explained the wealth redistribution objective of federal taxes in a magazine article:

> The second principal purpose of federal taxes is to attain more equality of wealth and of income than would result from economic forces working alone. The taxes which are effective for this purpose are the progressive individual income tax, the progressive estate tax, and the gift tax. What these taxes should

---

1 Table 523. Government Transfer Payments to Individuals by Type: 1990 to 2005, Social Insurance & Human Services: Government Transfer Payments, Social Assistance, The 2008 Statistical Abstract, US Census Bureau [Internet]; available from http://www.census.gov/compendia/statab/tables/08s0523.pdf; accessed 14 July 2008.

2 Table 466. Internal Revenue Gross Collections by Type of Tax: 2001 to 2006, Federal Government Finances & Employment: Federal Budget — Receipts, Outlays, and Debt, The 2008 Statistical Abstract, US Census Bureau [Internet]; available from http://www.census.gov/compendia/statab/tables/08s0466.pdf; accessed 29 June 2008.

3 Table 523. Government Transfer Payments to Individuals by Type: 1990 to 2005, Social Insurance & Human Services: Government Transfer Payments, Social Assistance, The 2008 Statistical Abstract, US Census Bureau [Internet]; available from http://www.census.gov/compendia/statab/tables/08s0523.pdf; accessed 14 July 2008.

be depends on public policy with respect to the distribution of wealth and of income. These taxes should be defended and attacked in terms of their effect on the character of American life, not as revenue measures.[1]

The evidence above shows quite clearly why the bankers wanted the Sixteenth amendment ratified. Income tax collections were to be used to pay interest on their investments in US Treasury securities and to increase their reserves for creating new loans that earned even more interest. Although the income tax laws in themselves were to be a means for reallocating wealth, tax collections were also to be an apparatus for reallocating wealth through transfer payments to individuals. The underlying rationale for this entire scheme was, as Mr. Skousen stated in the quotation above, to have a means for "ruthlessly squeez[ing the middle class in America] out of existence."

Of course, this entire scheme could not have come about in the first place, if Congress had followed the Constitution and did only what it was authorized to do. Only by ignoring the Constitution, could Congress increase the size of government to unprecedented levels and finance the welfare-warfare state. However, since the people could only be taxed so far, money had to be borrowed to fund the over-spending. Consequently, in due course an enormous Federal Debt was created. Since a source of funds was now needed to pay the interest of the Debt, the personal income tax was created, with one of its purposes being, to pay this outlay.

What was the reason for having the Seventeenth Amendment in the bankers' plan? The answer is that it was needed to sever the representation of the states, as political entities, with the federal government in order to obstruct their ability to put an end to the bankers' plan by abolishing the Fed.

As we have seen, the Fed is a completely fiat monetary system without a scintilla gold or silver coin backing up the money supply it administers. Based on Article I, section 10, clause 1 that "No State shall ... make any Thing but gold and silver Coin a Tender in Payment of Debts," the states are constitutionally barred from recognizing Federal Reserve notes, coins, and checking accounts in the form of demand deposits or other check writing deposits as legal tender. Now that Senators are elected by the people of each state and thus represent the people and their concerns, this clause in the Constitution can be easily forgotten or ignored. This was not the case prior to the supposed ratification of the Seventeenth Amendment, when Senators were chosen by the state legislatures and they represented the states and their interests.

Professor Todd Zywicki of George Mason University has this to say about the one time custom of state legislatures providing directives to their Senators:

> The Senate was seen as the forum for the states to speak as sovereign entities. State governments ensured that senators represented their interests through the historic practice of "instructing" senators. Under this practice, state legislatures told senators how to vote on particular legislative items.[2]

Furthermore, he says, "Senators who failed to heed their instructions were usually forced to resign, even if their terms were not complete."[3] This custom of providing

---

1 "Taxes for Revenue Are Obsolete," by Beardsley Ruml, *American Affairs*, January, 1946, p.36. Quoted from G. Edward Griffin, *The Creature from Jekyll Island: A Second Look at the Federal Reserve*, Second Printing (Appleton, Wisconsin: American Opinion Publishing, Inc., 1994), 205.

2 Todd J. Zywicki, "Senators and Special Interests: A Public Choice Analysis of the Seventeenth Amendment" (pg. 1036), Professor Todd J. Zywicki's Publications [Internet]; available from http://mason.gmu.edu/~tzywick2/Oregon%20Senators.pdf; accessed 26 July 2008.

3 Ibid (pg. 1036).

instructions is apparently no longer practiced, at least not anywhere near the extent it was prior to the supposed ratification of the Seventeenth Amendment in 1913.

If Senators were still chosen by the state legislatures instead of by the people of each state as they are now, it is more likely that a constitutionally informed state legislature or perhaps even a group of such states acting through their state legislatures might order their Senators to pass legislation to abolish the Fed. This is precisely what the bankers did not want to happen, so the Seventeenth Amendment was "ratified" to make it more difficult for such a thing to occur.

Nevertheless, if the state legislatures would finally find the courage to follow the Constitution instead of merely giving it lip service, the Fed could be abolished even today. Based on Article I, section 10, clause 1 that "No State shall ... make any Thing but gold and silver Coin a Tender in Payment of Debts," each state legislature could pass a resolution informing Congress that from hence forward it will no longer recognize Federal Reserve notes, coins, and checking accounts in the form of demand deposits or other check writing deposits as legal tender. In order to have the needed effect, this action would have to be carried out by a large number of states — preferably a majority or larger. No doubt, a major constitutional crisis would be precipitated, but it would force Congress to act in the proper manner.

Chapter 17: Reclaiming America's Legacy

It behooves our citizens to be on their guard, to be firm in their principles, and full of confidence in themselves. We are able to preserve our self-government if we will but think so.
— *Thomas Jefferson, Letter to Thomas Mann Randolph, Jr., 1800.*

To gain an understanding of the importance the Founders attached to the establishment of the United States, one place to begin is to examine the Great Seal of the United States. Over a period of six years beginning in 1776, the Confederation Congress established three separate committees in succession to attempt to create an official seal for the new nation. Each one failed in the effort until Congress finally handed over the task to Charles Thomson, Secretary of Congress, in June 1782. Thomson selected what he felt were the best ideas from the three committees, added a touch of his own creativity into the mix, and presented his two-sided design for the Seal to Congress on June 20, 1782. Congress approved it that day.

Thomson did not actually submit a drawing to Congress for approval, but only a written description along with some comments on the symbolism and the mottos in his design. However, although drawings of the obverse (front), as well as an actual brass die of it, came into existence soon after Congress approved Thomson's work, this was not the case for the reverse (back). A drawing of the reverse did not appear until 1786, four years later — but because it has never been used as an official seal like the obverse, a die has never been cast to this day.

Since 1935, both sides of the Great Seal have been printed on the back of a one-dollar bill. If you look at the back of a dollar, you will see the obverse of the Great Seal on the right and the reverse on the left. Unfortunately, you will not see them in their true colors, because a dollar bill is printed only in white and green on its backside.

An article on the U. S. Department of State's web site, which is titled "The Great Seal of the United States," describes the imagery of the Great Seal in the following manner. It may be helpful, if you actually view a $1 bill while you read this description:

Symbolically, the seal reflects the beliefs and values that the Founding Fathers attached to the new nation and wished to pass on to their descendants. The report which Thomson submitted to the Congress explained the obverse this way: The ... stripes of the shield "represent the several states ... supporting a ... Chief [the upper part of the shield] which unites the whole and represents Congress." ... The shield, or escutcheon, is "born on the breast of an American eagle without any other supporters to denote that the United States of America ought to rely on their own Virtue."

The number 13, denoting the 13 original States, is represented in the bundle of arrows, the stripes of the shield, and the stars of the constellation. The olive branch and the arrows "denote the power of peace & war." The constellation of stars symbolizes a new nation taking its place among other sovereign states. The motto E Pluribus Unum [Translation: *Out of many, one*], emblazoned across the scroll and clenched in the eagle's beak, expresses the union of the 13 States....

The reverse, sometimes referred to as the spiritual side of the seal, contains the 13-step pyramid with the year 1776 in Roman numerals on the base. At the summit of the pyramid is the Eye of Providence in a triangle surrounded by a Glory (rays of light) and above it appears the motto *Annuit Coeptis* [Translation: *He (God) has favored our undertaking*]. Along the lower circumference of the design appear the words *Novus Ordo Seclorum* [Translation: *A new order of the ages*], heralding the beginning of the new American era in 1776.[1]

The reverse contains the most important information for our purposes. In his submittal to Congress, Thomson commented on the reverse as follows:

Reverse: The Pyramid signifies strength and duration. The eye over it and the motto [*Annuit Coeptis*] allude to the many signal interpositions of providence in favour of the American cause. The date underneath [1776] is that of the Declaration of Independence, and the words under it [*Novus Ordo Seclorum*] signify the beginning of the new American Era, which commences from that date. [2]

Thus, the Founders viewed the establishment of the United States as inaugurating an entirely new era in the history of the world and they even called it the "new American era."

The United States was expected by many to become a shining example to the peoples of the world. It was thought that the successful example of living under a free government would motivate others to move toward constitutional republics of their own. But the current US policy of going around the world meddling in the affairs of other nations and forcing them through fear and intimidation tactics to do our bidding belies this legacy; it smacks of arrogance and an aim to establish a world empire. Consider this quote by Thomas Jefferson from one of his letters:

A just and solid republican government maintained here will be a standing monument and example for the aim and imitation of the people of other countries; and I join ... in the hope and belief that they will see from our example that a free government is of all others the most energetic; that the inquiry which has been excited among the mass of mankind by our revolution and its consequences will ameliorate the condition of man over a great portion of the globe (Thomas Jefferson, Letter to John Dickinson, 1801).

---

1 "The Great Seal of the United States," US Department of State [Internet]; available from http://www.state.gov/documents/organization/27807.pdf; accessed 26 July 2008.

2 Journals of the Continental Congress 1774–1789, Thursday, June 20, 1782, Volume 22, Page 339-40, Library of Congress (Thomas) [Internet]; available from http://memory.loc.gov/cgi-bin/ampage?collId=lljc&fileName=022/lljc022.db&recNum=348&itemLink=r?ammem/hlaw:@field(DOCID+@lit(jc022113))%230220349&linkText=1; accessed 15 July 2008.

A similar quotation from one of James Madison's letters has relevance here as well:

> The free system of government we have established is so congenial with reason, with common sense, and with a universal feeling, that it must produce approbation and a desire of imitation.... Our country, if it does justice to itself, will be the officina-Libertatio [i.e., the workshop or office of freedom], to the Civilized World, and do more than any other for the uncivilized (James Madison, Letter to Peter Stephen DuPonceau, 1826).[1]

To summarize from the previous chapters the many ways in which the "Authentic Constitution" has been disregarded or distorted:

1. The United States has all but forgotten its founding principles: certain rights are inherent in all humans; they are unalienable; the sole function of government is to protect them; and if the government does not perform its function, the people can change it and institute another one in its place.

2. The United States has incorrectly emphasized democracy as its form of government rather than what the Founders really created: a Constitutional Republic. Unbridled democracy can be just as dangerous to liberty as a king or a dictator.

3. Congress has overstepped its bounds by passing numerous laws that it has no constitutional authority to pass. In so doing, it has spent far beyond its means and has loaded our posterity with an enormous debt that it may never be able to repay. Thus, instead of "secur[ing] the Blessings of Liberty to ourselves and our Posterity,"[2] Congress has turned US citizens into debt slaves.

4. Congress has given its power to create money to the unconstitutional Federal Reserve System (the Fed), which is really owned by cabal of private bankers. The Fed issues fiat currency (Federal Reserve notes) that is not backed by real commodity money (i.e., gold and silver), as the Constitution requires. Chronic inflation has been the unfortunate result of this unconstitutional transfer of power and, since Federal Reserve notes can only be issued by the Fed in exchange for US Treasury securities, the American people must pay interest on the currency (debt) in circulation.

5. Congress has implemented a federal income tax even through the Sixteenth Amendment, which supposedly authorized it, was not properly ratified.

6. Congress has gotten us into international "free trade" agreements like NAFTA and CAFTA-DR that allow international organizations to regulate trade for us, which completely bypasses our own constitutional and legislative processes. However, the Constitution stipulates that

---

1 Quoted from Adrienne Koch, *Jefferson and Madison: The Great Collaboration* (Old Saybrook, CT: Konecky & Konecky), 2. This source has only the last name of the recipient of the letter and it is spelt "De Ponceau." Through additional research, I was able to determine that this individual was actually Peter Stephen DuPonceau (born Pierre-Etienne Du Ponceau, 1760–1844). He was a French jurist, linguist, and philosopher who lived most of his life in the United States.

2 According to the Constitution's Preamble, "WE THE PEOPLE of the United States, in Order to form a more perfect Union, establish Justice, insure domestic Tranquility, provide for the common defense, promote the general Welfare, *and secure the Blessings of Liberty to ourselves and our Posterity*, do ordain and establish this Constitution for the United States of America" (italics mine).

Congress shall regulate our trade with foreign nations. In the area of internal trade, the federal government has usurped more and more of each state's constitutional authority to regulate trade within its own borders. Congress was only given the power to regulate trade "*among* the several States" (Article I, section 8, clause 3).

7. Congress routinely surrenders its power to declare war to the President. There are indeed instances when the President is authorized to mobilize military forces without a declaration of war. These would be on the rare occasions when a *national emergency* requiring *immediate action* exists, but for most situations, Congress must declare war. Simply passing a bill to give the President authority to use force at his discretion, like the Iraq War resolution, is *not* a proper declaration of war.

8. We no longer follow a noninterventionist foreign policy, which the Founders advocated. Under this type of a foreign policy, although we endeavor to be friends with and to trade with all nations, we do not get into any "entangling alliances" with them and we always mind our own business. A noninterventionist foreign policy is *not* isolationist, because we would not wall ourselves off from the rest of the world.

9. The right of able-bodied citizens to keep and bear arms is no longer encouraged and state militias, which are made up of the armed citizenry of each state, have an existence only on paper, even though the Constitution requires that the states actually maintain them. The National Guard, which is actually a reserve force for the army, only poses as the "Militia of the several States."

10. We allow Senators to be chosen by the people of the states rather than the state legislatures even though the Seventeenth Amendment, which supposedly authorized this change, was not properly ratified.

11. The US Supreme Court has treated the Fourteenth Amendment as valid law, even though it was not properly ratified. Furthermore, it has utilized the Amendment to allow the Bill of Rights to become more and more applicable to the states, even though each state actually has its own enumeration of rights. This process has been accomplished by means of the legal doctrine called "selective incorporation," which has created an artificial homogeny throughout the nation. The Founders did not advocate national uniformity in this sense. They expected that a state's Constitution and laws would espouse local ideas and standards of living.

12. We have allowed the Electoral College System to operate in a completely different manner than the Founders intended. However, it is very unlikely that we would be able to restore it to its original intended mode of operation. Under the circumstances, it would make sense to abolish the Electoral College system by a constitutional amendment and to institute a direct election of the President and Vice-President in its place. In addition, certain changes that were described in Chapter 13 should be made to improve our present manner of conducting all our federal elections.

13. Although a constitutional amendment needs to be ratified properly in order to give Congress the authority to control immigration as well as naturalization, which it already has power over (Article I, section 8, clause 4); this would only be a legal formality. It is still imperative that we gain control of our borders and enforce our immigration and naturalization

laws now. We have allowed the federal government to become lax in these areas and it has been very detrimental to our nation.

14. We have allowed the Supreme Court to be the sole arbiter of what the Constitution means even though no such power was given to it in the Constitution. As a result, we have become a Krytocracy (i.e., a nation ruled by judges) instead of what we are supposed to be: a Constitutional Republic.

The evidence is clear that we have betrayed our posterity, the world, and ourselves. Some of us may prefer to think the blame really rests on government, unforeseen circumstances, or the sinister forces working behind the scenes that were described in the previous chapter. Indeed, there is some modicum of truth to these viewpoints, but all the same the simple facts are that it is *we* who are the government, most of us still retain our reason and common sense, and the power to change things by exercising both our right to vote and our right to "petition the Government for a redress of grievances"[1] is still held by us.

Why then has this happened? The answer is twofold. First, we have not done the hard work required for self-government, which is constantly watching the performance of those we place in power and acting swiftly and appropriately if they should overstep the limits placed on them by the Constitution. A contravention should never be allowed to go uncorrected, since it creates a precedent that supposedly justifies future actions of a similar type. Second, we have placed our faith in men rather than the Constitution. This is surely not a reliable place to set our trust, since it is precisely because we are imperfect human beings that we need governments and constitutions in the first place. In *The Federalist Papers* (#51), James Madison made this point very clear:

> If men were angels, no government would be necessary. If angels were to govern men, neither external nor internal controls on government would be necessary.

An objective, written code protects us from our own human shortcomings, which unquestionably include greed and the desire for power. Turning again to Thomas Jefferson's advice:

> ... it would be a dangerous delusion were a confidence in the men of our choice to silence our fears for the safety of our rights: that confidence is every where the parent of despotism: free government is founded in jealousy and not in confidence; it is jealousy and not confidence which prescribes limited Constitutions to bind down those whom we are obliged to trust with power: that our Constitution has accordingly fixed the limits to which and no further our confidence may go.... In questions of power then let no more be heard of confidence in man, but bind him down from mischief by the chains of the Constitution.[2]

The only real solution is to return to the system that created the most prosperous and free nation in the history of the world. We should reestablish the "Authentic Constitution" and we should formally rescind the constitutional amendments that were not properly ratified (i.e., the Fourteenth, Sixteenth, and Seventeenth

---

1 According to the First Amendment, "Congress shall make no law ... abridging the freedom of speech, or of the press, or the right of the people peaceably to assemble, *and to petition the Government for a redress of grievances*" (italics mine).

2 *The Kentucky Resolutions of 1798*, The Papers of Thomas Jefferson Princeton University [Internet]; available from http://www.princeton.edu/~tjpapers/kyres/kyednote.html; accessed 16 July 2008.

Amendments)[1] and ratify those amendments that have been suggested in the previous pages — and perhaps others that may be required. We should also examine all our laws and treaties, discarding the unconstitutional ones, fixing those that need fixing, and approving new ones that may be necessary for the restoration of our Constitutional Republic.

What would be the some of the practical benefits that would ensue if the United States reestablished the "Authentic Constitution"?

- The idea that certain fundamental rights are unalienable but they come with responsibility, and require integrity and morality. As Samuel Adams said: "[N]either the wisest constitution nor the wisest laws will secure the liberty and happiness of a people whose manners are universally corrupt."
- By learning more about the Founding of the United States and what made the system of government the Founders created so exceptional, perhaps we would come to realize the important responsibilities we have as a self-governing people. More qualified and less self-interested individuals might run for office. Keeping close watch over public officials and voicing criticisms or complaints when necessary would be never-ending tasks. We would be diligent in electing individuals dedicated to the republican form of government.
- We would have a much smaller, less bureaucratic, less intrusive federal government. All federal programs that are not mandated by the Constitution would be abolished. Of course, it would be very disruptive to the economy to terminate all these programs at once, so we would need a transition period to bring about the changes gradually. If such a transition were done properly, those who will suffer as a result would be reduced to a bare minimum. However, if we continue on our present course, a financial disaster is sure to come. Then, those who will *not* suffer will be reduced to a bare minimum.
- We would have much lower federal taxes. The federal income tax would be abolished and the federal government would be financed mainly by tariffs, excise taxes, and perhaps sales taxes.
- The federal government would no longer be a source of charity, but *private* charities of all kinds would be promoted instead.
- We would have a noninterventionist foreign policy. Friendship and trade with other nations would be emphasized, but "entangling alliances" and meddling in the affairs of others would be avoided. All government foreign aid would be abolished, but private aid to other nations and peoples would be encouraged. The military would only be used to defend the United States.
- We would not get involved with any international "free trade" agreements that bypass our own constitutional and legislative processes. The President would negotiate commercial treaties with foreign nations with full oversight by Congress. Our approach would be balanced trade with the goal of keeping to a minimum any trade deficits and any jobs being lost abroad.

---

1 Even though these amendments were not properly ratified and thus were never a part of the Constitution, a consensus of all fifty states and the three branches of the federal government would doubtless need to be attained and some form of legal process undertaken to formally expunge them from the Constitution. The Fifteenth Amendment, which states that the right to vote "shall not be denied or abridged ... on account of race, color, or previous condition of servitude," was not properly ratified either, but a unique way of retaining it in the Constitution is provided in Chapter 12.

- Since the Federal Reserve System would be abolished, we would have a stable and dependable monetary system. There would be no fractional reserve banking and we would have a commodity monetary system fully backed by gold and silver. Americans would no longer be paying interest on money created out of debt and savings would be sheltered from loss of value due to inflation. In fact, under this type of monetary system it is possible that prices would gradually *decrease*, which means that we could look forward to the purchasing power of our money steadily rising instead of rapidly declining.

- In accordance with the Tenth Amendment,[1] the rights of the states would be fully recognized again. As long as something was not prohibited to a state by the Constitution or by its own Constitution, a state would be free to do it. We would have "liberal" states with numerous social programs and "conservative" ones with few such programs. There would be a healthy competition among them. Furthermore, the Bill of Rights would no longer be applied to the states. Each state's enumeration of rights would be authoritative for that state.

- Senators would again represent the states in Congress, because state legislatures instead of the people of the state would chose them. The House of Representatives would represent the people as it was supposed to do and we would once again have a truly bicameral Congress. The rights of the states would be safeguarded in this way.

- The right of able-bodied citizens to own guns would no longer be discouraged, but neither would the corresponding duty of these citizens to be members of their state's militia be overlooked. By revitalizing the state militias, made up of the armed citizenry of each state, the ideal body to handle homeland security at the state and local levels would be found.

- Immigration laws would be strictly enforced.

- The Supreme Court would no longer be the sole arbiter of what the Constitution means. The executive and legislative branches, being co-equal branches with the judiciary, would also be able to determine the constitutionality of acts or laws within their own sphere of authority.

- We would have a lot more freedom all around. The great motto of our society would be this: *You are free to do what you want as long as you do not use force to diminish or take away someone else's freedom.* Obviously, this type of freedom is not license, which is freedom without any restraints. License is an abuse of true freedom, which is properly called liberty. Our motto would be the guiding principle that would control our misuse of freedom.

History readily confirms what the Declaration asserts, "mankind are more disposed to suffer, while evils are sufferable, than to right themselves by abolishing the forms to which they are accustomed." In other words, until the suffering really hits home, human beings are prone to sit back and accept some modicum of discomfort. However, by carefully observing current events, as they are unfolding, it appears more and more apparent that ominous winds are indeed blowing ever faster and more forcefully. The menacing winds of tyranny are gaining ever steadily on the reassuring breezes of liberty. Most Americans seem oblivious to these disturbing changes. Perhaps, according to the words of the Declaration, they believe that the "evils are

---

1 The Tenth Amendment states, "The powers not delegated to the United States by the Constitution, nor prohibited by it to the States, are reserved to the States respectively, or to the people."

[still] sufferable." On the other hand, could there be a more serious reason for their lack of awareness?

Alexander Fraser Tytler (1747–1813), the Scottish jurist, historian, and professor at Edinburgh University, described the downward progression of all great nations in the following manner:

> Great nations rise and fall. [The average age of the world's greatest civilizations has been 200 years.] The people go from bondage to spiritual faith, [from spiritual faith] to great courage, from [great] courage to liberty, from liberty to abundance, from abundance to selfishness, from selfishness to complacency, from complacency to apathy, from apathy to dependence, [finally] from dependence back again to bondage.[1]

1 This is the second quotation usually attributed to Alexander Fraser Tytler. The first one was quoted in Chapter 3. The second sentence in brackets actually belongs at the end of the first quotation, but it makes better sense here. In addition, spiritual *faith* is used more often in the quotation than spiritual *truth*, so I have used the former in this quotation. See Loren Collins, "The Truth About Tytler," Loren Collins [Internet]; available from http://lorencollins.net/sundries.html; accessed 5 July 2008.

GLOSSARY

Al-Aqsa Mosque	A mosque in Jerusalem that is the third holiest site in Islam. Although in a general sense the Al-Aqsa Mosque refers to the entire religious complex called the Al-Haram al-Sharif, which includes the famous Dome of the Rock, it refers in particular to the large mosque on the southern end that can hold more than five thousand worshippers.
Alien	A person who is not a US citizen or a US national.
Al-Masjid al-Harām	A mosque in Mecca that is the holiest site in Islam.
Al Qaeda	(from Arabic, meaning "the base") An Islamic terrorist organization led by Osama bin Laden that is said to be behind various attacks on civilian and military sites worldwide, but most notably 9/11 in 2001.
Amendment	A change in the Constitution that is done in accordance with Article V.
Anarchy	A condition of a society in which there is no government or law.
Annuit Coeptis	(Latin) A motto that appears on the reverse of the Great Seal of the United States and means, "He (God) has favored our undertaking."
Aristocracy	A form of government in which all power is held by an elite upper class.
Articles of Confederation and Perpetual Union	The document that describes the system of government that was in operation in the United States from March 1, 1781 until the Constitution, which was ratified on June 21, 1788, officially took its place.

Athenian Assembly	The main governing body of Athens in the fifth century B.C. The government of ancient Athens provides us with a nearly perfect example of a pure or complete democracy.
Bailment	The possession of property is transferred to someone else (the bailee) for some stated purpose, but the person who transfers the property (the bailor) retains ownership and can take legal action against the former, if the property in his care is broken or destroyed.
Bastille	A fortress used as a prison in Paris that was stormed by a Parisian mob on July 14, 1789. This act is considered the beginning of the French Revolution.
Bicameral Legislature	A legislature consisting of two separate chambers (e.g., the Senate and the House of Representatives), as opposed to a unicameral legislature having only one chamber (e.g., the legislature operating during the period of the Articles of Confederation).
Bill (also Joint Resolution)	A measure proposed in Congress that requires the approval of both houses and the President's signature to become law.
Bill of Attainder	An act of a legislature that sentences a person for a crime without a trial.
Bills of Credit	Paper money that is not backed one hundred percent by gold or silver.
Bill of Rights	The first ten amendments to the Constitution that were ratified by the states on December 15, 1791. Their purpose was to place additional curbs on the powers of the federal government in order to guarantee certain rights of the people.
Bimetallism	A monetary system that uses two metals as the standard of value, usually gold and silver, and sets the relative value of the metals by using a fixed mint ratio.
Board of Governors (also the Federal Reserve Board)	The seven-member board that manages the Federal Reserve system (the Fed).
CAFTA-DR (Dominican Republic — Central America — United States Free Trade Agreement)	A trade agreement that is essentially an expansion of NAFTA to the Central American countries of Guatemala, El Salvador, Honduras, Costa Rica, Nicaragua and the Dominican Republic. It apparently went into effect on October 7, 2007, when Costa Rica, the last participating nation to approve it, did so. Congress transferred its own constitutional power to "regulate Commerce with foreign Nations" (Article I, section 8, clause 3) to an international organization, when it approved this agreement.
Capitation Tax	(from the Latin word meaning "head") A tax assessed on each person or "head" without regard to income or status.

Census (also Enumeration)	According to the Constitution, an official count of the population performed every ten years to determine the apportionment population for allocating congressional representatives and direct taxes among the states.
Chagas	A parasitic disease from South America that is propagated by insect bites and blood transfusions. It can be deadly, if it is not treated in the early phases of the infection.
Checks and Balances	A system set into the Constitution that allows each branch of government — the executive, legislative, and judicial, through certain specified mechanisms (i.e., "check and balances"), to guard against the possible excesses of the other branches.
Civil War	The war fought in the United States between the Union (North) and the Confederacy (South). It is also known as the War Between the States. Hostilities began on April 12, 1861, when Confederate forces attacked Ft. Sumter in South Carolina, and ended, when the Confederacy surrendered at Appomattox, Virginia on April 9, 1865.
Coinage Act of 1792	In accordance with the power granted to it in the Constitution "To coin Money [and] regulate the Value thereof" (Article I, section 8, clause 5), Congress passed this Act on April 2, 1792, which established the first Mint and currency system of the United States.
Committee of Public Safety	The main governing body in France during the period of the French Revolution known as the Reign of Terror (1793-4). The committee was responsible for ordering thousands of executions on the guillotine.
Concurrent Constitutional Review	The view that each branch of the government can determine for itself the constitutionality of some act or law that comes before its purview and that no branch is the final arbiter of what the Constitution means. In the event of a deadlock, only the people via the amendment process found in Article V of the Constitution can resolve it.
Concurrent Resolution	A measure proposed in Congress that requires the approval of both houses, but does not require the President's signature and is not legally binding.
Confederate States of America (also the Confederacy)	Eleven southern states that seceded from the Union prior to or soon after the Civil War began on April 12, 1861. They were in order of secession South Carolina, Mississippi, Florida, Alabama, Georgia, Louisiana, Texas, Virginia, Tennessee, Arkansas, and North Carolina.

Congressional — Executive Agreement (CEA)	An agreement between the United States and one or more other countries that is not considered a treaty and is thus exempt from the requirement of a two-thirds vote in the Senate (Article II, section 2, clause 2 in the Constitution), which is normally the case for approving a treaty. Since a CEA is classified as statutory law, its passage requires only a majority vote in both houses.
Constitution (general term)	A document that describes the fundamental principles and laws of a nation or smaller political sub-division and the structure and operation of its government.
Constitutional Republic	An indirect or representative democracy in which all power is dispersed and limited by the rule of law, which is set down in a written Constitution.
Consumer Price Index (CPI)	The main measurement of inflation used by the government.
Continental	The name given to the paper money issued by the Continental Congress during the Revolutionary War.
Customs Duty (also Duty, Impost or Tariff)	A tax assessed on imported goods to raise revenue or to safeguard domestic manufacturing from overseas competition.
Debt Ceiling	The maximum amount of US Treasury securities (i.e., bills, notes, bonds, and savings bonds) that can be sold to the public via the Bureau of the Public Debt, which is a division of the US Treasury. Congress can increase the Debt Ceiling by passing appropriate legislation.
Declaration of Independence	The document adopted by the Second Continental Congress on July 4, 1776 that formerly declared the separation of the American Colonies from Great Britain.
Demagogue	A charismatic person who is able to gain political influence by exciting the passions and prejudices of the people.
Dictatorship	A form of government in which a single individual holds all power.
Direct Tax	A tax assessed on persons or their property and paid straight to the government by the individuals that are assessed the tax.
Dollar	The monetary unit of the United States that was officially established by the Coinage Act of 1792. In this Act, a dollar was defined as 371.25 grains of pure silver and it coincided with the Spanish milled silver dollar (the Peso), which had been used as currency in the United States prior to the ratification of the Constitution.

Duty of Tonnage	A tax on a merchant ship's storage space capacity.
Eagle	A gold coin that was authorized by the Coinage Act of 1792. It had a value of ten dollars and a weight of 247.5 grains of pure gold. Half eagles and quarter eagles were authorized by the Act as well.
Electoral College	The name given to the group of electors chosen by the people of each state and the District of Columbia, who actually elect the President and Vice President of the United States.
Emigrate	Leaving one country for another and usually settling there permanently.
E Pluribus Unum	(Latin) The motto that appears on the obverse of the Great Seal of the United States and means, "out of many, one."
Executive Order	In its legitimate form, a presidential directive that gives guidance to the departments of the executive branch in implementing laws passed by Congress. However, executive orders are often unconstitutional in that they create new law without congressional authorization.
Ex Post Facto Law	(in Latin, ex post facto means "from what is done afterward") a law that can be utilized retroactively in some way. For example, a law is passed making the consumption of alcoholic beverages illegal starting from a date prior to when the law was actually passed.
Excise Tax	A tax assessed on the manufacture, sale, or consumption of specific commodities, such as liquor or tobacco.
Faithless Elector	An Elector in the Electoral College who casts a vote for a presidential candidate other than his party's candidate.
Fatwa	(in Islam) a binding religious edict.
Federal Funds Rate	The interest rate banks charge other banks to borrow money overnight from excess reserves they have at the Fed. The FOMC sets the *target* Federal Funds Rate and endeavors to attain it by using the monetary tools at its disposal. The result is the actual Federal Funds Rate, which usually comes close to the projected goal.
Federalism	The division of power between the central government of a country (e.g., the federal government) and a number of smaller entities that govern specific parts of the country (e.g., the states).
Federal Open Market Committee (FOMC)	The twelve-member committee of the Federal Reserve system (the Fed) that determines the nation's overall monetary policy.

Federal Reserve System (also the Fed)	The central banking system of the United States that was created by the Federal Reserve Act passed on December 23, 1913. The Fed issues fiat currency (Federal Reserve notes) that is not backed by real commodity money (i.e., gold and silver), as the Constitution requires. Only Congress was given the power to "coin money" and "regulate the Value thereof" in the Constitution (Article I, section 8, clause 5).
Fiat Money	Paper money that is declared legal tender by government decree.
Fractional Reserve Banking	Each unit of currency in circulation represents less than one hundred percent or only a "fraction" of all bank reserves, which is gold and silver in a commodity-based monetary system. As a result, the value of the currency, and thus its purchasing power, is reduced because the total supply of currency has increased beyond the amount needed for a one hundred percent reserve.
French Revolution	A revolution begun in France with the storming of the Bastille on July 14, 1789 that brought down the French Monarchy, but that led to the terrible Reign of Terror (1793-4) and finally the rise to power of Napoleon Bonaparte, who crowned himself Emperor of the French on December 2, 1804.
Full-bodied Coin	The market value of the metal in which the coin is made is equal to the monetary value of the coin.
Grace Commission Report (also the President's Private Sector Survey on Cost Control (PPSS)	A report commissioned by President Ronald Reagan in 1982 and presented to Congress in 1984 that was highly critical of the government's financial condition. The commission was lead by J. Peter Grace, the well-known, American industrialist.
Great Seal of the United States	The two-sided design of Charles Thomson, Secretary of Congress, that was approved as the official Seal of the United States by Congress on June 20, 1782. The obverse (front) is still used to stamp official government documents and since 1935, both sides of the Seal have appeared on the back of a one-dollar bill.
Green Card	The identification card that a Lawful Permanent Resident (LPR) receives in due course and that must be kept in his/her possession at all times.
Gresham's Law	A law regarding coinage that states if a metal has a market value less than its mint value, and is thus overvalued at the mint, it will tend to remain as money in circulation. On the other hand, if a metal that has a market value more than its mint value, and is thus undervalued at the mint, it will tend to be withdrawn from circulation and used for commercial purposes or hoarded.

Gross Domestic Product (GDP)	The total market value of all goods and services that a nation produces within a particular period.
Immigrate	Entering one country from another and usually settling there permanently.
Importation	Buying merchandise from a foreign country and bringing it into your own for resale.
Independence Hall	Originally, the Pennsylvania State House in Philadelphia where the Declaration of Independence and the Constitution were debated, adopted and signed. It is now a national landmark.
Indian Appropriation Act of 1871	An Act passed by Congress that made it a policy of the federal government to no longer recognize Indian tribes as sovereign nations, and thus to no longer negotiate treaties with them. Henceforth, Indian policy would be set by federal statute or executive order. However, treaties passed prior to 1871 were still considered valid.
Indian Citizen Act of 1924	An Act that made citizens of all Indians born within the United States and gave them voting rights.
Indirect or Representative Democracy	A form of government in which the majority of the people hold all power, but they transfer this power to elected representatives who run the government in their place.
Indirect Tax	A tax assessed on commodities and usually paid by the taxpayer to a tax collector, who then remits it to the government. Although the term "indirect" is never explicitly mentioned in the Constitution, duties, imposts, and excises are mentioned in Article I, section 8, clause 1, and they are indirect taxes.
Inflation	A rise in consumer prices, and thus a decrease in the purchasing power of money, due to an increase in the supply of currency and credit that is greater than the current value of goods and services.
Infringe	(v. tr.) To contravene or go beyond the restrictions, violate; (v. intr.) to intrude on someone or something, trespass.
Jihad	(in Islam) A holy war.
Judicial Review	The process of deciding a specific case that comes before a court and, if need be, declaring a statute relevant to the case unconstitutional if it is in conflict with the Constitution. True judicial review only binds the parties to the case, not the other branches of government or anyone else, although the judiciary can choose to be bound by its past decisions (see stare decisis). Today judicial review is usually confused with judicial supremacy (see below).

Judicial Supremacy	The view that the judicial branch of the government is the final arbiter as to what the Constitution means and that the other branches of government and everyone else are bound by what the courts decide.
Korean War	A military conflict between North and South Korea that started when the North invaded the South on June 25, 1950 and ended when a ceasefire was signed on July 27, 1953. The United States along with some other nations entered the war to enforce a United Nations resolution.
Krytocracy	A form of government in which the judges hold all power.
Law and Equity	(in law) The two components of the judicial power of the United States (Article III, section 2, clause 1 of the Constitution). "Law" refers to the written law, i.e., the Constitution followed by the statutes and treaties made according to its precepts. "Equity," on the other hand, refers to the principle of fair-mindedness rather than the strict, automatic application of the written law. The courts employ both components, but generally apply Equity when no satisfactory resolution is available in Law.
Lawful Permanent Resident (LPR)	An alien who, though not entitled to all the rights and privileges of a citizen, is allowed to live permanently in the United States and to take employment. Such a person in due course receives an identification card commonly called a "green card" that must be kept on his/her possession at all times.
Law of Nations	International law.
Letter of Marque and Reprisal	The authority granted by a government to a private ship owner (a privateer) to undertake military operations against enemy vessels, which would usually include capturing the ships and seizing their cargo. This Letter protected the private ship owner from being branded a pirate, if the enemy captured him. A pirate could be executed immediately without any trial.
Liberty	Freedom without license, which is the abuse of true freedom (liberty).
Lusitania	A British ocean liner that was sunk by a German U-boat on May 7, 1915. Of the 1,959 passengers on board, 1,198 were killed, including 128 Americans. This was one of the provocations that led President Woodrow Wilson to ask Congress to declare war on Germany. It did so on April 6, 1917 and the United States entered the First World War.
Majority	Receiving at least half plus one of the votes cast.
Migrate	Moving to or from a country one or more times.

Militia	A military force made up of ordinary citizens bearing arms instead of professional soldiers.
Militia Act of 1792	In accordance with the power granted to it in the Constitution "To provide for organizing, arming, and disciplining, the Militia, and for governing such Part of them as may be employed in the Service of the United States..." (Article I, section 8, clause 16), Congress passed this Act on May 8, 1792, which established a uniform Militia throughout the United States.
Monarchy	A form of government in which all power is held by a single individual, usually a king or queen, who rules by inheritance.
Money	A medium that make possible the unimpeded exchange of goods and services by providing a common measurement of value.
Monroe Doctrine	The doctrine advocated by President James Monroe in his seventh Annual Message to Congress on December 2, 1823. It advised the European powers to desist from subjugating or inhabiting any lands in the Western Hemisphere and to deem any such actions as a threat to the security of the United States.
NAFTA (North American Free Trade Agreement)	A trade agreement between the United States, Mexico, and Canada that went into effect on January 1, 1994. By approving this agreement, Congress transferred its own constitutional power to "regulate Commerce with foreign Nations" (Article I, section 8, clause 3) to an international organization.
National (Federal) Debt	When expenditures are more than revenues, the government must borrow money to pay for the deficiency of funds. A national debt is created, when money is borrowed. The power to borrow money and thus create a national debt is found in Article I, section 8, clause 2, which states, "[Congress shall have Power] To borrow Money on the credit of the United States." This is accomplished by selling US Treasury securities (i.e., bills, notes, bonds, and savings bonds) to the public via the Bureau of the Public Debt, which is a division of the US Treasury.
Naturalization	The process by which a foreigner becomes a citizen.
Natural Law	Laws that originate from nature that are binding on human activity in tandem with laws that human beings create. The Declaration of Independence refers to the "Laws of Nature," but adds "and of Nature's God," indicating that it is beyond the power or authority of humans, including the ruler, to take them away.
Navajo Reservation (Nation)	The largest Indian reservation, comprising a land area of approximately seventeen million acres and including portions of Arizona, Utah, and New Mexico.

"Necessary and Proper" Clause (also the Elastic Clause)	Article I, section 8, clause 18 of the Constitution, which states, "[Congress shall have Power] To make all Laws which shall be necessary and proper for carrying into Execution the foregoing Powers, and all other Powers vested by this Constitution in the Government of the United States, or in any Department or Officer thereof."
Nonimmigrant Visa	A document issued to an alien that allows him/her to enter the United States temporarily for a specific purpose. There are numerous visa classifications. For example, an H-2A visa is for a temporary or seasonal agricultural worker and an F-1 visa is for an academic student.
Novus Ordo Seclorum	(Latin) A motto that appears on the reverse of the Great Seal of the United States and means, "a new order of the ages."
Nugatory	Having no authority; of no use; pointless; futile.
Oligarchy	A form of government in which a few persons (i.e., a clique) hold all power.
Originalism	The idea that the Constitution should be understood in accordance with the meaning advanced by those who wrote and ratified it. In addition, each constitutional amendment should be understood in the same manner (i.e., in accordance with the meaning advanced by those who wrote and ratified it).
Plurality	Receiving the most votes, but less than half the votes cast (only possible if more than two choices are available).
Pocket Veto	A procedure mentioned in the Constitution (Article I, section 7, clause 2) that allows the President, provided that the Congress has adjourned, to simply hold on to ("pocket") a piece of legislation and thus disapprove it without having to return it to Congress with his objections.
Poll Tax	A type of capitation (head) tax assessed on a person as a precondition for voting. The Twenty-Fourth Amendment made it illegal to deny anyone the right to vote for not paying a poll tax.
Prime Rate	The interest rate banks charge to their principle customers and the reference point banks use to determine their other interest rates.
Property Tax	A tax assessed on a person's real or personal property.
Pure or Complete Democracy	A form of government in which the majority of the people hold all power.

Question of Fact	(in law) A question regarding what actually happened during an alleged incident in a jury trial (also known by the Latin term, de facto, which means "from the fact").
Question of Law	(in law) A question regarding what the legal ramifications will be for the alleged incident in a jury trial (also known by the Latin term, de jure, which means "from the law").
Quota	The maximum amount of a product that can be imported into a country during a certain period.
Radical Republicans	A group of Republicans in Congress after the Civil War who believed the South should be treated harshly for seceding from the Union.
Reign of Terror	An extremely violent period during the French Revolution (1793-4), in which anywhere from 14,000 to 40,000 people were sentenced to death on the guillotine for allegedly supporting the Monarchy or opposing the Revolution.
Revolutionary War	The war begun on April 19, 1775 with the Battle of Lexington and Concord and ended on September 3, 1783 with the signing of the Treaty of Paris that gave the American Colonies their independence from Great Britain.
Sales Tax	A wide-ranging excise tax assessed on the sale of all, or nearly all, commodities.
Selective Incorporation	The doctrine that the rights secured by the first eight Amendments in the Bill of Rights are included or "incorporated" in the "due process" and "equal protection" clauses found in Section 1 of the Fourteenth Amendment.
Separation of Powers	The doctrine that the government be split into three distinct and co-equal branches — the executive, legislative, and judicial — in order to restrain any one branch from gaining undue influence.
Specie	Coined money.
Stare Decisis	(in Latin, "stare decisis" means "to stand by things that have been settled") The doctrine of adhering to the findings of prior court decisions (i.e., precedent) in deciding subsequent cases in which the facts are similar.
Supremacy Clause	Article VI, clause 2 of the Constitution, which states, "this Constitution, and the Laws of the United States which shall be made in Pursuance thereof; and all Treaties made, or which shall be made, under the Authority of the United States, shall be the supreme Law of the Land; and the Judges in every State shall be bound thereby, any Thing in the Constitution or Laws of any State to the Contrary notwithstanding."

Taliban	An Islamic movement that ruled Afghanistan from approximately 1996 to 2001. They were toppled by the invasion of Afghanistan, which began on October 7, 2001.
The Federalist Papers	A group of essays that were written by Alexander Hamilton, James Madison, and John Jay from 1787 to 1788 in order to plead the case for ratifying the new system of government under the Constitution.
Token Coin	The market value of the metal in which the coin is made is less than the monetary value of the coin.
Trade Promotion Authority (TPA, also "Fast Track" Authority)	The authority given to the President by Congress to negotiate trade agreements with other countries with minimal endorsement from the latter. Such an authorization is clearly unconstitutional. Even though the President is indeed given the power "to make Treaties," it is only "by and with the Advice and Consent of the Senate" (Article II, section 2, clause 2 of the Constitution), and in any case, only Congress is given the power "To regulate Commerce with foreign Nations" (Article I, section 8, clause 3 of the Constitution).
Transfer Payments	Money paid to individuals by the government that is not given as compensation for goods or services and that the latter never uses itself, but "transfers" from one group of people to another to provide the latter with certain monetary benefits.
Treaty	A written agreement between two or more countries regarding their common interests, including, resolving border disputes, acquiring land, carrying out trade, establishing policies regarding immigration and citizenship, ownership and inheritance, and instituting copyright and patent protections.
Treaty of Paris	The treaty, signed on September 3, 1783, that officially ended the Revolutionary War.
Treaty of Versailles	The peace treaty, signed on June 28, 1919, that officially ended World War I.
Unalienable Rights	Rights inherent to all human beings that cannot be surrendered, transferred, or taken away by anyone or by any circumstance.

Union	Prior to and after the Civil War, a name given to the entire United States of America. During the Civil War, a name given to the twenty-three states that did not secede from the United States and join the Confederate States of America. The twenty-three loyal states were California, Connecticut, Delaware, Illinois, Indiana, Iowa, Kansas, Kentucky, Maine, Maryland, Massachusetts, Michigan, Minnesota, Missouri, New Hampshire, New Jersey, New York, Ohio, Oregon, Pennsylvania, Rhode Island, Vermont, and Wisconsin.
United Nations (UN)	An international organization with its headquarters in New York City that was established in 1945 to facilitate dialogue and cooperation regarding global security, economic concerns, and social issues among the 192 member states.
US Constitution	The document that describes the fundamental principles and laws of the United States and the structure and operation of the federal government. When the Constitution was ratified by the states on June 21, 1788, it replaced the Articles of Confederation and Perpetual Union. However, the government of the Constitution did not actually start on that date, but almost a year later. The new Congress assembled on March 4, 1789, George Washington was inaugurated President on April 30, and the first Supreme Court met on February 2, 1790.
US National	US citizens and citizens of certain possessions of the United States.
USS Cole	An American ship that was being refueled in the Yemeni port of Aden on October 12, 2000, when two Muslim men drove a motorboat full of explosives into it, blew a 40-by-60 foot hole in its port side, and killed 17 sailors and 39 others in the blast.
USS Maine	An American ship that sank in Havana Harbor, Cuba on February 15, 1898 due to an explosion. Two hundred and sixty-six men were killed in the disaster, and it set the course for our eventual entry into the Spanish-American War.
Veto	A procedure mentioned in the Constitution (Article I, section 7, clauses 2 and 3) that allows the President to disapprove a piece of legislation sent to him by Congress either by refusing to sign it and returning it with his objections, or by holding on to it if Congress has adjourned (see Pocket Veto).

War Powers Resolution	An unconstitutional resolution passed by Congress in 1973 that allows the President to unilaterally introduce armed forces into situations where Congress has not yet declared war or even where no *national emergency* requiring *immediate action* exists, which would allow the President to act on his own without a war declaration. The President is required to submit a report to Congress within forty-eight hours of introducing the forces into the area and is expected to remove them within sixty days after the report is submitted, unless Congress extends the period by thirty days. In any case, the President must remove the forces from the area, if Congress passes a concurrent resolution that directs him to do so.
World War I	A worldwide conflict that took place from 1914 to 1918 and started when Archduke Franz Ferdinand, the heir to the Austro-Hungarian throne, was assassinated on June 28, 1914. The war was fought between the Allied (Entente) Powers, which included France, the United Kingdom, Russia, Italy, and the United States; and the Central Powers, which included Germany, Austria-Hungary, the Ottoman Empire, and Bulgaria. The Allied (Entente) Powers were the victors and a ceasefire was signed on November 11, 1918. The peace treaty, known as the Treaty of Versailles, was not signed until June 28, 1919. World War I remade the map and reorganized the governments of Europe to an extent that was unprecedented as a consequence of any previous European wars.
World War II	A worldwide conflict that took place from 1939 to 1945 between the Allies, which included the United Kingdom, Russia, and the United States; and the Axis Powers, which included Japan, Italy, and Germany. The war started when Germany invaded Poland on September 1, 1939. The Allies were the victors. The major Axis Powers, Germany and Japan, signed surrender documents on May 7 and September 2 of 1945, respectively. Because of World War II, Europe's infrastructure and economy were destroyed and Japan was the first nation that experienced the horrors of nuclear weapons.
Writ of Habeas Corpus	(in Latin, habeas corpus means "you may have the body") a legal document that requests the authorities to bring a person who was arrested before the court in order to determine whether he was illegally detained or not.

WTO (World Trade Organization)	An international organization that handles about sixty trade agreements for 152 member nations. The WTO came into existence because of GATT (General Agreement on Tariffs and Trade) 1994, which was the result of the Uruguay Round of trade negotiations from 1986 through 1994.

BIBLIOGRAPHY

Books

Amos, Gary T. *Defending the Declaration*. Charlottesville: Providence Foundation, 1994.

Badnarik, Michael. *Good to be King: The Foundation of our Constitutional Freedom*. Cranston, Rhode Island: The Writers' Collective, 2004.

Banister, Joseph R. *Investigating the Federal Income Tax*. First Edition. 1999.

Bastiat, Frederic. *The Law*. 15th Edition. Irvington-On-Hudson, New York: Foundation for Economic Education, Inc., 1990.

Benson, Bill and Beckman, M. J. 'Red' Beckman, *The Law That Never Was*. Fourth Printing. South Holland, IL: Constitutional Research Assoc., 2001.

Benson, Bill. *Proof the 17th Amendment Was Not Ratified*. South Holland, IL: Constitutional Research Assoc., 1986.

Berger, Raoul. *Government By Judiciary: The Transformation of the Fourteenth Amendment*. Indianapolis: Liberty Fund, Inc., 1997.

Bork, Robert H. *The Tempting of America: The Political Seduction of the Law*. New York: The Free Press, 1990.

Browne, Harry. *The Great Libertarian Offer*. Great Falls, Montana: LiamWorks, 2000.

Buchanan, Patrick J. *Where the right went wrong: how neoconservatives subverted the Reagan revolution and hijacked the Bush presidency*. New York: Thomas Dunne Books, 2005.

Carson, Clarence B. *A Basic History of the United States*. Five volumes. Wadley, Alabama: American Textbook Committee, 1986.

Charter of the United Nations and Statute of the International Court of Justice. New York: United Nations.

The Constitution of the Commonwealth of Massachusetts. Published by Michael J. Connolly, Massachusetts Secretary of State, January, 1984.

The Constitution of the United States with Index and The Declaration of Independence. First Edition. Malta, ID: National Center for Constitutional Studies, 2002.

Diggins, John Patrick, ed. *The Portable John Adams.* New York: Penguin Books, 2004.

DiLorenzo, Thomas J. *The Real Lincoln: A New Look at Abraham Lincoln, His Agenda, and an Unnecessary War.* Roseville, California: Prima Publishing, 2002.

— *How Capitalism Saved America: The Untold History of Our Country, from the Pilgrims to the Present.* New York: Three Rivers Press, 2004.

— *Lincoln Unmasked: What You're Not Supposed to Know About Dishonest Abe.* New York: Crown Forum, 2007.

Dobbs, Lou. *Exporting America: Why Corporate Greed Is Shipping American Jobs Overseas.* New York: Warner Books, 2004.

Eaton, William. *Who Killed the Constitution? The Judges v. The Law.* Washington, D.C.: Regnery Gateway, 1988.

Ellison, Jr., J.D., Edward and Kurowski, John William. *Prosperity Restored by the State Rate Tax Plan.* Free State Constitutionists Media Publishing Co.,1985.

Epperson, Ralph. *The Unseen Hand: An Introduction to the Conspiratorial View of History.* Tucson: Publius Press, 1985.

— *The New World Order.* Tucson: Publius Press, 1990.

Farah, Joseph. *Taking America Back: A Radical Plan to Revive Freedom, Morality, and Justice.* Nashville: WND Books, 2003.

The Federal Reserve System: Purpose & Functions. Second Printing. Washington, D. C.: Board of Governors of the Federal Reserve System, 1985.

Federer, William J. *America's God and Country: Encyclopedia of Quotations.* St. Louis: Amerisearch, Inc., 2000.

Flexner, James Thomas. *Washington: The Indispensable Man.* Boston: Back Bay Books, 1974.

Flynn, Ted. *Hope of the Wicked: The Master Plan to Rule the World.* Sterling, Virginia: MaxKol Communications, Inc., 2000.

Gause, Andrew, *The Secret World of Money.* Hilton Head Island, S.C.: SDL Press, 1996.

Griffin, G. Edward. *The Creature from Jekyll Island: A Second Look at the Federal Reserve.* Second Printing. Appleton, Wisconsin: American Opinion Publishing, Inc., 1994.

Hamilton, Alexander; Madison, James; and Jay, John. *The Federalist Papers.* Introduction and commentary by Gary Wills. Fifth Printing. New York: Bantam Books, 1987.

Heffner, Richard D. *A Documentary History of the United States.* Expanded Edition. New York: A Mentor Book, 1965.

Jaikaran, M.D., Jacques S. *Debt Virus: A Compelling Solution to the World's Debt Problems.* Lakewood, CO: Glenbridge Publishing Ltd., 1995.

Johnson, Paul. *George Washington: The Founding Father.* New York: HarperCollins Publishers, 2005.

Johnson, Roger T. *Historical Beginnings ... The Federal Reserve.* Revised Edition. Boston: Federal Reserve Bank of Boston, 1990.

Kelly, Alfred H; Harbison, Winfred A. *The American Constitution: Its Origins & Development.* Fourth Edition. New York: W. W. Norton & Company, Inc., 1970.

Kennedy, James Ronald and Kennedy, Walter Donald. *Why Not Freedom! America's Revolt Against Big Government.* Gretna, LA: Pelican Publishing Company, Inc., 1995.

Ketcham, Ralph, Editor. Introduction by Ralph Ketcham. *The Anti-Federalist Papers and the Constitutional Convention Debates.* New York: A Mentor Book, 1986.

Klos, Stanley L. *President Who? Forgotten Founders.* Carnegie, PA: Estoric.com, 2004.

Koch, Adrienne. *Jefferson and Madison: The Great Collaboration.* Old Saybrook, CT: Konecky & Konecky.

Larson, Martin A. *The Federal Reserve and the Manipulated Dollar.* Third Printing. Greenwich, Connecticut: Devin-Adair, Publishers, 1983.

— *Jefferson Magnificent Populist.* Greenwich, Connecticut: Devin-Adair, Publishers, 1984.

Lee, Robert W. *The United Nations Conspiracy.* Belmont, MA: Western Islands, 1981.

Madison, James. *Notes of Debates in the Federal Convention of 1787.* Introduction by Adrienne Koch. Bicentennial Edition. New York: W. W. Norton & Company, 1987.

Mayer, David N. *The Constitutional Thought of Thomas Jefferson.* Charlottesville: University Press of Virginia, 1994.

Melton, Jr. Buckner F., ed. *The Quotable Founding Fathers: A Treasury of 2,500 Wise and Witty Quotations from the Man and Women Who Created America.* Washington, D.C.: Potomac Books, Inc., 2004.

Meyers, Marvin, ed. *The Mind of the Founder: Sources of the Political Thought of James Madison,* rev. ed. Hanover and London: Brandeis University Press by University Press of New England, 1981.

Murphy, Paul L. *The Constitution in Crisis Times 1918 — 1969.* New York: Harper Torchbooks, 1972.

Napolitano, Judge Andrew P. *Constitutional Chaos: What Happens When the Government Breaks Its Own Laws.* Nashville: Thomas Nelson, 2006.

— *The Constitution in Exile: How the Federal Government Has Seized Power by Rewriting the Supreme Law of the Land.* Nashville: Nelson Current, 2006.

— *A Nation of Sheep.* Nashville: Thomas Nelson, 2007.

Nichols, Dorothy M. *Modern Money Mechanics.* June 1992 revision was prepared by Anne Marie L. Gonczy. Chicago: Federal Reserve Bank of Chicago, 1992.

Novak, Michael. *On Two Wings: Humble Faith and Common Sense at the American Founding.* San Francisco: Encounter Books, 2002.

Padover, Saul K. *The Living US Constitution.* Second Revised Edition by Jacob W. Landynski. New York: A Mentor Book, 1983.

Pape, Robert A. *Dying to Win: The Strategic Logic of Suicide Terrorism.* New York: Random House, 2005.

Parks, Lawrence. *What Does Mr. Greenspan Really Think?* New York: FAME, 2001.

Paul, Ron. *Gold, Peace, and Prosperity: The Birth of a New Currency.* Foreword by Henry Hazlitt. Preface by Murray Rothbard. Lake Jackson, Texas: Foundation for Rational Economics and Education, Inc., 1981.

— *Ten Myths About Paper Money & One Myth About Paper Gold.* Lake Jackson, Texas: Foundation for Rational Economics and Education, Inc., 1983.

— *Freedom Under Siege: The U.S. Constitution After 200 Years.* Lake Jackson, Texas: Foundation for Rational Economics and Education, Inc., 1987.

— *A Foreign Policy of Freedom: Peace, Commerce, and Honest Friendship.* Lake Jackson, Texas: The Foundation for Rational Economics and Education (FREE), 2007.

— *The Revolution: A Manifesto.* New York: Grand Central Publishing, 2008.

Paul, Rep. Ron and Lehrman, Lewis. *The Case for Gold: A Minority Report of the U.S. Gold Commission.* Second printing. Washington, D.C.: Cato Institute, 1983.

Popp, Dr. Edward E. *Money: Bona Fide or Non-Bona Fide.* Washington, Port Wisconsin: Wisconsin Education Fund, 1970.

— *The Great Cookie Jar: Taking the Mysteries Out of the Money System.* Introduction by G. Edward Griffin. Washington, Port Wisconsin: Wisconsin Education Fund, 1978.

Quick, William J, Bridwell, R. Randall. *Judicial Dictatorship.* Second paperback printing. New Brunswick, New Jersey: Transaction Publishers, 2003.

Quigley, Carroll. *Tragedy and Hope: A History of the World in Our Time.* New York: The Macmillan Company, 1966.

Rand, Ayn. With additional articles by Nathaniel Branden, Alan Greenspan, and Robert Hessen. *Capitalism: The Unknown Ideal.* New York: A Signet Book, 1967.

Rothbard, Murray N. *For a New Liberty: The Libertarian Manifesto.* Revised Edition. San Francisco: Fox & Wilkes, 1978.

— *The Mystery of Banking.* New York: Richardson and Snyder, Dutton, 1983.

— *What Has Government Done to Our money?* Auburn, Alabama: Praxeology Press of the Ludwig von Mises Institute, Auburn University, 1990.

— *The Case Against the Fed.* Auburn, Alabama: Ludwig von Mises Institute, 1994.

Rycroft, Robert S. and the Staff of Research & Education Association Dr. M. Fogiel, Director. *Super Review of Macroeconomics.* Piscataway, New Jersey: Research & Education Association, 2003.

Ryter, Jon Christian, *whatever happened to America?* Tampa: Hallberg Publishing Corporation, 2001.

Samons II, Loren J. *What's Wrong with Democracy? From Athenian Practice to American Worship.* Berkeley and Los Angeles: University of California Press, 2004.

Schiff, Irwin. *The Kingdom of Moltz.* Art by Andrew Ice. Hamden, Connecticut: Freedom Books, 1980.

Skousen, W. Cleon, Reviewer. *The Naked Capitalist.* Salt Lake City: Published as a private edition by the Reviewer, 1970.

— *The Making of America: The Substance and Meaning of the Constitution.* Washington, D. C.: The National Center for Constitutional Studies, 1985.

Sorenson, Leonard R. *Madison on the "General Welfare" of America.* Lanham, MD: Rowman & Littlefield Publishers, Inc., 1995.

Stedman, W. David, Lewis, LaVaughn G., eds. *Rediscovering the Ideas of Liberty.* Asheboro, NC: W. David Stedman Associates, 1995.

Stephens, George M. *Locke, Jefferson and the Justices: Foundations and Failures of the US Government.* Preface by Newt Gingrich. New York: Algora Publishing, 2002.

Turk, James & Rubino, John. *The Coming Collapse of the Dollar and How to Profit from It.* New York: A Currency Book, 2004.

Vieira, Jr., Dr. Edwin. *Pieces of Eight: The Monetary Powers and Disabilities of the United States Constitution.* Fredericksburg, Virginia: Sheridan Books, Second Revised Edition, 2002.

— *How to Dethrone the Imperial Judiciary.* San Antonio: Vision Forum Ministries, 2004.

— *Constitutional "Homeland Security", Volume One, The Nation in Arms.* Ashland, Ohio: Bookmasters, Inc., 2007.

Wilson, Jr., Vincent. *The Book of the Founding Fathers.* Second Printing. Brookeville, Maryland: American History Research Associates, 1985.

— *The Book of the Presidents.* Maps by Peter Guilday. Tenth Edition. Brookeville, Maryland: American History Research Associates, 1989.

Woods Jr., Ph.D, Thomas E. *The Politically Incorrect Guide™ to American History.* Washington, D.C.: Regnery Publishing, Inc., 2004.

Internet

ABC News, http://abcnews.go.com/

Alan Keyes Archives, http://www.renewamerica.us/archives/

American Cause, http://www.theamericancause.org/index.htm

American Conservative, http://www.amconmag.com/index.html

American Conservative Union Foundation, http://acuf.org/index.asp

American Ideal of 1776: The Twelve Basic American Principles, http://www.lexrex.com/enlightened/AmericanIdeal/index.html

American Presidency Project, http://www.presidency.ucsb.edu/

Avalon Project at Yale Law School, http://www.yale.edu/lawweb/avalon/avalon.htm

Ballot Access News, http://www.ballot-access.org/

Barefoot's World, http://www.barefootsworld.net/index.html

Barefoot's World Links, http://www.barefootsworld.net/bftw1.html

Board of Governors of the Federal Reserve System, http://www.federalreserve.gov/

Bureau of Indian Affairs, http://www.doi.gov/bia/index.html

Bureau of the Public Debt, U.S. Department of the Treasury, http://www.publicdebt.treas.gov/

Cato Institute, http://www.cato.org/index.html

CBS News, http://www.cbsnews.com/

Center for Immigration Studies, http://www.cis.org/

Christian Science Monitor, http://www.csmonitor.com/

Citizens Against Government Waste, http://www.cagw.org/site/PageServer?pagename=homePage

Citizen Review Online, http://www.citizenreviewonline.org/current_news.html

City Journal, http://www.city-journal.org/

CNN.com, http://www.cnn.com/

CoinFacts.com, http://www.coinfacts.com/

Commission on Presidential Debates, http://www.debates.org/index.html

Committee for Monetary Research & Education, http://www.cmre.org/

Common Dreams.org News Center, http://www.commondreams.org/

Constitution Society, http://www.constitution.org/

Countries of the World, http://www.theodora.com/wfb/

Cornell University Law School, http://www.law.cornell.edu/

Debt Money, ancient meme, http://landru.i-link-2.net/monques/index.html - GOOD%20NEWS!

Defense Science Board of the Department of Defense, http://www.acq.osd.mil/dsb/

Dictionary.com, http://dictionary.reference.com/

Dixieland Law Journal, http://home.hiwaay.net/%7Ebecraft/

Downsize DC, http://www.downsizedc.org/

Electronic Text Center, University of Virginia Library, http://etext.virginia.edu/

FAME (Foundation for the Advancement of Money Education), http://www.fame.org/

FDIC (Federal Deposit Insurance Corporation), http://www.fdic.gov/index.html

Federal Election Commission, http://www.fec.gov/index.shtml

Federal Reserve Bank of Minneapolis, http://www.minneapolisfed.org/index.html

Federal Reserve Bank of St. Louis, http://stlouisfed.org/

Federation for American Immigration Reform (FAIR), http://www.fairus.org/site/PageServer?pagename=research_researchf6ad

Filibuster Cartoons, http://www.filibustercartoons.com/

Financial Management Service, A Bureau of the U.S. Department of the Treasury, http://fms.treas.gov/index.html

FindLaw, http://www.findlaw.com/#

First Things, http://www.firstthings.com/

Foundation For Economic Education, http://www.fee.org/

Founders' Constitution, http://press-pubs.uchicago.edu/founders/

FOX News.com, http://www.foxnews.com/

Freedom Above Fortune, http://www.freedomabovefortune.com/

Freedom Alliance, http://www.freedomalliance.org/about.htm

Global Exchange, http://www.globalexchange.org/

GPOS 225 James Madison and the Great Events of His Era, http://www.jmu.edu/madison/gpos225-madison2/index.htm

GreatSeal.com, http://www.greatseal.com/index.html

Heritage Foundation, http://www.heritage.org/

Homeland Security, http://www.dhs.gov/index.shtm

Hoover Institution, http://www.hoover.org/

Independent Institute, http://www.independent.org/

Inflation Calculator, http://www.westegg.com/inflation/

Information for Students, Professor Joseph V. O'Brien, Dept. of History, John Jay College of Criminal Justice, http://web.jjay.cuny.edu/-jobrien/index.html

Internal Revenue Service (IRS), http://www.irs.gov/

Internet Modern History Sourcebook, http://www.fordham.edu/halsall/mod/modsbook.html

John Adams, Letter to the Officers of the First Brigade of the Third Division of the Militia of Massachusetts (October 11, 1798), http://personal.pitnet.net/primarysources/adamsmilitia.html

John Birch Society, http://www.jbs.org/

John Williams' Shadow Government Statistics, http://www.shadowstats.com/cgi-bin/sgs

Kussel's Indian Law Home Page, http://www.kussel.com/

LewRockwell.com, http://www.lewrockwell.com/

Libertarian International, http://www.libertarian.to/

Liberty Amendment, http://libertyamendment.org/

Library of Congress, Thomas, http://thomas.loc.gov/

Loren Collins, http://lorencollins.net/

Ludwig von Mises Institute, http://www.mises.org/

Mary Ann Liebert, Inc. publishers, http://www.liebertonline.com/

MSNBC, http://www.msnbc.msn.com/

National Rifle Association (NRA-ILA), http://www.nraila.org/

NBC.com, http://www.nbc.com/

New American, http://www.thenewamerican.com/

NewsMax.com, http://www.newsmax.com/

NewsWithViews, http://newswithviews.com/

Papers of George Washington, http://gwpapers.virginia.edu/index.html

Papers of Thomas Jefferson Princeton University, The Kentucky Resolutions of 1798, http://www.princeton.edu/-tjpapers/kyres/kyednote.html

PBS, http://www.pbs.org/

Pepperdine University School of Public Policy, The New Deal, http://publicpolicy.pepperdine.edu/faculty-research/new-deal/

Pew Hispanic Center, http://pewhispanic.org/

Phyllis Schlafly Report, http://www.eagleforum.org/psr/index.html

Professor Todd J. Zywicki Home Page, http://mason.gmu.edu/-tzywick2/index.html

Public citizen, http://www.citizen.org/index.cfm

Randy E. Barnett, http://randybarnett.com/texts.htm#articles

Representative Ron Paul, http://www.house.gov/paul/index.shtml

Restoring America to Constitutional Principles (Devvy's Project), http://www.devvy.com/

Bruce Schneier , http://www.schneier.com/index.html

Serendipity, http://www.serendipity.li/index.html

Six Kinds of United States Paper Currency, http://www.friesian.com/notes.htm Statue of Liberty National Monument and Ellis Island, The National Park Service, http://www.nps.gov/archive/stli/prod02.htm

TreasuryDirect, http://www.treasurydirect.gov/

ThisNation.com, http://www.thisnation.com/index.html

Thomas Jefferson On Politics & Government, http://etext.virginia.edu/jefferson/quotations/index.html

U. S. Courts, http://www.uscourts.gov/index.html

U.S. Census Bureau, http://www.census.gov/

U.S. Citizenship and Immigration Services (USCIS), http://www.uscis.gov/portal/site/uscis

Statistical Summary of America's Major Wars , http://www.civilwarhome.com/warstats.htm

U.S. Department of State, http://www.state.gov/

U.S. Dept. of Labor, Bureau of Labor Statistics, http://www.bls.gov/

U.S. Electoral College, Office of the Federal Register, U.S. National Archives and Records Administration (NARA), http://www.archives.gov/federal-register/electoral-college/index.html

U.S. General Services Administration (GSA), http://www.gsa.gov/Portal/gsa/ep/home.do?tabId=0

U.S. Government Accountability Office (GAO), http://www.gao.gov/index.html

U.S. Government Printing Office (GPO Access), http://www.gpoaccess.gov/index.html

University of Oklahoma, College of Law, http://www.law.ou.edu/

Upstate Citizens for Equality, http://www.upstate-citizens.org/

USA TODAY, http://www.usatoday.com/

USAGOLD, http://www.usagold.com/

USAID (United States Agency for International Development), http://www.usaid.gov/index.html

Wallbuilders, http://www.wallbuilders.com/

We The People, http://www.givemeliberty.org/

Welcome to the United Nations, http://www.un.org/english/

Welcome to uhuh.com, http://www.uhuh.com/index.htm

White House, http://www.whitehouse.gov/index.html

"The Electoral College" by William C. Kimberling, Deputy Director FEC Office of Election Administration, http://www.fec.gov/pdf/eleccoll.pdf

World Public Opinion. org, http://www.worldpublicopinion.org/?nid=&id=&lb=hmpg

World Trade Organization, http://www.wto.org/index.htm

WorldNetDaily.com, http://www.worldnetdaily.com/

World War I Casualties Page, http://www.nvcc.edu/home/cevans/Versailles/great-war/casualties.html

Acknowledgements

Special thanks to Dr. Edwin Vieira, Jr. for giving his permission to quote from the book *How to Dethrone the Imperial Judiciary* (San Antonio: Vision Forum Ministries, 2004); and from the articles "Will The North American Union Be American Patriots' Last Stand?" NewsWithViews.com [Internet]; http://newswithviews.com/Vieira/edwin49.htm; "Are You Doing Your Constitutional Duty For 'Homeland Security'?" Part 1, NewsWithViews.com [Internet]; http://newswithviews.com/Vieira/edwin11.htm; and "Are You Doing Your Constitutional Duty For 'Homeland Security'?" Part 2, NewsWithViews.com [Internet]; http://newswithviews.com/Vieira/edwin12.htm.

Also, special thanks to Dr. Kelley Ross for giving permission to use four images of Federal Reserve notes from the web site titled Six Kinds of United States Paper Currency [Internet]; http://www.friesian.com/notes.htm.